TEXTUAL CRITICISM AND THE NEW TESTAMENT TEXT

TEXT-CRITICAL STUDIES

Michael W. Holmes, General Editor

Editorial Board:

Todd R. Hanneken
Juan Hernández Jr.
Roderic L. Mullen
W. Andrew Smith

Number 12

TEXTUAL CRITICISM AND THE NEW TESTAMENT TEXT

Theory, Practice, and Editorial Technique

Eberhard W. Güting

SBL PRESS

Atlanta

Copyright © 2020 by Society of Biblical Literature

All rights reserved. No part of this work may be reproduced or transmitted in any form or by any means, electronic or mechanical, including photocopying and recording, or by means of any information storage or retrieval system, except as may be expressly permitted by the 1976 Copyright Act or in writing from the publisher. Requests for permission should be addressed in writing to the Rights and Permissions Office, SBL Press, 825 Houston Mill Road, Atlanta, GA 30329 USA.

Library of Congress Cataloging-in-Publication Data

Names: Güting, Eberhard W., 1934– author.
Title: Textual criticism and the New Testament text : theory, practice, and editorial technique / by Eberhard W. Güting.
Description: Atlanta : SBL Press, 2019. | Series: Text-critical studies ; Number 12 | Includes bibliographical references and index.
Identifiers: LCCN 2019000479 (print) | LCCN 2019004571 (ebook) | ISBN 9780884143536 (ebk.) | ISBN 9781628372366 (pbk. : alk. paper) | ISBN 9780884143529 (hbk. : alk. paper)
Subjects: LCSH: Bible. New Testament—Criticism, Textual.
Classification: LCC BS2325 (ebook) | LCC BS2325 .G88 2019 (print) | DDC 225.4/86—dc23
LC record available at https://lccn.loc.gov/2019000479

Contents

Preface vii
Places of Initial Publication ix
Select Bibliography of Publications by Eberhard W. Güting xi
Abbreviations xv

1. An Introduction to the Textual Criticism of the New Testament 1

2. The Geographical Horizon of Luke's List of the Nations
   (Acts 2:9–11) 25

3. A New Edition of the Parchment Fragments London
   Brit. Libr. Pap. 2240 from the Wadi Sarga containing
   New Testament Text 53

4. Amen, Benediction, Doxology: A Text-Critical Investigation 79

5. The Editorial Account as a Commentary on the Constitution of
   Text and Apparatus in Editions of the Greek New Testament 121

6. Weakly Attested Original Readings of the Manuscript D 05
   in Mark 147

7. The Relevance of Literary Criticism for the Text of the New
   Testament: A Study of Mark's Traditions on John the Baptist 167

8. Open Questions in the Discussion of New Testament Text-
   Critical Methodology 199

9. The Standing of the Textual Critic Heinrich Greeven 231

10. The Methodological Contribution of Günther Zuntz to the
    Text of Hebrews 247

11. Texts of the First Hand and Texts of the Second Hand in the
    Textual Criticism of the New Testament 271

12. The International Status of New Testament Textual Criticism
    in Practice and in Theory since Karl Lachmann 293

13. Print Editions and Online Editions of the *Novum Testamentum
    Graece*: Facing New Challenges 313

14. The Form of the New Testament Acclamation κύριος Ἰησοῦς:
    A Text-Critical Investigation 331

Author Index 337

Preface

The essays collected (and in many cases translated) here represent some of the fruit of more than three decades of engagement with the documents that preserve the text of the New Testament and the methodological and historical challenges they present.* For their kind support of *Textual Criticism and the New Testament Text: Theory, Practice, and Editorial Technique*, I thank all those who have given their aid. First, I name my American translator, Professor Robert L. Brawley (Albert G. McGaw Professor of New Testament Emeritus, McCormick Theological Seminary), of Durham, North Carolina. Next, I name Miss Diana C. Lumsden, BA, of Osnabrück, who standardized all of my English texts. Third, I thank Professor Michael W. Holmes (University Professor of Biblical Studies and Early Christianity emeritus, Bethel University, and Director of Scholars Initiative, Museum of the Bible), of St. Paul, Minnesota, who recommended my work by an expert report, who edited my texts with great care, and who assisted in the production.

Due recognition is given to all who kindly gave permission to republish materials: Nozomu Kabayashi, Director, Shinkyu Shuppansha, Tokyo; Professor Dr. Cilliers Breytenbach, Berlin; Professor Dr. Dr. h.c. Werner Eck, FBA, Köln; Professor Dr. Winfried Woesler, Osnabrück; Vandenhoeck & Ruprecht, Göttingen; Brill Academic Publishers, Leiden; and Bloomsbury Continuum Publishers, London.

---

* See further the select bibliography of publications on pages xi–xiii below. A full CV is available at www.eberhardwgueting.de.

Places of Initial Publication

1. *The Substance of the New Testament*. Translated into Japanese by Maekawa Yutaka (Tokyo: Shinkyu Shuppansha, 2012), 7–36.
2. "Der geographische Horizont der Völkerliste des Lukas (Acta 2:9–11)," *ZNW* 66 (1975): 149–69.
3. "Neuedition der Pergamentfragmente Brit. Libr. Pap. 2240 aus dem Wadi Sarga mit neutestamentlichem Text (Tafel I)," *ZPE* 75 (1988): 97–114.
4. "Amen, Eulogie, Doxologie: Eine textkritische Untersuchung," in *Begegnungen zwischen Christentum und Judentum in Antike und Mittelalter: Festschrift für Heinz Schreckenberg*, ed. Dietrich-Alexander Koch and Hermann Lichtenberger, SIJD 1 (Göttingen: Vandenhoeck & Ruprecht, 1993), 133–62.
5. "Der editorische Bericht als Kommentar zur Textkonstitution und zum Apparat in Editionen des Neuen Testaments," *Editio* 7 (1993): 94–108.
6. "Weakly Attested Original Readings of the Manuscript D 05 in Mark," in *Codex Bezae: Studies from the Lunel Colloquium June 1994*, ed. David C. Parker and Christian-Bernard Amphoux, NTTS 22 (Leiden: Brill, 1996), 217–31.
7. "The Relevance of Literary Criticism for the Text of the New Testament: A Study of Mark's Traditions on John the Baptist," in *Studies in the Early Text of the Gospels and Acts: The Papers of the First Birmingham Colloquium on the Textual Criticism of the New Testament*, ed. David G. K. Taylor, Texts and Studies 3/1 (Birmingham: University of Birmingham Press, 1999; repr. Piscataway, NJ: Gorgias, 2013), 142–67.
8. "Offene Fragen in der Methodendiskussion der neutestamentlichen Textkritik," in *Editio* 19 (2005): 77–98.
9. Previously unpublished.
10. "The Methodological Contribution of Günther Zuntz to the Text of Hebrews," *NovT* 48 (2006): 359–78.

11. "Texte erster Hand, Texte zweiter Hand in der Textkritik des Neuen Testaments," in *Materialität in der Editionswissenschaft*, ed. Martin Schubert, Beihefte zu Editio 32 (Berlin: de Gruyter, 2010), 405–19.
12. "Die Internationalität der neutestamentlichen Textkritik zwischen Praxis und Theorie seit Karl Lachmann," in *Internationalität und Interdisziplinarität der Editionswissenschaft*, ed. Michael Stolz and Yen-Chun Chen, Beihefte zu Editio 38 (Berlin: de Gruyter, 2014), 161–69.
13. "Druckausgaben und Onlineeditionen des Novum Testamentum Graece vor neuen Herausforderungen," in *Vom Nutzen der Editionen: Beiträge zur Bedeutung moderner Editorik für die Erforschung von Literatur- und Kulturgeschichte*, ed. Thomas Bein, Beihefte zu Editio 39 (Berlin: de Gruyter, 2015), 47–57.
14. Previously unpublished.

Select Bibliography of Publications by Eberhard W. Güting*

Bruce, F. F., and Eberhard Güting. *Ausserbiblische Zeugnisse über Jesus und das frühe Christentum, einschließlich des apokryphen Judasevangeliums*. 5th ed. Giessen: Brunnen, 2007.

Greeven, Heinrich, and Eberhard Güting. *Textkritik des Markusevangeliums*. Theologie, Forschung und Wissenschaft 11. Münster: LIT, 2005.

Güting, Eberhard. "Amen, Eulogie, Doxologie. Eine textkritische Untersuchung." Pages 133–62 in *Begegnungen zwischen Christentum und Judentum in Antike und Mittelalter: Festschrift für Heinz Schreckenberg*. Edited by Dietrich-Alexander Koch and Hermann Lichtenberger. SIJD 1. Göttingen: Vandenhock & Ruprecht, 1993.

———. *A Complete Concordance to Flavius Josephus*, vol. 1. Edited by Karl Heinrich Rengstorf in collaboration with Erwin Buck, Eberhard Güting, and Bernhard Justus. Leiden: Brill, 1973.

———. "Druckausgaben und Online-Editionen des Novum Testamentum Graece vor neuen Herausforderungen." Pages 47–57 in *Vom Nutzen der Editionen: Beiträge zur Bedeutung moderner Editorik für die Erforschung von Literatur- und Kulturgeschichte*. Edited by Thomas Bein. Beihefte zu Edito 39. Berlin: de Gruyter, 2015.

———. "Der editorische Bericht als Kommentar zur Textkonstitution und zum Apparat in Editionen des neuen Testaments." *Editio* 7 (1993): 94–108.

———. "Der geographische Horizont der sogenannten Völkerliste des Lukas (Acta 2, 9–11)." *ZNW* 66 (1975): 149–69.

———. "Die Internationalität der neutestamentlichen Textkritik seit Karl Lachmann." Pages 161–69 in *Internationalität und Interdisziplinarität der Editionswissenschaft*. Edited by Michael Stolz and Yen-Chun Chen. Beihefte zu Editio 38. Berlin: de Gruyter 2014.

———. "An Introduction to the Textual Criticism of the New Testament." Pages 6–36 in *What Is the Substance of the New Testament? Studies in Editorial Science and in the Textual Criticism of the New Testament*. By Eberhard W.

---

* A complete bibliography is available at www.eberhardwgueting.de/complete.html.

Güting. Translated into Japanese by Maekawa Yutaka. Tokyo: Shinkyo Shuppansya, 2012.

———. "Kritik an den Judäern in Jerusalem: Literarkritische Beiträge zu einem unabgeschlossenen Gespräch über den Evangelisten Johannes." Pages 158–201 in *Israel als Gegenüber: Vom Alten Orient bis in die Gegenwart; Studien zur Geschichte eines wechselvollen Zusammenlebens*. Edited by Folker Siegert. SIDJ 5. Göttingen: Vandenhoeck & Ruprecht, 2000.

———. "The Methodological Contribution of Günther Zuntz to the Text of Hebrews." *NovT* 48 (2006): 359–78.

———. *Die Mischna: Text, Übersetzung und ausführliche Erklärung mit eingehenden geschichtlichen und sprachlichen Einleitungen und textkritischen Anhängen*. Seder 1, Traktat 6: Terumot. Berlin: Töpelmann, 1969.

———. "Neuedition der Pergamentfragmente Brit. Libr. Pap. 2240 aus dem Wadi Sarga mit neutestamentlichem Text (Tafel I)." *ZPE* 75 (1988): 97–114.

———. "Offene Fragen in der Methodendiskussion der neutestamentlichen Textkritik." *Editio* 19 (2005): 77–98.

———. "The Relevance of Literary Criticism for the Text of the New Testament: A Study of Mark's Traditions on John the Baptist." Pages 142–67 in *Studies in the Early Text of the Gospels and Acts: The Papers of the First Birmingham Colloquium on the Textual Criticism of the New Testament*. Edited by David G. K. Taylor. Texts and Studies 3/1. Birmingham: Birmingham University Press, 1999. Repr., Piscataway, NJ: Gorgias, 2013.

———. Review of *A Commentary on Textual Additions to the New Testament*, by Philip Wesley Comfort. *TLZ* 143 (2018): 619–20.

———. Review of *Das Verhältnis der koptischen zur griechischen Überlieferung des Neuen Testaments: Dokumentation und Auswertung der Gesamtmaterialien beider Traditionen zum Jakobusbrief und den beiden Petrusbriefen*, by Franz-Jürgen Schmitz. *TLZ* 129 (2004): 1071–73.

———. Review of *Erziehung, Lebenswelt und Kriegseinsatz der deutschen Jugend unter Hitler: Anmerkungen zur Literatur*, by Heinz Schreckenberg. *SJT* 62 (2009): 259–61.

———. Review of *Griechisch-deutsches Wörterbuch zu den Schriften des Neuen Testaments und der frühchristlichen Literatur*, 6th ed., by Walter Bauer. *TBei* 21 (1990): 45–47.

———. Review of *Marcion und sein Apostolos: Rekonstruktion und historische Einordnung der marcionitischen Paulusbriefausgabe*, by Ulrich Schmid. *NovT* 39 (1997): 397–405.

———. Review of *Textual Scholarship and the Making of the New Testament*, by David C. Parker. *TLZ* 138 (2013): 1238–39.

———. Review of *The Book of Acts as Church History/Apostelgeschichte als Kirchengeschichte*, edited by Tobias Nicklas and Michael Tilly. *NovT* 47 (2005): 170–83.

———. Review of *The Greek New Testament with Dictionary*, 5th ed. *TLZ* 140 (2015): 64–65.

———. Review of *The Text of Galatians and Its History*, by Stephen C. Carlson. *TLZ* 141 (2016): 151–52.

———. "Texte erster Hand, Texte zweiter Hand in der Textkritik des Neuen Testaments." Pages 405–19 in *Materialität in der Editionswissenschaft*. Edited by Martin Schubert. Beihefte zu Editio 32. Berlin: de Gruyter, 2010.

———. "Weakly Attested Original Readings of the Manuscript D 05 in Mark." Pages 217–31 in *Codex Bezae: Studies from the Lunel Colloquium June 1994*. Edited by David C. Parker and Christian-Bernard Amphoux. NTTS 22. Leiden: Brill, 1996.

———. "Zu den Voraussetzungen des systematischen Denkens Adolf Schlatters." *NZSTh* 15 (1973): 132–147.

———. "Zum hermeneutischen Ansatz Joachim Wachs." *ZRGG* 30 (1978): 68–71.

Güting, Eberhard, and David L. Mealand. *Asyndeton in Paul: A Text-Critical and Statistical Enquiry into Pauline Style*. SBEC 39. Lewiston, NY: Mellen, 1998.

Junack, Klaus, Eberhard Güting, Ulrich Nimtz, and Klaus Witte. *Das Neue Testament auf Papyrus, II: Die paulinischen Briefe, Teil 1, Röm., 1 Kor., 2. Kor.* ANTF 12 Berlin: de Gruyter, 1989.

Abbreviations

1 Apol.	Justin, *Apologia i*
1 Clem.	1 Clement
Acts John	Acts of John
AGJU	Arbeiten zur Geschichte des Antiken Judentums und des Urchristentums
AGLB	Aus der Geschichte der Lateinischen Bibel
AHAW.PH	Abhandlungen der Heidelberger Akademie der Wissenschaften, Philosophisch-Historische Klasse
AKG	Arbeiten zur Kirchengeschichte
AnBib	Analecta Biblica
Ant.	Josephus, *Jewish Antiquities*
ANTF	Arbeiten zur neutestamentlichen Textforschung
ANRW	*Aufstieg und Niedergang der römischen Welt: Geschichte und Kultur Roms im Spiegel der neueren Forschung.* Part 2, *Principat*. Edited by Hildegard Temporini and Wolfgang Haase. Berlin: de Gruyter, 1972–.
APAW.PH	Abhandlungen der Preussischen Akademie der Wissenschaften, Philosophisch-Historische Klasse
Apos. Con.	Apostolic Constitutions and Canons
b.	Babylonian Talmud
Barn.	Epistle of Barnabas
BDF	Blass, Friedrich, Albert Debrunner, and Robert W. Funk. *A Greek Grammar of the New Testament and Other Early Christian Literature.* Chicago: University of Chicago Press, 1961.
BDAG	Danker, Frederick W., Walter Bauer, William F. Arndt, and F. Wilbur Gingrich. *Greek-English Lexicon of the New Testament and Other Early Christian Literature.* 3rd ed. Chicago: University of Chicago Press, 2000.
Ber.	Berakot

BETL	Bibliotheca Ephemeridum Theologicarum Lovaniensium
BFCT	Beiträge zur Förderung christlicher Theologie
BHT	Beiträge zur historischen Theologie
Bib	Biblica
B.J.	Josephus, Bellum judaicum
BMus	Bibliothèque du Muséon
BR	Biblical Research
BT	The Bible Translator
BTS	Biblical Tools and Studies
BWANT	Beiträge zur Wissenschaft vom Alten und Neuen Testament
BZ	Biblische Zeitschrift NS
BZNW	Beihefte zur Zeitschrift für die neutestamentliche Wissenschaft und die Kunde der älteren Kirche
CBET	Contributions to Biblical Exegesis and Theology
CBQ	Catholic Biblical Quarterly
Cels.	Origen, Contra Celsum
CIJ	Corpus Inscriptionum Judaicarum. Edited by Jean-Baptistes Frey. 2 vols. Rome: Pontifical Biblical Institute, 1936–1952.
CJAn	Christianity and Judaism in Antiquity
CNT	Commentaire du Nouveau Testament
Comm.	Commentarium, Commentarii
Comm. Jo.	Origen, Commentarii in evangelium Johannem
Comm. Matt.	Origen, Commentarium in evangelium Matthaei
Comm. Rom.	Origen, Commentarii in Romanos
Conc. Nic.	Concilium Niceaenum
CQR	Church Quarterly Review
CRAI	Comptes rendus des séances de l'Académie des Inscriptions et Belles-Lettres
CSEL	Corpus Scriptorum Ecclesiasticorum Latinorum
Dial.	Dialogus cum Tryphone
Did.	Didache
Diogn.	Diognetus
DMOA	Documenta et Monumenta Orientis Antiqui
EBib	Études Bibliques
ECM	Novum Testamentum Graecum: Editio Critica Maior
ECM²	Novum Testamentum Graecum: Editio Critica Maior, 2nd ed.

EFNT	Estudios de Filologia Neotestamentaria
EKKNT	Evangelisch-katholischer Kommentar zum Neuen Testament
fasc.	fascicle
FNT	*Filología Neotestamentaria*
FRLANT	Forschungen zur Religion und Literatur des Alten und Neuen Testaments
GCS	Die griechischen christlichen Schriftsteller der ersten Jahrhunderte
Geogr.	Strabo *Geographica*
GGA	*Göttingische gelehrte Anzeigen*
Gk. Apoc. Ezra	Greeek Apocalypse of Ezra
GTA	Göttinger Theologische Arbeiten
Haer.	Irenaeus, *Adversus haereses (Elenchos)*
HdO	Handbuch der Orientalistik
HKNT	Handkommentar zum Neuen Testament
HNT	Handbuch zum Neuen Testament
HThKNT	Herders Theologischer Kommentar zum Neuen Testament
HTR	*Harvard Theological Review*
HUCA	*Hebrew Union College Annual*
Huck-Greeven	Huck, Albert, ed. Synopsis of the First Three Gospels with the Addition of the Johannine Parallels. Rev. by Heinrich Greeven. 13th ed. Tübingen: Mohr, 1981.
ICC	International Critical Commentary
Inst.	*Institutio oratoria*
JAC	*Jahrbuch für Antike und Christentum*
JBL	*Journal of Biblical Literature*
JGRChJ	*Journal of Greco-Roman Christianity and Judaism*
JR	*Journal of Religion*
JRS	*Journal of Roman Studies*
JSNT	*Journal for the Study of the New Testament*
JSNTSup	Journal for the Study of the New Testament Supplement Series
JTS	*Journal of Theological Studies*
JWKG	*Jahrbuch für Westfälische Kirchengeschichte*
KD	Barth, Karl. *Kirchliche Dogmatik*. 14 vols. Zurich: TVZ, 1932–1967.

KEK	Kritisch-exegetischer Kommentar über das Neue Testament
KNT	Kommentar zum Neuen Testament
LD	Lectio Divina
Legat.	Philo, *Legatio ad Gaium*
LQ	*Lutheran Quarterly*
LSJ	Liddell, Henry George, Robert Scott, and Henry Stuart Jones. *A Greek-English Lexicon*. New edition revised and augmented. Oxford: Clarendon, 1940.
m.	Mishnah
Ign. *Eph.*	Ignatius, *To the Ephesians*
Ign. *Magn.*	Ignatius, *To the Magnesians*
Marc.	*Adversus Marcionem*
Mart. Pol	Martyrdom of Polycarp
Meg.	Megillah
MM	Moulton, James H., and George Milligan. *Vocabulary of the Greek Testament*. London: Hodder & Stoughton, 1930. Repr. Peabody, MA: Hendrickson, 1997.
MPSW	Mitteilungen aus der Papyrussammlung der Nationalbibliothek in Wien (Papyrus Erzherzog Rainer)
MSU	Mitteilungen des Septuaginta-Unternehmens
MThS	Münchener Theologische Studien
Myst.	*de Mysteriis*
NA^{26}	*Novum Testamentum Graece*, Nestle-Aland, 26th ed.
NA^{27}	*Novum Testamentum Graece*, Nestle-Aland, 27th ed.
NA^{28}	*Novum Testamentum Graece*, Nestle-Aland, 28th ed.
NEchtB	Neue Echter Bibel
Neot	*Neotestamentica*
NGWG.PH	*Nachrichten der Gesellschaft der Wisssenschaften in Göttingen—Philologisch-Historische Klasse*
NIGTC	New International Greek Text Commentary
NKZ	*Neue Kirchliche Zeitschrift*
NovT	*Novum Testamentum*
NovTSup	Supplements to Novum Testamentum
NTD	Das Neue Testament Deutsch
NTF	Neutestamentliche Forschungen
NTGF	New Testament in the Greek Fathers
NTS	*New Testament Studies*
NTTS	New Testament Tools and Studies

NZSTh	*Neue Zeitschrift für systematische Theologie und Religionsphilosophie*
Odes Sol.	Odes of Solomon
OrChr	*Oriens Christianus*
Pan.	Epiphanius, *Panarion*
Pesiq. Rab.	Pesiqta Rabbati
PG	Migne, Jacques-Paul, ed. *Patrologia graeca*. 161 vols. Paris: Migne: 1857–1886.
PW	*Paulys Real-Encyclopädie der classischen Altertumswissenschaft*. New edition by Georg Wissowa and Wilhelm Kroll. 50 vols. in 84 parts. Stuttgart: Metzler and Druckenmüller, 1894–1980.
RAC	*Reallexikon für Antike und Christentum*. Edited by Theodor Klauser et al. Stuttgart: Hiersemann, 1950–.
RB	*Revue Biblique*
REJ	*Revue des études juives*
RGG	*Religion in Geschichte und Gegenwart*. Edited by Hans Dieter Betz. 4th ed. Tübingen: Mohr Siebeck, 1998–2007.
RPP	*Religion Past and Present: Encyclopedia of Theology and Religion*. Edited by Hans Dieter Betz et al. 14 vols. Leiden: Brill, 2007–2013.
SBEC	Studies in the Bible and Early Christianity
SBLCP	Society of Biblical Literature Centennial Publications
SBLGNT	The Greek New Testament: SBL Edition
SBS	Stuttgarter Bibelstudien
SCS	Septuagint and Cognate Studies
SD	Studies and Documents
Shabb.	Shabbat
SHAW.PH	Sitzungsberichte der Heidelberger Akademie der Wissenschaften: Philosophisch-historische Klasse
SIJD	Schriften des Institutum Judaicum Delitzschianum
SJT	*Scottish Journal of Theology*
SNTSMS	Society for New Testament Studies Monograph Series
SPAW	*Sitzungsberichte der preussischen Akademie der Wissenschaften*
STAR	Studies in Theology and Religion
StPatr	*Studia Patristica*

Str-B	Strack, Hermann L., and Paul Billerbeck. *Kommentar zum Neuen Testament aus Talmud und Midrasch*. 6 vols. Munich: Beck, 1922–61.
SUNT	Studien zur Umwelt des Neuen Testaments
t.	Tosefta
Taʿan	Taʿanit
T. Abr.	Testament of Abraham
TBei	*Theologische Beiträge*
TC	*TC: A Journal of Biblical Textual Criticism*
TCSt	Text-Critical Studies
T. Dan	Testament of Dan
TDNT	Kittel, Gerhard, and Gerhard Friedrich, eds. *Theological Dictionary of the New Testament*. Translated by Geoffrey W. Bromiley. 10 vols. Grand Rapids: Eerdmans, 1964–1976.
TDOT	Botterweck, G. Johannes, Helmer Ringgren, and Heinz-Josef Fabry, eds. *Theological Dictionary of the Old Testament*. Translated by John T. Willis et al. 15 vols. Grand Rapids: Eerdmans, 1974–2006.
THAT	*Theologisches Handwörterbuch zum Alten Testament*. Edited by Ernst Jenni, with assistance from Claus Westermann. 2 vols. Munich: Chr. Kaiser Verlag; Zürich: Theologischer Verlag, 1971–1976.
THKNT	Theologischer Handkommentar zum Neuen Testament
ThR	*Theologische Rundschau*, new series
T. Job	Testament of Job
TLOT	*Theological Lexicon of the Old Testament*. Edited by Ernst Jenni, with assistance from Claus Westermann. Translated by Mark E. Biddle. 3 vols. Peabody, MA: Hendrickson, 1997.
TLZ	*Theologische Literaturzeitung*
TRE	*Theologische Realenzyklopädie*. Edited by Gerhard Krause and Gerhard Müller. Berlin: de Gruyter, 1977–.
Trin.	*De Trinitate*
TS	Texts and Studies
TS	*Theological Studies*
TSK	*Theologische Studien und Kritiken*
T. Sol.	Testament of Solomon

ThWAT	Botterweck, G. Johannes, Helmer Ringgren, and Heinz-Josef Fabry, eds. *Theologisches Wörterbuch zum Alten Testament*. 10 vols. Stuttgart: Kohlhammer, 1970–2000.
TU	Texte und Untersuchungen
TUGAL	Texte und Untersuchungen zur Geschichte der altchristlichen Literatur
TWNT	Kittel, Gerhard, and Gerhard Friedrich, eds. *Theologisches Wörterbuch zum Neuen Testament*. Stuttgart: Kohlhammer, 1932–1979.
TynBul	*Tyndale Bulletin*
TZ	*Theologische Zeitschrift*
UBS³	*The Greek New Testament*, United Bible Societies, 3rd ed.
UBS⁴	*The Greek New Testament*, United Bible Societies, 4th ed.
UBS⁵	*The Greek New Testament*, United Bible Societies, 5th ed.
WD	*Wort und Dienst*, new series
WdF	Wege der Forschung
WMANT	Wissenschaftliche Monographien zum Alten und Neuen Testament
WUNT	Wissenschaftliche Untersuchungen zum Neuen Testament
ZBK	Zürcher Bibelkommentare
ZKG	*Zeitschrift für Kirchengeschichte*
ZNW	*Zeitschrift für die neutestamentliche Wissenschaft und die Kunde der älteren Kirche*
ZPE	*Zeitschrift für Papyrologie und Epigraphik*
ZRGG	*Zeitschrift für Religions- und Geistesgeschichte*
ZWTh	*Zeitschrift für wissenschaftliche Theologie*

– 1 –
An Introduction to the Textual Criticism of the New Testament

Introduction

As is the case with other texts inherited from antiquity, the writings of the New Testament do not come into our hands unaltered. What precisely their authors wrote is unknown often enough. Copies copied from copies discovered in various localities, mainly in Egypt, present a confusing abundance of variant readings. Many decades before the pioneering edition of Karl Lachmann, editors of the Greek New Testament began to collect variant readings into their apparatuses. In the course of the finds of the nineteenth and twentieth centuries these lists of witnesses have accumulated tremendously. Today the apparatuses of editions do not collect merely Greek witnesses. The testimony of early translations, of lectionaries, of New Testament quotations in the writings of Greek and Latin church fathers are recorded.[1] The use of citations from the New Testament, however, requires a careful method.[2] Textbooks introduce a student to editions and their apparatuses.[3]

---

1. Barbara Aland et al., eds., *Novum Testamentum Graecum: Editio Critica Maior. Edited by the Institute for New Testament Textual Research, Installment 1. IV. Catholic Letters: James; Part 1: Text; Part 2: Supplementary Material*, 2nd ed. (Stuttgart: Deutsche Bibelgesellschaft, 2013); B. Aland et al., eds. *Novum Testamentum Graece*, 28th ed. (Stuttgart: Deutsche Bibelgesellschaft, 2012) [= NA^{28}]; B. Aland et al., eds., *The Greek New Testament*, 5th ed. (Stuttgart: Deutsche Bibelgesellschaft; United Bible Societies, 2014) [= UBS^5]; Michael W. Holmes, ed., *The Greek New Testament: SBL Edition* (Atlanta: Society of Biblical Literature; Bellingham, WA: Logos Bible Software, 2010).

2. Gordon D. Fee, revised by Roderic L. Mullen, "The Use of the Greek Fathers for New Testament Textual Criticism," in *The Text of the New Testament*

A student about to engage in written homework needs the discussion of textual variation as found in commentaries. In addition, the editors of the *Greek New Testament* of the United Bible Societies have published a *Textual Commentary* that lists important literature, and discusses and decides on a select number of variant readings.[4]

Text-critical methods need to be employed and, likewise, to be taught.

---

in Contemporary Research: Essays on the Status Quaestionis, ed. Bart D. Ehrman and Michael W. Holmes, 2nd ed., NTTS 42 (Leiden: Brill, 2013), 351–73; Amy M. Donaldson, "Explicit References to New Testament Variant Readings among Greek and Latin Church Fathers" (PhD diss., University of Notre Dame, 2009); online https://tinyurl.com/sbl7012c. Problems met with in quotations from translations into languages of Near Eastern cultures from antiquity are discussed in Ehrman and Holmes, *Text of the New Testament in Contemporary Research*.

3. Ehrman and Holmes, *Text of the New Testament in Contemporary Research*; Barbara Aland, "Text Criticism of the Bible. II. New Testament," *RPP* 12:576–78; B. Aland, "Textkritik der Bibel, II. Neues Testament," *RGG* 8:200–207; David C. Parker, *Textual Scholarship and the Making of the New Testament: The Lyell Lectures Oxford Trinity Term 2011* (Oxford: Oxford University Press, 2012); J. Keith Elliott, *New Testament Textual Criticism: The Application of Thoroughgoing Principles; Essays on Manuscripts and Textual Variation*, NovTSup 137 (Leiden: Brill, 2010); David C. Parker, *Manuscripts, Texts, Theology: Collected Papers 1977–2007*, ANTF 40 (Berlin: de Gruyter, 2009); Parker, *An Introduction to the New Testament Manuscripts and Their Texts* (Cambridge: Cambridge University Press, 2008); Bart D. Ehrman, *Studies in the Textual Criticism of the New Testament*, NTTS 33 (Leiden: Brill, 2006); Bruce M. Metzger and Bart D. Ehrman, *The Text of the New Testament: Its Transmission, Corruption, and Restoration*, 4th ed. (Oxford: Oxford University Press, 2005); Eldon J. Epp, *Perspectives on New Testament Textual Criticism: Collected Essays 1962–2004*, NovTSup 116 (Leiden: Brill, 2005); B. Aland, "Textgeschichte/ Textkritik der Bibel, II. Neues Testament," *TRE* 33:155–68; Kurt Aland and Barbara Aland, *The Text of the New Testament: An Introduction to the Critical Editions and to the Theory and Practice of Modern Textual Criticism*, 2nd ed. (Grand Rapids: Eerdmans; Leiden: Brill, 1989), 32–35 and 317–37; Léon Vaganay, *An Introduction to New Testament Textual Criticism*, rev. and updated by Christian-Bernard Amphoux and Jenny Heimerdinger, trans. Jenny Heimerdinger, 2nd ed. (Cambridge: Cambridge University Press, 1991), 52–86; Martin L. West, *Textual Criticism and Editorial Technique: Applicable to Greek und Latin Texts* (Stuttgart: Teubner, 1973).

4. Bruce M. Metzger, *A Textual Commentary on the Greek New Testament: A Companion Volume to the United Bible Societies' Greek New Testament (Fourth Revised Edition)*, 2nd ed. (Stuttgart: Deutsche Bibelgesellschaft, 1994).

1. Introduction to the Textual Criticism of the New Testament

Tried and tested among these is the analysis in detail of the mistakes and errors of ancient scribes. Bernhard Weiss, Eberhard Nestle, Bruce M. Metzger, and many others pioneered such analysis. These authors identified slips and intentional changes in manuscripts, and even noticed improvements, and classified them.

Textual criticism of the New Testament aims at an overall presentation of the various aspects of early textual transmission. It describes diverse factors that influenced the early copying process in antiquity. For many decades textual criticism endeavoured to reconstruct the original texts of New Testament authors with energy and with skill. While scholarly interest recently shifted and began to devote intensive study to the cultural contexts of early diversity in traditions, this essay seeks to resume philological approaches to textual criticism, and in doing so makes use of proven procedures.[5]

Several recent surveys, in investigating specific sets of data, adapted the methods used to the topics chosen. In a survey of the occurrence of "Amen" in New Testament contexts, attention was given to *Formgeschichte*.[6] In an examination of primary and secondary asyndeta as elements of Pauline style, statistical procedures were introduced.[7] An extensive investigation of the textual criticism of the Gospel of Mark analyzed a multiplicity of linguistic and stylistic aspects of Mark's language.[8] This method gained recognition.[9]

---

5. For the shift in emphasis, see Parker, *Textual Scholarship*; Eldon J. Epp, "It's All about Variants: A Variant-Conscious Approach to New Testament Textual Criticism," *HTR* 100 (2007): 275–308; Tobias Nicklas and Michael Tilly, eds., *The Book of Acts as Church History/Apostelgeschichte als Kirchengeschichte: Text, Textual Traditions, and Ancient Interpretations/Text, Texttraditionen und antike Auslegungen*, BZNW 120 (Berlin: de Gruyter, 2003).

6. Eberhard Güting, "Amen, Eulogie, Doxologie: Eine textkritische Untersuchung," in *Begegnungen zwischen Christentum und Judentum in Antike und Mittelalter: Festschrift Heinz Schreckenberg*, ed. Dietrich-Alex Koch and Hermann Lichtenberger, SIJD 1 (Göttingen: Vandenhoeck & Ruprecht, 1993), 133–62 [ch. 4 in this collection].

7. Eberhard W. Güting and David L. Mealand, *Asyndeton in Paul: A Text-critical and Statistical Enquiry into Pauline Style*, SBET 39 (Lewiston, NY: Mellen, 1998).

8. Heinrich Greeven and Eberhard Güting, eds., *Textkritik des Markusevangeliums*, Theologie, Forschung und Wissenschaft 11 (Münster: LIT, 2005).

9. Thus Wolfgang Schrage, "Geleitwort," in Greeven and Güting, *Textkritik des Markusevangeliums*, 1–2.

It is recommended to those teaching textual criticism that they use the technique of an investigation in order to make it possible for the student to make a decision on text-critical issues. In order to profit from this experience, attention must be paid to the style of a New Testament text, to the type of text, and to the author. Every text reveals its individuality more or less distinctly.[10] To read a Greek text means in the first place to pay attention to the semantics, to the grammar, to the structure of the literary form, and to the scope of the intended communication. Resources need to be to hand. In principle such a reading aims at an adequate understanding of a complete text.

For textual criticism, however, it is necessary to examine in detail whether a text as transmitted may be considered correct. This issue belongs to the jurisdiction of a demanding philology. Classical philology examines traditions from antiquity in three steps: *Recensio, examinatio, emendatio.* Among the authors who represent this methodology numerous New Testament scholars must be mentioned. In Germany the researches of Adolf Deissmann, Friedrich Blass, and Adolf von Harnack once set the pace. In England the classical scholar Günther Zuntz represented this philological methodology to a significant degree.[11] It is the task of *examinatio* as a scientific *procedure* to ask whether the language of a textual unit, in its elements and in its entirety, may be described as correct.[12] Conspicuous speech may at times be out of keeping with the known language of an author. On the other hand, within this framework it may be entirely proper, chosen for reasons of stylistic design. To expect a student who did not receive any training in classical studies to excel here would be ill-advised. Therefore textual criticism deserves to be taught. Let us begin!

---

10. Marius Reiser, *Sprache und literarische Formen des Neuen Testaments: Eine Einführung* (Paderborn: Schöningh, 2001).

11. Michael W. Holmes, "The Text of the Epistles Sixty Years After: An Assessment of Günther Zuntz's Contribution to Text-Critical Methodology and History," in *Transmission and Reception: New Testament Text-critical and Exegetical Studies*, ed. Jeffrey Wayne Childers and David C. Parker (Piscataway, NJ: Gorgias, 2006), 89–113; Eberhard Güting, "The Methodological Contribution of Günther Zuntz to the Text of Hebrews," *NovT* 51 (2006): 359–78 [ch. 10 in this collection]; Günther Zuntz, *Lukian von Samosata und das Neue Testament*, ed. Barbara Aland and Klaus Wachtel, AHAW.PH 2 (Heidelberg: Winter, 1995).

12. Paul Maas, *Textual Criticism*, trans. Barbara Flower (Oxford: Clarendon, 1958); Maas, *Textkritik*, 4th ed. (Leipzig: Teubner, 1960).

It has been known for a long time that the Fourth Gospel presents its themes in a sublime manner. Prominent elements of its literary design are the numerous *asyndeta*. Greek sentences normally form a network of interwoven sentences. Unconnected sentences, in contrast, have something startling: ἀπεκρίθη Ἰησοῦς, John 1:50; τῇ ἐπαύριον, John 1:43; ἤγαγεν αὐτόν, John 1:42; θεὸν οὐδεὶς ἑώρακεν πώποτε, John 1:18. Scribes frequently add: καί, δέ, οὖν, τέ.[13]

1. The Adverb πάλιν: Strictly Adverbial Uses

We shall investigate uses of the adverb πάλιν within the text of the Fourth Gospel. Lexical meanings of the word move in the spectrum "back, again, further, moreover, in turn, on the other hand."[14] In numerous passages the word πάλιν has been uniformly transmitted. In all of these, language patterns regarding the position of the word within the sentence may be analyzed; second, regarding the structure of the sentences in which the word appears; and, third, regarding uses that serve merely to connect narratives and other units of speech. Occasionally πάλιν appears in places in which alternatively connecting particles have been introduced into the sentence. We have to investigate whether πάλιν in these passages has been added in the process of copying.

This question is related to a problem already mentioned. As will be demonstrated, πάλιν is used not only to link words and phrases, but also to connect literary units. Hellenistic Greek authors have alternative parts of speech at their disposal to achieve a similar effect, namely, the use of particles as sentence connectives. It is desirable, in passages that employ πάλιν, to ask whether asyndeta have been transmitted in one part of the tradition and whether these represent the original text of the gospel. If οὖν, καί, or δέ appear in one part of the tradition, these particles may be secondary additions. The present investigation, however, does not intend to survey fully the insertion of secondary particles into the text of the Fourth Gospel. It is an interesting question, of course, whether scribes inserted

---

13. Regarding the function and use of asyndeta in Greek authors, see Güting and Mealand, *Asyndeton in Paul*, 1–8.

14. BDAG, 752–53; Kurt Aland and Barbara Aland, eds., *Griechisch-deutsches Wörterbuch zu den Schriften des Neuen Testaments und der [übrigen] frühchristlichen Literatur von Walter Bauer*, 6th ed. (Berlin: de Gruyter, 1988), 1227–28; LSJ, 1292; MM, 475–76.

connecting particles that destroyed asyndeton, since it was observed long ago that asyndeta are a frequent device in the style of this gospel.¹⁵

A concordance informs us that πάλιν in the Gospel of John occurs forty-five times. From the apparatus of Nestle-Aland we gather the information that four times a πάλιν was rejected by the editors, namely, in John 1:21; 8:28; 9:26; 12:22. May we consider these textual decisions as correct? Have all of the forty-five occurrences been justifiably accepted?¹⁶

The adverb πάλιν forms a close link semantically to the predicate. In John 4:13, for instance, we read: "Everyone who drinks this water will be thirsty again."¹⁷ Or, in John 10:17–18, the Son, somewhat majestically, remarks that nobody is able to rob him of his life. "I have the right to lay it down, and I have the right to receive it back again." To travel again to Judea means much the same as to return there (John 11:7–8). A divine voice sounds encouragement from heaven: "I have glorified it, and I will glorify it again." (John 12:28). The connection of ἔρχομαι to its adverb denotes "to return" (John 14:3). The adverb is employed in the term "to see again" (John 16:22). To come into the world and to leave it again are combined similarly (John 16:28). In all of these passages the adverb is placed directly before the verb. The tradition is uniform. It is firm, too, when in one of the Johannine parting speeches the closeness of the παρουσία is spoken of. "Soon" and "again soon" are matched (John 16:16, 17, 19).

A close semantic link of πάλιν to its verb may be noticed in John 4:3. The passage mentions a return to Galilee. This narrative turn is prepared by a phrase that forms a parallel: ἀφῆκεν τὴν Ἰουδαίαν. Several witnesses, however, do not present any πάλιν here: B* A G H K U 037 039 041 044 0141 28 157 579 700 1346 1424 q sy ʰ bo ᵐˢˢ geo² *pm*. Apart from B* this set of witnesses represents a relatively late form of the text. The textual critics Bart Ehrman, Gordon Fee, and Michael Holmes examined the quota-

---

15. Reiser, *Sprache und literarische Formen*, 66, 212, 213; Friedrich Blass, *Philology of the Gospels* (London 1898; repr. Amsterdam: Grüner, 1969), 236: "That John's style is asyndetic you will recognize at once, wherever you open his book."

16. Kurt Aland, ed., *Vollständige Konkordanz zum griechischen Neuen Testament: Unter Zugrundelegung aller modernen kritischen Textausgaben und des Textus Receptus*, ANTF 4 (Berlin: de Gruyter, 1978–1983); K. Aland, *Computer-Konkordanz: Vollständige Konkordanz zum griechischen Neuen Testament* (Berlin: de Gruyter, 1977); Carl Hermann Bruder, *Tamieion ton tes kaines diathekes lexeon, sive concordantiae omnium vocum Novi Testamenti Graeci* (Leipzig: Bredt, 1888).

17. Unless otherwise noted, all translations are mine.

tions of this passage by Origen and stated that Origen's manner of quoting precludes any answer to the question whether πάλιν was part of his text.[18] Πάλιν, then, belongs to the original text and is to be retained. We note that occasionally we have to decide against the excellent witness B.[19]

In John 9:27 the tradition fluctuates as to the word order. A minority of witnesses, namely, P[75] and B, two important Egyptian witnesses, and also achm[2] bo[ms], have τί οὖν πάλιν θέλετε ἀκούειν; In omitting this οὖν, other witnesses present τί πάλιν θέλετε ἀκούειν; So ℵ A K L M N U W 039 044 28 33 69 124 157 579 1071 1424 fam[1] fam[13] *pm*. The author emphasizes the verb θέλετε by using it twice. A word order that seems more natural is found in P[66] (D) 038 047 0211 e a r[1]: τί θέλετε πάλιν ἀκούειν; It is questionable, though, whether this variant is a Western improvement of the text, or whether it is original. The grammar of Blass and Debrunner preferred the Egyptian variant without discussing this textual problem.[20] It is recommended to follow the Egyptian text here. On the other hand, the Western text and its differing word order could be defended equally well.

At first glance the use of πάλιν in John 10:39 seems comparable to the examples established above. The adverb directly precedes the verb. Yet to speak of a "renewed" stoning is not really meaningful language. Also we meet in this passage a marked diversity of variant readings. This πάλιν, therefore, a secondary intrusion, will be discussed within the next section.

2. The Adverb πάλιν: Uses Designed to Structure a Narrative

The Fourth Gospel regularly uses πάλιν to give structure to narratives. Movements in their precise sequence are vividly portrayed. The Roman prefect appears outside the praetorium in front of the multitude and enters the building again. He appears anew and leaves the multitude (John 18:28–40). A blind man who had received sight is questioned by his neighbors, by Pharisees, by other Pharisees. His parents are interviewed, and again the cured man. The tradition is firm here: John 9:15, 17, 27. The adverbs used to form strands of action are as a rule firmly transmitted in this gospel, compare John 4:46 (2:2); 6:15 (6:3); 10:19 (7:43 and 9:16);

---

18. Bart D. Ehrman, Gordon D. Fee, and Michael W. Holmes, *The Text of the Fourth Gospel in the Writings of Origen*, vol. 1, NTGF 3 (Atlanta: Scholars Press, 1992), 112 n. 4.

19. Thus Metzger, *Textual Commentary*, 176–77.

20. BDF §338.2.

11:38 (11:33); 12:39 (12:38); 13:12 (13:4); 18:7 (18:4); 18:27 (18:17 and 18:25); 19:37 (19:36); 20:10 (20:2); 20:21 (20:19).

A secondary πάλιν in John 1:21 is meant to tie together a course of events. The additional word in ℵ W^s e it sy^p is poorly attested. This πάλιν is not found in sy^s, in f q aur vg and in a remarkable number of ancient witnesses, among them P^{66} P^{75} B C A and numerous other majuscule manuscripts.[21] The text of Origen's commentary on John, too, supports the omission of πάλιν.[22]

Another πάλιν in John 8:28 is also insufficiently attested. Here the additional word links together several sayings of Jesus. The addition is attested by ℵ* D 28 sy^s and sy^p, but is not found in e or in most of the Old Latin witnesses.

In John 9:26, too, an additional πάλιν serves to tie a narrative together. It is superfluous, though, and it is missing in good witnesses, in P^{75} ℵ* B D W 579 sy^s co, in e and in most of the Old Latin witnesses. In f q aur, *iterum* is found.

Chapter 10 of the Fourth Gospel features a series of monologues of Jesus, which mainly introduce him as the Good Shepherd. Various units are only loosely connected. Some parts lack any narrative setting, while other parts are set in narrative passages. Several times a πάλιν appears, the transmission of which is not entirely clear. Its textual status needs to be examined.

The passage John 10:11–18 may be seen as a narrative unit. Verse 19 resumes the narrative setting and tells of a reaction of the Judeans, which reminds the reader of similar reactions: πάλιν (John 7:43 and 9:16). The transmission of this πάλιν is firm, with the exception of D, which omits it. Here a secondary οὖν is found in many witnesses, among them P^{66} A (D) K M U 037 038 039 041 044 fam^1 fam^{13} sy^h pbo bo. The connecting particle is missing in P^{75} ℵ B L W 157 579 1071 e it sy$^{s.p}$ sa achm^2. The attestation of the particle is partly old, but the Egyptian group of witnesses, supported by the Western attestation of W e it sy$^{s.p}$ achm^2, deserves preference: πάλιν is secondary.[23]

In contrast to these texts, the passage John 10:7–10 appears to be a

---

21. Metzger, *Textual Commentary*, 170, leans for its decision on the age and the wide geographical distribution of these witnesses.

22. Origen, *Comm. Jo.* 6.10.62 (ed. Preuschen, p. 119); see Ehrman, Fee, and Holmes, *Text of the Fourth Gospel in the Writings of Origen*, 63.

23. Metzger, *Textual Commentary*, 197. In a situation such as this, where a

supplement drawn up by Johannine redactors who ignore in a remarkable fashion the concepts of figurative speech in John 10:1–6 and 10:11–18. This supplement includes part of the wording of verse 7, εἶπεν οὖν αὐτοῖς ὁ Ἰησοῦς: so P^{45vid} P^{66c} ℵ^2 W 1 565 1241 *l* 2211 it. A secondary πάλιν is discernible as a disturbing element. It appears in varying positions in this sentence. P^{6vid} P^{75} (B) read εἶπεν οὖν πάλιν ὁ Ἰησοῦς, while D G L M U Y 037 038 044 579 700 892^s a sy co *pm* have εἶπεν οὖν πάλιν αὐτοῖς ὁ Ἰησοῦς. Another word order, εἶπεν οὖν αὐτοῖς πάλιν ὁ Ἰησοῦς is attested by A K 039 0250 sy^p. Here the Egyptian witness ℵ* gives εἶπεν αὐτοῖς πάλιν ὁ Ἰησοῦς, while P^{66*} e read εἶπεν αὐτοῖς ὁ Ἰησοῦς. And, finally, εἶπεν οὖν αὐτοῖς ὁ Ἰησοῦς πάλιν is attested by 33 1424 sy^h and (omitting οὖν) fam^{13}.[24] The additional οὖν is also not found in P^{66*} ℵ* e sy^s. Within the Old Latin tradition, *iterum* is omitted in ff^2, but it is found in a d. The Sinai Syriac (sy^c) text opens its sentence with "again." This πάλιν is clearly meant to connect this supplementary text to the narrative sequence, similar in effect to the connective οὖν. This πάλιν should not be accepted.

Such variance in word order is rather typical of a process of transmission that received secondary intrusions. The supplement began asyndetically (without οὖν), as is seen in P^{66*} ℵ* e sy^s. In a passage like this, it is necessary to depart from the position of Brooke Foss Westcott and Fenton John Anthony Hort and their successors and to prefer an ancient Western tradition. We read: εἶπεν αὐτοῖς ὁ Ἰησοῦς.[25]

The monologue of Jesus in John 10:1–6, 11–18 was completed by resuming the narrative. The reaction of the audience is reported. Twice his listeners are about to seize and to stone Jesus on account of his high claims (John 10:31, 39). An adverb πάλιν as mentioned above is firm in the tradition (John 10:19).[26] Three times an adverb πάλιν is made use of to underscore a narrative sequence. All of these occurrences appear uncertain as to the text. In John 10:31 πάλιν is omitted by P^{45} D 038 e it (except

---

balance of witnesses emerges, the observation gains weight that particles are more often added than lost.

24. See NA^{28}, Appendix II: Variae lectiones minores, 827.

25. The textual criticism of Westcott and Hort preferred as a rule the Egyptian variant readings and sought to justify this by the theory of an early "neutral" text, see Brooke Foss Westcott and Fenton John Anthony Hort, eds., *The New Testament in the Original Greek: Volume 1, Text; Volume 2, Introduction [and] Appendix* (Cambridge: Macmillan, 1881).

26. See above, §2, p. 2 note 2.

f) sy^s sa^{ms} pbo bo (John 8:59 alluded to). This speaks clearly against an original status of the word.

In John 10:39 an alternative οὖν found in some of the witnesses cannot be accepted as an original part of the text either: οὖν D 28 69 124 788 *l* 844 e it sa^{ms} bo; οὖν πάλιν P^{66} A K M U 036 037 039 041 044 fam^1 fam^{13} f sy^h sa^{ms} pm.[27] In John 10:39 several witnesses lack the adverb: P^{45vid} P^{75} ℵ* D 579 1241 e it achm^2.[28] This definitely decides against an original status. Here, too, an original asyndeton was removed by οὖν or καί or δέ respectively. Asyndetic ἐζήτουν is testified to by P^{75vid} B M U 036 038* 039 045 28 157 180 700 1292 1342 pbo bo^{ms} *pm*. In John 10:40 πάλιν is missing in P^{66} 036 047 e sy$^{s.p}$ achm^2.

A narrative concisely told in John 12:22 begins a sentence by placing two verbs asyndetically. Greek and Latin witnesses removed this typically Johannine stylistic device in different ways. The additional πάλιν is missing in P^{75vid} P^{66c} B Q* L A a c l r^1 sy^s. In a few Old Latin witnesses it appears in various positions. It is missing in the African witness e.

In John 12:38 + 40, by introducing two quotations from Isaiah, the author creates a sequence of reflection. The introductions to these are linked by a πάλιν (John 12:39). A singular variant of Codex Bezae introduces a stylistic alternative: D καὶ γάρ. A singular variant reading, however, is not acceptable here.

In a conspicuous section of the passion narrative, πάλιν is employed in order to illustrate the conduct of the Roman prefect. The author endeavors to bring the correct adherence to purity requirements on the part of Jewish prosecutors into focus (John 18:28). Since they refuse to enter the praetorium, Pilate addresses them outside the building, but in order to conduct the trial, he enters it. The movements of the Roman prefect are given in detail: ἐξῆλθεν οὖν ... εἰσῆλθεν οὖν πάλιν ... καὶ τοῦτο εἰπὼν πάλιν ἐξῆλθεν πρὸς τοὺς Ἰουδαίους ... καὶ ἐξῆλθεν πάλιν ... καὶ εἰσῆλθεν εἰς τὸ πραιτώριον πάλιν (John 18:29, 33, 38; 19:4, 9). It is questionable here, whether or not the first occurrence of πάλιν in John 18:33 belongs to the original text. The adverb is missing in the minuscules 33 and 1424; the other witnesses present it in three different positions. In P^{52} P^{66vid} B C* D^s L W 037 0109 fam^{13}

---

27. NA^{28}; UBS^5; and Metzger, *Textual Commentary*, include οὖν in square brackets, as the editors were not confident about its original status, see p. 198.

28. Regarding the quotation of the testimony of P^{75}, see William J. Elliott and David C. Parker, *The New Testament in Greek, IV: The Gospel according to St. John; Vol. One; The Papyri*, NTTS 20 (Leiden: Brill, 1995), 237.

579 *l*844 e it, it appears as the third word of the sentence. Since the most ancient Johannine papyrus P⁵² is among the witnesses and the Old African and Old Latin witnesses have the word, the decision is clear: the word is part of the original text. It is supported, too, by the form of the whole narrative, as it is firmly transmitted in John 18:38 b, in 19:4, and in 19:9.

In John 18:40 the author depicts the tumult that is raised by an angry crowd. Is πάντες λέγοντες the text we ought to read here or is it πάλιν λέγοντες? One of the two words is an intrusion. Πάλιν is attested by P⁶⁰ ℵ B L W 045 0109 118 579 1071. Both words are lacking in 1241 and in achm². Both words are transmitted in A (Dˢ) 036 037 038 0250 f vg syʰ *pm*.

Two traditions are in opposition to each other. Instead of πάντες our best Egyptian witnesses have πάλιν, but they are alone in this. Instead of πάλιν our best Western witnesses have πάντες, namely, e and all Old Latin witnesses; this variant reading is supported additionally by P⁶⁶ᵛⁱᵈ G K N U 041 044 fam¹ fam¹³ 33 565 700 *l*844 and syᵖ sa pbo bo. The papyrus P⁶⁶ was copied about the year 200. D exists as a supplement here: πάλιν λέγοντες πάντες.²⁹ The Sinai Syriac text does not transmit any text here.³⁰

It is evident that πάλιν intruded rather frequently into the Johannine text, and regarding the word πάντες, of course, nothing comparable could be stated. Also πάλιν seems to be misplaced in this passage. Not before chapter 19 does the shouting of the crowd get out of hand (John 19:6, 12, 15). We have to accept the Western text here, our most ancient text.

A threefold commission of the risen Lord to Peter is shaped into an impressive scene (John 21:15–17). Three times the disciple is questioned, three times he receives instructions to be the shepherd of the flock. The author writes succinctly. Three times without designating the subject, the answer is repeated: λέγει αὐτῷ.

These questions seem to be counted: δεύτερον, τὸ τρίτον. In John 21:16 an additional πάλιν doubles this enumeration. It is questionable, however, whether this πάλιν belongs to the original text. It is lacking in D, in e, and in c. Both Old Latin manuscripts read *secundo*. On the other hand, δεύτερον is missing in ℵ* syˢ *pc*. This latter variant reading, on account of its poor attestation, cannot be recommended. The omission may be explained as a reaction of scribes who were irritated by a twofold enumeration. The

---

29. NA²⁸, Anhang: Variae lectiones minores, 828.
30. The text of the papyrus P⁹⁰ cannot be quoted here, reading only π[; see Elliott and Parker, *Papyri*, 385.

fluctuation of our tradition regarding the position of the πάλιν reveals that it was added to the text: ℵ C* W 038 b f present πάλιν at the beginning of the sentence, B A K L M N X 036 037 039 041 044 *pm* have πάλιν as the third word.

Early in the twentieth century Blass was a classical scholar of high renown. Though much of the material that has been published since then was unknown to him, this author arrived at the same conclusion: λέγει αὐτῷ δεύτερον.[31]

3. The Adverb πάλιν: A Tie That Connects Literary Units

A third function of πάλιν must still be considered, namely, its use as a connective of literary or, more specifically, narrative units. This πάλιν is regularly found within the first sentence of a textual unit at one of the prominent positions.

Often such a πάλιν is found together with a particle meant to create *syndesis*. In John 8:12, for instance, a conversation with Pharisees is introduced by a πάλιν that opens the sentence. The sentence structure is syndetical. A syndetically introduced passage reports a conversation with hostile Judeans in John 8:21; at the third position in this sentence we find a πάλιν. A syndetical sentence opens a further narrative unit in John 20:26. At the fifth position in that sentence we find πάλιν. The report of a miraculous cure may be completed by a summarizing remark. A second sign takes place. Beside the numeral a πάλιν appears as the second word in the sentence. The author formulates asyndetically, appropriate to a concluding remark (John 4:54).

It may thus be questioned whether the πάλιν in John 1:35, which connects two episodes, is, indeed, original. It appears as the third word of an asyndetical sentence. Yet it is lacking in P[5vid] P[75] 036 044 1071 e b r[1] sy[s.c.p] bo[ms]. The Egyptian witnesses are reinforced by numerous Western witnesses, among these all Syriac witnesses. This constellation carries decisive weight. That word does not belong to the original text.[32]

---

31. Fridericus Blass, *Euangelium secundum Iohannem cum variae lectionis delectu* (Leipzig: Teubner, 1902), 107.

32. The commentary of Origen on Matthew does not support this decision: Origen quotes a text that includes πάλιν. See Origen, *Comm. Mat* 10,1,442 (ed. Klostermann, p. 1), and Ehrman, Fee, and Holmes, *Text of the Fourth Gospel in the Writings of Origen*, 80. Elliott calls attention to the reading of P[120], which sup-

1. Introduction to the Textual Criticism of the New Testament 13

A further transition that connects narratives by using πάλιν seems to be preserved in John 21:1. The passage 20:30–31, formally designed as a book ending, reveals that the narratives of chapter 21 were written by some Johannine redactors. The first verse of this supplement, however, is not transmitted without variant readings. The concluding sentence of this unit states that this appearance of the risen Lord is the third and also the last in a series of three (John 21:14). We identify the two narratives implied in this remark with the texts of John 20:11–18 and 20:19–23 and 20:24–29. "Revelation" as a keyword carries weight in the context of the theology of the Fourth Gospel. Yet some disorder is obvious in view of four reported revelations. A solution to this problem may be sought in the suggestion that the narrative John 20:24–29 dates back to a later origin than that of John 21:1–14.

In what manner are Johannine redactors seen to use the connective πάλιν? This adverb, firm in our tradition, is found in a syndetically opened sentence in John 20:26. A πάλιν found in John 21:1, however, is not firm. It is missing in G 1424 sy^s sa pbo bo^{ms}. It is not missing in the Old Latin tradition including the Old African witness e. Hence it must be considered to be old. It is found, too, in one of our oldest witnesses, in P^{66}, according to the text reconstructed in the *editio princeps*:

μ[ετα ταυτ]α εφαν[ε]ρω[σ]εν[εαυ
τον παλινις]τοις μαθητα[ις επι
της θαλασσης] της τιβεριαδ[ος
εφανερωσεν δε ο]υτως.[33]

Its position, as transmitted, varies within this verse, a mark of early disturbance. D presents πάλιν as the third word of the sentence; ℵ as the fourth word; B C* A H K L M N U 037 038 039 041 33 565 700 1071 present it as a fifth word; and W 044 as the seventh word. Complicated processes of transmission are discernible. These variant readings are numerous. Hence

---

ports the omission with P^5 and P^{75}: "Spacing suggests P^{120} omits πάλιν with P^{75} Ψ" (*New Testament Textual Criticism*, 172).

33. *Editio princeps* of P^{66}: Victor Martin, *Papyrus Bodmer II: Evangile de Jean; chap. 1–14 et chap. 15–21*, 2 vols. (Cologny-Genève: Bibliotheca Bodmeriana, 1956); Martin, *Papyrus Bodmer II: Evangile de Jean; Chap. 1–14 et chap. 15–21: Supplément* (Cologny-Genève: Bibliotheca Bodmeriana, 1962).

we raise the question, which text represents the original version of the first sentence of this chapter.

Only a small selection of variant readings is listed in some of our editions. They give what is considered important. If difficulties are discernible, it is recommended to fall back on the best editions of the past, above all the *Octava* of Constantin von Tischendorf. Tischendorf investigated the disturbances in this tradition and noticed that this passage suffered ancient additions. The sentence originally lacked a subject. Ἰησοῦς and ὁ Ἰησοῦς, respectively, were supplied later. In D M and in the African witness e these words are missing. The indirect object τοῖς μαθηταῖς, as Tischendorf noted, has been supplied in two versions, with and without αὐτοῦ. And this indirect object is lacking in e aur and in numerous manuscripts of the Vulgate.

We are presented with a multitude of data, difficult to analyze, not merely with two alternatives. In such cases it is recommended to arrange variant readings according to their length and then to analyze. We examine the apparatus of Tischendorf, the data collected by Reuben J. Swanson and the lists of variant readings as given by the International Greek New Testament Project.[34]

First we delete all witnesses that carry the supplement ἐγερθεὶς ἐκ νεκρῶν. These are 036 and the minuscule manuscripts 2 1241 1346 1424 fam[13]. Then we scrutinize the Byzantine majority text. This testifies to μετὰ ταῦτα ἐφανέρωσεν ἑαυτὸν πάλιν ὁ Ἰησοῦς τοῖς μαθηταῖς ἐπὶ τῆς θαλάσσης τῆς Τιβεριάδος· ἐφανέρωσεν δὲ οὕτως, so P[66] A K L N 038 039 041 0250 fam[1] 33 157 565 Koine. We distinguish from these, other old witnesses, mainly Western, which add an αὐτοῦ to the indirect object, so: C[3] D G H M U X 044 700 1071 *l*844 *l*2211 it sy[s.p] co. In contrast to these, the African witness e lacks an indirect object, lacks *suis*. Since numerous manuscripts of the Vulgate have no *discipulis suis*, Tischendorf presumed that this object is not part of the original text. He printed τοῖς μαθηταῖς. Likewise he surmised that this passage lacked a subject originally. The variation of

---

34. Reuben J. Swanson, *New Testament Greek Manuscripts: Variant Readings Arranged in Horizontal Lines Against Codex Vaticanus; John* (Sheffield: Sheffield Academic; Pasadena: William Carey International University Press, 1995), 282–83; Elliott and Parker, *Papyri*, 410; Ulrich B. Schmid, William J. Elliott and David C. Parker, *The New Testament in Greek, IV: The Gospel according to St. John; Volume Two: The Majuscules*, NTTS 37 (Leiden: Brill, 2007), 542–43.

Ἰησοῦς/ὁ Ἰησοῦς supports this conclusion.³⁵ We have to delete from this sentence both the indirect object and the subject.

If πάλιν was an original part of this sentence, where does it belong? The Byzantine tradition supplies it with a strong attestation. It is found at the fifth position. But what does it mean that B C*, that D, that ℵ, that W 044 present it at different positions? What does it mean that G 1424 sy^s sa pbo bo^ms lack this word? Πάλιν is an ancient intrusion. I consider the variant reading that lacks this word as the original wording and recognize as the text of the redaction:

μετὰ ταῦτα ἐφανέρωσεν ἑαυτὸν ἐπὶ τῆς θαλάσσης τῆς Τιβεριάδος· ἐφανέρωσεν δὲ οὕτως.

This μετὰ ταῦτα placed asyndetically is modeled upon similar introductions (John 2:12; 3:22; 5:1, 14; 6:1; 7:1; 11:7; 19:28, 38; 20:26). Before World War I, Blass, the classical scholar, presented the same conclusion.³⁶

4. Inquiries Addressed to This Text-Critical Method

The text-critical method presented here deliberately receives some important developments of the twentieth century. It accepts the view that the original texts of the New Testament, insofar as they have been preserved by the tradition, may be found in principle among witnesses from all traditions of the ancient world.

In contrast to the textual theory of Westcott and Hort, it is not assumed that the original wording of "neutral" forms of the text regularly may be identified in Egyptian witnesses. Rather it is assumed that so-called Western witnesses not affected by authoritative Egyptian traditions occasionally do preserve the most ancient wording. It is assumed, too, that occasionally Byzantine witnesses preserve the most ancient text. The philologist Zuntz proved that this proposition is fully justified.³⁷

---

35. Constantin von Tischendorf, *Novum Testamentum Graece: Ad antiquissimos testes denuo recensuit; Apparatum criticum omni studio perfectum apposuit; Commentationem Isagogicam praetexuit Constantinus Tischendorf*, 8th ed. (Leipzig: Giesecke & Devrient, 1869), 959: "nullam caussam fuisse hoc loco auferendi nomen Iesu patet, hinc vix errat cui D et e rectum habere videantur."

36. Blass, *Evangelium secundum Iohannem*, 105.

37. Günther Zuntz, *The Text of the Epistles: A Disquisition upon the Corpus*

Textual criticism depends upon data. These have been collected in the published volumes of the *Editio critica maior*, in the apparatuses of Greek, Latin, Syriac, Coptic, Old Armenian, Old Georgian editions of the New Testament, and also in other invaluable publications such as the *Biblia Patristica* of a Strasbourg group of researchers, the Münster series *Text und Textwert* and *Das Neue Testament auf Papyrus* as well as *Arbeiten zur neutestamentlichen Textforschung*, further the publications of the *Vetus Latina Institute* at the Erzabtei Beuron, the series *New Testament Tools and Studies*, formerly edited by Metzger and, after him, by Ehrman and Eldon J. Epp, and finally, to enumerate some of the most important reference series, the "Third Series" of *Text and Studies*, edited by David C. Parker and David G. K. Taylor.

By means of a methodical analysis, textual criticism gains insight from these data into ancient processes of transmission and reception. To identify losses of ancient text and alterations requires first a sufficient amount of experience in recognizing scribal mistakes, efforts to smooth out texts, to improve stylistically, to add relevant material from other gospels or from other contexts, to alter dogmatically ambiguous wording, even to heighten narrative highlights.[38] Sometimes scribes, remembering relevant material, anticipate stylistic effects that authors intended to appear at a later moment.[39]

Paulinum, Schweich Lectures of the British Academy 1946 (London: Oxford University Press, 1953), 12: "The rejection *en bloc* of the Byzantine text similarly tends to rob us of a most helpful instrument. This rejection is due to Johann Griesbach, who, as we saw, considered the late text to derive from the two earlier 'recensions' combined. We shall see that this view is erroneous and thus gain another clue to the early history of the tradition." Zuntz presented in detail proof for his proposition, see pp. 49–57.

38. The topic of dogmatically ambiguous wording was presented in its various aspects by Bart Ehrman, *The Orthodox Corruption of Scripture: The Effect of Early Christological Controversies on the Text of the New Testament* (New York: Oxford University Press, 1993). Sometimes scribes discern a dramatic moment in some narrative and decide to underscore this stylistic effect. In Luke 24:15, e.g., among several additions the words καὶ αὐτός are found, a phrase unattested by D. The most ancient form of this passage has been kept by e c sy[s. c] sa.

39. Occasionally copyists, by introducing an element of the text of an author prematurely, disturb the stylistic effect aimed at by the author, cf., e.g., the ἔτι of 1 Cor 3:2, a secondary addition to that verse. See Güting, "Methodological Contribution," 363 n. 16. Heinrich Greeven called attention to a passage in Mark 2:9 that presents a later phrase (from Mark 2:11) prematurely, namely, the words καὶ

This procedure was described by Zuntz as a "fruitful circle." For, while various phenomena analyzed in detail apparently receive full attention as conclusions are sought critically, at the same time a full view of an object is striven for, a view capable of justifying judgments allotted to the details. Textual analysis thus seeks to meet scientific standards in rejecting subjective assumptions.[40]

An important function in the course of this analysis is reserved to the process of considering ancient translations. As Harnack emphasized, and as Johann Griesbach noticed, the Old Latin tradition is destined to take an essential part here. Quite often original variant readings are found mainly in older witnesses, first of all in the African e. Occasionally it is discerned that secondary variant readings begin to appear in later witnesses of the Old Latin tradition. Within the Old Syriac tradition of the New Testament, which has undergone careful research by the Münster *Institut für Neutestamentliche Textforschung*, it is not at all unusual that a development from the Cureton Syriac or the Sinai Syriac to later versions is discerned. By means of quotations from the writings of church fathers, transmitted forms of New Testament texts may be localized as to region or date. This method was developed by scholars like Cuthbert H. Turner, Burnet H. Streeter, and Zuntz and proven to be fruitful.

This method proceeds eclectically, and is not ashamed of being accused of eclecticism. A manuscript that in a given unit of variation testifies to an excellent text, may in the next unit introduce variant readings clearly discernible as secondary. Constellations of witnesses united in their testimony to the critically established text keep changing constantly. Text-critical methodology keeps clear of subjective presumptions. The question, however, whether a given text may be attributed to an author or not, certainly a problem of sober philology, is dependent upon extensive linguistic knowledge.

To all appearances this text-critical method gives attention predominantly to text-centered issues, to semantic, to grammatical, to stylistic, and to contextual questions, with the effect that considerations that evaluate the outward attestation lose their significance. It must be emphasized, however, that the analysis of relevant aspects of the text requires a considerable

---

ἆρον τὸν κράββατόν σου, see Greeven, "Die Heilung des Gelähmten nach Matthäus," *WD* 4 (1955): 65–78, = Greeven, in *Das Matthäusevangelium*, ed. Joachim Lange, WdF 525 (Darmstadt: Wissenschaftliche Buchgesellschaft, 1980), 205–22; Greeven and Güting, *Textkritik des Markusevangeliums*, 139–41.

40. Zuntz, *Text of the Epistles*, 12, 13.

amount of experience in the use of data. Again and again the question must be raised, whether the result of an analysis is, indeed, supported by the given set of witnesses, or whether the attestation, on the contrary, is apt to contradict these conclusions. Only if our analysis of outward attestation and our examination of inward criteria both retain a balanced weight, are false conclusions avoidable.

Whoever proceeds to examine variant readings in some text with the purpose of deciding text-critical issues, will not necessarily encounter phenomena correlated to each other. The method introduced here, on the contrary, chooses first a topic and then an adequate procedure. Hence distant phenomena lose their isolation. An interrelation of text-critical phenomena becomes visible that enables one to compare decisions. Last, but not least, faulty conclusions become conspicuous as texts are linguistically or stylistically compared.

5. Results

The question remains: what results were achieved by the method here chosen? First, we have to state that the decision of the edition Nestle-Aland, not to accept πάλιν into the text in John 1:21, 8:28, 9:26, and 12:22, must be approved of.[41] A πάλιν in a strictly adverbial use is printed twelve times in the edition Nestle-Aland (John 4:13; 10:17, 18; 11:7, 8; 12:28; 14:3; 16:16, 17, 19, 22, 28). It is questionable whether in two other instances πάλιν does properly belong to the text. On account of its attestation it is to be kept in John 4:3. It is also to be kept in John 9:27. In this latter passage, however, possibly a different word order is to be preferred.[42]

The Nestle-Aland edition prints sixteen references to πάλιν used to give structure to narratives, all of them firm in their transmission (John 4:46; 6:15; 9:15; 10:19; 11:38; 12:39; 13:12; 18:7, 27, 38; 19:4, 9, 37; 20:10, 21). Twelve other references in need of testing regarding their textual status are partly original (John 12:39; 18:33).[43] All the other references involve secondary variant readings. These additions must be attributed to ancient scribes, not to the author of the Fourth Gospel. The relatively high number of such additions proves that copyists interpreted such narrative

---

41. See the discussion in §2 above, pp. 7–12.
42. See the discussion near the end of §2 above, p. 8.
43. See the discussion in §2 above, pp. 10–11.

sequences as coherent events and were interested in underscoring their coherence. This result is in harmony with the observation that scribes tended to link together their texts and that they used as alternatives to πάλιν various secondary particles, such as οὖν, καί, and δέ (John 9:27; 10:7, 19, 31, 39; 12:22).

The Nestle-Aland edition prints four references to a πάλιν used to link literary units, all of them firm in their transmission (John 4:54; 8:12, 21; 20:26). Two other references are secondary additions of copyists (John 1:35; 21:1). They do not originate with the author of the Fourth Gospel nor with the text of the ancient editors.[44]

Bibliography

Aland, Barbara. "Text Criticism of the Bible. II. New Testament." *RPP* 12:576–78.

———. "Textgeschichte/ Textkritik der Bibel, II. Neues Testament." *TRE* 33:155–68.

———. "Textkritik der Bibel, II. Neues Testament." *RGG* 8:200–207.

Aland, Barbara, Kurt Aland, Gerd Mink, Holger Strutwolf, and Klaus Wachtel, eds. *Novum Testamentum Graecum: Editio Critica Maior; Edited by the Institute for New Testament Textual Research; IV. Catholic Letters; Installment 1: James; Part 1: Text; Part 2: Supplementary Material*. 2nd ed. Stuttgart: Deutsche Bibelgesellschaft, 2013.
Installment 2. The Letters of Peter. Part 1: Text; Part 2: Supplementary Material. Stuttgart: Deutsche Bibelgesellschaft, 2000.
Installment 3. The First Letter of John. Stuttgart: Deutsche Bibelgesellschaft 2003.
Installment 4. The Second and Third Letter of John. The Letter of Jude. Stuttgart: Deutsche Bibelgesellschaft, 2005.

Aland, Barbara, Kurt Aland, Johannes Karavidopoulos, Carlo M. Martini, and Bruce M. Metzger, eds. *The Greek New Testament*. 5th ed. Stuttgart: Deutsche Bibelgesellschaft; United Bible Societies, 2014.

———, eds. *Novum Testamentum Graece*. 28th ed. Stuttgart: Deutsche Bibelgesellschaft, 2012.

Aland, Kurt. *Computer-Konkordanz: Vollständige Konkordanz zum griechischen Neuen Testament*. Berlin: de Gruyter, 1977.

---

44. See the discussion in §3 above, pp. 13–15.

———, ed. *Vollständige Konkordanz zum griechischen Neuen Testament: Unter Zugrundelegung aller modernen kritischen Textausgaben und des Textus Receptus*. ANTF 4. Berlin: de Gruyter, 1978–1983.

Aland, Kurt, and Barbara Aland, eds. *Griechisch-deutsches Wörterbuch zu den Schriften des Neuen Testaments und der [übrigen] frühchristlichen Literatur von Walter Bauer*. 6th ed. Berlin: de Gruyter, 1988.

———. *The Text of the New Testament: An Introduction to the Critical Editions and to the Theory and Practice of Modern Textual Criticism*. 2nd ed. Grand Rapids: Eerdmans; Leiden: Brill, 1989.

Blass, Friedrich. *Euangelium secundum Iohannem cum variae lectionis delectu*. Leipzig: Teubner, 1902.

———. *Philology of the Gospels*. London, 1898. Repr. Amsterdam: Grüner, 1969.

Blass, Friedrich, and Albert Debrunner. *Grammatik des neutestamentlichen Griechisch: Joachim Jeremias zum 75. Geburtstag*. 18th ed. Edited by Friedrich Rehkopf. Göttingen: Vandenhoeck & Ruprecht, 1990.

Bruder, Carl Hermann. *Tamieion ton tes kaines diathekes lexeon, sive concordantiae omnium vocum Novi Testamenti Graeci*. Leipzig: Bredt, 1888.

Donaldson, Amy M. "Explicit References to New Testament Variant Readings among Greek and Latin Church Fathers." PhD diss., University of Notre Dame, 2009. https://tinyurl.com/sbl7012c.

Ehrman, Bart D. *The Orthodox Corruption of Scripture: The Effect of Early Christological Controversies on the Text of the New Testament*. New York: Oxford University Press, 1993.

———. *Studies in the Textual Criticism of the New Testament*. NTTS 33. Leiden: Brill, 2006.

Ehrman, Bart D., Gordon D. Fee, and Michael W. Holmes. *The Text of the Fourth Gospel in the Writings of Origen*. Vol. 1. NTGF 3. Atlanta: Scholars Press, 1992.

Ehrman, Bart D., and Michael W. Holmes, eds. *The Text of the New Testament in Contemporary Research: Essays on the Status Quaestionis*. 2nd ed. NTTS 42. Leiden: Brill, 2013.

Elliott, J. Keith. *New Testament Textual Criticism: The Application of Thoroughgoing Principles; Essays on Manuscripts and Textual Variation*. NovTSup 137. Leiden: Brill, 2010.

Elliott, William J., and David C. Parker. *The New Testament in Greek, IV: The Gospel according to St. John; Vol. One; The Papyri*. NTTS 20. Leiden: Brill, 1995.

Epp, Eldon J. "It's All about Variants: A Variant-Conscious Approach to New Testament Textual Criticism." *HTR* 100 (2007): 275–308.

———. *Perspectives on New Testament Textual Criticism: Collected Essays 1962–2004*. NovTSup 116. Leiden: Brill, 2005.

Fee, Gordon D., revised by Roderic L. Mullen. "The Use of the Greek Fathers for New Testament Textual Criticism." Pages 351–73 in *The Text of the New Testament in Contemporary Research: Essays on the Status Quaestionis*. Edited by Bart D. Ehrman and Michael W. Holmes. 2nd ed. NTTS 42. Leiden: Brill, 2013.

Greeven, Heinrich. "Die Heilung des Gelähmten nach Matthäus." *WD* 4 (1955): 65–78; = pages 205–22 in *Das Matthäusevangelium*. Edited by Joachim Lange. WdF 525. Darmstadt: Wissenschaftliche Buchgesellschaft, 1980.

Greeven, Heinrich, and Eberhard Güting, eds. *Textkritik des Markusevangeliums*. Theologie, Forschung und Wissenschaft 11. Münster: LIT, 2005.

Güting, Eberhard. "Amen, Eulogie, Doxologie: Eine textkritische Untersuchung." Pages 133–62 in *Begegnungen zwischen Christentum und Judentum in Antike und Mittelalter: Festschrift Heinz Schreckenberg*. Edited by Dietrich-Alex Koch and Hermann Lichtenberger. SIJD 1. Göttingen: Vandenhoeck & Ruprecht, 1993.

———. "The Methodological Contribution of Günther Zuntz to the Text of Hebrews." *NovT* 51 (2006): 359–78. [Ch. 10 in this collection.]

Güting, Eberhard W., and David L. Mealand. *Asyndeton in Paul: A Text-critical and Statistical Enquiry into Pauline Style*. SBET 39. Lewiston, NY: Mellen, 1998.

Holmes, Michael W., ed. *The Greek New Testament: SBL Edition*. Atlanta: Society of Biblical Literature; Bellingham, WA: Logos Bible Software, 2010.

———. "The Text of the Epistles Sixty Years After: An Assessment of Günther Zuntz's Contribution to Text-Critical Methodology and History." Pages 89–113 in *Transmission and Reception: New Testament Text-critical and Exegetical Studies*. Edited by Jeffrey Wayne Childers and David C. Parker. Piscataway, NJ: Gorgias, 2006.

Maas, Paul. *Textkritik*. 4th ed. Leipzig: Teubner, 1960.

———. *Textual Criticism*. Translated by Barbara Flower. Oxford: Clarendon, 1958.

Martin, Victor. *Papyrus Bodmer II: Evangile de Jean; chap. 1–14 et chap. 15–21*. 2 vols. Cologny-Genève: Bibliotheca Bodmeriana, 1956.

———. *Papyrus Bodmer II: Supplement; Evangile de Jean, chap. 14–21, Nouvelle édition augmentée et corrigée avec reproduction photographique complète du manuscript (chap. 1–21)*. Cologny-Genève: Bibliotheca Bodmeriana, 1962.
Metzger, Bruce M. *A Textual Commentary on the Greek New Testament: A Companion Volume to the United Bible Societies' Greek New Testament (Fourth Revised Edition)*. 2nd ed. Stuttgart: Deutsche Bibelgesellschaft, 1994.
Metzger, Bruce M., and Bart D. Ehrman. *The Text of the New Testament: Its Transmission, Corruption, and Restoration*. 4th ed. Oxford: Oxford University Press, 2005.
Nicklas, Tobias, and Michael Tilly, eds. *The Book of Acts as Church History/Apostelgeschichte als Kirchengeschichte: Text, Textual Traditions, and Ancient Interpretations/Text, Texttraditionen und antike Auslegungen*. BZNW 120. Berlin: de Gruyter, 2003.
Parker, David C. *An Introduction to the New Testament Manuscripts and Their Texts*. Cambridge: Cambridge University Press, 2008.
———. *Manuscripts, Texts, Theology: Collected Papers 1977–2007*. ANTF 40. Berlin: de Gruyter, 2009.
———. *Textual Scholarship and the Making of the New Testament: The Lyell Lectures Oxford Trinity Term 2011*. Oxford: Oxford University Press, 2012.
Reiser, Marius. *Sprache und literarische Formen des Neuen Testaments: Eine Einführung*. Paderborn: Schöningh, 2001.
Schmid, Ulrich B., William J. Elliott, and David C. Parker, eds. *The New Testament in Greek, IV: The Gospel according to St. John; Vol. Two: The Majuscules*. NTTS 37. Leiden: Brill, 2007.
Schrage, Wolfgang. "Geleitwort." Pages 1–2 in *Textkritik des Markusevangeliums*. Edited by Heinrich Greeven and Eberhard Güting. Theologie, Forschung und Wissenschaft 11. Münster: LIT, 2005.
Swanson, Reuben J. *New Testament Greek Manuscripts: Variant Readings Arranged in Horizontal Lines Against Codex Vaticanus; John*. Sheffield: Sheffield Academic; Pasadena: William Carey International University Press, 1995.
Tischendorf, Constantin von. *Novum Testamentum Graece: Ad antiquissimos testes denuo recensuit; Apparatum criticum omni studio perfectum apposuit; Commentationem Isagogicam praetexuit Constantinus Tischendorf*. 8th ed. Leipzig: Giesecke & Devrient, 1869.

Vaganay, Léon. *An Introduction to New Testament Textual Criticism.* 2nd ed. Rev. and updated by Christian-Bernard Amphoux and Jenny Heimerdinger. Translated by Jenny Heimerdinger. Cambridge: Cambridge University Press, 1991.
West, Martin L. *Textual Criticism and Editorial Technique: Applicable to Greek und Latin Texts.* Stuttgart: Teubner, 1973.
Westcott, Brooke Foss, and Fenton John Anthony Hort, eds. *The New Testament in the Original Greek: Volume 1, Text; Volume 2, Introduction [and] Appendix.* Cambridge: Macmillan, 1881.
Zuntz, Günther. *Lukian von Antiochien und der Text der Evangelien.* Edited by Barbara Aland and Klaus Wachtel. AHAW.PH 2. Heidelberg: Winter, 1995.
———. *The Text of the Epistles: A Disquisition upon the Corpus Paulinum.* Schweich Lectures of the British Academy 1946. London: Oxford University Press, 1953.

Selected Bibliography of Greek and Latin Manuscripts of John

Aland, Kurt, Barbara Aland, and Klaus Wachtel, eds., *Text und Textwert der griechischen Handschriften des Neuen Testaments: V. Das Johannesevangelium; Teststellenkollation der Kapitel 1–10.* ANTF 35–36. Berlin: de Gruyter, 2005.
Burton, Philip H., Hugh Alexander Gervase Houghton, Rosalind F. Maclachlan, and David C. Parker, eds. *Die Reste der altlateinischen Bibel: 19; Evangelium secundum Johannem, Fascicle 1: Jn 1,1–4,48; Fascicle 2: Jn 4,49–9,44.* Freiburg: Herder, 2011, 2013.
Comfort, Philip W., and David P. Barrett, eds. *The Text of the Earliest New Testament Greek Manuscripts: A Corrected, Enlarged Edition of The Complete Text of the Earliest New Testament Greek Manuscripts.* Wheaton: Tyndale, 2001.
Elliott, J. Keith. "Bible United: Codex Sinaiticus Online: a Gold Standard for Ancient Texts in the Digital Age." *Times Literary Supplement,* January 29, 2010, 14.
———. *A Bibliography of Greek New Testament Manuscripts.* 3rd ed. NovTSup 160. Leiden: Brill, 2015.
———. "Four New Papyri Containing the Fourth Gospel and Their Relevance for the Apparatus Criticus." Pages 170–74 in *New Testament Textual Criticism: The Application of Thoroughgoing Principles; Essays*

on Manuscripts and Their Textual Variation. Edited by J. Keith Elliott. NovTSup 137. Leiden: Brill, 2010.

Elliott, William J., and David C. Parker, eds. *The New Testament in Greek. IV: The Gospel According to St. John; Vol. 1: The Papyri.* NTTS 20. Leiden: Brill, 1995.

Jaroš, Karl, Johann Hintmaier, Brigitte Jaroš, Karin Pichlwagner, Urs Stingelin, und Ulrich Victor. *Das Neue Testament nach den ältesten griechischen Handschriften.* Ruhpolding: Rutzen; Würzburg: Echter, 2006. [CD]

Matzkow, Walter, and Kurt Aland, eds. *Itala: Das Neue Testament in altlateinischer Überlieferung nach den Handschriften herausgegeben von Adolf Jülicher: IV. Johannesevangelium.* Berlin: de Gruyter, 1963.

Parker, David C., ed., *The Critical Editions of the New Testament Online: The Greek Text, Versions, and Transcriptions of Manuscripts.* Leiden: Brill, 2015. http://www.brill.com/products/online-resources/critical-editions-new-testament-online (subscription required).

Porter, Stanley E., and Wendy J. Porter, eds. *New Testament Greek Papyri and Parchments: New Editions.* 2 vols. MPSW 29–30. Berlin: de Gruyter, 2008.

Schmid, Ulrich B., William J. Elliott, and David C. Parker, eds. *The New Testament in Greek, IV: The Gospel According to St. John; Vol. 2: The Majuscules.* NTTS 37. Leiden: Brill, 2007.

Swanson, Reuben J., ed., *New Testament Greek Manuscripts: Variant Readings Arranged in Horizontal Lines Against Codex Vaticanus: John.* Sheffield: Sheffield Academic; Pasadena, CA: William Carey International University Press, 1995.

– 2 –
The Geographical Horizon of Luke's List of the Nations (Acts 2:9–11)

For a long time New Testament research has been persuaded that Luke's so-called "list of the nations" (Acts 2:9–11)[1] was transmitted with textual corruptions. But even though over and over suggestions have been made toward the recovery of the original text, an all-around satisfactory and

---

For Professor D. Dr. W. G. Kümmel, 16 May 1975.

1. For bibliographic references see Eduard Lohse, "πεντηκοστή," *TDNT* 6:44–53; Klaus Haacker, "Das Pfingstwunder als exegetisches Problem," in *Verborum Veritas: Festschrift für G. Stählin*, ed. Otto Böcher and Klaus Haacker (Wuppertal: Brockhaus, 1970), 125–31; Jacob Kremer, *Pfingstbericht und Pfingstgeschehen: Eine exegetische Untersuchung zu Apg 2:1–13*, SBS 63/64 (Stuttgart: Katholisches Bibelwerk, 1973); Werner Stenger, "Beobachtungen zur sogenannten Völkerliste des Pfingstwunders (Apg 2:7–11)," *Kairos* 21 (1979): 206–14; Joseph A. Fitzmyer, SJ, "The Ascension of Christ and Pentecost," *TS* 45 (1984): 409–40; Pieter W. Van der Horst, "Hellenistic Parallels to the Acts of the Apostles (2.1–47)," *JSNT* 25 (1985): 49–60; John G. Gager, "Jews, Gentiles, and Synagogues in the Book of Acts," *HTR* 79 (1986): 91–99; Hans Conzelmann, "Excursus: The List of Nations," in *A Commentary on the Acts of the Apostles*, Hermeneia (Philadelphia: Fortress, 1987), 14–15; James M. Scott, "Luke's Geographical Horizon," in *The Book of Acts in its First Century Setting*, ed. David W. J. Gill and Conrad Gempf, vol. 2 of *The Book of Acts in Its Graeco-Roman Setting*, ed. Bruce W. Winter (Grand Rapids: Eerdmans; Carlisle: Paternoster, 1994), 483–544; Justin Taylor, "The List of the Nations in Acts 2:9–11," *RB* 106 (1999): 408–20; Christian Wolff, "λαλειν γλωσσαις in the Acts of the Apostles," in *Paul, Luke, and the Graeco-Roman World: Essays in Honour of J. M. Wedderburn*, ed. Alf Christophersen et al., JSNTSup 217 (London: Sheffield Academic, 2002), 189–220; Gary Gilbert, "The List of Nations in Acts 2: Roman Propaganda and the Lukan Response," *JBL* 121 (2002): 497–529; Richard I. Pervo, "Excursus: The List of Nations," in *Acts: A Commentary*, Hermeneia (Minneapolis: Fortress, 2009), 66–68.

compelling solution of the problems connected with this text has not yet been achieved. In the following I suggest a new emendation and give reasons for it.

1. Appraisal of the "List of Nations" in Past Research: Material Taken Over

With some attacks against interpreters who could explain everything, Friedrich Blass maintained in 1892 that Ἰουδαίαν in Acts 2:9 was not original.[2] This assertion, which at that time was already old,[3] was later introduced in his grammar of New Testament Greek. It also appears in the most recent edition of this grammar.[4] Numerous exegetes have agreed with this opinion, have formulated objections, and have suggested emendations.[5]

---

2. Friedrich Blass, "Zur Textkritik von Apostelgeschichte 2:5," *NKZ* 3 (1892): 830.

3. Carl Clemen, "Die Zusammensetzung von Apg 1–5," *TSK* 68 (1895): 318 n. 1.

4. BDF §261.4.

5. Adolf von Harnack, *Beiträge zur Einleitung in das Neue Testament, IV: Untersuchungen zur Apostelgeschichte und zur Abfassungszeit der synoptischen Evangelien* (Leipzig: Hinrichs, 1911), 65–69; Julius Wellhausen, *Kritische Analyse der Apostelgeschichte* (Berlin: Weidmannsche Buchhandlung, 1914), 4; Alfred F. Loisy, *Les Actes des Apôtres* (Paris: Nourry, 1920), 190; Heinrich von Baer, *Der Heilige Geist in den Lukasschriften*, BWANT 39 (Stuttgart: Kohlhammer, 1926), 88; Albert C. Clark, *The Acts of the Apostles* (Oxford: Clarendon, 1933), 338; Kirsopp Lake, "The Gift of the Spirit on the Day of Pentecost," in *Additional Notes to the Commentary*, Vol. 5 of *The Beginnings of Christianity Part I: The Acts of the Apostles*, ed. F. J. Foakes-Jackson and Kirsopp Lake (London: Macmillan, 1933), 113; E. Haenchen, *The Acts of the Apostles: A Commentary* (Philadelphia: Westminster, 1971), 166–175; C. K. Barrett, *A Critical and Exegetical Commentary on the Acts of the Apostles*, ICC (Edinburgh: T&T Clark, 2004), 1:117–25; Pervo, *Acts*, 66–68.

Conzelmann was convinced that the text of Acts needs emendation: "In many passages the text is clearly corrupt" (*Acts of the Apostles*, xxxv). He referred to Acts 3:16; 4:25; 10:36–41; 19:40.

Bruce M. Metzger gives a list of emendations on the passage: *A Textual Commentary on the Greek New Testament: A Companion Volume to the United Bible Societies' Greek New Testament (Fourth Revised Edition)*, 2nd ed (Stuttgart: Deutsche Bibelgesellschaft, 1994), 253–54; and Metzger, "Ancient Astrological Geography and Acts 2:9–11," in *Apostolic History and the Gospel: Biblical and His-*

2. The Geographical Horizon

Nevertheless, the relatively new handbook of New Testament textual criticism already mentioned argues in this passage for the textus receptus.[6]

---

torical Essays Presented to F. F. Bruce on His Sixtieth Birthday, ed. W. Ward Gasque and Ralph P. Martin (Grand Rapids: Eerdmans, 1970), 133, see also Walter Bauer, *Wörterbuch zu den Schriften des Neuen Testaments und der übrigen urchristlichen Literatur*, 5th ed. (Berlin: Töpelmann, 1963), 749. Ἰδουμαίαν (Caspar, Spitta, Lagercrantz); Ἰωνίαν (Cheyne); Βιθυνίαν (Hemsterhuis, Valckenaer); Κιλικίαν (Mangey); Λυδίαν (Bentley, Bryant); Ἰνδίαν (Erasmus, Schmid—with Chrysostom); Γορδυαίαν (Greve, Burkitt); Ἰαοῦδι (Gunkel); Ἀδιαβαίαν (Eberhard Nestle); Ἀραμαίαν (Hatch).

Also the tradition of the church fathers provides variant readings, but these apparently have only the value of conjectures. Apart from the already mentioned Ἰνδίαν we find Ἀρμενίαν (Tertullian, Augustine) and Συρίαν (Jerome); so also James H. Ropes, *The Text of Acts*, vol. 3 of Foakes-Jackson and Lake, *Beginnings of Christianity* (1926), 14. Incidentally Ropes defends the textus receptus.

This list still permits adding the conjecture of Martin Dibelius, namely, Γαλλίαν or Γαλατίαν ("Der Text der Apostelgeschichte," in *Studies in the Acts of the Apostles*, ed. Heinrich Greeven, trans. Mary Ling [London: SCM Press, 1956], 91). In regard to paleography the scribal error that Dibelius assumed is certainly possible. However, in view of the deliberate construction of the list, little supports the view that the countries of Asia Minor were spearheaded by Galatia.

6. Metzger *Textual Commentary*, 253–54 [editor's note: by "new handbook" Güting means Metzger's *Textual Commentary*, 1st ed. (1971), 293–94]. Among others, the following have defended the textus receptus: Johannes Weiss, *Über die Absicht und den literarischen Charakter der Apostelgeschichte* (Göttingen: Vandenhoeck & Ruprecht, 1897), 5–6; Heinrich J. Holtzmann, *Die Apostelgeschichte*, 3rd ed., HKNT 1 (Tübingen: Mohr, 1901), 32; Ernst von Dobschütz, "Zu der Völkerliste Act 2:9–11," ZWTh 45 (1902): 407–10; Karl L. Schmidt, *Die Pfingsterzählung und das Pfingstereignis* (Leipzig: Hinrichs, 1919), 15–16; Ropes *Text of Acts*, 14; Kirsopp Lake and Henry J. Cadbury, *English Translation and Commentary*, vol. 4 of Foakes-Jackson and Lake, *Beginnings of Christianity*, 19; Otto Bauernfeind, *Die Apostelgeschichte*, THKNT 5 (Leipzig: Deichert, 1939), 33–35; Lohse, "πεντηκοστή," 6:50–51 n. 44 [= TDNT 6:51 n. 44]; S. G. Wilson, *The Gentiles and the Gentile Mission in Luke-Acts*, SNTSMS 23 (Cambridge: Cambridge University Press, 1973), 122–23. The older defense of this tradition—for instance Weiss—assumed that sources stood behind the "list," the "speeches," and the "narratives," with which Luke the redactor found himself in disagreement. "The speech and narrative that lay before him meant *Jews* from every nation, but he himself sees the gathering as an assembly of all nations of the earth, among them *he* now names also Ἰουδαῖοί τε καὶ προσήλυτοι, and in a rather awkward place at that. But if one does not wish to read the καί, in 2:5, the Ἰουδαῖοι would still stand in the older report and would

The cause of this can basically be only one thing: up to this point the suggestions for improvement have not been convincing.

A solution for the problem of the text can only be achieved if the immediate and broader context of the list is incorporated into the research. Above all a clear answer must be given to the question whether Luke has inserted a transmitted piece for his purposes, or whether he wrote here independently. For instance, Adolf von Harnack was convinced that the author did not employ a source but here—as in the entire second chapter—to a large extent composed freely.[7] By contrast, with respect to this text recent authors reckon mostly with an editorial revision of material that is taken over.[8] Most authors claim in relation to it that Luke relied on a geographical source that is unknown to us.[9] But some maintain that Luke took an excerpt from a quite specific astrological work that was also used by Paulus Alexandrinus, an author of the fourth century.

In view of the thesis just mentioned, which was advanced especially by Stefan Weinstock,[10] but also by some other authors, reference can be made to Bruce M. Metzger's essay cited above; on closer comparison, however, the similarity of the two lists is less conspicuous than one might initially think.[11] Only five names are common to both lists.[12]

We ourselves want to keep an eye on the form of the "list." Only in this way is a solution possible. But first it must be asked whether the

---

have been overlooked, then would have been deleted by ℵ, of course completely in accord with the mind of the author" (6–7, emphasis original). In view of the speech as well as the narrative, this view has been given up. Language and style in fact display a completely Lukan character (so summarized by Lohse, "πεντηκοστή," 6:51 [= *TDNT* 6:51). But with respect to the "list of nations," the older opinion has held on rather tenaciously. I can only surmise that the determination to take the transmission as unscathed (that is, here the Ἰουδαίαν in v. 9), is responsible for the retention of this "source."

7. Harnack, *Untersuchungen zur Apostelgeschichte*, 65–69, 153, 183.

8. So most of the authors mentioned in n. 6 above.

9. Similarly Haenchen *Acts of the Apostles*, 169 n. 5, who incidentally takes Ἰουδαίαν with Harnack as an insertion (170 n. 2).

10. Stefan Weinstock, "The Geographical Catalogue in Acts II.9–11," *JRS* 38 (1948): 43–46.

11. For the taking over of this proposal see Haenchen, *Acts of the Apostles*, 169 n. 5, and Metzger "Ancient Astrological Geography," 124 n. 4.

12. Metzger, "Ancient Astrological Geography," 132.

method of redaction history should not also be brought forward to make advances in treating this matter. The demand to inquire into and thus to clarify the original *Sitz im Leben* can today of course only resolve subordinate issues. This holds notably for Acts. Ever since it was recognized that fixed units that could be related to a formative circle are hardly available in Acts,[13] the question of Luke's authorial intention has come into the foreground.

Above all the commentaries of Ernst Haenchen and Hans Conzelmann have sought to establish the thesis that the onset of the gentile mission, the justification of which Luke wanted to present, is not portrayed until Acts 10 and following. In my opinion, the more important this insight is, the less it does justice to the meaning of Acts 2 in the entirety of the two volumes of Luke. This needs to be more closely established later.[14]

But now it must be asked whether the insight into Luke's work of composing, which Haenchen himself adroitly established,[15] has been sufficiently applied to our material. Both authors open up the source that Luke used with a certainty that borders on the astounding. Is it certain that Luke had a source here? The weightiest argument for this claim is still the reference (indeed difficult to understand) to Ἰουδαίαν.

Conzelmann remarked quite assertively:

Here Luke is dependent upon a list of nations which reflects the political situation of an earlier time (there is no mention of Macedonia/Achaia).

---

13. Martin Dibelius, "Style Criticism in Acts," in *Studies in the Acts of the Apostles*. Jacob Jervell uses this essay for an attack against the method of form criticism. Here fundamental insights were dismissed; Jervell, *Luke and the People of God: A New Look at Luke-Acts* (Minneapolis: Augsburg, 1972). On the question of sources in Acts the bibliographical information from Erich Grässer remains important ("Die Apostelgeschichte in der Forschung der Gegenwart," *ThR* 26 [1960]: 93–167).

14. See below, 43–47.

15. "When he came to the Pentecost episode, Luke found himself confronted with a difficult task. He wanted to present one of the most important incidents since the departure of Jesus: the coming of the Spirit. He had to depict it vividly so that it would rise unforgettably before the eyes of his readers. But this was not enough: he would have not succeeded in his task unless at the same time the meaning of this incident was plain to them. He could not count on much help from sources: there was no ancient or uniform tradition" (Haenchen, *Acts of the Apostles*, 173).

It describes the constituency of the twelve kingdoms, excluding Europe. Such lists come from the geographers and the historians of Alexander and of the twelve kingdoms."[16]

Indeed Ernst Haenchen does not know from where Luke gets his list. However, he reconstructs the form that he would have wanted to give it, and is also able to itemize the changes that come from Luke himself. From the source, which "presumably ... contained names only of countries, not signs of the zodiac," he took "twelve names: 1. Parthians. 2. Medes. 3. Elamites. 4. Mesopotamia. 5. Cappadocia. 6. Pontus. 7. Asia. 8. Phyrgia. 9. Pamphylia. 10. Egypt. 11. Libya Cyrenaica. 12. Rome."[17] The fact that Rome is placed at the end demonstrates that this list in this form goes back to Luke.[18] Also Luke transformed the Persians from his source into Parthians.[19] Medes and Elamites were entities from the past, which Luke took from the Septuagint.[20] Ἰουδαίαν in verse 9 should be deleted: "Judaea has long been acknowledged a late insertion."[21] Also the Cretans and Arabs should be deleted.[22] Because the summary designation of the enumerated nations as "Jews and proselytes" precedes these words, after the summary they have no acceptable meaning. The result is a list of twelve, which describes the origin of the Jerusalem community in a crowd of diaspora Jews gathered in Jerusalem. The gentile mission "did not ... begin until Peter baptized Cornelius (Chapter 10)."[23]

The outcome of the acceptance of this view in later Lukan studies is that for the question regarding the purpose of Acts, or regarding the

---

16. Conzelmann, *Acts of the Apostles*, 14.
17. Haenchen, *Acts of the Apostles*, 169–70 n. 5.
18. Haenchen, *Acts of the Apostles*, 169–70 n. 5.
19. Haenchen, *Acts of the Apostles*, 169–70 n. 5.
20. Haenchen, *Acts of the Apostles*, 169–70 n. 5.
21. Haenchen, *Acts of the Apostles*, 170.
22. Haenchen, *Acts of the Apostles*, 135. Here already it should be noted that what Haenchen takes exception to would be invalidated if Otto Eissfeldt's explanation were to be applied. Haenchen argues against this article (Eissfeldt, "Kreter und Araber," *ThLZ* 72 [1947]: 207–12) in such a way that he states: "Otto Eissfeldt's interpretation, which finds here named seafarers in the West and desert-dwellers in the East, is merely a stopgap" (Haenchen, *Acts of the Apostles*, 171 n. 1). Linguistic and factual considerations are ignored. Incidentally, he follows Wellhausen, *Kritische Analyse*, 4.
23. Haenchen, *Acts of the Apostles*, 171.

overall design, which determines the composition of this book, this list no longer needs to be investigated. Ulrich Wilckens for instance, investigated the convictions of Luke effective in the patterns of the speeches without going into the details of the list.[24] Even Eckhard Plümacher, who investigated the Lukan episode style in a noteworthy way, assessed the list of nations as material taken from a source that as such was of no further interest.[25]

However, it is in no way superfluous to consider whether some kind of geographical conception or perhaps geographical knowledge went into this list—knowledge that is still noteworthy. We would like, therefore, to deal with the question, which names the list contains and what should be inferred from it. But first it must be asked, what results for us from the form of the "list."

2. Form-Critical Considerations

The question of what the "list of the nations" intends to accomplish is not even asked by many authors in the first place. Johannes Weiss, still before the time of form critical investigations, spoke in this context of a "convention of all the peoples of the earth."[26] For his part, J. Thomas, who does not want to delete the Ἰουδαίαν of the textus receptus, still is able to say a lot about the rhetorical form of the catalog, but does not ask what the list is about. For him, it is certain:

---

24. Ulrich Wilckens, *Die Missionsreden der Apostelgeschichte: Form- und traditionsgeschichtliche Untersuchungen*, 2nd ed., WMANT 5 (Neukirchen-Vluyn: Neukirchener Verlag, 1963), 32 n. 3.

25. Eckhard Plümacher, *Lukas als hellenistischer Schriftsteller: Studien zur Apostelgeschichte*, SUNT 9 (Göttingen: Vandenhoeck & Ruprecht, 1972), 107: "Those who are astonished speak in vv. 7–11; Luke adeptly places the 'catalog of nations' that he had before him in their mouth, so that as far as possible it loses its own dryness and above all does not break into the scene." The remark on p. 107 n. 119 contrasts with this: "Thereby it is of course presupposed, that the 'itinerary' is not a source however constituted but was first formulated by the author of Acts (on this see [Hans] Conzelmann, *Die Apostelgeschichte* [2nd ed. (Tübingen: Mohr Siebeck, 1972)], pp. 5–6 with bibliography)." On Acts 2 see in addition the remarks on pp. 106–8 and 124.

26. Weiss, *Über die Absicht und den literarischen Charakter der Apostelgeschichte*, 5–6.

Catalogues are not, as one could deduce from the treatment in scholarly literature, a paraenetic matter, but a common *rhetorical form*. Most of the amorphous structure that can be observed is peculiar to it. It does not serve to provide the reader with an incoherent summation for his or her use and for arbitrary division and selection. Rather, it aims at demonstrating a self-contained whole: According to Acts 2:9–11, the entirety of Judaism that is dispersed across the nations is reached by the action of the Spirit.[27]

However, it is not simply to be taken for granted that it deals with a catalog freely designed from a rhetorical point of view—so Thomas—or a list of the lands that are located under the twelve signs of the zodiac—so Weinstock—or a "list of nations" or an excerpt of some such as the exegetical tradition would have it.

Of course our tradition does contain a list of nations, only it is in Gen 10. And this list after all has the intention to be complete in the sense that it names all of Noah's grandsons and relates all of the best-known nations to these sixteen ἥρωες ἐπώνυμοι. Philo, who in his *Legat.* 36 (= §§276–293) enumerates the most important lands of the Jewish diaspora, gives probably the best comparable parallel to our "list": long-windedness though proper to the older forms of such lists, would miss the mark in the case of Acts. It is essential that the reader, who is not a scholar, does not weary in his or her attention, quite especially if this reader should be a distinguished person. The names enumerated in Luke's list of the nations are found in various texts of antiquity, texts among others of Jewish and of Roman origin.[28] Jewish texts typically refer to the sons of Noah: Sem, Ham, and Japhet. Noah's progeny settled in every region of the earth (Gen 9:19). These lists vary, of course, as to the names quoted (1 Chr 1:1–2:2; Philo, *Legat.* 36 [= §§276–293]; Josephus, *B.J.* 2.345–401; Jub. 8–9; 1QM II, 10–14).

Luke spares no pains to formulate the material vividly: the episode style suits the taste of a fastidious audience.[29] But an exhausting comprehensive totality is never put before them. To allude to something well known is enough. Philo does this when he enumerates the most significant

---

27. J. Thomas, "Formgesetze des Begriffs-Katalogs im N.T.," *TZ* 24 (1968): 16, emphasis original.

28. Scott, "Luke's Geographical Horizon," 499, 501, 507, 509.

29. Cf. especially Plümacher, *Lukas als hellenistischer Schriftsteller.*

2. The Geographical Horizon

lands of the Jewish diaspora, with no hassle and elegantly. Luke does this, too, so it seems to me. Here not even the slightest effort to say everything is in view.

There was no reason for geographical science, and particularly for an astrology that today would evoke a smile, to make the material more intelligible by abridging it. These sciences intended to portray the entire known world.[30] It is obvious that Luke does not wish to do this.

Differently from Philo, Luke appreciates how to open up his material. He refrains from a strict, somewhat mechanical stringing together of data. Instead he picks out particular elements here and there, as if it were a matter of arranging a spray of flowers. So the impression of a totality, about which Thomas speaks, unfolds. The geographers and philosophers are capable of arousing this impression if at the same time they are stylists.[31] Admittedly catalogs seldom appear among them. They have more to relate than names.

Even at places where these authors go back to actual lists of Roman provincial administrations, they knew how to conceal the origin of this material as far as possible.[32] The difference of a list according to form and function from what Luke has is considerable.

I would like to demonstrate the distinctiveness of the literary form employed by an outstanding geographer, who actually offers an enumeration, an enumeration to be sure, of material that is well known to the reader. Here much rests on the ease of the arrangement.[33]

Strabo intends to name the countries of the Mediterranean that Homer already knows. He presupposes familiarity with this topic. At the same time he suggests in what way he himself takes a stand as an author in the

---

30. This holds at any rate for authors such as Ptolemy.

31. The geographer Strabo as well as the poet Manilius understood themselves as philosophers. This gave breadth to their scholarship. Manilius marks the intersection between astronomy and philosophy. The insightful interpretation of Franz-Frieder Lühr shows that he had more to offer than the average astronomer at the beginning of the imperial age; Lühr, *Ratio und Fatum: Dichtung und Lehre bei Manilius* (Berlin: de Gruyter, 1969).

32. Cf. the excursuses to the official lists used by Pliny and Ptolemy in the well-known book of A. H. M. Jones, *The Cities of the Eastern Roman Provinces*, 2nd ed., rev. Michael Avi-Yonah et al. (Oxford: Clarendon, 1971), appendixes I and II.

33. Strabo, *Geogr.* I.1.1–10.

tradition of Homeric philology—everything with ease, that is, elegantly. He begins with something known to his ancient readers—that is, with the Pillars of Hercules—goes with them along the coast of Libya, Egypt, and Phoenicia and is soon at the part of Asia Minor that lies across from Cyprus. The regions of the Solymi, Lycia, and Caria follow, then the stretch of coast between Mycale and Troas with its islands, then the Propontis and the Black Sea all the way to Kolchis. Homer also was acquainted with the Cimmerian Gulf, so naturally then also with the Cimmerians, who indeed in his own time had overrun all of Ionia; he mentions the name of the people. And after the enumeration of many other countries—Homer also was acquainted with more names than he listed—the author ends again at the starting point, with the riches of the Iberian Peninsula. There he ends elegantly: he did not give an account of a sea journey,[34] because, evidently, the description of the coasts and the mouths of rivers, the naming of ports and the mountain peaks and ranges visible in the distance as orientation points belonged to a nautical journey.

Strabo mentions sixteen territories, and quite casually he criticizes the famous Eratosthenes on some point, to which he will return. He thinks that Eratosthenes was at fault in the claim that a poet would only entertain. In reality poetry is a kind of elementary philosophy. We see in Strabo how a section like this conveys information. Even a competent geographer passes over a lot of detail.[35]

What can now be gained from an enumeration so formulated? Evidently, quite different things, depending on which circle of readers it reaches. Satisfaction over the stylistic proficiency of the author, over the congenial relaying of the material, which one easily slips over, is certainly the smallest part of what it accomplishes. For the connoisseur, for whom a rich personal reading came to his or her aid, many points of comparison would have arisen, stimulations and confirmations of what was already known. For others, the sheer enumeration of lands would have aroused an outlook, adventures, memories; for others still, dreams of faraway places.

All of this is to a degree familiar to an author. The mode of viewing that addresses the reader enables the author to give design. A definite style corresponds to a defined knowledge. But a successful enumeration always

---

34. He gives a casual review on this older geographical form in I.1.21.
35. So expressly I.1.10.

2. The Geographical Horizon

proceeds from the known to something new, which uncovers a new facet of the matter.

I do not intend to try to check out which Homeric reminiscences Strabo passes over. At any rate Luke does not say everything he knows. It is easy to demonstrate this.

If Luke wishes to enumerate languages, as it appears at first glance, Lycaonian (14:11), Galatian (16:6; 18:23), and Hebrew (21:40; 26:14) are missing. Who would want to say to him that he left out Greek? If he wishes to name peoples, as it also appears, the Samaritans are missing, whom he introduces in the gospel and in the programmatic verse in 1:8. Also Cyprians, Cilicians, Syrians, Phoenicians, Ethiopians, Pisidians, Lycaonians, and Galatians are missing. Also Mysians and Bithynians, Macedonians and Thracians, Rhodians (Carians) and Lycians are absent, and, in case the last pair are not original, Cretans and Arabs also are missing. All of these are peoples whom the book presupposes or mentions.

But then which option is encountered in the list? Are at least the territories of Asia Minor approximately complete? One will not want to say that with five territories itemized. The fact that the regions of Bithynia and Cilicia that were indispensable for the Roman military are absent makes this questionable. Even if Cilicia emerged as a new Roman administrative unit lately under Vespasian, what geographer could have left it out? What strategist could have overlooked Bithynia? Of the important regions of the interior Galatia, Lycaonia, and Paphlagonia are conspicuously missing. Now one could of course designate the barbarian regions of the West as Phrygia. But that was indeed a very vague way of speaking, and at least the absence of the Galatians would be inexcusable.

The list can only be understood as a possible itemization of territories in Asia Minor if it consciously intended to provide simply a selection but basically meant a totality. At this point my view agrees with the ideas that Thomas brought forward on the nature of the catalog.[36] I can agree with the thesis that the list precisely in its succinct exemplary form intends to present a totality. However, now the question to ask would be, which totality Luke has in mind.

---

36. See Thomas, "Formgesetze des Begriffs-Katalogs im N.T." However, a kind of arbitrariness in the handling of things affects his remarks. What Thomas wishes to say about the rhythm of the list is unintelligible to me. Any reference to ancient prosody is missing.

3. Investigation of the Names Presented in the Enumeration

Parthians, Medes, and Elamites open the catalog. What can be gathered from this group of names? First, it needs to be established that this cannot be a combination of the old empires taken from the Septuagint. Whatever source one chooses to assume, Assyria and Babylonia should not be missing. Of course it is possible to object that the fourth member of the chain, οἱ κατοικοῦντες τὴν Μεσοποταμίαν, catches up what is missing. But no ancient geographical list is conceivable that would have deleted the names of both these nations—when other nations are already named.

But Parthians, Medes, and Elamites are simply not standard names in the geographical literature. To be sure, these are the only ones among the names mentioned here that lie outside the Roman Empire and the domains of the Diadochi. However, among other conceivable names, the three nations listed are precisely those that since the time of Cyaxares maintained the administration of the Median and later of the Persian Empire. But in this form they do not constitute a traditional triad. The geographers—as well as the astronomers—are much more exhaustive. Above all they did not fail to mention Iberians or Spanish in the west, Indians in the east, Scythians in the north, and Ethiopians in the south. What is named here is not a triad of empires but of peoples and of their cultures. After the defeat of Crassus (53 BCE) and the disastrous inroads of the two following years that resounded everywhere, the Parthians were considered a threat to the Roman Empire. Josephus is aware of many details about their impact in the regions of Syria and of Asia Minor. The ancient Persians by contrast were listed under this name, as Strabo demonstrates. In the introductory parts of his geography, he replaces the name of the Persians with that of the Parthians as soon as he arrives at the more recent past.

But if the emphasis on this group of three mediated no political point of view, what then speaks against seeing here, not only in a general way people of ancient cultures in the east, but languages, namely, languages of Luke's time?[37] From the start it is probable that the Jewish diaspora was

---

37. This widespread opinion of an earlier time was advanced more recently, e.g., by Schmidt, Lake, and Étienne Trocmé. Schmidt, *Pfingsterzählung und das Pfingstereignis*, 17: "There is no doubt that the narrator had all of these languages in mind." Lake, in connection with a passage from Midrash Tanḥuma 26c: "It will be noted that this parallel is much more striking if it be accepted that those who understood the glossolalia of the Apostles were Gentiles as well as Jews" ("Gift of

acquainted with details about the nations of the East.³⁸ It is possible that Luke also relied on such information.

As an example I would like to mention a baraita from the Babylonian Talmud, Shabb. 115a:

היו כתובין גיפטית מדית עיברית עילמית יוונית אף על פי שלא ניתנו לקרות בהן מצילין אותן מפני הדליקה

"If they [i.e., biblical scrolls] are written in Coptic, Median, Hebrew [i.e., Aramaic], Elamite, Greek—even though it is not permitted to read them [i.e., liturgically], one rescues them from fire [danger] [even on the Sabbath]."

Whatever one can otherwise learn from this old text, obviously this has to do with translated portions of the Pentateuch and—as another Baraita demonstrates—also the scroll of Esther.³⁹

---

the Spirit," 116). Trocmé, *Le 'Livre des Actes' et l'histoire* (Paris: Presses Universitaires de France, 1957), 201–7. I must, however, distance myself from Trocmé's handling of the question of sources. Jean Potin also holds the same view (*Le fête Juive de la Pentecôte: Étude des textes liturgiques*, LD 65 [Paris: Cerf, 1971], 311). In an exemplary way this latter work strives to evaluate the targumim by differentiating different traditions.

38. In addition to the information of Billerbeck, Str-B, vol. 2, cf. Jean Juster, *Les Juifs dans l'Empire Romain: Leur condition juridique, économique, et sociale*, 2 vols. (Paris: Geuthner, 1914). Further literature has been assembled by Heinrich Kasting, *Die Anfänge der urchristlichen Mission* (Munich: Kaiser, 1969).

39. See b. Meg. 18a: גיפטית לגיפטים ‹מדית למדים› עברית לעברים עילמית לעילמים יוונית ליוונים "Coptic scrolls [should be read] only to Copts, Median ones only to Medes, Hebrew ones only to Hebrews, Elamite ones only to Elamites, Greek ones only to Greeks." This regulation demonstrates a possibility of getting around the ancient prohibition against the reading of Bible translations. Actually there was an ancient prohibition that is transmitted in the same passage, which must be older: "Reading in Coptic, Hebrew, Elamite, Median, or Greek language is forbidden." Both passages are from Lajos Blau, *Zur Einleitung in die heilige Schrift* (Budapest: Alkalay, 1894), 70–72, to which von Dobschütz referred ("Zu der Völkerliste Act 2:9–11"). One of the two passages is also quoted in Str-B 2.608. It needs to be emphasized that there are no linguistic monuments in the Median language (Ilya Gershevitch, "Old Iranian Languages," in *Literatur*, vol. 1 of *Iranian Studies*, HdO 4/1 [Leiden: Brill, 1968], 2–3). On the remainder of Ancient and Middle Iranian, which was spoken in the region of Susa, see Erica Reiner, "The Elamite Language," in *Altkleinasiatische Sprachen*, HdO 2/1 (Leiden: Brill, 1969), 54–118. It should be

So it appears reasonable, in view of the other peoples mentioned by Luke, to go into this question. It is easy to say which of Mesopotamia's languages Luke could have thought of if he actually wanted to refer to a language. Because Akkadian had long ceased to exist, only Aramaic dialects come into view. To what degree that period comprehended how to make linguistic differentiation, is of course difficult to say.

On the basis of some recent research on languages of Asia Minor, considerably more can be said today about the following names than could be hoped for some decades ago.[40] When almost seventy years ago Karl Holl searched for traces of languages of Asia Minor in the church fathers, he could compile only very little and quite isolated evidence.[41] For the West—that is, the part rapidly hellenized after Alexander's conquest—he was able to name only one person who exclusively spoke Mysian (PG 114:1428B). However, Holl could not exclude the possibility that the speaker mentioned here spoke a dialect of Bithynian-Phrygian—and it has long been known that Phrygian survived until these times.[42]

Along with this, one ought to consider seriously the very long survival of Isaurian and Lycaonian. Holl cites as evidence legends of the sixth century. Beside Galatian, for which Holl mentions Lucian, *Alexander* 51,[43] only the long survival of Cappadocian is certain. Of course Thracian and

---

no secret that long before our time we have to reckon with the demise of Elamite. However, Franz Heinrich Weissbach, "Elymais," PW 5.2:2486, gives documentary evidence that Elamite lived on in Islamic times.

40. Because here bibliographical information becomes obsolete relatively rapidly, I mention only Günter Neumann, *Untersuchungen zum Weiterleben hethitischen und luwischen Sprachgutes in hellenistischer und römischer Zeit* (Wiesbaden: Harrassowitz, 1961).

41. Karl Holl, "Das Fortleben der Volkssprachen in Kleinasien in nachchristlicher Zeit," *Hermes* 43 (1908): 240–54; repr. in *Gesammelte Aufsätze zur Kirchengeschichte* (Tübingen: Mohr, 1928), 2:238–48.

42. Otto Haas has remarked on the lingering on and dying out of Phrygian, *Die phrygischen Sprachdenkmäler*, Balkansko Ezikoznanie 10 (Sofia: Académie bulgare des sciences, 1966), 18, 21, 59–60, 71–73 [Prof. Dr. Alfred Heubeck, Erlangen kindly gave me this reference].

43. Fritz M. Heichelheim, "Geschichte Kleinasiens von der Eroberung durch Kyros II. bis zum Tode des Herakleios I, 547 v.Chr.–641 n.Chr.," in *Orientalische Geschichte von Kyros bis Mohammed*, ed. Albert Dietrich, Geo Widengren, and Fritz M. Heichelheim, HdO 4 (Leiden: Brill, 1966), 75, mentions Phrygian and Latin as languages alongside of Celtic.

Scythian dialects had encroached on the south side of the coast of the Black Sea at certain times. However, it is questionable whether during the first century such linguistic islands can be reckoned with. Holl mentions no documentary evidence.

This is also improbable for Asia proper in the time of the Principate. The homogeneous Greek culture must have been established right into the borders of Phrygian and Galatian regions. Our inscriptions run out long before the period in question. But Luke speaks precisely of Asia (2:9).

At least Arrian mentions the dialect of the city of Side,[44] which apparently had survived deep into the Hellenistic period.[45] When Luke mentions Pamphylia, the most important city of which was Side, this could go back to bits of information.

We can thus mention Cappadocia, Phrygia, and Pamphylia as regions in which indigenous languages lingered on for a long time. How do things stand with other regions?

It is difficult to specify more precisely the point in time of the demise of barbarian languages in Pontus. The reign of Mithradates Eupator (d. 63 BCE) with his determination to amalgamate Iranian and Hellenistic cultures had a strong impact on the following period. Strabo's family, which came from the ancient royal city Amaseia, is a notable example of

---

44. Arrian, *Anabasis* 1.26.4. On this, see P. Kretschmer, "Nochmals die Hypachäer und Alaksandus," *Glotta* 24 (1936): 230–34.

45. On this question, see the insightful work of P. H. J. Houwink ten Cate, *The Luwian Population Groups of Lycia and Cilicia Aspera During the Hellenistic Period*, DMOA 10 (Leiden: Brill, 1961), esp. 1–50, 188–215. Along with the linguistic investigations that are most important for the work, Houwink ten Cate features interesting findings concerning the survival of Luwian linguistic islands in isolated regions of the Taurus Mountains. The survival also of Lycian and Cilician languages appears certain well into the Hellenistic period. The reference on p. 188 is important in view of the limits of sources preserved for us. Cf. also Heichelheim "Geschichte Kleinasiens von der Eroberung," 74–77. Recent discoveries in the language of Side that at the latest come from the second century are discussed by Claude Brixhe, "L'alphabet épichorique de Sidé," *Kadmos* 8 (1969): 54–84; Brixhe, "Un nouveau document épichorique de Sidé," *Kadmos* 8 (1969): 143–51; as well as by Günter Neumann, "Zur Entzifferung der sidetischen Inschriften," *Kadmos* 7 (1968): 75–95. On the "official" use of Greek on coins minted after 216 BCE, cf. Brixhe's reference on p. 144 n. 9. I am grateful to Prof. Dr. A. Heubeck, who kindly made me aware of these essays as well as the bibliographic material mentioned in notes 41 and 51 (at the end).

this amalgamation. Strabo, who himself traveled in this region, reports that there were no cities in Cataonia and the Melitene, apart from a few exceptions. This is characteristic for the "Hellenism" of that region. Cataonia, which he separates from Pontic Cappadocia as Great Cappadocia, spoke no other language, according to his statements, than the regions of the former kingdom of Pontus insofar as they were Cappadocians.[46] This information is important. It seems that there was no cultural divide between the former regions of Mithradates II and Cappadocia in his time.[47] This would mean that Luke here was inadequately informed about the linguistic homogeneity of these two regions. This, of course, does not speak against the possibility that Luke meant languages. Later still, Arrian mentions in his *Periplus* numerous barbarian tribes.[48]

Time and again scholarship has been concerned with the question which word might have stood originally at the place of the corrupt Ἰουδαίαν. It appears to me beyond doubt that Ἰουδαίαν embodies a corruption: A convincing interpretation of the anarthrous Ἰουδαίαν is not possible. For Harnack's opinion—that the word is to be deleted simply as a gloss—cannot be maintained. The list mainly consists of a series of pairs. Where Luke emphasizes, he arranges the names of nations to stand alone: Mesopotamia and Rome receive this distinction.

Therefore the question needs to be asked, which region of Asia Minor could have opened the original series of six items. Numerous suggestions have been made in the past. On paleographic grounds, however, most of them have little power of persuasion as long as we make the presumption of a scribal error. Indeed since a conscious substitution of the original by a copyist is conceivable, perhaps Jerome may have preserved the original text: *habitantes* in Syria. A reaction of a Jewish Christian copyist to this

---

46. Strabo, *Geogr.* 12.1.2.

47. On this, see Edward H. Bunbury, *A History of Ancient Geography*, 2nd ed. (London: Murray, 1883), 294–96. Whether Luke knew anything about barbarian languages of the northeast coast of the Black Sea, which Strabo mentions, is of course quite unclear.

48. The barbarians from the Asiatic coast of the Black Sea who lived between Trapezunt and Tanais are mentioned in the *Periplus maris Euxini* 2.1–3; 18.3 (ed. A. G. Roos and G. Wirth) vol. 2, 112–13, 121. Arrian explains the defective Greek of some altar inscriptions in Trapezunt in terms of the dominance of barbarian idioms (1.2, p. 103).

name is at least imaginable. However, Greek and Aramaic were spoken in Syria. There was no need of a miracle of tongues.

Burkitt's conjecture of Γορδυαίαν has recently been advanced again by E. F. F. Bishop. Some Arabic manuscripts of the Bodleian Library exhibit a corresponding form for Kurdistan. On this, however, it must be said that this word, as long as it is not documented elsewhere, most probably first appeared in this specific tradition.[49] With respect to the geography of Asia Minor, Bentley's conjecture of Λυδίαν has a claim to serious consideration. Here a writing error is actually easily imagined. However, at least two considerations speak against Λυδίαν. First, Λυδίαν was later a part of the Roman province Asia, which Luke mentions. Second, it appears as quite improbable that the Lydian language was preserved until the Roman period. No geographical or cultural factors could have produced resistance to the penetration of Greek.[50]

I would like to suggest here another word worthy of consideration: Λυκίαν.

The introduction of an enumeration of nations of Asia Minor with this word appears to be fitting to a high degree. Precisely in the Roman period and with Roman eyes the Lycians were referred to with respect. Not only was the Lycian city league a pattern of an ancient and distinctively democratic constitution. In an earlier age, in writing on constitutional principles, Aristotle had concerned himself especially with the Lycians. Homer mentions this nation honorably. Above all, the Lycians—in any case the city league—had never supported the pirating nuisance of the Cilicians. In distinction from Side, such ships were not permitted to land in Lycian ports. Pompey's ventures were backed up by a huge contingent of Lycian ships.

The natural position of its region and the political distinction of its constitutional bodies created a certain independent originality. The Lycian cities appear to have preserved many of their traditions into the Byzantine period. Thus, the survival of the Lycian language into the time of Luke is conceivable.[51]

---

49. E. F. F. Bishop, "Professor Burkitt and the Geographical Catalogue," *JRS* 42 (1952): 84–85.

50. M. Dibelius "Text der Apostelgeschichte," 82, rejects the conjecture Λυδίαν on purely paleographic grounds. However, this view does not convince me. The possibility of damaged letters cannot be excluded.

51. Lycian inscriptions originate from the fifth and fourth centuries BCE and break off toward the end of the fourth century BCE. However, perhaps alongside

The additional names in the list present no problems. The mention of Egypt in such a context refers not to the Hellenic language but to Coptic, which also plays a role in rabbinic sources. Libya, which had a significant role in the Jewish diaspora, is not an unambiguous geographical term. Luke also knows this and therefore makes it precise: he has his interest fixed on the Pentapolis. Here a dialect close to Berber must have been spoken.

The Romans, who alone are present as "travelers," constitute the climax of the list. Among the others, with the exception of the first three names, it is claimed that they must have been temporary residents of Jerusalem. In our ears this may sound like an overstatement. However, from the first it need not be assumed that Luke had a precise overview of temporary or permanent foreigners in Jerusalem. At least in Acts 6:9 we are informed that there must have been different synagogues made up of compatriots.

I agree with Otto Eissfeldt that the conclusion of the list is original. Jews and proselytes, people from the West as well as from the East are gathered together, in order to experience the fulfillment of the promise given in 1:8.

---

the use into a late period of Lycian proper names, one fact speaks for my conjecture, which W. Arkwright expresses thus: "Excepting the Hittites with their twenty thousand cuneiform tablets, the Lycians have left much larger remains of their language than any other nation in Asia Minor." ("Lycian Epitaphs," in *Anatolian Studies Presented to Sir William Mitchell Ramsay*, ed. W. H. Buckler and W. M. Calder [Manchester: University Press, 1923], 15). See also the information in Jones, *Cities of the Eastern Roman Provinces*. For me it is significant that Günter Neumann, "Lykisch," in *Altkleinasiatische Sprachen*, 359, reckons with the possibility of a lengthy survival of Lycian. The passage in Cicero (*In Verrem* 4.10.21), *Lycii Graeci homines*, can hardly be related to full blown Hellenization as Neumann does. In context it has to do with the definite disavowal of Cilician piracy. Potentially of course it would be possible also to consider another explanation, namely, the stories circulating in antiquity about the Greek origin of the Lycians, see on this Kretschmer, "Nochmals die Hypachäer und Alaksandus." A stele excavated in 1973 ought to provide a decisive advance for the linguistic analysis of Lycian, which reports the founding of a cult of Βασιλεὺς Καύνιος and of Ἀρκέσιμας in the Létoon of Xanthos in the Greek, Aramaic, and Lycian languages. This trilingual report, which Prof. Dr. Heubeck also called to my attention, comes from the middle of the fourth century, see Henri Metzger, "La stèle trilingue récemment découverte au Létoon de Xanthos: Le texte grec," *CRAI* 118 (1974): 82–93.

4. The Context of the Enumeration: Acts 2 in Relation to Lukan Theology

Long ago Harnack and Heinrich von Baer indicated that this chapter has a central function for the outline of Acts. Our understanding of Luke's theology must find an important reference point here.

The thesis of Conzelmann, Haenchen, and others, that here an event is depicted that is important only for the Jerusalem church but not for the Greek church, is correct only with reservations. To begin with, for support of this claim a text-critically disputed variation must be addressed. I take the Ἰουδαῖοι from verse 5, as do many other exegetes, to be text-critically untenable. The external attestation of the word itself is striking: the word is missing in ℵ it^ph; C and E have it in another place. The internal grounds that speak against the word are even stronger. Ἰουδαῖοι ἀπὸ παντὸς ἔθνους is an impossible collocation. The Jewish people themselves legally constitute an ἔθνος.[52] Also it is rather remarkable if Luke introduces the Jews who live in Jerusalem and expressly characterizes them as pious. That was really quite self-evident. It is different if we understand the κατοικοῦντες succinctly as dwelling without full rights of citizenship. Where κατοικοῦντες appears in geographical contexts, this meaning is not rare. This is the meaning with which we have to do here.[53]

In this context, ἄνδρες εὐλαβεῖς should by all means be understood as a further designation for semiproselytes, similar to οἱ σεβόμενοι or οἱ φοβούμενοι τὸν θεόν. Luke appears to use the expression in this way also in Acts 8:2.[54] In spite of these arguments most exegetes take the word to be original. Holtzmann even claimed that the absence of Ἰουδαῖοι in the Sinaiticus is a facilitating improvement of the text.[55] Indeed the word stands in other manuscripts in another place without facilitating anything. Such variations in the word order are among the most important indicators for the introduction of glosses into the text.

---

52. A. N. Sherwin-White offers a consideration of the Roman perception of the unity of the ἔθνη in the empire, *The Roman Citizenship*, 2nd ed. (Oxford: Clarendon, 1973), 437–44. In this the diverse origin of the Latin concept of *gens* and of the Greek concept is emphasized.

53. Walter Gutbrod ("Ἰσραήλ," *TDNT* 3:379) points to the striking use of Ἰουδαῖοι: "Acts 2:5 could possibly be the only exception."

54. So Blass, "Textkritik von Apostelgeschichte 2:5," 828.

55. Holtzmann, *Apostelgeschichte*, 32. So also, e.g., Schmidt, *Pfingsterzählung und das Pfingstereignis*, 19.

Another argument against the textus receptus emerges from our insight into the authorial intent of Luke. Rather than saying how a multilingual mix of nations had taken up residence in Jerusalem as must accord with his intention, he explains here from the outset how something such as this is intelligible: it has to do with Jews. In reality not until close to the end of the list does the author indicate this. Jews and proselytes constitute the most important component of the foreign-speaking population of Jerusalem. I would like to set forth the hypothesis that also the choice of ἄνδρες εὐλαβεῖς in the introduction of the list of nations stands in agreement with this authorial intention of Luke. The author here chooses a word that is not a *terminus technicus* for proselytes, like οἱ σεβόμενοι or οἱ φοβούμενοι τὸν θεόν.

Consequently, what would result for us is the statement that the eyewitnesses who were present at the fulfillment of the promise were foreigners from the entire realm of the Roman Empire and even beyond. Luke does not expressly say that these foreigners had affiliated themselves with the Jerusalem community. Its first new members will have been precisely proselytes in the technical sense and Jews. In the second place, σεβόμενοι τὸν θεόν came into consideration along with them. One could say that the foreigners are not understood and are not mentioned as members of the original community. In Luke's intention foreigners as eyewitnesses underscore the outstanding meaning of the event. To say this in Luke's terms: God creates for himself a people from among the nations.[56] Not until later does God bring this purpose to fruition. Pentecost is only a modest beginning on the way to this. Nevertheless, Pentecost is a beginning.

This interpretation can be reinforced by referring to the Pentecost speech itself. Indeed, alongside the ἄνδρες Ἰουδαῖοι the address in 2:14 names a group that is apparently distinct from them, namely, καὶ οἱ κατοικοῦντες Ἰερουσαλὴμ πάντες. Later, however, Peter speaks only to ἄνδρες ἀδελφοί or ἄνδρες Ἰσραηλῖται as the case may be. Indeed the hearers of the Pentecost sermon also respond: τί ποιήσωμεν, ἄνδρες ἀδελφοί; The foreigners have disappeared! To express this differently, one must say: Jews are the spokespersons of these ἄνδρες εὐλαβεῖς. Humanity breaks down into Jews and non-Jews, as in the list. Thus where the non-Jews can be designated as σεβόμενοι τὸν θεόν; indeed where they constitute a new unity with Jews to form the people of God of the end times, the Jewish element retains

---

56. Acts 15:14, cf. Gen 11:6.

2. The Geographical Horizon

the leadership role. This does correspond to the time of the beginning. Furthermore, this picture is in accord with an ancient theological concept.

This theological concept has been known for a long time as an ancient Christian pattern of thought. Ancient Jewish notions of the meaning of Jerusalem in the end time quite clearly had a decisive meaning in the thoughts of the early community in Jerusalem about mission. The expansion of the Christian proclamation beyond the borders (Acts 1:8) was not the expectation, but rather the streaming of all the nations to Zion. This theory must have continued to have an impact even when de facto this self-limitation of the Christian proclamation was broken by the activity of Stephen's circle, and when some men from Cyprus and Cyrene also presented the Christian proclamation to nonproselytes.[57] Luke reports in detail on resistance against these developments. One can say that the justification of the gentile mission constitutes the central concern of the entire book.[58]

But theologically this means that Luke endows the ancient "mission theory" that is based on Holy Scripture with a new "historical" interpretation. The ancient view that the fulfillment of the promise of the end time in the pouring out of the Spirit would have to lead to a centripetal movement, namely, a pilgrimage to Jerusalem, is correct. It has been fulfilled in the original Jerusalem community.[59]

But now this period has come to an end. The Spirit does not characterize only the event in the early Jerusalem community but is rather a constitutive element of the entire movement, which finally leads to the Pauline mission. The promised Holy Spirit has conducted this movement in all of its particulars.

These things have repeatedly been dealt with in the literature. I limit myself, therefore, to some brief comments. Still, a problem that Luke does not explicitly mention has to be touched on. We must assume that he nevertheless engaged it intensively. As the format of his two volumes shows,

---

57. Acts 11:20.

58. The view that the justification of the gentile mission, specifically the Pauline mission, constitutes the goal of Acts was first established by M. Schneckenburger, see A. J. Mattill, "The Purpose of Acts: Schneckenburger Reconsidered," in Gasque and Martin, *Apostolic History and the Gospel*, 108–22.

59. In his gospel, Luke has also left aside a certain amount of tradition in favor of this view, see Ferdinand Hahn, *Das Verständnis der Mission im Neuen Testament*, WMANT 13 (Neukirchen-Vluyn: Neukirchener Verlag, 1963), 111–12.

Luke had to deal with the still-continuing effect of opponents of the Pauline mission who were able to base their protest on Scripture. Thumping on the precepts of the law appears to have scarcely impressed him. However, we have to assume that his treatment of the events of the end times was consciously directed against dissenting views. If Luke himself composed the speech in Acts 2:14–39, which we assume, a significant function accrues for the explicit citation of a specific text. The quotation is an eschatological text: "I will pour out my spirit on all flesh" (Joel 3:1–5 [ET 2:28–32]). The conclusion of the speech comes back around to this quotation (Acts 2:39). The μακράν that is added (from Isa 57:19) is essential for Luke. It bears a part of the burden of proof for his main thesis: Since Pentecost God summons the ἔθνη.

We do not encounter the opponents' argument in Acts. However, the Pauline epistles themselves contain the most important textual evidence of representatives of a "centripetal mission," namely, in Rom 9–11. I cannot here go into Paul's complex and debated argument in this controversial matter.[60] Luke's line of thought is comparatively simple. Paul derives more from the passage in Joel (Rom 10:12–15).

Still Luke provides an important contribution for the debate itself. He can demonstrate that the efficacy of the Spirit in Jesus's activity and in the history of the ancient church does not abrogate the Scripture. What others see as intermingling and use to oppose the legitimacy of the emerging church, Luke turns into a sequence. The modern concept of redemptive history (*Heilsgeschichte*) is used for this. Luke does not use the pristine period in order to idealize. The events of that time have their meaning in the first instance for that epoch.[61] They ought not to become opponents of what is new.

Some have thought that here Luke harks back to the story of the confusion of languages in Gen 11. However, the text of Acts 2 has scarcely any echoes that point in this direction.[62] Moreover, Luke does not take up the table of the nations in Gen 10. The fact that the count of sixteen

---

60. Unfortunately Joachim Jeremias in his book that is important in this connection, *Jesu Verheissung für die Völker*, 2nd ed. (Stuttgart: Kohlhammer, 1959), did not go into this issue.

61. As is well known, Hans Conzelmann has established this view in detail. Conzelmann, *Die Mitte der Zeit: Studien zur Theologie des Lukas*, 5th ed. (Tübingen: Mohr, 1964); ET: *The Theology of St. Luke* (Philadelphia: Fortresss, 1982).

62. J. G. Davies has attempted to establish this view, "Pentecost and Glosso-

peoples recurs in Acts 2 can be coincidental.⁶³ At most the house in which the disciples were located might be understood as the counterpart to the prideful tower.

As a matter of fact, Luke will have perceived the parallel. This is shown by the mere fact that he actually features a "table of the nations." However, evidently he thinks nothing of the expectation of a unified human language, which must have been considered by some as the decisive sign of the end times.⁶⁴ Luke has a different emphasis. For him it does not fall on overcoming language barriers in themselves. The hope for a restored humanity, which he shares and about which he speaks, has meaning for him only when with this restoration corporate praise of God's great deeds comes about (2:11). For this, however, the turning around of this perverse and corrupt generation is necessary, the turning to the one whom none other than God has made Lord and Messiah (2:36).

A final question remains open. How did Luke envision the end-time miracle about which he reports in our chapter? The answer to this question is certainly not irrelevant. Nevertheless, I have left it in the background in order to be able to highlight what Luke himself emphasizes in his interpretation. He gives this interpretation in the form of the Pentecost sermon. The fact that this interpretation is also available—though indeed cautiously—in the dramatic presentation itself is for this reason not contested. The dramatic presentation in its entirety was not a part of the investigation in this study.⁶⁵

---

lalia," *JTS* 3 (1952): 228–31. Some of the documentation has nothing to do with Acts 2 or Gen 11.

63. Holtzmann, *Apostelgeschichte*, 32, has referred to the agreement in numbers.

64. T. Jud. 25.

65. Answering to the question of whether the linguistic means of expression, as in Homer's Apollo hymn, betrays that the author wanted to present a miracle of understanding, Hans Jürgen Tschiedel has compared both texts. Thereby, the Apollo hymn turns out to be a remarkable parallel with respect to the history of religions and its content. In his view of Acts, Tschiedel follows Overbeck's opinion that here there is a miracle of hearing. In view of the languages mentioned by Luke this appears to me unlikely. However, this does not detract from the value of the parallel indicated here. Tschiedel, "Ein Pfingstwunder im Apollonhymnus (*Hymn. Hom. Ap.* 156–164 und Apg. 2:1–13)," *ZRGG* 27 (1975): 22–39.

5. Results

Luke identifies the whole of humanity as the addressees of the new period of redemptive history initiated by the pouring out of the Spirit, the representatives of whom—ἀπὸ παντὸς ἔθνους—gathered in Jerusalem on the Day of Pentecost. The word Ἰουδαῖοι in Acts 2:5 proves to be a later gloss, which is to be deleted from our text. For the corrupt Ἰουδαίαν in Acts 2:9, Λυκίαν is surmised to be original. The thesis that at Pentecost Luke allows only for the foundation of the Jerusalem community is therefore invalid. The result for Luke's theology is: Luke gives the standard view that the pouring out of the Spirit has to lead to the centripetal movement of peoples to Zion, "its historical location." The ancient expectation of a centripetal movement that was constitutive for the self-understanding of the original community has actually been replaced by a centrifugal movement. With his portrayal Luke has given a warrant for this.

This produces an insight that is by no means uninteresting for ancient geography: The search for Luke's geographical source needs to be abandoned. Luke himself has become the source. We read his "list" as an enumeration of spoken languages of that time, which Luke himself has composed and for which he could utilize information from the territory of the Jewish diaspora.

Bibliography

Arkwright, W. "Lycian Epitaphs," Pages 15–25 in *Anatolian Studies Presented to Sir William Mitchell Ramsay*. Edited by W. H. Buckler and W. M. Calder. Manchester: University Press, 1923.

Baer, Heinrich von. *Der Heilige Geist in den Lukasschriften*. BWANT 39. Stuttgart: Kohlhammer, 1926.

Barrett, C. K. *A Critical and Exegetical Commentary on the Acts of the Apostles*. 2 vols. ICC. Edinburgh: T&T Clark, 2004.

Bauer, Walter. *Wörterbuch zu den Schriften des Neuen Testaments und der übrigen urchristlichen Literatur*. 5th ed. Berlin: Töpelmann, 1963.

Bauernfeind, Otto. *Die Apostelgeschichte*. THKNT 5. Leipzig: Deichert, 1939.

Bishop, E. F. F. "Professor Burkitt and the Geographical Catalogue." *JRS* 42 (1952): 84–85.

Blass, Friedrich. "Zur Textkritik von Apostelgeschichte 2:5." *NKZ* 3 (1892): 826–30.

Blau, Lajos. *Zur Einleitung in die heilige Schrift*. Budapest: Alkalay, 1894.
Brixhe, Claude. "L'alphabet épichorique de Sidé." *Kadmos* 8 (1969): 54–84.
———. "Un nouveau document épichorique de Sidé." *Kadmos* 8 (1969): 143–51.
Bunbury, Edward H. *A History of Ancient Geography*. 2nd ed. London: Murray, 1883.
Clark, Albert C. *The Acts of the Apostles*. Oxford: Clarendon, 1933.
Clemen, Carl. "Die Zusammensetzung von Apg 1–5." *TSK* 68 (1895): 297–357.
Conzelmann, Hans. *Die Apostelgeschichte*. 2nd ed. Tübingen: Mohr Siebeck, 1972.
———. *A Commentary on the Acts of the Apostles*. Hermeneia. Philadelphia: Fortress, 1987.
———. *Die Mitte der Zeit: Studien zur Theologie des Lukas*. 5th ed. BHT 17. Tübingen: Mohr, 1964. English trans. *The Theology of St. Luke*. Philadelphia: Fortresss, 1982.
Davies, J. G. "Pentecost and Glossolalia." *JTS* 3 (1952): 228–31.
Dibelius, Martin. *Studies in the Acts of the Apostles*. Edited by Heinrich Greeven. Translated by Mary Ling. London: SCM, 1956.
Dobschütz, Ernst von. "Zu der Völkerliste Act 2:9–11." *ZWTh* 45 (1902): 407–10.
Eissfeldt, Otto. "Kreter und Araber." *TLZ* 72 (1947): 207–12.
Fitzmyer, Joseph A., SJ. "The Ascension of Christ and Pentecost." *TS* 45 (1984): 409–440.
Gager, John G. "Jews, Gentiles, and Synagogues in the Book of Acts." *HTR* 79 (1986): 91–99.
Gershevitch, Ilya. "Old Iranian Literature." Pages 1–30 in *Literatur*. Vol. 1 of *Iranian Studies*. HdO 4/1. Leiden: Brill, 1968.
Gilbert, Gary. "The List of Nations in Acts 2: Roman Propaganda and the Lukan Response." *JBL* 121 (2002): 497–529.
Grässer, Erich. "Die Apostelgeschichte in der Forschung der Gegenwart." *ThR* 26 (1960): 93–167.
Gutbrod, Walter. "Ἰσραήλ." *TDNT* 3:369–91.
Haacker, Klaus. "Das Pfingstwunder als exegetisches Problem." Pages 125–31 in *Verborum Veritas: Festschrift für G. Stählin*. Edited by Otto Böcher and Klaus Haacker. Wuppertal: Brockhaus, 1970.
Haas, Otto. *Die phrygischen Sprachdenkmäler*. Balkansko Ezikoznanie 10. Sofia Académie bulgare des sciences, 1966.

Haenchen, Ernst. *The Acts of the Apostles: A Commentary*. Philadelphia: Westminster, 1971.
Hahn, Ferdinand. *Das Verständnis der Mission im Neuen Testament*. WMANT 13. Neukirchen-Vluyn: Neukirchener Verlag, 1963.
Harnack, Adolf von. *Beiträge zur Einleitung in das Neue Testament, IV: Untersuchungen zur Apostelgeschichte und zur Abfassungszeit der synoptischen Evangelien*. Leipzig: Hinrichs, 1911.
Heichelheim, Fritz M. "Geschichte Kleinasiens von der Eroberung durch Kyros II. bis zum Tode des Herakleios I, 547 v.Chr.–641 n.Chr." Pages 32–98 in *Orientalische Geschichte von Kyros bis Mohammed*. Edited by Albert Dietrich, Geo Widengren, and Fritz M. Heichelheim. HdO 4. Leiden: Brill, 1966.
Holl, Karl. "Das Fortleben der Volkssprachen in Kleinasien in nachchristlicher Zeit." *Hermes* 43 (1908): 240–54. Republished in *Gesammelte Aufsätze zur Kirchengeschichte*, 2:238–48. Tübingen: Mohr, 1928.
Holtzmann, Heinrich J. *Die Apostelgeschichte*. 3rd ed. HKNT 1. Tübingen: Mohr, 1901.
Horst, Pieter W. van der. "Hellenistic Parallels to the Acts of the Apostles (2.1–47)." *JSNT* 25 (1985): 49–60.
Houwink ten Cate, P. H. J. *The Luwian Population Groups of Lycia and Cilicia Aspera During the Hellenistic Period*. DMOA 10. Leiden: Brill, 1961.
Jeremias, Joachim. *Jesu Verheissung für die Völker*. 2nd ed. Stuttgart: Kohlhammer, 1959.
Jervell, Jacob. *Luke and the People of God: A New Look at Luke-Acts*. Minneapolis: Augsburg, 1972.
Jones, A. H. M. *The Cities of the Eastern Roman Provinces*. 2nd ed. Rev. by Michael Avi-Yonah et al. Oxford: Clarendon, 1971.
Juster, Jean. *Les Juifs dans l'Empire Romain: Leur condition juridique, économique, et sociale*. 2 vols. Paris: Geuthner, 1914.
Kasting, Heinrich. *Die Anfänge der urchristlichen Mission*. Munich: Kaiser, 1969.
Kremer, Jacob. *Pfingstbericht und Pfingstgeschehen: Eine exegetische Untersuchung zu Apg 2:1–13*. SBS 63/64. Stuttgart: Katholisches Bibelwerk, 1973.
Kretschmer, P. "Nochmals die Hypachäer und Alaksandus." *Glotta* 24 (1936): 203–51.
Lake, Kirsopp. "The Gift of the Spirit on the Day of Pentecost." Pages 111–21 in *Additional Notes to the Commentary*. Vol. 5 of *The Begin-*

2. The Geographical Horizon 51

nings of Christianity Part I: The Acts of the Apostles. Edited by F. J. Foakes-Jackson and Kirsopp Lake. London: Macmillan, 1933.

Lake, Kirsopp, and Henry J. Cadbury. *English Translation and Commentary.* Vol. 4 of *The Beginnings of Christianity Part I: The Acts of the Apostles.* Edited by F. J. Foakes-Jackson and Kirsopp Lake. London: Macmillan, 1920.

Lohse, Eduard. "πεντηκοστή." *TDNT* 6:44–53.

Loisy, Alfred F. *Les Actes des Apôtres.* Paris: Nourry, 1920.

Lühr, Franz-Frieder. *Ratio und Fatum: Dichtung und Lehre bei Manilius.* Berlin: de Gruyter, 1969.

Mattill, A. J. "The Purpose of Acts: Schneckenburger Reconsidered." Pages 108–22 in *Apostolic History and the Gospel: Biblical and Historical Essays Presented to F. F. Bruce on His 60th Birthday.* Edited by W. Ward Gasque and Ralph P. Martin. Grand Rapids: Eerdmans, 1970.

Metzger, Bruce M. "Ancient Astrological Geography and Acts 2:9–11." Pages 123–33 in *Apostolic History and the Gospel: Biblical and Historical Essays Presented to F. F. Bruce on His Sixtieth Birthday.* Edited by W. Ward Gasque and Ralph P. Martin. Grand Rapids: Eerdmans, 1970.

———. *A Textual Commentary on the Greek New Testament: A Companion Volume to the United Bible Societies' Greek New Testament (Fourth Revised Edition).* 2nd ed. Stuttgart: Deutsche Bibelgesellschaft, 1994.

Metzger, Henri. "La stèle trilingue récemment découverte au Létoon de Xanthos: Le texte grec." *CRAI* 118 (1974): 82–90.

Neumann, Günter. "Lykisch." Pages 358–96 in *Altkleinasiatische Sprachen.* HdO 2/1. Leiden: Brill, 1969.

———. *Untersuchungen zum Weiterleben hethitischen und luwischen Sprachgutes in hellenistischer und römischer Zeit.* Wiesbaden: Harrassowitz, 1961.

———. "Zur Entzifferung der sidetischen Inschriften." *Kadmos* 7 (1968): 75–95.

Pervo, Richard I. *Acts: A Commentary.* Hermeneia. Minneapolis: Fortress, 2009.

Plümacher, Eckhard. *Lukas als hellenistischer Schriftsteller: Studien zur Apostelgeschichte.* SUNT 9. Göttingen: Vandenhoeck & Ruprecht, 1972.

Potin, Jean. *Le fête Juive de la Pentecôte: Étude des textes liturgiques.* LD 65. Paris: Cerf, 1971.

Reiner, Erica. "The Elamite Language." Pages 54–118 in *Altkleinasiatische Sprachen.* HdO 2/1. Leiden: Brill, 1969.

Ropes, James H. *The Text of Acts*. Vol. 3 of *The Beginnings of Christianity Part I: The Acts of the Apostles*. Edited by F. J. Foakes-Jackson and Kirsopp Lake. London: Macmillan, 1926.
Schmidt, Karl L. *Die Pfingsterzählung und das Pfingstereignis*. Leipzig: Hinrichs, 1919.
Scott, James M. "Luke's Geographical Horizon." Pages 483–544 in *The Book of Acts in Its First Century Setting*. Edited by David W. J. Gill and Conrad Gempf. Vol. 2 of *The Book of Acts in Its Graeco-Roman Setting*. Edited by Bruce W. Winter. Grand Rapids: Eerdmans; Carlisle: Paternoster, 1994.
Sherwin-White, A. N. *The Roman Citizenship*. 2nd ed. Oxford: Clarendon, 1973.
Stenger, Werner. "Beobachtungen zur sogenannten Völkerliste des Pfingstwunders (Apg 2:7–11)." *Kairos* 21 (1979): 206–14.
Taylor, Justin. "The List of the Nations in Acts 2:9–11." *RB* 106 (1999): 408–20.
Thomas, J. "Formgesetze des Begriffs-Katalogs im N.T." *TZ* 24 (1968): 15–28.
Trocmé, Étienne. *Le "Livre des Actes" et l'histoire*. Paris: Presses Universitaires de France, 1957.
Tschiedel, Hans Jürgen. "Ein Pfingstwunder im Apollonhymnus (*Hymn. Hom. Ap.* 156–164 und Apg. 2:1–13)." *ZRGG* 27 (1975): 22–39.
Weinstock, Stefan. "The Geographical Catalogue in Acts II.9–11." *JRS* 38 (1948): 43–46.
Weiss, Johannes. *Über die Absicht und den literarischen Charakter der Apostelgeschichte*. Göttingen: Vandenhoeck & Ruprecht, 1897.
Weissbach, Franz Heinrich. "Elymais." PW 5.2:2458–86.
Wellhausen, Julius. *Kritische Analyse der Apostelgeschichte*. Berlin: Weidmannsche, 1914.
Wilckens, Ulrich. *Die Missionsreden der Apostelgeschichte: Form- und traditionsgeschichtliche Untersuchungen*. 2nd ed. WMANT 5. Neukirchen-Vluyn: Neukirchener Verlag, 1963.
Wilson, S. G. *The Gentiles and the Gentile Mission in Luke-Acts*. SNTSMS 23. Cambridge: Cambridge University Press, 1973.
Wolff, Christian. "λαλειν γλωσσαις in the Acts of the Apostles." Pages 189–220 in *Paul, Luke, and the Graeco-Roman World: Essays in Honour of J. M. Wedderburn*. Edited by Alf Christophersen, Carsten Claussen, Jörg Frey, and Bruce Longenecker. JSNTSup 217. London: Sheffield Academic, 2002.

3
A New Edition of the Parchment Fragments London Brit. Libr. Pap. 2240 from the Wadi Sarga Containing New Testament Text

Whenever a newly discovered manuscript is to be published, some essential steps are required. These include material, measurements, date, a paleographical assessment of its script, a transcription, and, if possible, the reconstruction of an ancient corpus or scroll that it represents. Often a thorough restoration of ancient remains demands all possible skill. If the find concerns a New Testament text, it is necessary to define its relation to related witnesses. Any new finds are bound to improve our insight into ancient transmission processes. How one should proceed is demonstrated by the reedition of a Pauline fragment from the Wadi Sarga.

1. Description of the Manuscript 0201

In 1922 W. E. Crum and H. Idris Bell published Coptic and Greek texts from the Wadi Sarga, among which are two severely disintegrated parchment fragments with Greek texts from Paul's 1 Corinthians.[1] The transcript at that time provided parts of 1 Cor 12:2–3, 6–13; and 14:20–29. The first

---

1. W. E. Crum and H. Idris Bell, eds., *Wadi Sarga: Coptic and Greek Texts from the Excavations Undertaken by the Byzantine Research Account* (Copenhagen: Gyldendalske, 1922), 32–42. See also Herbert J. M. Milne, ed., *Catalogue of the Literary Papyri in the British Museum* (London: The Trustees, 1927), 183 no. 216, and *British Museum Catalogue of Additions to the Manuscripts in the Years 1921–1925* (London: The Trustees, 1950), 363. The latter publication identifies 1921 as the date of acquisition. As R. Campbell Thompson reports in his "Introduction" (in Crum and Bell, *Wadi Sarga*, 1) all of the texts were discovered in the excavations of the Byzantine Research Account in the winter of 1913–1914.

two transcribed lines of the first leaf as well as the text from a fragment 3 could not be correlated by the editors with any specific part of 1 Corinthians. Furthermore, other lines were described as illegible.[2] However, the readings that were provided were carefully substantiated.[3] Plates of the Greek text were not published.[4] The published texts have the number 0201 in the official list of manuscripts of the New Testament.[5] They were put to use as a witness in *The Greek New Testament*, edited by K. Aland et al. (London, 1966) and *Novum Testamentum Graece*, edited by K. Aland et al. (26th ed., Stuttgart, 1979).[6]

Of note is not only the sound text, which is close to the text of manuscripts DFG, but also the age of the fragment, which has been dated to the fifth century by the editors.[7] A trip to London in October, 1987 enabled me to confirm my supposition that a study of the original would be profitable with regard to readings left out of the *editio princeps*. These readings are—and this must be emphasized—in part unrecognizable in existing photographs. In the following these readings are considered in detail.

I am grateful to members of the Department of Western Manuscripts of the British Library for their kind help and for allocating technical arrangements, and also for the excellent photographs of an especially

---

2. Fragment 1, side a, col. 1: "[14 lines too much defaced for any confident reading.]"; fragment 1, side a, col. 2: "[12 lines too much defaced for any confident reading.]" so Crum and Bell, *Wadi Sarga*, 35. "Besides this fragment a few yet smaller scraps remain, too small and too much defaced to yield anything of interest," p. 42.

3. Crum and Bell, *Wadi Sarga*, 37–42.

4. Neither of the two accompanying volumes of plates contains a photograph of text 9; neither does the catalogue by Milne in *Catalogue of the Literary Papyri*. However, the Department of Western Manuscripts keeps two photographs of the front sides of papyrus 2240 (1) and 2240 (2) available. See *Prints from Manuscript Negatives*, vol. 19, p. 108.

5. Kurt Aland et al., *Kurzgefasste Liste der griechischen Handschriften des Neuen Testaments*, 2nd ed., ANTF 1 (Berlin: de Gruyter, 1994), 36 n 6.

6. According to J. Keith Elliott, *A Survey of Manuscripts Used in Editions of the Greek New Testament*, NovTSup 57 (Leiden: Brill, 1987), 24, the manuscript has not been used in other editions of the New Testament in spite of its sound text. Incidentally, the statement that 0201 is not cited in UBS[1-2] is incorrect: my copies of UBS[1] (as also UBS[3]) cite 0201 at 1 Cor. 12:9.

7. Crum and Bell, *Wadi Sarga*, p. 33. So also Milne, *Catalogue of the Literary Papyri*, and *British Museum Catalogue*.

3. New Edition of the Parchment Fragments London Brit. Libr. Pap. 2240

severely damaged part of the manuscript procured from the Photographic Service (black and white, ultraviolet, infrared).

1.1. Measurements and State of Preservation of the Fragments

Today's user of the Department of Western Manuscripts has access to two parchment leaves behind glass that are framed and that are severely fragmented and are therefore held together by strips of tape two to eight millimeters wide. Thus two folios are produced, which are numbered by the editors as fragment 1 and fragment 2.[8] As some of the Greek characters—which the editors did not decipher—show, originally both leaves made up one single folio, over which a lost folio of the original codex lay. The lost leaf contained precisely the text that is missing between the reverse side of fragment 1 (1 Cor 12:13) and the front side of fragment 2 (1 Cor 14:19).

A piece that the editors designated fragment 3, which they were not able to put into place, can be inserted in lines 12 and 13 of column 1 of fragment 1, side a. The reverse side completes the text of lines 12–14 from fragment 1, side b, column 2 as well as lines 12 and 13 from fragment 2, side a, column 1. The difficulty of fitting in fragment 3, which Bell could not remedy, is resolved by the fact that the characters ϕ[on line 12 and ϵ[on line 13, which can be observed on the right of the opposite side of what appears to be an intercolumnium between columns of fragment 3, are the remainder of the inner column of fragment 2, side a, column 1. This allows fragment 1 and fragment 2 to be understood as originally attached to each other. The alphabet characters are in fact not relics of a third column.[9]

A small shred taped to the upper left of fragment 2, side a, with a page number PMZ is not located in the correct place. As the remains of characters show, it was located over the space between columns 1 and 2 on fragment 2, side a.

Furthermore, the frame of fragment 1 contains five small fragments, which I also was not able to arrange in lacunae, because the reverse sides exhibit almost no vestiges of characters.

The leaf of parchment to which all fragments appear to belong was part of a Pauline manuscript in two columns, which presented the text in every case in nineteen lines. In spite of severe damage it can be determined

---

8. According to Bell, five pieces were joined together for fragment 1 and two pieces for fragment 2. See Crum and Bell, *Wadi Sarga*, 32.

9. Crum and Bell, *Wadi Sarga*, 42.

that before lettering the manuscript was carefully lined. The twenty horizontal lines running into the inner edge were defined on the outer edge by a line that was drawn down to the leaf below. Similar perpendicular lines apparently defined the ends of all columns. I observe a perpendicular double line as the inner edge of the reverse side of 2240 (1). A double line as the outer edge also appears to be preserved at the bottom on leaf 2240 (2) on the reverse side. In other places where these lines would be expected one searches in vain.

The copyist located his characters at the top exactly between the horizontal lines, but at the bottom they are located on the lines. At the ends of the lines on the right, he was often forced to place the letters closer together. This was the way in which the copyist was able to end the lines.

Because the tattered remnants have obviously become distorted, the measurements of the fragments remain uncertain.[10] The following approximate measurements can be specified.

The top margin on fragment 1, side a, measured at least 12 mm, the lower margin on fragment 1, side a, measured at least 17 mm; the intercolumnium between the columns of fragment 1, side a, 10 mm, fragment 2, side b, from 7 to 13 mm; the inner margin on fragment 1, side a, and fragment 2, side b (the reverse), measured 10 mm, the outer margin on fragment 1, side a, measured at least 12 mm, on fragment 2, side b (the reverse), measured a maximum of 40 mm. Because the writing surface of fragment 1, side a, column 2 can be measured as 42 x 99 mm, the page must have had a format of at least 14 x 13 cm, that is, broader than the height.[11] Fragment 3 measures a maximum of 34 x 34 mm.

1.2. Orthography and Punctuation

Accents and breathing marks do not occur. Twice a dieresis is found (over ϊΟΥΔΑΙΟΙ in 12:13, and over ϊΛΙѠ[ΤΗϹ] in 14:24) and once the apostrophe is used as a separator between two consonants. Dots of medium height have sometimes been preserved. Yet this is not always easy to ascertain. *Nomina sacra* are abbreviated as usual: Θ̄Ϲ̄ Θ̄Ῡ Θ̄Ѡ̄ Κ̄Ϲ̄ Π̄ΝᾹ Π̄Ν̄Ϲ̄ Π̄Ν̄Ῑ Χ̄Ϲ̄. Ν at the end of a line is occasionally replaced by the stroke

---

10. Crum and Bell, *Wadi Sarga*, 32.

11. Bell calculates 15 x 15 cm (Crum and Bell, *Wadi Sarga*, 32), likewise Aland, *Kurzgefasste Liste*, 53. Eric G. Turner, *The Typology of the Early Codex* (Philadelphia: University of Pennsylvania Press, 1977), 160, gives it as 14 x 14 cm.

3. New Edition of the Parchment Fragments London Brit. Libr. Pap. 2240

for abbreviations. Frequently the well-known vowel confusions occur: ⲈⲒ > Ⲓ, ⲒⲆⲰⲖⲀ in 12:2; Ⲓ > ⲈⲒ, ⲨⲘⲈⲒⲚ (in addition to ⲨⲘⲒⲚ) in 12:3; ⲆⲒⲀⲔⲢⲈⲒⲤⲒⲤ (in addition to ⲀⲚⲀⲔⲢⲒⲚⲈⲦⲀⲒ) in 12:10, ⲄⲚⲰⲢⲈⲒⲌⲰ in 12:3, ⲄⲈⲒⲚⲈⲦⲀⲒ in 14:25; ⲀⲒ > Ⲉ, ⲆⲒⲆⲞⲦⲈ (in addition to ⲆⲒⲆⲞⲦ[Ⲁ]Ⲓ) in 12:7; Ⲉ > ⲀⲒ, ⲄⲈ]ⲒⲚⲈⲤⲐⲀⲒ in 14:20, ⲘⲀ[ⲒⲚⲈⲤ]ⲐⲀ[Ⲓ] in 14:23. However, the common long ⲈⲒ in verb stems corresponds to the duration of the tone of the older New Testament manuscripts (cf. ⲄⲈⲒⲚⲈⲤⲐⲈ[1], P[46] ℵ A B* and ⲄⲈⲒⲚⲈⲤⲐⲀⲒ, G in 14:20; ⲄⲈⲒⲚⲈⲤⲐⲈ[2], P[46] B and ⲄⲈⲒⲚⲈⲤⲐⲀⲒ, A in 14:20; ⲀⲚⲀⲔⲢⲈⲒⲚⲈⲦⲀⲒ, B* in 14:24; ⲄⲈⲒⲚⲈⲦⲀⲒ, P[46] ℵ A B* D* F G 0201 in 14:25; ⲄⲈⲒⲚⲈⲤⲐⲰ, P[46] A B* D* F G in 14:26; ⲤⲈⲒⲄⲀⲦⲰ, P[46] B* D* in 14:28; ⲆⲒⲀⲔⲢⲈⲒⲚⲈⲦⲰⲤⲀⲚ, P[46] B* in 14:29). And for the interchange between Ⲟ and Ⲱ, or between Ⲏ and the correlated Ⲓ-sounds, only the uncertain references ⲪⲀⲚⲈⲢⲞⲤⲒⲤ in 12:7 and ⲈⲢⲘⲎⲚⲈⲒⲀ in 12:10 may be listed. Subjunctives have the correct vowels. With regard to consonants, the orthography is absolutely correct. Therefore the orthography is remarkably careful and good.

1.3. Dating

0201 evidences a perpendicular, calligraphically well-formed biblical uncial script. Ⲟ Ⲥ Ⲉ Ⲑ are well-rounded. A light upstroke on the horizontal rises up smoothly to a more sturdy perpendicular script. The ends of Ⲥ and Ⲉ each have points. Full symmetry of the forms is achieved.

Vertical strokes are sturdy and comparatively short. With the condensed arrangement of the letters, this gives the script a somewhat compact character. Only Ⲩ and Ⲫ have longer descending strokes. Ⲣ and Ⲩ agree in their measures with the other letters, but occasionally show a tendency to lengthen the descending stroke. The ends of Ⲩ and Ⲧ at the top run out in sturdily developed points.

It is significant that the Ⲙ, while keeping to symmetry, develops the downward line running from the upper left more sturdily than the line running upward toward the upper right. The writing comes close to the scripts of PBerol. 16353 recto (from the beginning of the fifth century) and of PVindob. G 26055 verso (around 425) delineated by G. Cavallo and is to be located in the first half of the fifth century.[1]

---

12. See Guglielmo Cavallo, *Ricerche sulla maiuscola biblica* (Firenze: Le Monnier, 1967), 72 and 74, plates 51 and 58. Aland, *Kurzgefasste Liste*, 53, and Turner,

58   Textual Criticism and the New Testament Text

2. Transcription with Annotations on the Readings

2.1. Transcription[13]

Fragment 1, side a, column 1   inner column
  1   ΔΕΧΕ[C]ΘΕ   11:33
  2   ΕΙΔΕΤ[ΙCΠΕΙΝΑ]   11:34
  3   ΕΝΟΙ[ΚѠΕCΘΙΕΤѠ]
  4   [ΙΝΑ]ΜΗΕ[ΙCΚΡΙΜΑ]
  5   [CΥΝΕΡΧΗCΘΕ]
  6   ΤΑ[
  7
  8
  9
 10
 11
 12   (Α)[ΓΝΟΕΙΝ ΟΙΔΑΤΕ]   12:2
 13   (ΟΤΕΕ)[ΘΝΗΗΤΕ]
 14   [ΠΡΟCΤ]ΑΙΔ[Ѡ]
 15   [ΛΑΤΑΑ]ΦѠΝΑ
 16   [ѠCΑΝΗΓΕCΘΕ]
 17   ΑΠΑΓΟΜΕΝΟΙ
 18   ΔΙΟΓΝѠΡΕΙΖѠ   12:3
 19   ΥΜΕΙΝ·ΟΤΙΟΥ

Fragment 1, side a, column 2   outer column
  1   [ΔΙ]CΕΝΠΝΙΘΥ
  2   ΛΕΓΕΙΑΝΑΘΕ
  3
  4
  5
  6   12:4
  7   [ΔΕ]ΧΑ[ΡΙ]CΜ[Α]ΤѠ

Typology,160, also locate the manuscript in the fifth century. See also note 5 (on the enumeration of this manuscript) and note 11 (regarding the description of the early codex by Eric Turner).

13. Letters that are recognizable from the other fragments are given again in parentheses in places where they fit.

3. New Edition of the Parchment Fragments London Brit. Libr. Pap. 2240   59

```
 8
 9
10
11  [καιοα]υ[τ]οςκ̄c̄θ̄c̄
12  [διαιρες]ειϲε̄            12:6
13  [εργηματω]νε[ι]
14  [cιν]καιοαυτ[oc]θ̄c̄
15  εν[ε]ργωνεcτ[ι]
16  παν[τα]ενπ[αcιν]
17  εκα[cτ]ωδεδιδ[οτ]ε       12:7
18  ηφανερocιcτου
19  π̄ν̄cπρocτocyμ
```

Fragment 1, side b, column 1   outer column
```
 1  φορον·ωμεν                12:8
 2  γαρδιατουπ̄ν̄c
 3  διδοτ[α]ιλογο[c]
 4  coφ[ιαcαλλωδ]ε
 5  λογο[cγνωcεω]c
 6  κατα[τοαυ]τοπ̄ν̄α
 7  ετερωπιcτι[c]             12:9
 8  ε[ντ]ωαυτωπ̄[ν̄]ι
 9  [αλλωχαριcμαται]
10  αματωνε[ντω]
11  αυτωπ̄ν̄ι[αλλω]            12:10
12  δεενεργημ[α]
13  ταδυνα[μ]ε[ωc]
14  αλλωπροφ[ητεια]
15  αλλωδιακρειcιc
16  [τ]ων[πνευματω]ν
17  ετερωγενηγλωc
18  cωναλλωδεερ
19  μηνειαγλωc
```

Fragment 1, side b, column 2   Inner column
```
 1  cω[ν]πανταδε              12:11
 2  τα[υτα]ενεργει
 3  το[ενκ]αιτοαυτο
 4  [π̄ν̄α]διαιρουν
```

5 Є[ΚΑ]ϹΤѠΚΑΘѠ[Ϲ]
 6 [ΒΟΥΛЄ]ΤΑΙΚΑΘΑ   12:12
 7 [ΠЄΡΓΑ]ṚΤ[ΟϹѠΜ]Α
 8
 9
10
11
12 [Τ].. [ΠΟΛΛΑΟΝΤ](Α̣)
13 ЄΝЄϹΤ[ΙΝ](ϹѠΜΑ·)
14 ΟΥΤѠϹ̣[Κ](Α̣Ι[Ο]Χ̅Ϲ̅)
15 Κ̣ΑΙΓΑ[ΡЄΝΙΠ̅Ν̅Ι]
16 Π̣Α̣ΝΤ[ЄϹΗΜЄΙϹ]
17 ЄΙϹ̣ЄΝϹѠ[Μ]Α
18 ЄΒΑΠΤΙ̣[Ϲ]ΘΗΜЄ̅·
19 ЄΙ̣ΤЄΪΟΥΔΑΙΟΙ·

visible at the right of line 3:
 3 Κ[

Fragment 2, side a, column 1   inner column
                                          ΡΜΖ
 1
 2
 3 (Κ)
 4
 5
 6 [ЄΝΓΛѠϹϹΗ]Α̣   14:20
 7 [ΔЄΛΦΟΙΜ]ΗΠΑ[Ι]
 8 [ΔΙΑΓЄΙΝЄ]ϹΘΑΙ
 9 [ΤΑΙϹΦΡЄϹ]ΙΝΑΛ
10 [ΛΑΤΗΚΑ]Κ̣ΙΑΝΗ
11 [ΠΙΑΖЄΤЄΤΑΙ]Ϲ̣Δ̣Є̣
12 (Φ)[ΡЄϹΙΝΤЄΛЄΙΟΙ]
13 (Є)ΝΤѠ[ΝΟΜѠ]   14:21
14 [ΓЄ]ΓΡΑΠ[ΤΑΙΟΤΙ]
15 [Є]Ν[ЄΤ]ЄΡ[ΑΙϹΓΛ]Ѡ̣Ϲ
16 ϹΑΙϹΚΑΙЄΝΧЄΙ
17 ΛЄϹ̣ΙΝЄΤЄ[Ρ]Ѡ̣Ν̣
18 [ΛΑΛ]Η̣ϹѠΤ̣[ѠΛΑѠ]
19 ΤΟΥΤѠΚΑ̣[ΙΟΥΔΟΥ]

Fragment 2, side a, column 2 outer column
1 [ΤⲰС]ΕΙСΑ[ΚΟΥϹΟΝ]
2 [ΤΑΙ]ΜΟΥ[ΛΕΓΕΙ]
3 [Ο]ΘϹΔΙ[ΟΔΙΓΛⲰС] 14:22
4 ϹΑΙ[ΕΙϹϹΗ]ΜΕΙ[ΟΝ]
5 ΕΙϹ[ΙΝΟΥΤ]ΟΙϹΠΙϹ
6 ΤΕΥΟΥϹΙ[ΝΑΛΛΑΤ]ΟΙϹ
7 ΑΠΙϹΤΟΙϹ[ΗΔΕΠΡ]Ο
8 ΦΗΤΕΙΑ[ΟΥΤΟΙϹΑ]
9 ΠΙ[Ϲ]ΤΟ[ΙϹΑΛΛΑΤ]ΟΙϹ
10 ΠΙϹΤΕ[ΥΟΥϹΙΝ]ΕΑΝ 14:23
11 ΟΥΝ[ϹΥΝΕΛ]ΘΗΗ
12 ΕΚΚΛ[ΗϹΙΑΟ]ΛΗΕΠΙ
13 ΤΟΑΥΤ[Ο]ΚΑΙΠΑΝ
14 ΤΕϹΛΑΛⲰϹΙΝΓΛⲰϹ
15 ϹΑΙϹΕΙϹΕΛΘⲰϹΙΔΕ
16 ΚΑΙΙΔΙⲰΤΑΙΗΑΠΙ[Ϲ]
17 ΤΟΙΟΥ[ΚΕΡ]ΟΥ[ϹΙΝ]
18 ΟΤΙΜΑ[ΙΝΕϹ]ΘΑ[Ι]
19 ΕΑΝΔΕΠΑΝΤΕϹ 14:24

Fragment 2, side b, column 1 outer column
1 [ΠΡΟ]ΦΗ[ΤΕΥⲰϹΙΝΕΙϹ]
2 [ΕΛΘ]ΗΔΕ[ΤΙϹΑΠΙϹ]
3 [ΤΟϹΗ]ΪΔΙⲰ[ΤΗϹ]
4 Ε[ΛΕΓΧΕΤΑΙ]ΥΠΟ
5 Π[ΑΝΤⲰΝΑΝ]ΑΚΡΙ
6 [ΝΕΤΑΙΥΠ]ΟΠΑΝ
7 [ΤⲰΝ]ΤΑΚΡΥΠΤΑ 14:25
8 [ΤΗϹΚΑΡ]ΔΙΑϹΑΥΤΟΥ
9 ΦΑ[ΝΕΡΑ]ΓΕΙΝΕΤΑΙ
10 Κ[ΑΙΟΥΤⲰ]ϹΠΡΟ
11 ΠΕ[ϹⲰΝΠΡ]ΟϹΚΥ
12 ΝΗϹ[ΕΙΤⲰ]ΘΩΑ
13 ΠΑΓ[Γ]ΕΛ[Λ]ⲰΝΟΤ[Ι]
14 ΘϹΟΝΤⲰ[Ϲ]ΕΝΥ
15 ΜΙΝΕϹΤΙΝ·ΤΙΟΥ 14:26
16 ΕϹΤΙΑΔΕΛΦΟΥ
17 [Ο]ΤΑ[ΝϹΥΝ]ΕΡΧΗϹ

             18 ΘΕ[ΕΚΑΣ]ΤΟΣ· ΨΑΛ
             19 ṀΟΝΕΧΕΙΔΙΔΑ

Fragment 2, side b, column 2   inner column
              1
              2
              3
              4
              5 Π[ΑΝΤΑΠΡΟΣΟΙ]
              6 ΚΟΔ[ΟΜΗΝΓΕΙ]
              7 ṆẸΣ[ΘΩ ΕΙΤΕ]   14:27
              8 ΓΛΩṢ[ΣΗΤΙΣΛΑ]
              9 ΛΕΙΚΑ[ΤΑΔΥΟΗ]
             10 [Τ]ΟΠ[ΛΕΙΣΤΟΝ]
             11 [ΤΡΕΙΣΚΑΙΑΝ](ạ)
             12 [ΜΕΡΟΣΚΑΙ](ẸΙΣ)
             13 [ΔΙΕΡΜΗ]ΝΕΥ(ΕΤΩ)
             14 [ΕΑΝΔΕ]ΜΗḤ[ΔΙΕΡ]   14:28
             15 Μ[ΗΝΕ]Υ[ΤΗΣΣΕΙ]
             16 ΓΑṬ[Ω]ΕΝΕ̣ΚḲΛ[Η]
             17 ṢΙΑΕΑΥΤΩΔΕΛΑ
             18 [ΛΕΙΤ]ΩΚΑΙΤ[ΩΘ͞Ω]
             19 [ΠΡΟ]ΦΗΤΑΙ̣ΔΕΔ̣[ΥΟ]   14:29

Fragment 3, side a, column 1   inner column
             12 Ạ[ΓΝΟΕΙΝ ΟΙΔΑΤΕ]   12:2
             13 ΟṬΕṢ[ΘΝΗΗΤΕ]
                 visible at the left of this:

Fragment 3, side a, column 2, torn off   inner column
             11 [ΤΡΕΙΣΚΑΙΑΝ]ạ   14:27
             12 [ΜΕΡΟΣΚΑΙ]ẸΙΣ
             13   ]ΕΤΩ

Fragment 3, side b, column 2   inner column
             12 [Τ].. [ΠΟΛΛΑΟΝΤ]ạ   12:12
             13   ]ΣΩΜΑ·
             14   ]ạ̣Ι[Ο]Χ͞Σ
                 visible at the right of this:

3. New Edition of the Parchment Fragments London Brit. Libr. Pap. 2240   63

Fragment 3, side b, column 1   inner column
12 ⲫ[
13 ⲉ[14:21

2.2. Explanatory Notes on the Readings

Fragment 1, side a, column 1
Lines 12–13. The insertion of a small fragment (fragment 3) in this place is confirmed by its reverse. The discoloration of the parchment fits in with what is adjacent: line 12 ⲁ, line 13 ⲟⲧⲉⲉ. At the same time, the fragment can be identified as a portion torn off fragment 2, side b, column 2. The following letters may be read: at the end of line 12, ⲁ, at the end of line 13, ⲉⲓⲥ, and at the end of line 14, ⲉⲧⲱ.
Lines 17–19. Bell deciphered only line 1 ⲙⲁⲧ!..., line 2 ⲱⲧ!..., lines 17–19.

Fragment 1, side a, column 2
Line 2. Bell gave no readings for lines 2–13.
Line 14. As Bell indicated, ⲕⲁⲓ is certain. ⲟ after ⲕⲁⲓ is also clear. Apparently ⲑ̄ⲥ̄ stood at the end of the line. One sees traces of the stroke indicating the abbreviation of the *nomen sacrum*. After that there is no space for an ⲟ on the fragment, which has no writing.
Line 15. The first letter on line 15 is an ⲉ, not an ⲟ.
Line 16. Bell: ⲧⲁ ⲡⲁⲛ[ⲧⲁ].
Line 17. An ⲉ is discernible at the end of line 17, Bell: ⲇⲓⲁ[ⲟ]ⲧⲁⲓ.
Line 18. Ọ: Because the parchment is damaged here, an ⲱ is also possible (so Bell).

Fragment 1, side b, column 1
Line 7. No space is available for a [ⲇⲉ] before ⲡⲓ[ⲥ]ⲧⲓ[ⲥ] (so Bell). Thus it was absent in the text.
Line 9. Bell reads [ⲁⲗⲗⲱ]ⲭⲁⲣ[ⲓ]ⲥⲙ[ⲁⲧⲁ ?], very uncertain. He asserts that the ⲇⲉ must have been missing. On the basis of the amount of space, Bell takes ⲭⲁⲣⲓⲥⲙ[ⲁ] to be more plausible than ⲭⲁⲣⲓⲥⲙ[ⲁⲧⲁ]. The first reading is well known in Latin witnesses. ⲭⲁⲣⲓⲥⲙⲁ is read by Marcion according to Tertullian, *Marc.* 5.8.
Line 10. Against Bell, line 10 begins with ⲁ, therefore not ⲓⲁⲙⲁⲧⲱⲛ.
Line 11. 0201, instead of varying the terminology, reads twice τῷ αὐτῷ

πνεύματι. Bell was unable to recognize the stroke for the abbreviation of a *nomen sacrum*. After Π̄Ν̄Ι one sees a *spatium*.

Line 13. It is impossible to say whether in common with P⁴⁶ D F G b, 0201 had ΔΥΝΑΜΕѠC or, in common with the other witnesses, ΔΥΝΑΜΕѠΝ.

Line 16. The position of Ν at the end of line 16 speaks for a written-out form of ΠΝΕΥΜΑΤѠΝ (different from Bell). As a rule plural forms are not abbreviated.

Line 19. Perhaps ΜΙΝΕΙΑ. The parchment is damaged.

Fragment 1, side b, column 2

Line 3. ΤΟ at the beginning of the line can be discerned. Beyond the line there is a distinct Κ, not identified by Bell. It belongs to line 3 of fragment 2, side a, column 1. Placing it at the Κ[ΑΙ of 14:19 presents no difficulty.

Line 4. The stroke indicating an abbreviation of the *nomen sacrum* over Π̄ΝΑ is discernible.

Line 5. Bell reads [ΕΚΑCΤ]Ѡ ΚΑΘѠ[C], but he is uncertain whether the letter before ΚΑΘѠ[C] should be rendered as Α or Ѡ.

Line 12. Bell gave no reading for line 12. Lines 8–12 are torn off. The opposite side of the piece that fits into fragment 1, side a, column 1, at lines 12 and 13 provides an Α for line 12 and a well-preserved CѠΜΑ· with a point in the center for line 13 and remains of ΑΙ[ ]Χ̄C̄ for line 14. To the right of the inner edge the fragment presents a Φ at the level of line 12 and at the level of line 13 an Ε. Both letters are torn off from the left edge of fragment 2, side a, column 1. The position of Α to the right over the Α of CѠΜΑ· makes it possible to assess tentatively what is missing from line 12.

Bell had correctly determined the position of CѠΜΑ·, but he abandoned this identification because he thought he had to place the word in the space of a left-hand column. He did not recognize that the letters Φ and Ε were correctly arranged beyond the inner edge of fragment 1, side b, column 2 (see Crum and Bell, *Wadi Sarga*, 42).

Line 15. The text can scarcely be identified.

Fragment 2, side a, column 1

Lines 1–5. From the Κ of fragment 1 on, the text is missing for five lines.

Line 11. At the end of the line ΤΑΙ]CΑΕ can be read with difficulty, Bell: ΤΑΙC|ΑΕ (new line).

Line 12. ⲫ is found beyond the inner edge of fragment 1, side a, column 2 on the piece fitted in at lines 12–14.

Line 13. The same goes for the Ⲉ; ⲚⲦⲰ is preserved on fragment 2, side a, column 1. Bell: [Ⲡⲓ]ⲚⲎⲤ̣[ⲐⲈ ⲈⲚⲚⲞⲘⲰ].

Line 19. Bell's concerns over the length of line 19 are not justified; lines 11 and 12 are just as long. Ⲕⲁ[ⲒⲞⲨⲆⲞⲨ] ∥ [ⲦⲰⲤ] needs to be filled in, not Ⲕⲁ[ⲒⲞⲨⲆⲈ] ∥ [ⲠⲰ ?] (against Crum and Bell, *Wadi Sarga*).

Fragment 2, side a, column 2

Line 1–3. A small piece that also contains a page number (ⲢⲘⲌ) can be fitted into the upper part of the leaf. On line 1 it contains ⲈⲒⲤⲀ, on line 2 ⲘⲞⲨ, on line 3—easily legible—ⲐⲤⲀⲒ. It is baffling that the stroke indicating the abbreviation of the *nomen sacrum* is not discernible over ⲐⲤ. However, the position is made certain by the reverse, which is also legible. The reverse fits into fragment 2, side b, column 1. The position of the piece allows recognition that the page number stood above the space between the columns of fragment 2, side a.

Line 1. It is not possible to say whether 0201 had ⲀⲔⲞⲨⲤⲈⲦⲀⲒ or ⲀⲔⲞⲨⲤⲞⲚⲦⲀⲒ.

Line 3. Bell's reading [? Ⲟ]Ⲓ̅Ⲥ̅ ⲀⲒ[Ⲟ is not to be retained, compare also the singular reading Ⲟ ⲀⲨⲦⲞⲤ ⲔⲨⲢⲒⲞⲤ ⲐⲈⲞⲤ at 1 Cor 12:5 in line 11 of fragment 1, side a, column 2.

Fragment 2, side b, column 1

Lines 1–3. The reverse of the piece mentioned at fragment 2, side a, column 2 contains the Greek letters ⲪⲎ from line 1, ⲎⲆⲈ from line 2, Ⲓ̅Ⲇ̅Ⲓ̅Ⲱ from line 3.

Line 1. The line is noticeably long, but compare line 8 below as well as line 6 on fragment 2, side a, column 2. Bell considers a defective singular reading, perhaps ⲠⲢⲞⲪⲎⲦⲀⲒ.

Line 2. Bell reckons with the absence of ⲦⲒⲤ in line 2.

Line 8. This and the following lines appear on quite darkened parchment and can scarcely be deciphered. My indications are rather tentative.

Line 13. There was no Ⲟ after ⲞⲦⲒ. The parchment is preserved. Bell: [Ⲟ].

Line 14. Sufficient traces of Ⲑ̅Ⲥ̅ are preserved, Bell: [Ⲑ̅Ⲥ̅].

Line 16. There was no Ⲛ before ⲀⲆⲈⲖⲪⲞⲨ (Bell: ⲀⲆⲈⲖⲪⲞⲒ), Bell: ⲈⲤⲦⲒⲚ. The parchment is perforated at the last letter of ⲀⲆⲈⲖⲪⲞⲨ. It is possible that the copyist wrote ⲀⲆⲈⲖⲪⲞⲒ.

Line 18. [ⲈⲔⲀⲤ]ⲦⲞⲤ and ⳨ⲀⲖ are separated by an apostrophe, not noticed by Bell.

Fragment 2, side b, column 2
Lines 1-4. Differently from what Bell indicates, four lines in the upper part of the column are lost (not five). This determination results from the quantity of text to be fitted in and from the careful lining. All columns preserved have nineteen lines.

Lines 11-13. By the location of a piece (for Bell: fragment 3) in the text of fragment 1, side a, column 1, lines 12-13, and its reverse in fragment 1, side b, column 2, lines 12-14, it is possible to reconstruct lines 11-13 more precisely than what Bell achieved. ⲈⲦⲰ is attached to the torn-off text of [ⲆⲒⲈⲢⲘⲎ]ⲚⲈⲨ, ⲈⲒⲤ constitutes the end of line 12, line 11 ends with Ⲁ. In 14:27 the text of 0201 manifests no divergences from the commonly printed text.

Line 8. It is not possible to say whether 0201 had ⲄⲖⲰⲤⲤⲎ or ⲄⲖⲰⲤⲤⲀⲒⲤ.

Line 14. Whether filling in [ⲆⲒⲈⲢ] or [ⲈⲢ] or [ⲞⲈⲢ] is in accordance with the text of 0201 must remain undecided. According to space requirements [ⲆⲒⲈⲢ] presents no difficulty (different from Bell).

3. The Text of Manuscript 0201

3.1. Textual Criticism[14]

12:2 0201 with K 0150 1 69 2464 improves the text, as stated by Wolfgang Schrage: "The omission of ὅτι (K 2646 pc) and likewise of ὅτε (F G 629 al a b d vg^{mss} sy^p) appear to alleviate the difficulty of the transmitted text."[15] Similarly Hans Conzelmann on the construction of the sentence. "FG 0142.0151.629 a b d sy^p offer a more satisfying, even if weakly attested, improvement."[16] Brooke Foss Westcott and Fenton John Anthony Hort

---

14. Readings of the manuscript that have not yet been corrected are designated with an asterisk [*], and corrections of copyist of the manuscript are designated with the sign [C*]. Corrections are numbered consecutively.

15. Wolfgang Schrage, *Der erste Brief an die Korinther*, EKKNT 7.3 (Neukirchen-Vluyn: Neukirchener Verlag, 1999), 120 n. 35.

16. Hans Conzelmann, *Der erste Brief an die Korinther*, 2nd ed. (Göttingen: Vandenhoeck & Ruprecht, 1981), 248 n. 2.

3. New Edition of the Parchment Fragments London Brit. Libr. Pap. 2240

conjectured ὅτι ποτέ.[17] A. T. Robertson and Alfred Plummer, in their commentary on 1 Corinthians, speak for this conjecture.[18]

12:3 λαλων om. DFG 0201 a. The omission has parallels in the New Testament. Evidently λεγω is missing in the exemplar for the Sahidic translation in Rom. 3:5, see Origen, who knew such manuscripts, in his commentary on Romans: Ταῦτα τὸ «Μ[ὴ] ἄδικος ὁ θεὸς ὁ ἐπιφέρων τὴν ὀργὴν κατὰ ἀνθρώπων;» [.] ... εἰ δὲ ὡς ἐν ἑτέροις εὕρομεν, «Μὴ ἄδικος ὁ θεὸς ἐπιφέρων τὴν ὀργήν; κατὰ ἀνθρώπο[ν] λέγω. Μὴ γένοιτο», τοιοῦ[το]ν ἂν ἔχοι νοῦν ἡ λέξις.[19] Origen's summary, as well as his individual expositions, are undergirded by this secondary reading.[20] Compare κατα των ανθρωπων 1739^mg. Similarly in the transmission of Ephraem a λαλῶν has disappeared. It must be restored.[21]

Apparently also in Heb 10:17 a *verbum dicendi* has been lost. In view of the interruption of a quotation by γάρ φησιν in 8:5, I conjecture as the beginning of 10:17 καί φησιν -, hence καί φησιν τῶν ἁμαρτιῶν αὐτῶν κτλ.

12:6 The early Alexandrian tradition (P^46 B 1739) has και ο. This reading is attested by C as well. και ο is probably an accommodation to v. 5.[22] Origen does not attest this reading (against Zuntz).[23]

---

17. Brooke Foss Westcott and Fenton John Anthony Hort, eds., *The New Testament in the Original Greek: Volume 1, Text; Volume 2, Introduction [and] Appendix*, 2nd ed. (Cambridge: Macmillan, 1896), 116.

18. A. T. Robertson and Alfred Plummer, *A Critical and Exegetical Commentary on the First Epistle of St. Paul to the Corinthians*, 2nd ed., ICC (Edinburgh: T&T Clark, 1911), 260.

19. Jean Scherer, *Le commentaire d' Origène sur Rom. III 5–V 7 d' après les extraits du Papyrus No 88748 du Musée du Caire et les fragments de la Philocalie du Vaticanus gr. 762* (Cairo: l'Institut Français d'Archéologie Orientale, 1957), P 1., pp. 25–27.

20. On this see Caroline P. Hammond Bammel, *Der Römerbrieftext des Rufin und seine Origenesübersetzung*, Vetus Latina (Freiburg im Breisgau: Herder, 1985), 215–16; cf. 40, 197, and 204.

21. T. S. Pattie, "Ephraem the Syrian and the Latin Manuscripts of 'De Paenitentia,'" *British Library Journal* 13 (1987): 8.

22. Hans Lietzmann, *An die Korinther*, 5th ed., HNT 9 (Tübingen: Mohr, 1969), 61; Günther Zuntz, *The Text of the Epistles: A Disquisition upon the Corpus Paulinum*, Schweich Lectures of the British Academy 1946 (London: Oxford University Press, 1953), 203.

23. Claude Jenkins, "Documentation: Origen on 1 Corinthians IV," *JTS* 10 (1908): 29.

12:6 The omission of ο by 0201 and the insertion of εστιν by B* 0201^vid, and in a different position by ℵ² K L 0150.0151, are correlated and are secondary.

12:6 The omission of τα before παντα links D* to 0201. The omission is secondary, as Zuntz has shown.²⁴

12:7 0201 συμφορον. The adjective σύμφορος is attested as Pauline in 1 Cor 7:35 by P¹⁵, ⁴⁶ ℵ* A B D* 33 and in 1 Cor 10:33 by P⁴⁶ ℵ* A B C. The later tradition was inclined to substitute forms of συμφέρω. This factor speaks for the originality of the singular reading. Admittedly, the Pauline use of the participle of συμφέρω is also in evidence: 2 Cor 12:1.

12:8 The word order of P⁴⁶ is to be rejected. Paul is fond of the chiastic structure.

12:9 δε after ετερω as well as after αλλω is secondary just as in the five positions in verse 10.²⁵ According to Robertson and Plummer the last δε of v 10 is "perhaps" original.²⁶

χαρισμα ιαματων (so Marcion, according to Tertullian, *Marc.* 5.8): d *alii gratia sanitatem,* f *alii gratiae sanitatem,* g *dona gratiae sanitatum* (g* *donat<io>*).²⁷ Since according to content the singular is preferable, this could have been introduced as a correction.

12:9 In view of the "diversified support for ἐνί," the committee of textual critics of the *Institut für neutestamentliche Textforschung* preferred this reading.²⁸

12:10 Here also the singular is preferable; ενεργια in D (ενεργεια FG), ενεργημα 056.0142 (supported by Phil 3:21) may have been introduced as a correction. However, δυναμεως in the present context can hardly have originated secondarily and consequently may be appealed to as original.²⁹

---

24. Zuntz, *Text of the Epistles,* 109–10.

25. So Zuntz, *Text of the Epistles,* 105–7, 215. Differently Conzelmann, *Der Erste Brief,* 252 n. 3.

26. Robertson and Plummer, *First Epistle,* 268.

27. Adolf von Harnack, *Marcion: Das Evangelium vom fremden Gott,* 2nd ed., TUGAL 45 (Leipzig: Hinrichs, 1924), 89*.

28. Bruce M. Metzger, *A Textual Commentary on the Greek New Testament: A Companion Volume to the United Bible Societies' Greek New Testament (Fourth Revised Edition),* 2nd ed. (Stuttgart: Deutsche Bibelgesellschaft, 1994), 497; Schrage, *Der Erste Brief,* 152 n. 213.

29. Zuntz, *Text of the Epistles,* 100.

3. New Edition of the Parchment Fragments London Brit. Libr. Pap. 2240

Certainly the interchange of singular and plural forms, as in other passages, caused difficulties for the copyists.

12:10 The reading διακρεισις in 0201, supported by ℵ C D* F G P 33.1175 sy^p sa, may be preferred on the basis of the content. Marcion reads this according to Tertullian, *Marc.* 5.8.[30] For the meaning of the expression see an essay of Gerhard Dautzenberg.[31] Later interest was concentrated upon the abundance of the acts of grace, rather than upon their unity.

On the other hand, the reading διακρίσεις, supported by P[46] A B D² Ψ 1739.1881 Byz sy^h bo, is preferred by Schrage.[32]

As the source for later amendments and corruptions, perhaps χάρισμα ἰαμάτων, ἐνεργήματα δυνάμεως, διάκρισις πνευμάτων would be conceivable.

12:10 0201 των πνευματων. Paul uses the plural form without the article (1 Cor 14:12, 32), differently from later literature.

12:10 It is arguable whether the word ἑρμηνεία or ἑρμηνευτής appeared in Paul. Theodor von Nägeli argued: "Not until the Byzantine grammarians did διερμηνευτής surface again (1 Cor 14:28 Eust. ad Il. 106,14)."[33]

Paul uses the verb διερμηνεύειν (1 Cor 12:30; 14:5, 13, 27), which also is attested in Lukan writings along with μεθερμηνεύειν (Luke 24:27; Acts 9:36). Elsewhere New Testament authors use passive forms of ἑρμηνεύειν (John 1:42; 9:7; Heb 7:2) or of μεθερμηνεύειν (Mark 5:41; 15:22; 15:34; Matt 1:23; John 1:38, 41; Acts 4:36; 13:8). Where Codex Bezae reformulates Luke 24:27, it uses ἑρμηνεύειν, though in Acts 18:6 D uses διερμηνεύειν for the interpretation of Scripture. In 1 John 1:38 the later tradition changes the original μεθερμηνεύειν into ἑρμηνεύειν. In 1 Cor 12:10 D* A have διερμηνία, and in 14:26 D has διερμηνίαν, FG διερμηνείαν. In 14:28, P[46] ℵ A D¹ K L Ψ 049.056.0150.0151.0243.0285.6.424.1739.1908 have διερμηνευτής.

Thus it seems likely that in the three places in which the tradition diverges, in each case ἑρμηνεία, ἑρμηνείαν, and ἑρμηνευτής or ὁ ἑρμηνευτής are the secondary forms. I assume that an original διερμηνία in 12:10 in the greater part of the tradition induced the incorrect δέ, which was then inserted secondarily in A. That a substitution of διερμηνείαν, διερμηνευτής

---

30. Harnack, *Marcion*, 89*.

31. Gerhard Dautzenberg, "Zum religionsgeschichtlichen Hintergrund der διάκρισις πνευμάτων (1 Cor 12:10)," *BZ* 15 (1971): 93–104.

32. Schrage, *Der Erste Brief*, 7.3:156 n. 236.

33. Theodor von Nägeli, *Der Wortschatz des Apostels Paulus: Beitrag zur sprachgeschichtlichen Erforschung des Neuen Testaments* (Göttingen: Vandenhoeck & Ruprecht, 1905), 50; see also pp. 32, 41.

happened at a time that was familiar with ἑρμηνεία as a *terminus technicus* of interpretation of Scripture, would be understandable. Attestation: διερμήνευσις Iamblichus *Myst.* 5.5, διερμηνευτικός Olympiodorus. Alchemista, p. 17 C, Hesychius διερμηνευτής s.v. ὑποφῆται. Of mediums (revealing himself), Serapion of Thmuis, *Euchologium* 13.4.

12:11 ἰδίᾳ only here in the New Testament, in the LXX only in 2 Macc 4:34, and also in Ign. *Magn.* 7.1; Epictetus I.16.15, 19; II.2.9, 10.4; 19.9. The classical ἰδίᾳ that receded in Koine times, is to be retained with Zuntz.[34] Some exegetes prefer, indeed, ἴδια.[35]

14:23 The paleographic similarity between ΟΥΝ and ϹΥΝ explains the fluctuation of the tradition at the beginning of this verse. The number of witnesses in which ΟΥΝ or ϹΥΝ is missing is too large for one to be able to assume dittography here. Since in this context there is no necessity for ΟΥΝ, and the widespread tendency of the tradition in individual witnesses introduces *simplicia*, I am inclined to take ελθη as secondary, even though its attestation is impressive. ουν is to be deleted. P[46] had ουν ελθη or συνελθη.

14:23 It is hard to imagine that Paul uses the aorist λαλησωσιν in verse 23 as in P[46] G, since the contrasting προφητευωσιν is in the present tense. It is probably secondary and evoked by the aorists in verses 23 and 24, compare 0150 προφητευσωσιν in 14:24.

14:23 An original ιδιωται standing alone could have generated the resulting text. The unexpected substantive is explained from the context.[36]

14:25 Without further ancient attestation the interesting προπεσών is to be taken as secondary.

14:25 In spite of Robertson and Plummer, and also Philipp Bachmann, the ὁ in verse 25 is not to be retained.[37]

14:26 The secondary intrusion of ὑμῶν is not found in 0201.[38]

---

34. Zuntz, *Text of the Epistles*, 98.
35. Schrage, *Der Erste Brief*, 7.3:164 n. 273.
36. Zuntz, *Text of the Epistles*, 40 and 61.
37. Robertson and Plummer, *First Epistle*, 319; Philipp Bachmann, *Der erste Brief des Paulus an die Korinther*, 3rd ed., KNT (Leipzig: Deichert, 1921), 421 n. 1.
38. Metzger, *Textual Commentary*, 499.

3. New Edition of the Parchment Fragments London Brit. Libr. Pap. 2240   71

3.2 Locating the Manuscript 0201 in the History of the Transmission

Because the collective attestation of one related group of witnesses cannot establish family relations of groups of manuscripts, the question concerning the nature of the text of the uncial 0201 must specifically be raised and must be settled by textual criticism. For this clarification a complete collation of all uncial manuscripts (including the unpublished Sinai fragments) is established as a basis and additionally of the following minuscule manuscripts: 6, 424, 424^c, 1739, and 1908. Professor J. Neville Birdsall has made the minuscule collation available, and for this I thank him sincerely. The minuscule collation, originally assembled in 1873 over against the Scrivener edition of the textus receptus, was reoriented to the readings of the NA^{26}.

An examination of the text of 0201 demonstrates first of all a great number of singular readings. A certain stylistic freedom of the copyist over against the tradition leaps into view. Thirteen divergences from the tradition in such a short section of text is more than a few. The substitution of ωστε by διο in 14:22 and of πεσων επι προσωπον by the stylistically sound προπεσων in 14:25 are among these. The omission of και and of an article in 12:6 and the addition of an article before πνευματων in 12:10 are also among these. The reading συμφορον in 12:7 could potentially be designated original. With respect to the content, the replacement of the title κυριος with reference to God's speech in an Old Testament citation by ο θεος in 14:21 and along with this perhaps the interrelated clarification of the κυριος title in 12:5 by the addition of θεος are striking. Whereas the text originally relates κυριος to the Lord of the community, the tradition of the copyist apparently relates κυριος θεος and the distribution of power (i.e., διαιρεσεις ενεργηματων) to God. A change in word order in 12:13 and two omissions in 12:13 and 14:20 are probably to be assessed as copyist errors. Naturally the exemplar used for the manuscript already contained a number of these changes, a matter I cannot go into further here. However, it must be said that two apparent copyist errors (φανεροσις in 12:7 and αδελφου in 14:26) are possibly due to the condition of preservation of the fragment and not to the copyist.

Can relationships to the proto-Alexandrian text be determined? Several times 0201 provides a good text along with a few other witnesses. 0201 shares only one textual error with the group P^{46} B 6.424^c 1739; in 12:6, 0201 (as in P^{46} C 81.365.630) has αυτος θεος ο ενεργων, but is differentiated from the witnesses mentioned by omitting the second ο. On the other hand, this manuscript shares the addition εστιν after ενεργων, which is found also in B 1739. The εστιν, inserted by other manuscripts in various places, is secondary. και ο also appears to be secondary.

With part of the group (P[46] B 1739) 0201 does without the addition of υμων that DFG and other witnesses have. 0201 also does not have the addition και ουτως (in 14:25) but is supported in this by the entire Alexandrian text as well as the group DFG.

However, in 12:9b, against the ενι of the best proto-Alexandrian witnesses (B 1739 [P[46] *omittit*]) 0201 has a secondary αυτω that also DFG and other witnesses support. And in 12:10, 0201 (supported by DFG) turns against the proto-Alexandrian διακρισεις, which became accepted incorrectly, and reads διακρισις with ℵ C. Also in 14:23 0201 does not support the (probably original) absence of η απιστοι (P[46 vid] B).

Of seven passages in which a secondary δε is attested by a number of the witnesses, in five of them 0201 has the original text without the addition. Among these 0201 is supported in 12:10 αλλω² by the entire proto-Alexandrian group and also by D F G; in 12:10 αλλω³ by the entire proto-Alexandrian group and also by D G F; in 12:10 ετερω is supported by the entire proto-Alexandrian group and also by D F G; in 12:9 ετερω is supported by the proto-Alexandrian group (with the exception of P[46]) and also by D* F G. By contrast 0201[vid] reads the αλλω in 12:9 without δε and in this, contrary to all other witnesses, is supported only by the group DFG. In these seven passages D provides the correct text without exception.

If the ουν in 14:23 is secondary and συνελθη is adopted as original, the witnesses B G*, with their reading ουν ελθη, still permit what is original to be recognized. Evidently 0201 also reads the secondary ουν [συνελ]θη.

Where the group P[46] B 6.424[c].1739 is divided, 0201 has secondary readings just as frequently as those which are original (cf. again ιδια 12:11, του ενός 12:12, ετέρων 14:21). Therefore, a relationship of the manuscript 0201 with the proto–Alexandrian text witnesses cannot be proved.

Whereas the examination of all known variants has come up with a negative conclusion, it is now possible to gain a positive result. Four textual errors prove membership in the manuscript group DFG. These are the readings: 12:3, 0201 om. λαλων with D F G a; 12:6, 0201 om. τα with D*; 12:11, 0201 om. ιδια with P[46] D*FG 1175 sy[p]; and 14:21, ετεραις γλωσσαις 0201[vid] with FG.

On the other hand, 0201 does not share noted *vitia* of FG:

— 12:9: 0201 certainly does not read χαρισματα τα with FG*.

3. New Edition of the Parchment Fragments London Brit. Libr. Pap. 2240

- 14:22: 0201 does not read εισιν εις, but εισιν with the remaining tradition.
- 14:23: 0201 does not read αυρουσειν with FG but on the basis of space probably reads ερ]ου[σιν.
- 14:27: 0201 does not have δαερμηνευτω with F, nor διερμηνευτω with G, but corresponds with the remaining tradition in reading διερμηνευετω.

Further secondary readings are confined to FG (12:2, αμορφα; 12:3, εν; 14:20, ινα ταις; 14:22, πιστοις), or to the group DFG (namely, 12:6, ο αυτος δε θεος; 12:10, ενεργεια; 12:11, ταυτα δε παντα; 12:11, om. το; and 14:23, ολη η εκκλησια), and are not supported by 0201.

It is evident that the text of 0201 is related to the archetype of the group DFG.

3.3. 0201 as a Pauline Manuscript

The number (possibly secondary[39]) preserved near the top of Fragment 2, side a, column 1—PMZ, 147—probably serves as a page number. It shows that the lost manuscript contained more than 1 Corinthians. What it contained, naturally, can only be surmised. On the basis of the capacity of 440 characters per Nestle page, the entire epistle to the Romans in addition to the text of 1 Cor 1:1–14:18 could be fitted into the missing leaves.[40] A *Corpus Paulinum* opening with the sequence of Romans and 1 Corinthians would be in accord with the arrangement of Athanasius. It is attested by the old chapter divisions of the manuscript B, by the canon list transmitted by Codex Claromontanus, and by the appendix of the fifty-ninth canon of

---

39. Crum and Bell, *Wadi Sarga*, 33.
40. The highly varying lengths of lines compel us to define an average length.

Fragment 1 a Column 1 Inner Column 9/13	ø 10:7
Fragment 1 a Column 2 Outer Column 10/14	ø 12:2
Fragment 1 b Column 1 Outer Column 9/14	ø 11:4
Fragment 1 b Column 2 Inner Column 9/13	ø 11:3
Fragment 2 a Column 1 Inner Column 8/13	ø 11:4
Fragment 2 a Column 2 Outer Column 11/16	ø 13:2
Fragment 2 b Column 1 Outer Column 10/15	ø 11:9
Fragment 2 b Column 2 Inner Column 9/13	ø 11:2

The number of characters in the outer column is on average 10 percent higher than that of the inner column.

Laodicea. This is at the same time the sequence of the great manuscripts ℵ A B C D F G, but not of P⁴⁶. As I have demonstrated elsewhere by the arrangement of a fragment 6, this was also the order of P⁶¹. The fragment constitutes the transition between Romans and 1 Corinthians. The documentation has not yet been published.⁴¹

Supplement I

Unique Readings of 0201⁴²

12:5	κυριος] add. θεος 0201
12:6	και¹] om. 0201ᵛⁱᵈ
12:6	ο²] om. 0201
12:7	φανερωσις] φανεροσις 0201ᵛⁱᵈ
12:7	συμφερον] συμφορον 0201, perhaps original
12:10	πνευματων] των πνευματων 0201ᵛⁱᵈ
12:13	εν ενι] ενι 0201ᵛⁱᵈ
12:13	ημεις παντες] παντες ημεις 0201ᵛⁱᵈ
14:20	γινεσθε] om. 0201ᵛⁱᵈ
14:21	κυριος] ο θεος 0201ᵛⁱᵈ
14:22	ωστε] διο 0201ᵛⁱᵈ
14:25	πεσων επι προσωπον] προπεσων 0201ᵛⁱᵈ
14:26	αδελφοι] αδελφου 0201ᵛⁱᵈ

---

41. On the arrangement of the *Corpus Paulinum*, see William H. P. Hatch, "The Position of Hebrews in the Canon of the New Testament," *HTR* 29 (1936): 133–51; H. J. Frede, "Die Ordnung der Paulusbriefe," in *Papers Presented to the 4th International Congress on New Testament Studies: Held at Oxford, 1969*, ed. Elizabeth A. Livingstone, TUGAL 112, Studia Evangelica 6 (Berlin: Akademie, 1973), 122–27; Harry Gamble, "The Redaction of the Pauline Letters and the Formation of the Pauline Corpus," *JBL* 94 (1975): 403–18; Kurt Aland, "Die Entstehung des Corpus Paulinum," in *Neutestamentliche Entwürfe* (Munich: Kaiser, 1979), 302–50; Alexander Sand, "Überlieferung und Sammlung der Paulusbriefe," in *Paulus in den neutestamentlichen Spätschriften*, ed. Karl Kertelge, Quaestiones disputatae 89 (Freiburg im Breisgau: Herder, 1981), 11–24. Wilhelm Schneemelcher, "Bibel III Die Entstehung des Kanons des Neuen Testaments und der christlichen Bibel," *TRE* 6:22–48.

42. The readings 12:7 φανεροσις and 14:26 αδελφου possibly go back not to the copyist but to parchment damage.

Supplement II

Secondary Readings of 0201 in Addition to the Singular Readings[43]

11:34	ει] add. δε ℵ² D¹ K L P 056.0150.0151.0201.6.424.1739.1908 b sy TR
12:2	οτι] om. K 0150.0201ᵛⁱᵈ 1.69.2464
12:3	λαλων] om. DFG 0201 a
12:6	ο δε] και ο P⁴⁶ B C 0201ᵛⁱᵈ 81.365.630.1175.1739
12:6	ενεργων] add. εστι(ν) B* 0201.1739
12:6	τα]om. D* 0201
12:9	ενι] αυτω ℵ C² D F G L P 056 0151 0201 6 424* 1908 sy TR
12:10	αλλω¹] add. δε P⁴⁶ ℵ A B C D² K L P Ψ 056.0150.0151.0201.6.424.1739.1908 TR
12:10	αλλω⁴]add.δε P⁴⁶ ℵ A C D¹ F G L P Ψ 056.0150.0201.6.424.1739.1908 TR
12:10	διερμηνεια] ερμηνεια C D² Ψ 056.0150.0201.6.424.1739.1908 TR; ερμηνια P⁴⁶ ℵ F G L P
12:11	ιδια] om. P⁴⁶ D* F G 0201.1175 syᵖ
14:21	ετερωγλωσσοις] ετεραις γλωσσαις F G 0201ᵛⁱᵈ
14:23	εαν] add. ουν P⁴⁶⁽?⁾ ℵ A B D K L P Ψ 049.056.0150.0151.0201.1908 TR
14:23	δε] add. και P⁴⁶ 0150.0201
14:23	ιδιωται] add. η απιστοι ℵ A D F G K L Ψ 049.056.0150.0151.020 1.0243.6.424.1739.1908 TR
14:25	οντως θεος εν υμιν εστιν] θεος οντως εν υμιν εστιν Ψ 0201

Bibliography

Aland, Kurt. "Die Entstehung des Corpus Paulinum." Pages 302–50 in *Neutestamentliche Entwürfe*. Munich: Kaiser, 1979.

Aland, Kurt, Matthew Black, Bruce M. Metzger, and Allen Wikgren. *The Greek New Testament*. London: United Bible Societies, 1966.

---

43. The critical assessment of the variants ὁ δέ in 12:6 and ἰδιῶται in 14:23 is not easy. Perhaps here 0201 has the original text.

Aland, Kurt, Matthew Black, Carlo Maria Martini, Bruce M. Metzger, Allen Wikgren, eds. *Novum Testamentum Graece*. 26th ed. Stuttgart: Deutsche Bibelgesellschaft, 1979

Aland, Kurt, with Michael Welte, Beate Köster, and Klaus Junack. *Kurzgefasste Liste der griechischen Handschriften des Neuen Testaments*. 2nd ed. ANTF 1. Berlin: de Gruyter, 1994.

Bachmann, Philipp. *Der erste Brief des Paulus an die Korinther*. 3rd ed. KNT. Leipzig: Deichert, 1921.

Bammel, Caroline P. Hammond. *Der Römerbrieftext des Rufin und seine Origenesübersetzung*. Vetus Latina. Freiburg im Breisgau: Herder, 1985.

British Museum Catalogue of Additions to the Manuscripts in the Years 1921–1925. London: The Trustees, 1950.

Cavallo, Guglielmo. *Ricerche sulla maiuscola biblica*. Firenze: Le Monnier, 1967.

Conzelmann, Hans. *Der erste Brief an die Korinther*. 2nd ed. KEK 5. Göttingen: Vandenhoeck & Ruprecht, 1981.

Crum, W. E., and H. Idris Bell, eds. *Wadi Sarga: Coptic and Greek Texts from the Excavations Undertaken by the Byzantine Research Account*. Copenhagen: Gyldendal, 1922.

Dautzenberg, Gerhard. "Zum religionsgeschichtlichen Hintergrund der διάκρισις πνευμάτων (1 Cor 12:10)." *BZ* 15 (1971): 93–104.

Elliott, J. Keith. *A Survey of Manuscripts Used in Editions of the Greek New Testament*. NovTSup 57. Leiden: Brill, 1987.

Frede, Hermann Josef. "Die Ordnung der Paulusbriefe." Pages 122–27 in *Papers Presented to the 4th International Congress on New Testament Studies: Held at Oxford, 1969*. Edited by Elizabeth A. Livingstone. TUGAL 112. Studia Evangelica 6. Berlin: Akademie, 1973.

Gamble, Harry. "The Redaction of the Pauline Letters and the Formation of the Pauline Corpus," *JBL* 94 (1975): 403–18.

Harnack, Adolf von. *Marcion: Das Evangelium vom fremden Gott*. 2nd ed. TUGAL 45. Leipzig: Hinrichs, 1924.

Hatch, William H. P. "The Position of Hebrews in the Canon of the New Testament." *HTR* 29 (1936): 133–51.

Jenkins, Claude. "Documentation: Origen on 1 Corinthians IV." *JTS* 10 (1908): 29–51.

Lietzmann, Hans. *An die Korinther*. 5th ed. HNT 9. Tübingen: Mohr, 1969.

Metzger, Bruce M. *A Textual Commentary on the Greek New Testament: A Companion Volume to the United Bible Societies' Greek New Testament*

3. New Edition of the Parchment Fragments London Brit. Libr. Pap. 2240

(Fourth Revised Edition). 2nd ed. Stuttgart: Deutsche Bibelgesellschaft, 1994.

Milne, Herbert J. M., ed. *Catalogue of the Literary Papyri in the British Museum*. London: The Trustees, 1927.

Nägeli, Theodor von. *Der Wortschatz des Apostels Paulus: Beitrag zur sprachgeschichtlichen Erforschung des Neuen Testaments*. Göttingen, Vandenhoeck & Ruprecht, 1905.

Pattie, T. S. "Ephraem the Syrian and the Latin Manuscripts of 'De Paenitentia.'" *British Library Journal* 13 (1987): 1–24.

Robertson, A. T., and Alfred Plummer. *A Critical and Exegetical Commentary on the First Epistle of St. Paul to the Corinthians*. 2nd ed. ICC. Edinburgh: T&T Clark, 1911.

Sand, Alexander. "Überlieferung und Sammlung der Paulusbriefe." Pages 11–24 in *Paulus in den neutestamentlichen Spätschriften: Zur Paulusrezeption im Neuen Testament*. Edited by Karl Kertelge. Quaestiones disputatae 89. Freiburg im Breisgau: Herder, 1981.

Scherer, Jean. *Le commentaire d' Origène sur Rom. III 5–V 7 d' après les extraits du Papyrus No 88748 du Musée du Caire et les fragments de la Philocalie du Vaticanus gr. 762*. Cairo: L'Institut Français d'Archéologie Orientale, 1957.

Schneemelcher, Wilhelm. "Bibel III Die Entstehung des Kanons des Neuen Testaments und der christlichen Bibel." *TRE* 6:22–48.

Schrage, Wolfgang. *Der erste Brief an die Korinther*. EKKNT 7.1–4. Neukirchen-Vluyn: Neukirchener Verlag, 1999.

Thompson, R. Campbell. "Introduction." Pages 1–5 in *Wadi Sarga: Coptic and Greek Texts from the Excavations Undertaken by the Byzantine Research Account*. Edited by W. E. Crum and H. Idris Bell. Copenhagen: Gyldendal, 1922.

Turner, Eric G. *The Typology of the Early Codex*. Philadelphia: University of Pennsylvania Press, 1977.

Westcott, Brooke Foss, and Fenton John Anthony Hort, eds. *The New Testament in the Original Greek: Volume 1, Text; Volume 2, Introduction [and] Appendix*. Cambridge: Macmillan, 1881. 2nd ed., 1896.

Zuntz, Günther. *The Text of the Epistles: A Disquisition upon the Corpus Paulinum*. Schweich Lectures of the British Academy 1946. London: Oxford University Press, 1953.

4
Amen, Benediction, Doxology:
A Text-Critical Investigation

For a long time text-critical handbooks have called attention to the fact that in the transmission of the New Testament numerous passages exhibit ἀμήν as a secondary reading.[1] Most of these secondary and often only poorly attested cases of ἀμήν are then also dropped from philologically responsible editions of the nineteenth and twentieth centuries, as a comparison with the *editio princeps* demonstrates.[2] Up until now only a few cases of

---

1. E.g., Eberhard Nestle, *Einführung in das griechische Neue Testament*, 3rd ed. (Göttingen: Vandenhoeck & Ruprecht, 1909), 169: "Additions such as 'amen' or 'amen, amen' ... are completely disregarded." Many of these cases of ἀμήν as secondary readings have never been received into editions of the New Testament, cf. Luke 7:28; 12:44; Heb 13:8; the secondary reading in Rev 1:18 appears in the printed edition of the textus receptus (1873), but not in the edition of Erasmus; cf. Rev 4:9; 4:10; 5:13; 7:10; 11:15; 15:7; 22:21. The last ἀμήν in this list appears only in Erasmus and in the 1873 printing of the textus receptus.

2. The following editions are the basis for this: Desiderius Erasmus Roterodamus, ed., *Novum instrumentum omne* (Basel: Froben, 1516; repr., Stuttgart: Frommann, 1986); Johann Albrecht Bengel, ed., *Η ΚΑΙΝΗ ΔΙΑΘΗΚΗ: Novum Testamentum Graecum* (Tübingen: Berger, 1734); Johann Jacob Griesbach, ed., *Η ΚΑΙΝΗ ΔΙΑΘΗΚΗ: Novum Testamentum Graece*, 4 vols. (Leipzig: Göschen, 1803–1807); Karl Lachmann, ed., *Novum Testamentum Graece et Latine*, 2nd ed., 2 vols. (Berlin: Reimer, 1842–1850); Constantin von Tischendorf, ed., *Novum Testamentum Graece: Ad antiquissimos testes denuo recensuit; Apparatum criticum omni studio perfectum apposuit commentationem isagogicam praetexuit Constantinus Tischendorf*, 8th ed., 3 vols. (Leipzig: Giesecke & Devrient, 1869–1894); Samuel Prideaux Tregelles, ed., *The Greek New Testament Edited from Ancient Authorities with the Latin Version of Jerome from the Codex Amiatinus* (London: Bagster, 1870); Frederick H. Scrivener, ed., *Η ΚΑΙΝΗ ΔΙΑΘΗΚΗ* (Cambridge: Deighton & Bell, 1873); Brooke Foss Westcott and Fenton John Anthony Hort,

secondary ἀμήν have been retained in editions.³ Others are printed in brackets as dubious.⁴ Likewise it has been recognized for a long time that

---

eds., *The New Testament in the Original Greek: Volume 1, Text; Volume 2, Introduction [and] Appendix* (Cambridge: Macmillan, 1881; 2nd ed., 1896); Hermann von Soden, ed., *Die Schriften des Neuen Testaments in ihrer ältesten erreichbaren Textgestalt*. 4 vols. (Göttingen: Vandenhoeck & Ruprecht, 1911-1913); George Dunbar Kilpatrick, ed., *Η ΚΑΙΝΗ ΔΙΑΘΗΚΗ*, 2nd ed. (London: British and Foreign Bible Society, 1958); Alexander Souter, *Novum Testamentum Graece*, 2nd ed. (Oxford: Clarendon, 1950; repr., 1962); Heinrich Josef Vogels, ed., *Novum Testamentum Graece et Latine*, 4th ed. (Freiburg im Breisgau: Herder, 1955); August Merk, ed., *Novum Testamentum Graece et Latine*, 9th ed. (Rome: Pontifical Biblical Institute, 1964); José Maria Bover, ed., *Novi Testamenti Biblia Graeca et Latina*, 5th ed. (Madrid: Consejo Superior de Investigaciones Cientificas, 1968); Giofranco Nolli, ed., *Novum Testamentum Graece et Latine* (Citta del Vaticano: Libreria Editrice Vaticana, 1981); NA[28]; Albert Huck, ed., *Synopsis of the First Three Gospels with the Addition of the Johannine Parallels*, rev. Heinrich Greeven, 13th ed. (Tübingen: Mohr, 1981); Kurt Aland, ed., *Synopsis Quattuor Evangeliorum*, 15th rev. ed. (Stuttgart: Deutsche Bibelgesellschaft, 1997); John Gwynn, ed., *The Apocalypse of St. John in a Syriac Version Hitherto Unknown* (Dublin, 1897; repr., Amsterdam: APA-Philo Press, 1981); George W. Horner, ed., *The Coptic Version of the New Testament in the Southern Dialect, Otherwise Called Sahidic and Thebaic*, 7 vols. (Oxford: Clarendon, 1911-1924; repr., Osnabrück: Zeller, 1969).

3. As is to be demonstrated, the following passages contain a secondary ἀμήν: Rom 15:33; the secondary additions in Rom 16:24 and 16:25-27; Gal 6:18; 1 Thess 3:13; Rev 1:6 and at the end of 7:12; in addition the fluctuating cases of ἀμήν at the conclusion of books. By contrast the ἀμήν in 2 Pet 3:18 and the ἀμήν before the liturgical acclamation in Rev 22:20 are to be retained.

4. NA[28] prints ἀμήν in brackets in the following passages: Matt 18:19; 1 Thess 3:13; the first printing of Kurt Aland et al., eds., *The Greek New Testament* (London: United Bible Societies, 1966) had no ἀμήν in Matt 18:19; 1 Thess 3:13. Walter Bauer, *Griechisch-deutsches Wörterbuch zu den Schriften des Neuen Testaments und der frühchristlichen Literatur*, ed. Kurt and Barbara Aland, 6th ed. (Berlin: de Gruyter, 1988), s. v. "ἀμήν," lists Matt 6:13; 28:20; Mark 16:20; Luke 24:53; John 21:25; Acts 28:31; Rom 16:24; 1 Cor 16:24; 2 Cor 13:13; Phil 4:23; Heb 13:25 as passages with a doubtful transmission. Earlier printings of this lexicon also accepted Matt 18:19 in this list. Erasmus printed Πάλιν λέγω ὑμῖν, which Griesbach, Tischendorf, and von Soden also advocated. Aland, *Synopsis*, lists as witnesses of the omission ℵ D L f¹ 579. 892 lat sy^p bo. This *Synopsis* (just like NA[28]) prints here the form of the text that Westcott and Hort and, following them, Vogels had: πάλιν [ἀμήν] λέγω ὑμῖν. B (Θ) 058 078 f¹³ 33.700.1006.1241.1342.1506 Koine it sy^{s.c} sa mae bo^{ms} attest here πάλιν ἀμὴν λέγω ὑμῖν. Tregelles and Greeven

the doxologies and benedictions that are found in the New Testament have in part been augmented, in part altered, and in part generally built up secondarily.[5] Of course this holds true for patristic literature likewise, in that it was altered to conform with later expectations.

Over time doxologies tend toward fuller development; older ones are concise.[6] This fact makes it possible to understand modifications in a literary critical fashion. It makes it possible also to evaluate text-critical variation in patristic transmission. Whereas this essay primarily addresses the text of the New Testament, only a few examples regarding patristic literature will be given in order to document the processes of augmentation that have been observed.[7]

Such formulas and phrases of praise to God, in keeping with the Old Testament ברוך-formula that declare God's praise by means of verbal adjectives (εὐλογητός, αἰνητός, ἐπευκτός, θαυμαστός) or participles (mostly εὐλογημένος) are here designated as "benedictions."[8] By contrast I designate as "doxolo-

---

printed this text. By contrast, Bengel and Lachmann decided for ἀμὴν λέγω ὑμῖν, which Tischendorf explained as an erroneous text ("per errorem"). Since it is unknown which manuscripts read ἀμὴν λέγω ὑμῖν, the question of this text cannot be dealt with at this time.

5. In several regions the Lord's Prayer received a secondary doxology, in part without ἀμήν, see Aland, *Synopsis*, on Matt 6:13. On the secondary doxology in Rom 16:25–27 see J. Keith Elliott, "The Language and Style of the Concluding Doxology to the Epistle to the Romans," *ZNW* 72 (1981): 124–30. Elliott advocates the view that with the exception of Rev 1:16, the shorter form of the eternity formula is original if a part of the tradition transmitted a shorter form. This holds for Rom 16:27; 2 Cor 9:9; Gal 1:5; Eph 3:21; Phil 4:20; 1 Tim 1:17; 2 Tim 4:18; Heb 1:8; 13:21; 1 Pet 4:11; 5:11; 2 Pet 3:18.

6. 1 Esd 4:59: παρὰ σοῦ ἡ νίκη, καὶ παρὰ σοῦ ἡ σοφία, καὶ σὴ ἡ δόξα; Pr Man 15 (= Apos. Con. 2.22.14 = Odes Sol. 12.15): σοῦ ἐστιν ἡ δόξα εἰς τοὺς αἰῶνας· ἀμήν; 4 Macc. 18:24: ᾧ ἡ δόξα εἰς τοὺς αἰῶνας τῶν αἰώνων· ἀμήν; 1 Clem. 20:12: ᾧ ἡ δόξα καὶ ἡ μεγαλωσύνη εἰς τοὺς αἰῶνας τῶν αἰώνων· ἀμήν, and passim; Did.8:2 ὅτι σοῦ ἐστιν ἡ δύναμις καὶ ἡ δόξα εἰς τοὺς αἰῶνας; 9:2, 3; 10:2, 4 σοὶ ἡ δόξα εἰς τοὺς αἰῶνας; Did. 10:5 ὅτι σοῦ ἐστιν ἡ δύναμις καὶ ἡ δόξα εἰς τοὺς αἰῶνας. Concisely Diogn. 12:9 ᾧ ἡ δόξα εἰς τοὺς αἰῶνας. ἀμήν. So again Apos. Con. 8.3.3. Ceremoniously 1 Par. 29:11: σοί, κύριε ἡ μεγαλωσύνη καὶ ἡ δύναμις καὶ τὸ καύχημα καὶ ἡ νίκη καὶ ἡ ἰσχύς.

7. A secondary ἀμήν after an eternity formula is found in 1 Clem. 45:8, so also Alfred Stuiber, "Amen," *JAC* 1 (1958): 154 with further examples; 1 Clem. 64; 65:2 demonstrate how doxologies were augmented; the entire doxology in Mart. Pol. 21 is secondary.

8. Josef Scharbert, "ברך," *TWAT* 1.808–41 [= *TDOT* 2:279–308].

gies" the sentences or subordinate clauses (doxology formulas) that praise and magnify God by means of ascribing abstractions following the prototype δόξα.⁹ This distinction was introduced into the form criticism of the New Testament by Reinhard Deichgräber and was accepted by Philipp Vielhauer.¹⁰

Now the connection between eulogies and doxologies with respect to form is not to be overlooked. Hence for a long time no one distinguished the two forms. Form and function, of course, are closely related. However, no necessity exists to conclude a benediction or a doxology with an ἀμήν. The New Testament custom to associate doxologies with an ἀμήν does not persist for Christian literature outside the New Testament.¹¹ In the New Testament only a fraction of the benedictions end with ἀμήν.¹² The ἀμήν also takes over functions that display no direct connection with the praise of God and its forms of expression. Nevertheless it seems reasonable to review text-critically tangible transformations in usage and understanding of the formulas that have been named, because early Christianity took over benedictions, doxologies, and the amen from contemporary Judaism. It

---

9. Only passages that are introduced by εὐλογητός, εὐλογημένος display a liturgical formality. Septuagint passages (see n. 6 above), however, display a less formal usage: the doxological formula occurs. Benedictions and doxologies employ eternity formulas and both attract ἀμήν to themselves. It is not without reason therefore that Ernst Käsemann took the distinction to be only stylistic, see "Formeln II: Liturgische Formeln im NT," *RGG* (3rd ed.) 2:994.

10. See Reinhard Deichgräber, *Gotteshymnus und Christushymnus in der frühen Christenheit: Untersuchungen zu Form, Sprache und Stil der frühchristlichen Hymnen*, SUNT 5 (Göttingen: Vandenhoeck & Ruprecht, 1967), 24–59; Philipp Vielhauer, *Geschichte der urchristlichen Literatur* (Berlin: de Gruyter, 1975), 35. According to Deichgräber, p. 24 n. 2, Eric Werner, "The Doxology in Synagogue and Church," *HUCA* 19 (1945): 275–351, had already called for this distinction.

11. In the New Testament only the doxologies of Revelation remain without a concluding amen. Likewise Did. 8:2; 9:2, 3, 4; 10:2, 4, 5; Mart. Pol. 20:2. A series of "prières quotidiennes" from Qumran Cave 4, dated by the editor on paleographical grounds to between 100 and 75 BCE, show that benedictions were also recorded without ἀμήν, see 4Q 503,1–6, III, 7; 4Q503, 15–16, VI, 9, etc. Many of the texts quoted here—often severely damaged—display a doubled אמן, so 4Q 504, 1–2 recto, I, 7; 4Q 504, 4, 15; 4Q 507, 3, 2; 4Q 508, 20, 1; 4Q 509, 4, 5; 4Q 509, 131, II, 3; 4Q 511, 63, 4Q 511, 111, 9. The morning prayer that begins with ברוך in 4Q 503, III, 2 and often (cf. DJD 7:106) has a parallel in Apos. Con. 7.49, which has, however, a concluding doxology.

12. Rom 1:25; 9:5, cf. Luke 1:68; 2 Cor 1:3–4; 11:31; Eph 1:3–6; 1 Pet 1:3–5.

4. Amen, Benediction, Doxology

transmitted usage and understanding of this form within its own tradition. At the same time Jewish traditions affected its worship of God, influenced its teachers and prophets and its authors.[13]

1. Doxologies

1.1. The Regular Form of the Doxology

Following Deichgräber, brief sayings of praise that derive from Judaism are here described as "doxologies," for which three formal elements are essential:

> First the person to whom praise is ascribed is named in the dative (occasionally in the genitive). Only in Luke 2:14; Apc 7:10, 12; 19:1 is the one who receives praise placed after the word of praise, which is evidently due to the isolated location of these doxologies. A characteristic word of praise (a doxological predicate) follows, usually δόξα. A stipulation of time forms the conclusion, the formula regarding eternity. In most cases an "amen" is included.[14]

With this description of the typical form the issue should be recognized immediately, whether or not this concluding amen, understood as a response, constitutes a fourth element of form. In doxologies that are not embellished the "person ... to whom the praise applies" normally stands

---

13. Cf. Paul Glaue, "Amen nach seiner Bedeutung und Verwendung in der Alten Kirche," *ZKG* 44 (1925): 184-98; Erik Peterson, *ΕΙΣ ΘΕΟΣ: Epigraphische, formgeschichtliche und religionsgeschichtliche Untersuchungen*, FRLANT 41 (Göttingen: Vandenhoeck & Ruprecht, 1926), Index; Heinrich Schlier, "ἀμήν," *TWNT* 1.339-42 [= *TDNT* 2:335-38]; Jean-Paul Audet, "Esquisse historique du genre littéraire de la 'bénédiction' Juive et de l' 'eucharistie' Chrétienne," *RB* 65 (1958): 371-99; Stuiber, "Amen," 153-59; Stuiber, "Doxologie," *RAC* 4:210-26; Deichgräber, *Gotteshymnus und Christushymnus*, 24-27; Joachim Jeremias, "Kennzeichen der *ipsissima vox* Jesu," in *Abba: Studien zur neutestamentlichen Theologie und Zeitgeschichte* (Göttingen: Vandenhoeck & Ruprecht, 1966), 145-52; Jeremias and Gerhard Krause, "Amen," *TRE* 2:386-402; Elias J. Bickerman, "Bénédiction et prière," in *Studies in Jewish and Christian History*, AGJU 9 (Leiden: Brill, 1980), 2:313-23; Reinhard Deichgräber and St. G. Hall, "Formeln, Liturgische II. Neues Testament und Alte Kirche," *TRE* 11:256-65.

14. Deichgräber, *Gotteshymnus und Christushymnus*, 25.

after it outside of the statement of praise. The designation of God, to whom the praise always referred originally, is taken up by ᾧ or αὐτῷ, by σοί or σοῦ (ἐστιν).[15]

Deichgräber has shown that the formula is foreign to Palestinian Judaism. There is "no doxology in the Qumran texts published so far."[16] Old Testament passages that one can adduce as parallels are indeed "formally ... related to doxologies, however, the formulaic imprint is missing from them."[17]

Not until Hellenistic Judaism does one find precise parallels: παρὰ τοῦ θεοῦ·ᾧ ἡ δόξα εἰς τοὺς αἰῶνας τῶν αἰώνων ἀμήν (4 Macc 18:24); ὅτι σὲ ὑμνεῖ πᾶσα ἡ δύναμις τῶν οὐρανῶν, καὶ σοῦ ἐστιν ἡ δόξα εἰς τοὺς αἰῶνας·ἀμήν (Pr Man 15 = Odes Sol. 12:15); καὶ αὐτῇ ἡ ἰσχὺς καὶ τὸ βασίλειον καὶ ἡ ἐξουσία καὶ ἡ μεγαλειότης τῶν πάντων αἰώνων (3 Esdr. 4:40). All of the citations that are mentioned here are concluding phrases and were effective as such. They emphasize the confession to the God of Israel as underlined by the author (cf. 4 Macc 1:12) or in 3 Esdr. 4:40 the power of the truth, in which case then the ἀμήν is expected to be absent.

The doxology formula as a dependent clause is found quite frequently in the New Testament. In Gal 1:5 it concludes the elaborate epistolary prescript. In Heb 13:20 it forms the end of the concluding prayer request (in the optative). In 1 Pet 4:11 the doxology formula constitutes the apparent epistolary break precipitated by the paraenetic theme δοξάζειν. The paraenesis is, however, taken up again. The doxology formula introduced as a subordinate clause is also found in the Pastoral Epistles, and indeed refers to God at the conclusion of a series of hymnic praises of God in 1 Tim 6:16. Here this does not mark the conclusion of the main section of the epistle. In addition, the dependent clause located before the postscript as the conclusion of the main section does appear in 2 Tim 4:18, here particularly related to Christ, which characterizes a later phase (cf. 2 Pet 3:18; Rev 1:6).

The doxology formula also appears in independent sentences introduced by αὐτῷ, so in Paul, in the succession of Paul, and in non-Pauline tradition. In Rom 11:36 a hymn excellent in literary form leads to a conclusion by a doxology and at the same time ends this part of the epistle. A slightly enlarged doxology formula concludes the main section of the epistle

---

15. Differently 3 Esd. 4:59: σὴ ἡ δόξα.
16. Deichgräber, *Gotteshymnus und Christushymnus*, 36.
17. Deichgräber, *Gotteshymnus und Christushymnus*, 37.

in Phil 4:20—the postscript follows. In 1 Pet 5:10–11 an independently composed doxology as an element of an epistolary concluding promise (in the future) concludes the main section of the letter and directly precedes the postscript. The doxology to Christ in Rev 1:5–6 is richly embellished. Here the one who receives the δόξα (just as in Eph 3:20–21) is named in a participial periphrasis.

In only three passages does a doxology stand at the very end of an epistolary text, namely, in Jude 24–25, 2 Pet 3:18, and Rom 16:25–27 (secondary reading). These doxologies are not linguistically dependent on one another. Have we reached in this latest phase the form of the apparent prototype in 4 Macc. 18:24; Pr Man 15:3; 3 Esd. 4:40? The parallelism of the two solidly transmitted doxologies refers to their status as the epistolary conclusion; we observe pseudonymous literature departing from the epistolary style. Greetings or concluding blessings are lacking, even if the epistolary style is imitated in the epistolary opening (cf. 1 Pet 1:2). The idea suggests itself that the gradual development of the doxology formula as well as an increasingly independent doxology emerges in the epistolary literature that has been preserved. The understanding of its function and linguistic form must be sought in its liturgical context.

We ask: With which forms is the doxology most closely affiliated? Original functions need to be differentiated from secondary ones. Amplifications of the formula lead to the question, for what reasons the undeveloped formula has also been transmitted for so long? The use of the doxology formula as a stylistic device, (1) whereby texts gain structure, (2) whereby respect for tradition is maintained, (3) whereby epistolary communication is reinforced by an appeal to worship, reveals that here a central element of early Christian worship seeks expression. Finally, the close association of the doxology formula and its ἀμήν demonstrates the cultic origin and long-standing attachment of epistolary and literary forms to the worship event.

1.2. The Function of the Doxology

Although doxologies are found in almost all New Testament writings, the doxology formula as well as the ἀμήν appear not to be indispensable to an older phase of New Testament prayer.[18] Not until in later prayer texts do

---

18. See Lawrence A. Hoffman, "Gebet III. Judentum," *TRE* 12:42–47; Klaus Berger, "Gebet IV. Neues Testament," *TRE* 12:47–60.

they have a firm presence (Did. 8:2; 9:2, 3, 4; 10:2, 4, 5; 1 Clem. 61:3; Mart. Pol. 14:3). Jesus's prayers, in many cases literally shaped by the evangelists, have no doxologies and no ἀμήν as their conclusions (Matt 6:9–13 // Luke 11:2–4; Matt 11:25–26 // Luke 10:21–22; Mark 14:36 // Matt 26:39, 42; Luke 22:42; Mark 15:34 // Matt 27:46; Luke 23:46; John 11:41–42; 12:27–28; 17:1–26): private prayer has a formative effect.

However, the ἀμήν appears not without emphasis as an element of private prayer (Matt 11:26 // Luke 10:21; Mark 14:36 // Matt 26:39, 42; Luke 22:42). Doxologies are absent in the three cantica of Luke's Gospel and likewise in such community prayers as are inserted in the text of Acts (1:24–25; 4:24–30; cf. also 7:59, 60). This conforms to what we are able to discover within the Judaism of that time. There the benediction had an established place; the doxology had not; and the ἀμήν had its normal function as in Old Testament times with the acceptance of a blessing or a curse, with the affirmation and acceptance of a commission, and as a congregational response to benedictions and especially to the Aaronic blessing.

If from time to time an amen is in evidence as the conclusion of a prayer, such a case has to do with a response (Tob 8:8). The one who prays does not say amen. The μετ' αὐτοῦ, which requires a feminine subject, speaks against the *interpretatio Christiana* of this passage.[19] Not until the martyr Polycarp does one conclude one's own prayer with amen—after a doxology (Mart. Pol. 15:1).

The few examples that appear to contradict this are not formulated as prayers but speak in the third person, for example, "May the sanctuary soon be rebuilt in our days; Amen" (m. Ta'an. 4:8).[20] These are prayer requests that are taken up in the amen. This holds also for the majority of benedictions or requests for blessing that end with "amen" or "amen, amen" in the inscriptions collected in the *Corpus Inscriptionum Judaicarum*. One inscription from Haram ech Cherif from the sixth century, however, is formulated as a prayer:

---

19. Against Joachim Jeremias, "Amen 1. Biblisch-Theologisch," *TRE* 2:388, and Str-B 1:243 on this passage. Succinctly and correctly Günter Mayer, "Die Funktion der Gebete in den alttestamentlichen Apokryphen," in *Festgabe für Karl Heinrich Rengstorf zum 70. Geburtstag*, ed. Wolfgang Dietrich, Theokratia 2 (Leiden: Brill, 1973), 19: "on the lips of Tobias with the concluding amen of Sarah."

20. Cited according to Str-B 1:243.

4. Amen, Benediction, Doxology

God of the heavenly host! May you build this house during the life of Jacob ben Joseph and Theophylact and Sisinah and Anastasia! Amen and amen. Selah. (*CIJ* 2.1398)[21]

An ἀμήν at the conclusion is absent from the doxologies of the Didache,[22] from the Martyrdom of Polycarp (with the exception of 14:3),[23] and from some older versions of the secondary doxology in the Lord's Prayer.[24] Likewise from Rev 5:13; 7:10, 12,[25] and 19:1. As a response in answer to a chorus ἀμήν or ἀμήν ἀλληλουϊά are introduced. In Rev 5:14 the four living creatures respond, at which the twenty-four elders pay homage; in Rev 7:12 all the angels respond with ἀμήν and a doxology; in Rev 19:4 the elders and the four living creatures give praise by shouting ἀμήν ἀλληλουϊά. These parallels lead us also to designate ναί, ἀμήν in Rev. 1:7 as a response to 1:6. The author links a doxology and a promise (1:5–6 and 1:7). But thereby the ἀμήν in Rev 1:6 is discernible as secondary. The constraint of the form moved the copyist to insert what seemed necessary. Only a few witnesses attest a text without ἀμήν.[26] The solemn praise in Luke 2:14 lacks

---

21. Further passages according to Stuiber, "Amen," 157: *CIJ* 1.599, 630, 650, 661, 732; 2.828b, 845, 856, 857, 858, 859, 866, 867, 980, 987, 1199, 1203, 1204, 1398. However 2.982 needs to be deleted.

22. Did. 8:2; 9:2, 3, 4; 10:2, 4, 5. An ἀμήν as a response is placed next to the acclamation μαραναθά (10:6).

23. Ἀμήν is not present in Mart. Pol. 20:2 and there the sentence is continued from 22:1. The patchy witness, the fact that both are missing in m p, as well as the fact that due to the context a doxology to Christ would materialize, speak against the originality of the doxology that concludes with ἀμήν in 21:1. Furthermore, this text is dependent on 1 Clem. 65:2. Karl Bihlmeyer, *Die apostolischen Väter: Neubearbeitung der Funkschen Ausgabe*, 3rd ed. (Tübingen: Mohr, 1970), 70, received the doxology into the text.

24. According to Aland, *Synopsis*, 87: g¹ k sy^p.

25. Here the doxology is opened with ἀμήν; an additional ἀμήν at the conclusion following the witnesses C 2019 2051 2064 is to be judged as secondary. The testimony according to Josef Schmid, *Studien zur Geschichte des griechischen Apokalypse-Textes*, 3 vols., MThS 1 (Munich: Zink, 1955–1956). The commentaries accept the second ἀμήν without any objection.

26. I gather from Tischendorf's *Novum Testamentum Graece* the indication that the manuscript 33 and tol (a Vulgate manuscript) omit the ἀμήν. Bengel, *H KAINH ΔIAΘHKH*, 461 rejected this ἀμήν [β = eam, quae per codices firmior sit lectione textus, nec tamen plane certa]. By this he refers to editors of Coptic and Syriac manuscripts and to Latin manuscripts; cf. Horner, *Coptic Version of the*

an ἀμήν; here, however, the sentence continues. There are parallels for this omission in benedictions and doxologies.²⁷

1.3. Liturgical and Epistolary Forms

Deichgräber has analyzed the doxology formula and described its possible linguistic variations. He has indicated the frequency of the occurrence of doxologies. He has identified the genitive σοῦ as the probable older variant of the introduction of the form.²⁸ On inspection of the material it becomes clear, however, that some of the expansions and alterations are to be evaluated as literary pleonasm. The formula, inasmuch as it derives from the cult and by its form refers back to it, balks to a particular degree at its literary usage and adaptation.

It is striking that the four doxologies that structure the text of the Paschal homily of Melito escalate the doxological predicate only sparingly: it is doubled in the fourth passage. Like many of the doxologies of 1 Clement, they are all introduced with ᾧ.²⁹ For 1 Clement escalation with the doubling of the doxological predication also suffices (20:12; 61:3). According to the attestation of the Syriac translation the excessive expansions καὶ μεγαλωσύνη, κράτος καὶ τιμή, καὶ νῦν καί in chapter 64 and τιμή, κράτος καὶ μεγαλωσύνη, θρόνος αἰώνιος ἀπὸ τῶν αἰώνων εἰς τοὺς αἰῶνας τῶν αἰώνων in 65:2 are secondary. The solemn doxology in Mart. Pol. 14:3 is also restrained. It ends Polycarp's prayer in the form of a relative clause introduced by δι' οὗ and it employs one doxological predication.

The introductory formula δι' οὗ originates in post-New Testament times. The earliest examples that highlight the Christian character of the

---

New Testament, 7:258: In witness 2 some words are missing because of fragmentation. Gwynn, *Apocalypse of St. John*, 1 exhibits amen. Incidentally an opening response with ἀμήν is also found in Pesiq. Rab. 26 (ed. Buber 132ᵃ), cited according to Str-B 1:243.

27. 2 Cor 11:31; Mart. Pol. 22:1.

28. Cf. Deichgräber, *Gotteshymnus und Christushymnus*, 25. It is characteristic of the style of Revelation that it takes over this genitive repeatedly.

29. See Melito, *Passa-Homilie* (*Die Passa-Homilie des Bischofs Meliton von Sardes*), ed. Bernhard Lohse, Textus Minores 24 (Leiden: Brill, 1958), 10, 45, 65, 105; 1 Clem. 20:12; 32:4; 38:4; 43:6; 47:7; 50:7; Diogn. 12:9. The doxologies that are introduced by δι' οὗ in 1 Clem. 58:2; 61:3; 64; 65:2 are viewed as more recent; they define Christ as receiver of praise.

doxology turn out to be deficient in grammatical clarity. At least among the expositors of today the question arises, whenever an additional διὰ Ἰησοῦ Χριστοῦ is met with, as to whether ᾧ actually still refers to God. This question cannot be answered exegetically.[30] However, it is precisely the essence of doxologies that they praise God. Clement, whose forms can embody the same lack of clarity, wishes to understand all doxologies as consciously referring to God (1 Clem. 58:2; 61:3; 64; 65:2). In his text we have to understand the passages in 1 Clem. 20:12 and 50:7 accordingly.[31]

It is of some interest that the doxology formula exhibits a certain degree of resistance to changes. For this we have a further reference in the secondary doxology in Rom 16:25–27. Indeed some witnesses display a grammatically unobtrusive αὐτῷ; however, the abrupt ᾧ is to be judged as original. It belongs to the form.

Inasmuch as in worship the congregation had to acclaim God, variation and multiple doxology formulas were not needed, but rather brevity and clarity. The form had to call attention to itself. The *kedusha* from the *yotzer* prayer of Jewish worship with its combination of Ezra 3:12b and Isa 6:3 spoken alternately, demonstrates a parallel. This text is attested as old

---

30. Many authors hold the relationship of the ὁ ὤν in Rom 9:5 (see §2.2 below) and of ᾧ in Heb 13:21 and 1 Pet 4:11 to be unclear. Cf., e.g., D. Wilhelm Bousset, *Kyrios Christos: Geschichte des Christusglaubens von den Anfängen des Christentums bis Irenaeus*, 3rd ed., FRLANT 21 (Göttingen: Vandenhoeck & Ruprecht, 1926), 234 nn. 2 and 3; Deichgräber, *Gotteshymnus und Christushymnus*, 29; Elliott, "Language and Style," 128: "The reference at Heb 13:21 and at 1 Pet 4:11 is ambiguous but probably is to God." Vielhauer thinks differently in his *Geschichte der urchristlichen Literatur*, 35: "With the exception of 2 Tim 4:18 the doxologies always refer to God." Käsemann, "Formeln II," 994, mentioned only 2 Pet 3:21 as a doxology to Christ; Deichgräber and Hall, "Formeln, Liturgische II," 258, mentioned 2 Tim 4:18; 2 Pet 3:21; Rev 1:6. The following also considered 2 Tim 4:18 to be a doxology to Christ: Paul Wendland, *Die hellenistisch-römische Kultur in ihren Beziehungen zum Judentum und Christentum: Urchristliche Literaturformen*, 2nd and 3rd ed. , HNT 1.3 (Tübingen: Mohr, 1912), 416; Bousset, *Kyrios Christos*, 234 n. 3: "Probably 2 Tim 4:18;" Karl Ludwig Schmidt, "βασιλεία," *TWNT* 1.581 [= *TDNT* 1:581]; Deichgräber, *Gotteshymnus und Christushymnus*, 33; Franz Schnider and Werner Stenger, *Studien zum neutestamentlichen Briefformular*, NTTS 11 (Leiden: Brill, 1987), 181.

31. So also Deichgräber, *Gotteshymnus und Christushymnus*, 33.

in t. Ber.1:9.³² In the light of these parallels the text of Rom 16:25-27 supports Keith Elliott's assertion that the text derives from a liturgy.³³

If these contexts are correctly perceived, then the passages with ambiguous relative pronouns found after διὰ Ἰησοῦ Χριστοῦ also refer to God. It was a question of stylistic proficiency, whether the one who prayed or taught or read the liturgy had appropriately prepared the acclamation after ᾧ ἡ δόξα εἰς τοὺς αἰῶνας by means of appropriate predications. Indecision about the correct referent of ᾧ did not arise until the reference to God was no longer certain. Thus in the end, doxologies to Christ probably exist only in 2 Tim 4:18, 2 Pet 3:18, and Rev 1:6.³⁴ By contrast the succinct formula ᾧ ἡ δόξα εἰς τοὺς αἰῶνας points to the worship of God.

2. Benedictions

2.1. The Regular Form of the Benediction

"Benedictions" are distinguished from other expressions of praise to God by the constant use of the verbal adjective εὐλογητός or the participle εὐλογημένος that point to ברוך. They are found in the form of the independent nominal clause or in the form of relative clauses. A relative pronoun, the absence of a designation of God, and an eternity formula are constitutive for the form, but not an amen. The ברוך initially came into the cultic language of the Jerusalem temple from noncultic associations via the official language of the early monarchy. The verbal adjective is not found until the time of the LXX.³⁵ An abundance of material documents its use in the

---

32. Ismar Elbogen, *Der jüdische Gottesdienst in seiner geschichtlichen Entwicklung*, 3rd ed. (repr., Hildesheim: Olms, 1967), 61. Wilhlem Bousset, "Eine jüdische Gebetssammlung im siebenten Buch der Apostolischen Konstitutionen," *NGWG. PH* (1915): 435-41, also in Bousset, *Religionsgeschichtliche Studien: Aufsätze zur Religionsgeschichte des hellenistischen Zeitalters*, ed. Anthonie F. Verheule, NovTSup 50 (Leiden: Brill, 1979), 231-86; Arthur Marmorstein, "L'âge de la Kedoucha de l'Amida," *REJ* 97 (1934): 35-49.

33. Cf. Elliott, "Language and Style," 129-30.

34. In spite of the traditional formula ᾧ ἡ δόξα κτλ. the consistent differentiation between κύριος and ὁ κύριος (cf. 1:18) and the subject of the βασιλεία (τοῦ Χριστοῦ) (4:1) demonstrate the secondary understanding of the doxology formula in 2 Tim 4:18.

35. Deichgräber, *Gotteshymnus und Christushymnus*, 40 n. 2.

4. Amen, Benediction, Doxology

temple liturgy, in synagogue prayer, and in Jewish private prayer.[36] Perhaps benedictions were at times perceived as Jewish-Christian in character.[37] However, benedictions are present in late liturgical texts, and the fathers use the verb and the verbal adjective with classical distinction.[38]

It is not altogether easy to separate benedictions and doxologies formally. The eternity formula can be absent. However, it is found in the dependent brief benedictions of Paul (Rom 1:25; 9:5; 2 Cor 11:31). Paul normally attaches to benedictions in the form of subordinate clauses an ἀμήν (Rom 1:25; 9:5). When it is missing in 2 Cor 11:31, this is simply because the sentence is continued; thus, grammatically the formula is an insertion. The parallel in Mart. Pol. 22:1 has already been referred to above. If it is true that Rom 9:5 is transmitted corruptly, and this will be demonstrated below, then the identification of God is missing in all brief benedictions.

In amplified Christian benedictions, most of which exhibit ceremonial prayers, we come across extensive titles for God. For instance, in a Jewish Christian psalm in Luke 1:68: εὐλογητὸς κύριος ὁ θεὸς τοῦ Ἰσραήλ, and similarly in Paul in 2 Cor 1:3-4: εὐλογητὸς ὁ θεὸς καὶ πατὴρ τοῦ κυρίου ἡμῶν Ἰησοῦ Χριστοῦ, which is taken up verbatim in Paul's successors (Eph 1:3-6; 1 Pet 1:3-5). Here the text of prayers always begins with εὐλογητός and ἀμήν is absent. The eternity formula is also missing. What is essential for the form is the grammatical structure of the independent nominal clause that is initiated by the predication (verbal adjective or participle) as well as the identification of God. Amen and eternity formula can be omitted.

The passages from Ign. *Eph.* 1:3 and Barn. 6:10 are not dependent on New Testament exemplars: εὐλογητὸς γὰρ ὁ χαρισάμενος ὑμῖν ἀξίοις οὖσι τοιοῦτον ἐπίσκοπον κεκτῆσθαι (Ign. *Eph.* 1:3); and εὐλογητὸς ὁ κύριος ἡμῶν, ἀδελφοί, ὁ σοφίαν καὶ νοῦν θέμενος ἐν ἡμῖν τῶν κρυφίων αὐτοῦ (Barn. 6:10).

---

36. Cf. Str-B 1:242-44; 3:64, 456-61; Audet, "Esquisse historique," 371-99; Deichgräber, *Gotteshymnus und Christushymnus*, 40-43; Bickerman, "Bénédiction et prière," 313-23.

37. Cf. also Did. 10:6: ὡσαννὰ τῷ θεῷ Δαυίδ.

38. Cf. εὐλογητὸς ὁ θεὸς ὁ ὁδηγήσας ὑμᾶς εἰς τὴν ἀλήθειαν (Conc. Nic. [787] act. 1 [H. 4.49 B]): "Sciendum tamen est quod sermo hic benedictionis in scripturis diverse positus invenitur. Nam et deus benedicere vel homines, vel cetera quae creaverat, invenitur; et homines, vel ceterae creaturae deum benedicere iubentur. Sed Dei quidem benedictio aliquid muneris semper his qui ab eo benedicuntur impertit: homines vero deum benedicere, pro eo quod est laudare, et gratias referre dicuntur;" Origen, *Comm. Rom.* 9:14 (PG 14:1221A).

Barnabas relates εὐλογητός to Christ. Ignatius mentions the Christ who is lauded only by implication. This fact and the participial style still exhibit to us the Jewish origin.[39] As we have seen, at the end of the New Testament era benediction formulas as well as doxology formulas both lost a clear orientation toward God. The formulas may now be related expressly to Christ or to the κύριος ἡμῶν.

With the affinity of form and style between doxology formulas and benediction formulas, the question arises, by what functions the formulas are separated from one another. Linguistically the close connection of benedictions and doxologies has long been perceived and commented upon. εὐλογεῖν and δοξάζειν are used as synonyms: σὲ αἰνῶ, σὲ εὐλογῶ, σὲ δοξάζω (Mart. Pol. 14:3). The people of Smyrna describe the blessedness of the martyr Polycarp as follows: σὺν τοῖς ἀποστόλοις καὶ πᾶσιν δικαίοις ἀγαλλιώμενος δοξάζει τὸν θεὸν καὶ πατέρα παντοκράτορα καὶ εὐλογεῖ τὸν κύριον ἡμῶν Ἰησοῦν Χριστόν (Mart. Pol. 19:2). The verbs are also encountered as synonyms in Acts John 77 (ed. Lipsius and Bonnet; vol. 2.1, p. 189.23): δοξάζομέν σε καὶ αἰνοῦμέν σε καὶ εὐλογοῦμεν καὶ εὐχαριστοῦμεν τὴν πολλήν σου χρηστότητα ... ἅγιε Ἰησοῦ. Finally Didymus defines εὐλογεῖν by δοξάζειν: ὁ γὰρ θεὸς εὐλογεῖται μὲν ὑπὸ τῶν ἔργων αὐτοῦ, τοῦτ' ἔστιν δοξάζεται· εὐλογεῖ δὲ αὐτὸς τὰ οἰκεῖα κτίσματα, τοῦτ' ἔστιν ἁγιάζει (Trin. [PG 39.425B]). With the praise of the one God, one is aware of standing in the tradition of the postexilic community: εἰς τὸ δοξασθῆναι τὸ ὄνομα τοῦ ἀληθινοῦ καὶ μόνου (1 Clem. 43:6).

The unison amen, carried out in worship, is part of the acclamation that pays homage to the true God. This event is just as essential for Paul as for other New Testament authors. These authors intend to refer to messianic texts or such as are interpreted as messianic (e.g., Ps 68 [LXX 67]:35). I am reminded of Rom 15:6 and 2 Chr 5:13.[40] Justin (Dial. 34:6 [ed. Goodspeed, 129]) cites Ps 71:18 LXX εὐλογητὸς κύριος ... ὁ ποιῶν θαυμάσια μόνος, and continues: εὐλογοῦμεν τὸν ποιητὴν τῶν πάντων διὰ τοῦ υἱοῦ αὐτοῦ Ἰησοῦ Χριστοῦ καὶ διὰ πνεύματος τοῦ ἁγίου (1 Apol. 67.2 [ed. Goodspeed, 75]). Judaism can say: "There is nothing greater before God than the amen, with which the Israelites respond."[41]

No doubt it is not on account of a departure from Jewish prayer style that δόξα τῷ θεῷ comes so strongly into the foreground. Another factor will

---

39. Numerous benedictions are found in Psalms of Solomon; see, e.g., 6:6, εὐλογητὸς κύριος ὁ ποιῶν ἔλεον.

40. See Claus Westermann, "הלל," TLOT 1:375–76.

41. Cited according to Str-B.

have been operative in this, namely, the tradition of worship that reserved the use of εὐλογεῖν and εὐλογητός for use in Christian service. The doxology formula, by contrast, was regarded and used as a call to acclamations with amen, for which Rev 5:13; 7:10; 19:1 provide important evidence. Didache 10:6 and Justin (*1 Apol.* 67:4 [ed. Goodspeed, 75]) testify to the location of ἀμήν-acclamations within the celebration of the Eucharist and Melito (*On the Passover* 10, 45, 65, 105) attests to their location in the early Christian Quartodeciman Passover beginning on the 14th of Nissan. In this context the brief dependent doxology appears to preserve the form of the ancient style. By contrast, benedictions in Christian tradition are an element of hymns, of solemn prayers (e.g., the conclusion of prayer as in the Markan Liturgy of the Dêr-Balizeh Papyrus)[42] or also of homiletic language. From there they came into the tradition of epistolary forms.

2.2. The Text-Critical Problem of Romans 9:5

To this day the text of Rom 9:5 contains unresolved issues. The primary difficulty of the transmitted text lies in the fact that the four dependent clauses that name Israel's divine distinctions end with a christological benediction, although Paul employs the traditional benediction formula that praises God (9:4–5). At any rate the text suggests this understanding, although inexplicable stylistic peculiarities then remain.[43] Thus eminent exegetes and philologists have taken the text to be corrupt, among others Johann Jakob Wettstein, Richard Bentley, William Wrede, Johannes Weiss.[44] Presently the opinion has been accepted that the text is not corrupt. This opinion is hardly correct.[45]

---

42. Colin H. Roberts and Bernard Capelle, *An Early Euchologium: The Dêr-Balizeh Papyrus Enlarged and Reedited*, BMus 28 (Louvain: Bureaux de Muséon, 1949), 18–19, folio 1, verso, lines 9–10.

43. For further discussion Lagrange's appraisal has proved important, that Pauline doxologies are always related to what has been named beforehand and that they are always initiated with the predication. He deduces from that the christological sense of the doxology, and objects to assuming a new development after κατὰ σάρκα with asyndeton (Marie-Joseph Lagrange, *Épître aux Romains*, 6th ed., EtB 34 [Paris; Gabalda, 1950]: 277).

44. W. L. Lorimer mentions parallels for this kind of corruption outside of the New Testament ("Romans IX.3–5," *ZNW* 13 [1966–1967]: 385–86). The following hold the passage likewise to be corrupt: Hans-Werner Bartsch, "Röm 9,5

Whereas the ancient church found the proof text here for the recognition of Christ's divinity, a position that has been maintained until today, many exegetes hold the view to be unavoidable that in connection with the argument of Rom 9–11 a praise to the God of Israel is demanded by the context.[46] Such a praise, which appears as the climax of its argument about

---

und 1. Clem. 32,4: Eine notwendige Konjektur im Römerbrief," *TZ* 21 (1965): 401–9; J. Schniewind, "Diktate zum Römerbrief" (unpublished manuscript, 1937), cited by Bartsch, "Röm 9,5 und 1. Clem. 32,4," 406; Günther Harder, *Paulus und das Gebet*, NTF 10 (Gütersloh: Bertelsmann, 1936), 177–78; Karl Barth, *Der Römerbrief*, 2nd ed. (Munich: Chr. Kaiser Verlag, 1922; repr., Zürich: TVZ, 1954), 314–15; Barth, *KD*, 4 vols. (Zürich: Theologischer Verlag, 1976), cf. II.2:226; Johannes Weiss, "Beiträge zur paulinischen Rhetorik," in *Theologische Studien Bernhard Weiss zu seinem 70. Geburtstage* (Göttingen: Vandenhoeck & Ruprecht, 1897), 238; Weiss, *Das Urchristentum* (Göttingen: Vandenhoeck & Ruprecht, 1917), 363 n. 2; William Wrede, *Paulus*, 2nd ed. (Tübingen: Mohr, 1907), 82; Johann Jakob Wettstein, *Novum Testamentum Graecum* (Amsterdam: Dommerian, 1752), 2:64–65; Richard Bentley, *Bentleii Critica sacra: Notes on the Greek and Latin Text of the New Testament, Extracted from the Bentley MSS in Trinity College Library*, ed. Arthur Ayres Ellis (Cambridge: Deighton, Bell, & Co., 1862), 30, cited from Theodor Zahn and Friedrich Hauck, *Der Brief des Paulus an die Römer*, 3rd ed., KNT 6 (Leipzig, 1925), 434 n. 77; Jonas Slichtingius de Bukowiec, *Commentaria posthuma in plerosque Novi Testamenti libros* (Amsterdam: Philalethius, 1656–1865), 254; Lucius Mellierus Artemonius [= Samuel Crellius], *Initium Evangelii S. Joannis Apostoli ex antiquitate ecclesiastica restitutum indidemque nova ratione illustratum* (Amsterdam, 1726), 223–38. C. E. B. Cranfield, *A Critical and Exegetical Commentary on the Epistle to the Romans*, ICC 18 (Edinburgh: T&T Clark, 1980), 2:465–66, has analyzed the last two titles and has ascertained that neither of the two authors appear to have originated the conjecture. Walter Bauer (*Wörterbuch zu den Schriften des Neuen Testaments und der übrigen urchristlichen Literatur*, 5th ed. [Berlin: Töpelmann, 1963], 705) mentions additional literature; Bruce M. Metzger, *A Textual Commentary on the Greek New Testament: A Companion Volume to the United Bible Societies' Greek New Testament (Fourth Revised Edition)*, 2nd ed. (Stuttgart: Deutsche Bibelgesellschaft, 1994), 459–62.

45. The passage has been dealt with in detail by Bruce M. Metzger, "The Punctuation of Rom 9:5," in *Christ and Spirit in the New Testament: Studies in Honour of C. F. D. Moule*, ed. Barnabas Lindars (Cambridge: Cambridge University Press, 1973), 95–112; and by Otto Kuss, "Zu Römer 9:5," in *Rechtfertigung: Festschrift für Ernst Käsemann zum 70. Geburtstag*, ed. Johannes Friedrich (Tübingen: Mohr, 1976), 291–303. Cranfield provides a superb presentation of the exegetical problems of the text (*Romans*, 2:464–70).

46. So Ernst Käsemann, *An die Römer*, 4th ed. HNT 8a (Tübingen: Mohr,

4. Amen, Benediction, Doxology

Israel's privileges, would accompany well the sequence of the preceding dependent clauses.

Inexplicably, however, this text lacks any connection to the preceding text. If the word order corresponded to the independently placed doxology, for which numerous parallel texts outside and inside the New Testament are available for comparison, then only the asyndetic introduction would be noteworthy. But the real peculiarity is that the sentence structure is irregular. Blessings that are not construed as dependent clauses, which in hymnic contexts are often introduced asyndetically, regularly place the predication at the beginning of the sentence and thus follow a common type of nominal clause.

If one analyzes the sentence that comes down to us under the presupposition that it is transmitted to us in its original form, one perceives that its second part is a dependent blessing, accurately and correctly constructed: εὐλογητὸς εἰς τοὺς αἰῶνας·ἀμήν. With this the way to understanding is attained. A lost relative pronoun is needed at the beginning that would complement the conclusion of the sentence in a way that makes sense.

An anonymous writer has suggested an addendum in the form ὧν ὁ instead of ὁ ὤν, anonymous because it is certain that neither J. Schlichting nor J. Crell, who discussed it in the seventeenth century, were the originators (see note 44). The elegance of this conjecture consists in the fact that it presupposes a stylistically satisfactory order of Pauline dependent clauses, five in number, that at the same time aim at a noteworthy culmination. Stating this climax ὧν ὁ ἐπὶ πάντων θεός would also have generated the affront that caused the textual error.

However, this conjecture has been rejected. Ulrich Wilckens takes it as "as clever a solution of the problem of interpretation as arbitrary."[47] Otto Kuss takes it as "strikingly simple." "As is often the case with conjectures"

1980), 248; Ulrich Wilckens, *Der Brief an die Römer*, 4th ed., EKKNT 6.2 (Düsseldorf: Benziger; Neukirchen-Vluyn: Neukirchener Verlag, 2006), 189. Kuss ("Zu Römer 9.5," 292) and Cranfield (*Romans* 2:469) give passages from the fathers. Diodorus, founder of the exegetical school of Antioch, refers to a benediction to God, to which William Sanday and Arthur C. Headlam refer (*A Critical and Exegetical Commentary on the Epistle to the Romans*, 5th ed., ICC 5 [Edinburgh: T&T Clark, 1925], 234). So also Apollinaris and Photius, cf. Otto Michel, *Der Brief an die Römer*, 14th ed., KEK 4 (Göttingen: Vandenhoeck & Ruprecht, 1978), 296.

47. Wilckens, *Brief an die Römer*, 2:189 n. 833.

it "all too clearly and all too forcefully makes what one desires the father of the text. Beyond doubt, however, a correct feeling underlies it as to what should be expected and what should not be expected in the given context."[48] Hans Lietzmann also rejects "punctuation experiments (listed in Nestle's apparatus) or conjectures (as if God were the God of the Jews only)."[49]

Let us test these objections: (1) Lietzmann rejects punctuation experiments and in lieu of these inserts a dash. Actually only few passages have been discussed in more detail regarding their punctuation than this one. Since the essays of Ezra Abbot and the discussion of these by Westcott and Hort again and again a solution has been sought and based on this approach.[50] A period has been placed after κατὰ σάρκα by some commentators.[51] Also the first edition of *The Greek New Testament* of the United Bible Societies at least inserted a colon.[52] However the editors of the NA[28] edition have replaced this with a comma. Thereby, this edition opposes Paul's breaking off and beginning anew with an asyndeton.

(2) If one decides for a benediction that begins with asyndeton (so also Barn. 6:10), the problem is that the abnormalities in word order are almost without parallel, which Marie-Joseph Lagrange emphasized long ago.[53] Wilckens finds in Ps 68 (67 LXX):19 and Ps 72 (71 LXX):17 doxologies that begin with the subject.[54] This is correct for the first example. However, the alteration depends on the necessity of variation in connection with the *parallelismus membrorum* and means nothing in our context. Psalm 68 (67 LXX) ends with an independent blessing that preserves the form: εὐλογητὸς ὁ θεός. This holds also for Ps 72 (71 LXX):18-19. This view is supported by the fact that the assumption of a doxology to Christ, which the present context suggests, becomes unnecessary.[55] Such an assumption would be difficult to imagine for Paul.

---

48. Kuss, "Zu Römer 9:5," 299; see also p. 301.

49. Hans Lietzmann, *An die Römer*, 5th ed., HNT 8 (Tübingen: Mohr, 1971), 90.

50. Cf. Ezra Abbot, "On the Construction of Romans ix.5," *JBL* 1 (1881): 87-154.

51. Cf. Michel, *Brief an die Römer*, 290; Käsemann, *An die Römer*, 245; Wilckens, *Brief an die Römer*, 2:189.

52. Aland, *Greek New Testament*, 553.

53. Lagrange, *Épître aux Romains*, 227.

54. Wilckens, *Brief an die Römer*, 2:189 n. 836.

55. Cf. Kuss, "Zu Römer 9:5," 302.

With this appraisal the view gains weight that the transmission is corrupt here. Either a scribal error in early times or an intentional alteration was responsible for this corruption. If one follows the conjecture ὧν ὁ instead of ὁ ὤν, then one obtains a convincing climax: ὧν ὁ ἐπὶ πάντων θεὸς εὐλογητὸς εἰς τοὺς αἰῶνας· ἀμήν. Such a climax would not introduce any non-Pauline thought, as Rom 3:29 demonstrates. Such a thought would, however, be incomprehensible as a theological statement to a later generation of copyists. Clement, who read Rom 9:5 in this or another form and reshaped it for his writing (1 Clem. 32:4) features a doxology as the culmination.[56]

Finally what speaks in favor of the conjecture is that a succinct dependent doxology formula appears in all three passages—an authentic Pauline usage. Paul's successors did not take over this idiomatic usage. In this connection reference may be made to the Jewish phrase הוא ברוך הקודש, the antiquity of which Shaul Esh has established.[57] The meaning of this Pauline continuity with such an inner-Jewish phraseology could be explained exegetically. This will not be done here. However, it would be difficult to substantiate a satisfactory understanding of the transmitted text.

3. Blessings

3.1. Additional Blessing Formulas

The Pauline and non-Pauline epistolary literature contains varying blessing formulas that accumulate especially in the postscript. The following forms can be differentiated.

(1) The original blessing formula is designed as a nominal sentence. Its distinguishing mark is the preposition μετά or also ἐπί (Gal 6:16) and the personal pronoun of the second person designating the one who is blessed. God as the benefactor of the blessing or εἰρήνη, ἀγάπη, ἔλεος, χάρις as the content of the blessing in the nominative case introduce the formula. ἔσται can be added (2 Cor 13:11; Phil 4:9; T. Dan 5:2[58] [ἔσεσθε ἐν εἰρήνῃ, ἔχοντες τὸν θεὸν τῆς εἰρήνης]). Conditional blessings (Gal 6:16) also occur, which, however, requires that the second person of the addressee

---

56. Cf. Bartsch, "Röm 9,5," 409.

57. Shaul Esh, הקבה *'Der Heilige (er sei gepriesen)': Zur Geschichte einer nachbiblisch- hebräischen Gottesbezeichnung* (Leiden: Brill, 1957), 8–39.

58. Robert H. Charles, *The Greek Versions of the Testaments of the Twelve Patriarchs*, 2nd ed. (repr., Hildesheim: Olms, 1960), 136.

be given up.⁵⁹ The genuine Pauline epistles consistently end with a blessing that on account of its content has been designated as a word of grace.⁶⁰ Later a κύριος benediction also becomes established (2 Thess 3:16; 2 Tim 4:22; Barn. 21:9).

The benediction constitutes a second form, a form that is closely related to a supplication. One of its more frequent forms is the prayer for peace that is theologically oriented and in Pauline epistles frequently precedes the word of grace.⁶¹ Benedictions are characterized by a verb in the optative. These optatives are found in a letter dated to 124 BCE.⁶² The hymnic designation of God and a solemn abundance of the contents of the blessing as well as the preferred position in the transition to the epistolary postscript⁶³ characterize this form, a form that goes back on the one hand to the Aaronic benediction and its reception, and on the other hand to a tradition in personal letters.⁶⁴

(2) In distinction from blessings and benedictions, announcements of judgment or salvation are in the future.⁶⁵ There are, however, announce-

---

59. Käsemann, "Formeln II," 994, characterizes the passage in Galatians as a "Jewish greeting"; cf. Jude 2 and the sepulcher inscription of Faustinus in *CIJ* I no. 599: שלום על ישראל אמין; no. 650 שלום על ישראל אמן אמן (CE 383).

60. Schnider and Stenger, *Studien zum neutestamentlichen Briefformular*, speak of a supplication for grace (72) or of a concluding christological salutation (131–35). Vielhauer, *Geschichte der urchristlichen Literatur*, 66, speaks of a concluding wish. Harry Gamble (*The Textual History of the Letter to the Romans: A Study in Textual and Literary Criticism*, SD 42 [Grand Rapids: Eerdmans, 1977], 65) uses "χάρις benediction."

61. Cf. the transition in 1 Thess 3:11, 12 and 2 Macc 1:1-19.

62. Elias J. Bickerman, "Ein jüdischer Festbrief vom Jahre 124 v. Chr. (2 Macc. 1:1-9)," in *Studies in Jewish and Christian History*, AGJU 9 (Leiden: Brill, 1980), 2:136-58.

63. See 1 Clem. 64; Barn. 21:5.

64. See Gen 49:6, 8; Deut 28:7, 8, 9, 12, 13; 33:7, 16; Num 6:24-26; 1 QS II 2-4, cf. II 10, 18. However, aside from their liturgical use, such supplications for blessing are also at home in letters and are also found outside the Jewish tradition; cf. the examples in A. E. Cowley, *Aramaic Papyri of the Fifth Century B.C.* (Oxford; Clarendon, 1923; repr., Osnabrück: Zeller, 1967), nos. 17, 20, 21, 37, 38, 39, 40, 41. לך הושרת שליא שלום ושררת and ארן בכל ושאל שלום מראן אלה cited from Gamble, *Textual History*, 72 n. 76; Cf. again Gamble, *Textual History*, 67–73; Schnider and Stenger, *Studien zum neutestamentlichen Briefformular*, 87–91.

65. This is also suggested with respect to texts such as 2 Macc 2:16-18; Rom 16:20; 1 Thess 5:24; 2 Tim 4:18.

4. Amen, Benediction, Doxology

ments of salvation that are on account of their topic associated with benedictions.[66] As early as in Septuagint times, blessings are repeatedly expressed in the future.[67] And the transmission of the New Testament occasionally replaces the future with the optative.[68]

(3) The Pauline introductory greeting (*salutatio*), which has taken over elements of blessings, exhibits a certain independence. This is evident in the stereotyped form of the frequent nominal sentence χάρις ὑμῖν καὶ εἰρήνη.[69] The form is derived from the epistolary formula of the ancient letter.[70]

A liturgical origin has been assumed for some of these formulas. Regarding the Pauline word of grace, a definite place in the introductory part of the Lord's Supper liturgy could be established.[71] However, the view is accepted that primarily blessing formulas are at home in the context of the epistolary style. There appear to be no parallels before New Testament times for the combination χάρις καὶ εἰρήνη. It is Pauline.[72] Where no break in style can be perceived and the wording arises justifiably from the line of thought of the epistolary text, the text should be taken to be the original wording rather than a derived one.[73] Blessing formulas exhibit possibilities of epistolary enhancement just as much as doxological and benediction formulas. These are already found in Paul's writings. However, there is no need to pursue them in regard to our concerns.

---

66. 2 Cor 9:10; Phil 4:7; 4:19; 1 Peter 5:14. Eternity formulas occur in 2 Tim 4:18; 1 Peter 5:10.

67. Gen 49:7, 8, etc.; Deut 33:7, 10, etc.

68. Rom 16:20; 2 Cor 9:10; Phil 4:19.

69. Schnider and Stenger, *Studien zum neutestamentlichen Briefformular*, 25–41.

70. Klaus Berger, "Apostelbrief und apostolische Rede: Zum Formular frühchristlicher Briefe," *ZNW* 65 (1974): 196 and the discussion in Schnider and Stenger, *Studien zum neutestamentlichen Briefformular*, 26.

71. Cf. Did. 10:6 with 1 Cor 16:20b, 22, 23 and Rev 22:14–15, 20–21; Vielhauer, *Geschichte der urchristlichen Literatur*, 37–39; Käsemann, "Formeln II," 994: "1 Cor 16:22ff.; Rev 22:14ff. derive from the introduction of the eucharistic liturgy." Rather guardedly Gamble, *Textual History*, 144.

72. Cf. Schnider and Stenger, *Studien zum neutestamentlichen Briefformular*, 26, 89: "In spite of liturgical language the 'blessing' that closes the epistolary ending is specific for letters, and in fact for Jewish epistolary formulas, as 2 Macc 2:16–18 in particular attests."

73. Cf. Vielhauer, *Geschichte der urchristlichen Literatur*, 12.

The question remains to be investigated, as to whether Paul's blessing formulas were concluded with amen. If it is certain that epistolary conclusions with amen in New Testament epistolary literature are all secondary, the question remains to be investigated whether Pauline words of grace are occasionally accompanied by an amen.

3.2. On Galatians 6:18

Is the ἀμήν in Gal 6:18 that editions offer the original conclusion of a Pauline word of grace? The amen is absent from the witnesses G g Victorinus Ambrosiaster. If one surveys the genuine Pauline letters, then there appears to be a notably fixed linguistic usage. No Pauline letter ends without a proclamation of grace (Rom 16:20; 1 Cor 16:23; 2 Cor 13:13; Gal 6:18; Phil 4:23; 1 Thess 5:28; Phlm 25). The genitive attribute τοῦ κυρίου Ἰησοῦ and similar wording occurs, however, only in the genuine Pauline epistles and in 2 Thess 3:18. The second-person plural to the addressees also occurs without fail, but it also occurs in Col 4:18; 1 Tim 6:21; 2 Tim 4:22; Titus 3:15. It is missing in Heb 13:25 [according to P[46]*] and in Rev 22:21.[74]

Together with the blessing that varies slightly in each case, both catchwords of the salutation (χάρις καὶ εἰρήνη) are regularly taken up again in the postscript. The chiastic figure is used.[75] No word of grace ends with an amen. Since the attestation in Gal 6:18 is not firm, the ἀμήν is to be assessed as a secondary ἀμήν. It is to be deleted.[76]

---

74. Cf. Gamble, *Textual History*, 66 n. 54.

75. Cf. Rom 1:7 with 15:33 and 16:20; 1 Cor 1:3 with 16:33; 2 Cor 1:2 with 13:11 and 13; Gal 1:3 with 6:16 and 18; Phil 1:2 with 4:7 and 23; 1 Thess 1:1 with 3:12 and with 5:23, 24, 28; Phlm 3 with 25. Gamble, *Textual History*, 71–73; and Calvin J. Roetzel, *The Letters of Paul* (London: SCM, 1983), 25, have discussed this connection between the epistolary introduction and the conclusion.

76. According to Appendix II in the NA[28] (832) recent editions have allowed the ἀμήν of Gal 6:18 to remain unchallenged. Possibly Bengel alone recognized this ἀμήν as an addition. To be sure he printed the ἀμήν in the text. However he had already dismissed the ἀμήν from 1 Cor 16:24 (category α = "plane pro genuina habendam," relegated to a marginal reading) and 2 Cor 13:13 (category β = "eam, quae per codices firmior sit lectione textus, nec tamen plane certa," relegated to a marginal reading) and added "et sic in fine aliarum epistolarum." With this kind of designation Bengel's conclusion certainly remains somewhat unclear. Hans Dieter Betz, *Der Galaterbrief: Ein Kommentar zum Brief des Apostels Paulus*

3.3. On Romans 16:24

It appears to be unclear whether the concluding christological blessing (word of grace) in Rom 16:24 is a secondary addition or whether it was discarded by some later redaction, in which case it should be considered original. The editors of the New Testament have deleted it as secondary.[77] Many authors, who dealt with the text-critical problem came to the same conclusion.[78]

However, Harry Gamble attempted to prove that one of the transmitted forms of the text is original.[79] He decided in favor of the minuscule 629, the text of which he does not convey. We have come to know, however, that 629 does not contain the doxology 16:25–27 and that the blessing occurs only once, and in fact in 16:24. As an examination shows, the text is ἡ χάρις τοῦ κυρίου ἡμῶν Ἰησοῦ μετὰ πάντων ὑμῶν· ἀμήν. We have here to do with a late manuscript of the fourteenth century, the left column of which is Latin.[80] This manuscript contains no Greek doxology but has a Latin doxology that is similar to the text of F: "g̅i̅a̅ d̅n̅i̅ n̅r̅i̅ i̅h̅u̅i̅ cum omnibus vobis amen [16:24] Ei autem qui potens est affirmare iuxta evangelium

---

an die Gemeinden in Galatien (Munich: Kaiser, 1988), 556 decided that the αμην was not part of the original text. F. F. Bruce in his commentary assumed that this ἀμήν could be interpreted as an answering ἀμήν (*The Epistle to the Galatians: A Commentary on the Greek Text*, NIGTC 8 [Grand Rapids Eerdmans, 1982], 277). Cf. further my discussion of the ἀμήν within the epistolary conclusion in §4.1 below.

77. Bengel, Lachmann, Tregelles, Tischendorf, Westcott and Hort, and von Soden assessed Rom 16:24 as secondary.

78. Cf. Metzger, *Textual Commentary*, 476; Kurt Aland, "Der Schluss und die ursprüngliche Gestalt des Römerbriefs," in *Neutestamentliche Entwürfe* (Munich: Kaiser, 1979), 284–301; Larry W. Hurtado, "The Doxology at the End of Romans," in *New Testament Textual Criticism: Its Significance for Exegesis; Essays in Honour of Bruce M. Metzger*, ed. Eldon J. Epp and Gordon D. Fee (Oxford: Clarendon, 1981), 191–98.

79. Cf. Gamble, *Textual History*, 129–32.

80. Cf. Gamble, *Textual History*, 132: "Thus the primary form of the text at the conclusion of the letter was 16:20b + 21 + 23 + 24, without the doxology." Of all extant texts, only one preserves this sequence, and that probably by accident: ms 629, a fourteenth-century minuscule. Apart from this the tradition contains no extant witnesses to either the pure long form or the pure short form of the Roman letter.

meum et praedicationem ihu xri secundum revelationem misterii temporibus aeternis taciti quod nunc patefactum est per scripturas prophetarum secundum praeceptum etri di ad oboeditionem fidei in cunctis gentibus cogniti soli sapienti deo per ihs xrm Cui est honor et gloria in saecula saeculorum am" (16:25–27).[81] Gamble's argumentation suffers from the fact that he tabulates the positions of doxologies and benedictions but pays no attention to the forms of their text. It then collapses altogether, as 629 has two concluding benedictions, which he did not notice: ἡ χάρις τοῦ κυρίου ἡμῶν Ἰησοῦ Χριστοῦ μεθ' ὑμῶν (16:20).[82] Whereas good witnesses attest a form of the text in 16:20 that concludes without ἀμήν (P46 ℵ B 1881 ἡ χάρις τοῦ κυρίου ἡμῶν Ἰησοῦ μεθ' ὑμῶν), the altered position in 16:24 with the form of the text from (D) F G also led to the addition of ἀμήν: ἡ χάρις τοῦ κυρίου ἡμῶν μετὰ πάντων ὑμῶν· ἀμήν (in addition D has Ἰησοῦ Χριστοῦ after ἡμῶν). The text of 629 attests not the original text but a late conflation that embellishes the older form of the text by way of later forms of the text. This view is confirmed by the fact that D is written in the form of sense units, which this doxology is not.[83]

3.4. On Romans 15:33

Romans 15:33 presents a blessing, a petition for peace.[84] Such petitions for peace, as we have seen, belong to the stable framework of Pauline episto-

---

81. The Latin text of F is available in Frederick H. Scrivener, *An Exact Transcript of the Codex Augiensis to Which Is Added a Full Collation of Fifty Manuscripts* (Cambridge: Deighton & Bell, 1859), 50.

82. If the information is accurate that 630 has two concluding benedictions (Scrivener, *Exact Transcript*, 130 n. 9), the text-critical tabulation on the basis of which he argues is also incorrect on this point. Hurtado ("Doxology at the End of Romans," 196 n. 50) also noticed the mistake with respect to the manuscript 629.

83. See Lietzman, *An die Römer*, 131.

84. The ἀμήν appears in Erasmus, Bengel, Griesbach, Tischendorf, Westcott and Hort, NA28, but is discarded by Lachmann and Tregelles. Griesbach does not wish his acceptance of the ἀμήν to be considered as conclusive (category γ = "Litera γ designantur eae, quae probabilitate inferiores quidem illis, non tamen prorsus aspernandae, sed ulteriore examine dignae videntur"). Metzger leaves the question open, *Textual Commentary*, 475. Most commentaries print the amen: Lietzmann, *An die Römer*, 71; Lagrange, *Épître aux Romains*, 361; Michel, *Brief an die Römer*, 462; Käsemann, *An die Römer*, 388; Wilckens, *Brief an die Römer*, 2:123; Cranfield, *Romans*, 2:779.

lary formulas, they function as greetings. To be sure the resumption of the theme of peace within the conclusion is absent in 1 Corinthians and Philemon. However, before Pauline words of grace in such passages as Rom 16:20; 2 Cor 13:13; Gal 6:18; Phil 4:23; 1 Thess 5:28 we find the theme εἰρήνη in blessing formulas: Rom 15:33; 2 Cor 13:11; Gal 6:16; Phil 4:7, 9; 1 Thess 5:23. From this list we take it that the position and the form of these blessings in epistolary conclusions is not firm but is handled flexibly. Further, it is clear that the ἀμήν does not belong to petitions for peace. It is to be deleted here.

3.5. On 1 Thessalonians 3:12-13

The solemn benediction in 1 Thess 3:12 has its firm place in the epistolary style of Paul (Rom 15:5-6; 15:13; 1 Thess 5:23; 2 Thess 2:16-17; 3:5; 3:16a; Heb 13:20-21). If I see things correctly, except for the Pauline emulation in 2 Thessalonians and the reference from Hebrews, there appear to be no further references. A clear distinction from supplications is not possible. Benedictions (or an announcement of salvation, 1 Pet 5:10) have a reliably transmitted amen only when the text ends with a doxology (Heb 13:21).

In our passage only Tischendorf, following his manuscript ℵ* (and A D*), placed ἀμήν in the text.[85] The following editors have discarded this ἀμήν: Erasmus, the printed textus receptus, Bengel, Griesbach, Lachmann, Tregelles, Westcott and Hort, Nestle, Vogels, Merk, Bover. The first edition of *The Greek New Testament*[86] also made the same decision: [αμην]. However, Westcott and Hort distinguished ἀμήν as a marginal reading, von Soden and NA[28] reprinted the ἀμήν in brackets as doubtful.[87] Among the commentaries most have omitted the ἀμήν (Bernhard Weiss, Martin Dibelius, Béda Rigaux, Heinrich Schlier, Willi Marxsen, Gerhard Friedrich, Traugott Holtz).[88] Since neither parallel forms nor the attestation can support the ἀμήν, it is not to be retained here in 1 Thess 3:12-13.

---

85. ℵ and D exhibit a secondary ἀμήν in many other passages, cf. the passages mentioned in n. 1 (D in Luke 12:44, however, = 05 Codex Bezae).
86. Kurt Aland et al., *The Greek New Testament*, 1966, 709.
87. On this, see Metzger, *Textual Commentary*, 563.
88. Bernhard Weiss, *Textkritik der paulinischen Briefe*, TU 14.3 (Leipzig: Hinrichs, 1896), 104; Martin Dibelius, *Die Pastoralbriefe*, 4th ed., HNT 13 (Tübingen: Mohr, 1966), 18; Béda Rigaux, *Les Épîtres aux Thessaloniciens*, 2nd ed., EBib 33 (Paris: Cerf, 1960), 492; Heinrich Schlier, *Der Apostel und seine Gemeinde: Aus-*

4. Amen

4.1. Amen as the Epistolary Conclusion

The undisputed ἀμήν in the conclusion of a New Testament book appears in the twenty-sixth edition of the Nestle-Aland only in two places, in Gal 6:18 and Jude 25. I will show that the ἀμήν in Gal 6:18 does not belong in the text. It belongs in the apparatus. In 2 Pet 3:18 an ἀμήν was placed in the text as doubtful within brackets.[89] Later it was deleted.[90] It belongs in the text. The brackets, of course, are to be removed. In three further passages an ἀμήν stands as the conclusion of additions. In all three places this is secondary: Mark 16:20, Rom 16:24, and Rom 16:27.

The printing of the textus receptus of 1873 that serves the "International Greek New Testament Project" as the basis for collation goes far in introducing ἀμήν to designate endings of books.[91] However, this edition has no ἀμήν at the conclusion of Acts, James, and 3 John. Erasmus does not employ ἀμήν as often as does the edition that has been mentioned. It is found in the latter everywhere except at the conclusion of Matthew, Mark, Acts, James, and 3 John. It should be noted that Erasmus prints the longer

---

legung des ersten Briefes an die Thessalonicher (Leipzig: St. Benno Verlag, 1974), 57; Willi Marxsen, *Der erste Brief an die Thessalonicher*, ZBK 11.1 (Zurich: TVZ, 1979), 52; Gerhard Friedrich in Jürgen Becker, Hans Conzelmann, and Gerhard Friedrich, *Die Briefe an die Galater, Epheser, Philipper, Kolosser, Thessalonicher und Philemon*, 14th ed., NTD 8 (Göttingen: Vandenhoeck & Ruprecht, 1976), 232; Traugott Holtz, *Der erste Brief an die Thessalonicher*, EKKNT 13 (Zurich: Benziger, 1986), 148 n. 759; Ernst von Dobschütz, *Die Thessalonicherbriefe*, 7th ed., KEK 10 (Göttingen: Vandenhoeck & Ruprecht, 1909; repr., Leipzig: St. Benno Verlag, 1974), 153 considered the attestation of ἀμήν to be superior. James E. Frame, *A Critical and Exegetical Commentary on the Epistles of St. Paul to the Thessalonians*, 3rd ed., ICC 10 (Edinburgh: T&T Clark, 1953), 140, discussed the text-critical question without making a decision. Holtz, *Brief an die Thessalonicher*, n. 759: "The farewell ἀμήν that Nestle[26] took over in brackets in the text is hardly original. Paul places it after doxologies (Rom 1:25; 9:5; 11:36; Gal 1:5; Phil 4:20) or supplications for blessing (Rom 15:33; Gal 6:18); the textual transmission has frequently added it."

89. Metzger, *Textual Commentary*, 637.
90. NA[28], 715.
91. Cf. Scrivener, Η ΚΑΙΝΗ ΔΙΑΘΗΚΗ, fasc. 1, p. 87; fasc. 2, p. 141; fasc. 3, p. 232 etc.; see table 1 below.

ending of Mark without ἀμήν and the addition to Romans (16:25–27) with ἀμήν as the text. Why only Luke among the gospels receives an ἀμήν is left unexplained for the time being. However, in this connection it should be said that Erasmus understood himself to be an editor who claimed to review the text. This claim is put forward on the title page.

In that his editorial decisions on this question are based on manuscripts, in the gospels he evidently found only one conclusion with ἀμήν, namely, Luke 24:53. The manuscript B (03) deals with the endings of the gospels like the edition of Erasmus. It exhibits ἀμήν only in Luke 24:53. However, Erasmus did not know the Vaticanus. In the New Testament epistles the late tradition available for Erasmus differs from the text of Vaticanus, but not from the edition of the textus receptus that has been mentioned. In it the ἀμήν is lacking only in James and 3 John. It is unlikely that the older tradition or even the majority of the authors of New Testament writings placed an ἀμήν at the end of their writings. The inventory of the texts of old witnesses speaks against this.

The comparison with the text of apocryphal post-Old Testament literature also speaks against this. Third Maccabees 7:23 exhibits a benediction concluding with ἀμήν at the end of the book: εὐλογητὸς ὁ ῥύστης Ισραηλ εἰς τοὺς ἀεὶ χρόνους· ἀμήν. We find a doxology as the conclusion of a book in 4 Macc 18:24: ᾧ ἡ δόξα εἰς τοὺς αἰῶνας τῶν αἰώνων· ἀμήν; similarly T. Abr. 20:15; Greek Bar. 17:4; Gk. Apoc. Ezra 7:16. Manuscripts also have secondary doxologies in other texts. Finally, the conclusions of books have a mere ἀμήν inserted: Tob 14:15 (ℵ B secondary), Jdt 16:25 (B L secondary); T. Sol. 26.8 rec. B; T. Job 53.8.

How are passages to be assessed in which by many or all witnesses an ἀμήν is placed at the conclusion of the book?

4.2. On Jude 25

As far as we know there is a firmly transmitted ἀμήν as the conclusion of a New Testament book on only one occasion. With P[72] the entire transmission appears to be in agreement in placing an ἀμήν at Jude 25.[92] At other conclusions of books the tradition is divided. Thus a late book places an

---

92. This holds at least for the uncial manuscripts; cf. Winfried Grunewald and Klaus Junack, *Das Neue Testament auf Papyrus, Bd. 1: Die Katholischen Briefe*, ANTF 6 (Berlin: de Gruyter, 1986), 171.

ἀμήν at the conclusion with certainty. In this regard Jude is linked with 3 Macc 7:23 and 4 Macc 18:24 (cf. the conclusion of the exordium 1:12), it seems to take over distinctly Jewish and Jewish-Christian traditions, especially in the haggadic Midrash and in its quotation of the Greek Apocalypse of Enoch. This ἀμήν concludes a solemn doxology. The ἀμήν is to be considered as the conclusion of this doxology, but not in the first instance as a conclusion of a book.

4.3. On 2 Peter 3:18

The editions seem uncertain in the treatment of ἀμήν at the conclusion of 2 Peter. Whereas Erasmus, Bengel, and Lachmann put in ἀμήν, Griesbach exhibits a certain restraint. He puts in ἀμήν and places a γ to notify his verdict regarding the omission of ἀμήν: "Litera γ designantur eae, quae probabilitate inferiores quidem illis, non tamen prorsus aspernandae, sed ulteriore examine dignae videntur."[93] Tregelles rejected the ἀμήν and placed it in brackets. Tischendorf's *Novum Testamentum Graece* and Westcott and Hort deleted it. The twenty-sixth edition of Nestle-Aland again inserted it as doubtful in brackets. The twenty-eighth edition dropped it. The commentaries also proceed correspondingly.[94] In distinction from the twenty-sixth edition of Nestle-Aland, Erich Fuchs argued for the ἀμήν,[95] but then printed it in brackets. Hubert Frankemölle printed an ἀμήν without mentioning the text-critical problem.[96]

An important aspect of this problem is the fact that the manuscript B exhibits no ἀμήν.[97] Should B 82, 440, 522, 1175, 1739*vid be followed

---

93. Griesbach, *Η ΚΑΙΝΗ ΔΙΑΘΗΚΗ*, xix.

94. Cf. Hans Windisch, *Die Katholischen Briefe*, 3rd ed., HNT 15 (Tübingen: Mohr, 1951), 104; Horst Balz and Wolfgang Schrage, *Die Katholischen Briefe*, 11th ed., NTD 10 (Göttingen: Vandenhoeck & Ruprecht, 1982), 148; Walter Grundmann, *Der Brief des Judas und der zweite Brief des Petrus*, 3rd ed., THKNT 15 (Berlin: Evangelische Verlagsanstalt, 1986), 119; Karl Hermann Schelkle, *Die Petrusbriefe, Der Judasbrief*, HThKNT 8.2 (Darmstadt: Wissenschaftliche Buchgesellschaft, 2015), 235, do not print amen. Stuiber, "Amen," 154, explains the ἀμήν as "text critically uncertain."

95. Eric Fuchs and Pierre Reymond, *La Deuxième Epître de Saint Pierre, L'Epître de Saint Jude*, 2nd ed., CNT 8b (Geneva: Labor et Fides, 1988), 126.

96. Hubert Frankemölle, *1. Petrusbrief, 2. Petrusbrief, Judasbrief*, NEchtBNT 20 (Würzburg: Echter, 1987), 119.

97. NA[26]: om. B 1241, 1243, 1739*vid, 1881, 2298 pc vg[mss].

here? Second Peter ends with a doxology after a negative and a positive concluding exhortation. The concluding doxology stands alone as in Rom 11:36; Eph 3:21; Phil 4:20; 1 Tim 1:17; 1 Pet 5:11; Jude 24–25. All of these doxologies end with a firmly transmitted ἀμήν. Of course these doxologies that have been listed vary in their function: First Timothy 1:17 provides the high point of the prescript. Philippians 4:20; 1 Pet 5:11 conclude the epistolary exhortations and precede the postscript together with a promise. Jude 24–25 as also 2 Pet 3:18 are in place of a postscript, being used as substitutes. This is characteristic for the epistolary situation in these pseudonymous writings. Romans 11:36 and Eph 3:21 conclude the doctrinal parts of Romans and of Ephesians.

Doxologies in the New Testament that are introduced with a relative pronoun end without exception with a firmly transmitted ἀμήν. Galatians 1:5 closes the prescript, 1 Tim 6:16 a hymn to God, 2 Tim 4:18 a declaration of promise. Hebrews 13:21c constitutes a final doxology. First Peter 4:11 marks the goal of a *paraklesis*, namely, the δόξα θεοῦ as mediated through Jesus Christ, here, however, without reaching a break in the rhetorical disposition of the epistle. The secondary doxology in Rom 16:25–27 also ends with an ἀμήν. This uniform linguistic usage speaks for reckoning with an original ἀμήν in 2 Pet 3:18 against the witnesses B 1241, 1243, 1739*vid, 1881, 2298 pc vg^mss.

Finally the fact that 2 Peter is heavily dependent on Jude and also as a part of this dependence takes over its concluding doxology, speaks in favor of this decision. As far as we know this passage provides the only example of a transmission of a secondarily deleted ἀμήν. The motive for this deletion can only be conjectured. Perhaps B had in other places deleted a concluding amen, which had been exhibited by its exemplars. B transmits a final amen only in Luke, Jude, Romans, and Galatians.

4.4. On Galatians 6:18

The ἀμήν in Gal 6:18 is treated as original almost without exception.[98] Schlier, "Thus ἀμήν is to be explained as the conclusion of a prophetic word in Rev 1:7 and in the epistolary endings or conclusions in Rom 15:33;

---

98. Schlier, "ἀμήν," 340–41 [= TDNT 2:335–38]; Bauer, *Wörterbuch* (5th ed.), 90; Stuiber, "Amen" 154; Deichgräber, *Gotteshymnus und Christushymnus*, 27; Gamble, *Textual History*, 66; Schnider and Stenger, *Studien zum neutestamentlichen Briefformular*, 147–48, 181.

Gal 6:18; Rev 22:20."⁹⁹ The ἀμήν, however, in the passage quoted is not "the conclusion of a prophetic word" but, as the ναὶ ἀμήν shows, a response to a link of a doxology with an Old Testament promise. For the doxology in Rev 1:5–6, as we have seen above (§1.2), is not left without the responsorial ἀμήν. In each case of a new liturgical voice responses are repeatedly introduced by ναί or ἀμήν: 5:14; 7:12; 16:7; 19:4; 22:20a; 22:20b. They are not developed from the concluding amen of doxologies.¹⁰⁰ It is also not correct to designate the ἀμήν of doxologies as concluding amens. They are in their ancient understanding responsorial amens.¹⁰¹

Above (§3.2) we put the question to the test whether the ἀμήν in Gal 6:18 should be assessed as an element of a word of grace and therefore should be held as original. The answer was in the negative. The ἀμήν belongs to the secondary concluding amens from later transmission.

Most commentaries have considered the ἀμήν as original. Thereby the ἀμήν is construed as the last word of Galatians without the question being of any concern to the exegetes why Paul here turns away from what otherwise is his linguistic custom. He does not close his epistles with ἀμήν and he does not add ἀμήν to his word of grace. Franz Schnider and Werner Stenger note that this ἀμήν is striking, but they do not deal with the text-critical problem. Rather, they think of the ἀμήν as a resumption of Gal 1:5.¹⁰² A recent commentary on Galatians likewise presents the "amen" as part of the text.¹⁰³ Franz Mussner listed witnesses deviating from the majority text.¹⁰⁴ Finally Hans Dieter Betz presented the view that the ἀμήν probably

---

99. Schlier, "ἀμήν," 340–41 [= *TDNT* 2:335–38].

100. Against Schlier, "ἀμήν," 341 [= *TDNT* 2:338].

101. Correctly Stuiber, "Amen," 153: "If amen stands in the texts without a statement, this is to be spoken as an acclamation from others, knowledge of the living usage gives the correct explanation: amen is placed in the text under the anticipation of the acclamation. It is not necessary to specify that the speakers change."

102. Schnider and Stenger, *Studien zum neutestamentlichen Briefformular*, 147.

103. Peter Oakes, *Galatians*, Paideia (Grand Rapids: Baker Academic, 2015), 194. The secondary ἀμήν appears as an element of Paul's epistle in Stephen C. Carlson, *The Text of Galatians and Its History*, WUNT 2/385 (Tübingen: Mohr Siebeck, 2015), 272.

104. Cf. Franz Mussner, *Der Galaterbrief*, 5th ed., HThKNT 9 (Freiburg im Breisgau: Herder, 1988), 421 n. 87: "G g Victorin Ambrosiaster," probably following Metzger, *Textual Commentary*, 599.

did not belong to the original text[105] and thereby reverted to the view of H. A. W. Meyer in his commentary on Galatians.[106]

5. Conclusion

In an extensive study that is based on the methods of form-critical analysis, the New Testament use of ἀμήν is confronted with the texts of modern editions. We ascertain: Paul connects ἀμήν, when he does not broach the issue as such, with only two New Testament forms, with benedictions and doxologies. He understands it as a responsorial amen, that is, as a response of the congregation to the praise of God carried out liturgically. For him there are no doxologies to Christ. Where the responsorial amen does not appear, the reasons for this are evident in the context.

An ἀμήν as a response to prayers is spoken of in 1 Cor 14:16. The fact that there are no New Testament prayer texts with an original ἀμήν, and on the other hand that secondary doxologies in Matt 6:13 (not in Did. 8:2 and the other doxologies of the Didache; not in Mart. Pol. 22:1) display the ἀμήν, permit the assumption that also an ἀμήν in 1 Cor 14:15 is also meant, as with other acclamations, to have its liturgical place in worship. Consequently, the use of doxologies as conclusions of prayer, and likewise later as organizing elements of liturgies (Didache) and homilies (1 Clement), should not be assumed to originate in postapostolic literature, but were already in use in New Testament times.[107]

---

105. Cf. Hans Dieter Betz, *Galatians: A Commentary on Paul's Letter to the Churches in Galatia*, Hermeneia (Philadelphia: Fortress, 1975), 325.

106. "The letter that largely is so austere concludes with an address in which unaltered love for the brethren is expressed. Cf. 1 Cor 16:24." H. A. W. Meyer, *Brief an die Galater: Das Neue Testament Griechisch*, 3rd ed. (Göttingen: Vandenhoeck & Ruprecht, 1857), 257. This was adhered to until the ninth edition by Friedrich Sieffert (*Brief an die Galater, Das Neue Testament Griechisch*, 9th ed. [Göttingen: Vandenhoeck & Ruprecht, 1899), 365.

107. For support in the acquisition of materials for this essay, I express my gratitude to the Director of the Institute for New Testament Textual Research in Münster, Prof. Lic. Barbara Aland, as well as to my colleagues of the Münster Institute.

A Secondary Amen in Important Editions

	ER	TR	BE	GR	LA	TRE	TI	WH	VS	VO	SO	ME	BO	KI	NA28
Matt 6:13	+	+	+[108]	–	–	–	–	–	–	–	–	–	–	–	–
Matt 28:20	–	+	–	–	–	–	–	–	–	–	–	–	–	–	–
Mark 6:11	+	+	+[109]	–	[+]	–	–	–	–	–	–	–	–	–	–
Mark 16:20	–	+	–	–	–	–	–	[–][110]	[–]	_[111]	+	–	–	[–][112]	[–]
Luke 24:53	+	+	–	–	[+]	–	–	–	–	–	–	–	–	–	–
John 21:25	–	+	–	–	–	–	–	–	–	–	–	–	–	–	–
Rom 15:33	+	+	+	+[113]	[+]	–	+	+	+	+	+	+	+	–	+

Editions: ER = Erasmus; TR = Textus Receptus; BE = Bengel; GR = Griesbach; LA = Lachmann; TRE = Tregelles; TI = Tischendorf; WH = Westcott-Hort; VS = von Soden; VO = Vogels; SO = Souter; ME = Merk; BO = Bover; KI = Kilpatrick; NA28 = Nestle-Aland, 28th edition.

Signs and symbols: + indicates that ἀμήν is printed as text; – signifies that it is not accepted into the text; [ ] indicate that the word ἀμήν or a whole passage has been designated as a secondary addition.

108. Bengel expressed the view that the omission carries no inferior attestation compared to the amen.
109. Bengel expressed the view that the marginal reading shows a poorer attestation.
110. ἀμήν is a marginal reading.
111. Vogels designated this amen as secondary (so his personal copy).
112. Designated as secondary.
113. Griesbach considered the marginal reading as noteworthy, yet as less likely.

4. Amen, Benediction, Doxology

	ER	TR	BE	GR	LA	TRE	TI	WH	VS	VO	SO	ME	BO	KI	NA28
Rom 16:24	+	+	+[114]	+	–	–	–	–	–	–	–	–	–	–	–
Rom 16:25–27	+	+	–	–	+	+	+	+	[+]	+[115]	+	+	+	+	[+]
1 Cor 16:24	+	+	–	+	[+]	–	–	–	[+]	–	+	–	–	–	–
2 Cor 13:13	+	+	–	–	–	–	–	–	–	–	–	–	–	–	–
Gal 6:18	+	+	+	+	+	+	+	+	+	+	+	+	+	+	+
Eph 6:24	+	+	+	–	–	–	–	–	–	–	–	–	–	–	–
Phil 4:23	+	+	–	+	[+]	–	–	–	+	[+]	–	+	–	–	–
Col 4:18	+	+	+[116]	–	–	–	–	–	–	–	–	–	–	–	–
1 Thess 3:13	–	+	–	–	[+]	–	+	–[117]	[+]	–	–	–	–	–	[+][118]
1 Thess 5:28	+	+	+	–	–	–	–	–	[+]	[+]	–	–	–	–	–
2 Thess 3:18	+	+	+	+	+	–	–	–	–	[+]	–	–	–	–	–
1 Tim 6:21	+	+	–	–	–	–	–	–	[+]	–	–	–	–	–	–
2 Tim 4:22	+	+	–	–	–	–	–	–	–	–	–	–	–	–	–

---

114. Bengel considered the marginal reading as inferior in attestation.
115. Vogels designated this passage as secondary in his own copy.
116. Bengel called the attestation for the omission equally strong.
117. ἀμήν is a marginal reading.
118. NA[28], "Introduction," 54*: "Square brackets in the text ([ ]) except in the case of the Catholic Letters indicate that textual critics today are not completely convinced of the authenticity of the enclosed words."

Textual Criticism and the New Testament Text

	ER	TR	BE	GR	LA	TRE	TI	WH	VS	VO	SO	ME	BO	KI	NA28
Tit 3:15	+	+	−	−	[+]	−	−	−	−	−	−	−	−	−	−
Phlm 25	+	+	−	−	−	−	−	−	+	+	+	+	+	−	−
Heb 13:25	+	+	−	+[119]	−	+	−	−[120]	+	+	+	+	+	−	−
1 Pet 5:14	+	+	−	−	−	−	−	−	−	−	−	−	−	−	−
2 Pet 3:18[121]	+	+	+	+[122]	+	[+]	−	−	+	+	+	+	+	−	[+]
1 John 5:21	+	+	−	−	−	−	−	−	−	−	−	−	−	−	−
2 John 13	+	+	−	−	−	−	−	−	−	−	−	−	−	−	−
Rev 1:6	+	+	−	+	+	0[123]	+	+	+	+	+	+	+	+	+
Rev 1:18	−	+	−	−	−	0	−	+	−	−	−	−	−	−	−
Rev 7:12	+	+	−	+[124]	−	0	+	[+]	+	+	+	+	+	+	+
Rev 22:21	+	+	−	−	−	0	−	−	+	+	+	−	−	−	−

---

119. Griesbach considers the marginal reading as noteworthy, yet as less likely.
120. A marginal reading of Westcott and Hort.
121. I do not accept the view that this amen is secondary, but I listed the decisions of the editors regarding this passage.
122. Griesbach considered the marginal reading as noteworthy, yet as less likely.
123. I am not able to comment about the readings in the book of Revelation, since I lack any access to the second edition of this editor.
124. Griesbach considered this omission as textually quite unlikely.

Bibliography

Abbott, Ezra. "On the Construction of Romans ix.5." *JBL* 1 (1881): 87–154.
Aland, Barbara, Kurt Aland, Johannes Karavidopoulos, Carlo M. Martini, and Bruce M. Metzger, eds. *Novum Testamentum Graece*. 27th ed. Stuttgart: Deutsche Bibelgesellschaft, 2001.
Aland, Kurt. "Der Schluss und die ursprüngliche Gestalt des Römerbriefs." Pages 284–301 in *Neutestamentliche Entwürfe*. Munich: Kaiser, 1979.
———, ed. *Synopsis Quattuor Evangeliorum*. 15th rev. ed. Stuttgart: Deutsche Bibelgesellschaft, 1997.
Aland, Kurt, et al., eds. *The Greek New Testament*. London: United Bible Societies, 1966.
Artemonius, Lucas Mellierus [= Samuel Crellius]. *Initium Evangelii S. Joannis Apostoli ex antiquitate ecclesiastica restitutum indidemque nova ratione illustratum*. Amsterdam, 1726.
Audet, Jean-Paul. "Esquisse historique du genre littéraire de la 'bénédiction' Juive et de l' 'eucharistie' Chrétienne." *RB* 65 (1958): 371–99.
Balz, Horst, and Wolfgang Schrage. *Die Katholischen Briefe*. 11th ed. NTD 10. Göttingen: Vandenhoeck & Ruprecht, 1982.
Barth, Karl. *Der Römerbrief*. 2nd ed. Munich: Chr. Kaiser Verlag, 1922. Repr., Zurich: TVZ, 1954.
Bartsch, Hans-Werner. "Röm 9,5 und 1. Clem. 32,4: Eine notwendige Konjektur im Römerbrief." *TZ* 21 (1965): 401–9.
Bauer, Walter. *Griechisch-deutsches Wörterbuch zu den Schriften des Neuen Testaments und der frühchristlichen Literatur*. Edited by Kurt Aland and Barbara Aland. 6th ed. Berlin: de Gruyter, 1988.
———. *Wörterbuch zu den Schriften des Neuen Testaments und der übrigen urchristlichen Literatur*. 5th ed. Berlin: Töpelmann, 1963.
Becker, Jürgen, Hans Conzelmann, and Gerhard Friedrich. *Die Briefe an die Galater, Epheser, Philipper, Kolosser, Thessalonicher und Philemon*. 14th ed. NTD 8. Göttingen: Vandenhoeck & Ruprecht, 1976.
Bengel, Johann Albrecht, ed. *Η ΚΑΙΝΗ ΔΙΑΘΗΚΗ: Novum Testamentum Graecum*. Tübingen: Berger, 1734.
Bentley, Richard. *Bentleii Critica sacra: Notes on the Greek and Latin Text of the New Testament, Extracted from the Bentley MSS in Trinity College Library*. Edited by Arthur Ayres Ellis. Cambridge: Deighton, Bell, & Co., 1862.
Berger, Klaus. "Apostelbrief und apostolische Rede: Zum Formular frühchristlicher Briefe." *ZNW* 65 (1974): 190–231.

———. "Gebet IV. Neues Testament." *TRE* 12:47–60.
Betz, Hans Dieter. *Der Galaterbrief: Ein Kommentar zum Brief des Apostels Paulus an die Gemeinden in Galatien.* Munich: Kaiser, 1988.
———. *Galatians: A Commentary on Paul's Letter to the Churches in Galatia.* Hermeneia. Philadelphia: Fortress, 1975.
Bickerman, Elias J. "Bénédiction et prière." Pages 313–23 in *Studies in Jewish and Christian History.* AGJU 9. Leiden: Brill, 1980.
———. "Ein jüdischer Festbrief vom Jahre 124 v. Chr. (2 Macc 1:1–9)." Pages 136–58 in vol. 2 of *Studies in Jewish and Christian History.* 3 vols. AGJU 9. Leiden: Brill, 1980.
Bihlmeyer, ed. *Die apostolischen Väter: Neubearbeitung der Funkschen Ausgabe.* 3rd ed. Tübingen: Mohr, 1970.
Bousset, D. Wilhelm. "Eine jüdische Gebetssammlung im siebenten Buch der Apostolischen Konstitutionen." *NGWG.PH* (1915): 435–41.
———. *Kyrios Christos: Geschichte des Christusglaubens von den Anfängen des Christentums bis Irenaeus.* 3rd ed. FRLANT 21. Göttingen: Vandenhoeck & Ruprecht, 1926.
———. *Religionsgeschichtliche Studien: Aufsätze zur Religionsgeschichte des hellenistischen Zeitalters.* Edited by Anthonie F. Verheule. NovTSup 50. Leiden: Brill, 1979.
Bover, José Maria, ed. *Novi Testamenti Biblia Graeca et Latina.* 5th ed. Madrid: Consejo Superior de Investigaciones Cientificas, 1968.
Bruce, F. F. *Epistle to the Galatians: A Commentary on the Greek Text.* NIGTC 8. Grand Rapids: Eerdmans, 1982.
Carlson, Stephen C. *The Text of Galatians and Its History.* WUNT 2/385. Tübingen: Mohr Siebeck, 2015.
Charles, Robert H. *The Greek Versions of the Testaments of the Twelve Patriarchs.* 2nd ed. Repr., Hildesheim: Olms, 1960.
Cowley, A. E. *Aramaic Papyri of the Fifth Century B.C.* Oxford: Clarendon, 1923. Repr., Osnabrück: Zeller, 1967.
Cranfield, C. E. B. *A Critical and Exegetical Commentary on the Epistle to the Romans.* 2 vols. ICC 18. Edinburgh: T&T Clark, 1980.
Deichgräber, Reinhard. *Gotteshymnus und Christushymnus in der frühen Christenheit: Untersuchungen zu Form, Sprache und Stil der frühchristlichen Hymnen.* SUNT 5. Göttingen: Vandenhoeck & Ruprecht, 1967.
Deichgräber, Reinhard, and St. G. Hall. "Formeln, Liturgische II. Neues Testament und Alte Kirche." *TRE* 11:256–65.
Dibelius, Martin. *Die Pastoralbriefe.* 4th ed. HNT 13. Tübingen: Mohr, 1966.

4. Amen, Benediction, Doxology

Dobschütz, Ernst von. *Die Thessalonicherbriefe*. 7th ed. KEK 10. Göttingen: Vandenhoeck & Ruprecht, 1909. Repr., Leipzig: St. Benno Verlag, 1974.
Elbogen, Ismar. *Der jüdische Gottesdienst in seiner geschichtlichen Entwicklung*. 3rd ed. Repr., Hildesheim: Olms, 1967.
Elliott, J. Keith. "The Language and Style of the Concluding Doxology to the Epistle to the Romans." *ZNW* 72 (1981): 124–30.
Erasmus Roterodamus, Desiderius, ed. *Novum instrumentum omne*. Basel: Froben, 1516. Repr., Stuttgart: Frommann, 1986.
Esh, Shaul. הקבה *'Der Heilige (er sei gepriesen)': Zur Geschichte einer nachbiblisch- hebräischen Gottesbezeichnung*. Leiden: Brill, 1957.
Frame, James E. *A Critical and Exegetical Commentary on the Epistles of St. Paul to the Thessalonians*. 3rd ed. ICC 10. Edinburgh: T&T Clark, 1953.
Frankemölle, Hubert. *1. Petrusbrief, 2. Petrusbrief, Judasbrief*. NEchtB 20. Würzburg: Echter, 1987.
Fuchs, Eric, and Pierre Reymond. *La Deuxième Epître de Saint Pierre, L'Epître de Saint Jude*. 2nd ed. CNT 8b. Geneva: Labor et Fides, 1988.
Gamble, Harry. *The Textual History of the Letter to the Romans: A Study in Textual and Literary Criticism*. SD 42. Grand Rapids: Eerdmans, 1977.
Glaue, Paul. "Amen nach seiner Bedeutung und Verwendung in der Alten Kirche." *ZKG* 44 (1925): 184–98.
Griesbach, Johann Jacob, ed. *Η ΚΑΙΝΗ ΔΙΑΘΗΚΗ: Novum Testamentum Graece*. 4 vols. Leipzig: Göschen, 1803–1807.
Grundmann, Walter. *Der Brief des Judas und der zweite Brief des Petrus*. 3rd ed. THKNT 15. Berlin: Evangelische Verlagsanstalt, 1986.
Grunewald, Winfried, and Klaus Junack. *Das Neue Testament auf Papyrus, Bd. 1: Die Katholischen Briefe*. ANTF 6. Berlin: de Gruyter, 1986.
Gwynn, John, ed. *The Apocalypse of St. John in a Syriac Version Hitherto Unknown*. Dublin, 1897. Repr., Amsterdam: APA-Philo Press, 1981.
Harder, Günther. *Paulus und das Gebet*. NTF 10. Gütersloh: Bertelsmann, 1936.
Hoffman, Lawrence A. "Gebet III. Judentum." *TRE* 12:42–47.
Holtz, Traugott. *Der erste Brief an die Thessalonicher*. EKKNT 13. Zurich: Benziger, 1986.
Horner, George W., ed. *The Coptic Version of the New Testament in the Southern Dialect, Otherwise Called Sahidic and Thebaic*. 7 vols. Oxford: Clarendon, 1911–1924. Repr., Osnabrück: Zeller, 1969.

Huck, Albert, ed. *Synopsis of the First Three Gospels with the Addition of the Johannine Parallels*. Rev. Heinrich Greeven. 13th ed. Tübingen: Mohr, 1981.

Hurtado, Larry W. "The Doxology at the End of Romans." Pages 185–99 in *New Testament Textual Criticism: Its Significance for Exegesis; Essays in Honour of Bruce M. Metzger*. Edited by Eldon J. Epp and Gordon D. Fee. Oxford: Clarendon, 1981.

Jeremias, Joachim. "Amen 1. Biblisch-Theologisch." *TRE* 2:386–91.

———. "Kennzeichen der *ipsissima vox* Jesu." In *Abba: Studien zur neutestamentlichen Theologie und Zeitgeschichte*. Göttingen: Vandenhoeck & Ruprecht, 1966.

Jeremias, Joachim, and Gerhard Krause. "Amen." *TRE* 2:386–402.

Käsemann, Ernst. *An die Römer*. 4th ed. HNT 8a Tübingen: Mohr, 1980.

———. "Formeln II: Liturgische Formeln im NT." *RGG* (3rd ed.) 2:993–96.

Kilpatrick, George Dunbar, ed. Η ΚΑΙΝΗ ΔΙΑΘΗΚΗ. 2nd ed. London: British and Foreign Bible Society, 1958.

Kuss, Otto. "Zu Römer 9:5." Pages 291–303 in *Rechtfertigung: Festschrift für Ernst Käsemann zum 70. Geburtstag*. Edited by Johannes Friedrich. Tübingen: Mohr, 1976.

Lachmann, Karl, ed. *Novum Testamentum Graece et Latine*. 2nd ed. 2 vols. Berlin: Reimer, 1842–1850.

Lagrange, Marie-Joseph. *Épître aux Romains*. 6th ed. EtB 34. Paris; Gabalda, 1950.

Lietzmann, Hans. *An die Römer*. 5th ed. HNT 8. Tübingen: Mohr, 1971.

Lorimer, W. L. "Romans IX.3–5." *NTS* 13 (1966–1967): 385–86.

Marmorstein, Arthur. "L'âge de la Kedoucha de l'Amida." *REJ* 97 (1934): 35–49.

Marxsen, Willi. *Der erste Brief an die Thessalonicher*. ZBK 11.1. Zurich: TVZ, 1979.

Mayer, Günter. "Die Funktion der Gebete in den alttestamentlichen Apokryphen." Pages 16–25 in *Festgabe für Karl Heinrich Rengstorf zum 70. Geburtstag*. Edited by Wolfgang Dietrich. Theokratia 2. Leiden: Brill, 1973.

Melito. *Passa-Homilie* (*Die Passa-Homilie des Bischofs Meliton von Sardes*). Edited by Bernhard Lohse. Textus Minores 24. Leiden: Brill, 1958.

Merk, August, ed. *Novum Testamentum Graece et Latine*. 9th ed. Rome: Pontifical Biblical Institute, 1964.

Metzger, Bruce M. "The Punctuation of Rom 9:5." Pages 95–112 in *Christ and Spirit in the New Testament: Studies in Honour of C. F. D. Moule*.

Edited by Barnabas Lindars. Cambridge: Cambridge University Press, 1973.

———. *A Textual Commentary on the Greek New Testament: A Companion Volume to the United Bible Societies' Greek New Testament (Fourth Revised Edition)*. 2nd ed. Stuttgart: Deutsche Bibelgesellschaft, 1994.

Meyer, H. A. W. *Brief an die Galater: Das Neue Testament Griechisch*. 3rd ed. Göttingen: Vandenhoeck & Ruprecht, 1857.

Michel, Otto. *Der Brief an die Römer*. 14th ed. KEK 4. Göttingen: Vandenhoeck & Ruprecht, 1978.

Mussner, Franz. *Der Galaterbrief*. 5th ed. HThKNT 9. Freiburg im Breisgau: Herder, 1988.

Nestle, Eberhard. *Einführung in das griechische Neue Testament*. 3rd ed. Göttingen: Vandenhoeck & Ruprecht, 1909.

Nolli, Giofranco, ed. *Novum Testamentum Graece et Latine*. Città del Vaticano: Libreria Editrice Vaticana, 1981.

Oakes, Peter. *Galatians*. Paideia. Grand Rapids: Baker Academic, 2015.

Peterson, Erik. *ΕΙΣ ΘΕΟΣ: Epigraphische, formgeschichtliche und religionsgeschichtliche Untersuchungen*. FRLANT 41. Göttingen: Vandenhoeck & Ruprecht, 1926.

Rigaux, Béda. *Les Épîtres aux Thessaloniciens*. 2nd ed. EBib 33. Paris: Cerf, 1960.

Roberts, Colin H., and Bernard Capelle. *An Early Euchologium: The Dêr-Balizeh Papyrus Enlarged and Reedited*. BMus 28. Louvain: Bureaux de Muséon, 1949.

Roetzel, Calvin J. *The Letters of Paul*. London: SCM, 1983.

Sanday, William, and Arthur C. Headlam. *A Critical and Exegetical Commentary on the Epistle to the Romans*. 5th ed. ICC 5. Edinburgh: T&T Clark, 1925.

Scharbert, Josef. "ברך." *ThWAT* 1:808–41. [= *TDOT* 2:279–308.]

Schelkle, Karl Hermann. *Die Petrusbriefe, Der Judasbrief*. HThKNT 8.2. Darmstadt: Wissenschaftliche Buchgesellschaft, 2015.

Schlier, Heinrich. "ἀμήν." *TWNT* 1:339–42. [= *TDNT* 2:335–338.]

———. *Der Apostel und seine Gemeinde: Auslegung des ersten Briefes an die Thessalonicher*. Leipzig: St. Benno Verlag, 1974.

Schmid, Josef. *Studien zur Geschichte des griechischen Apokalypse-Textes*. 3 vols. MThS 1. Munich: Zink, 1955–1956.

Schmidt, Karl Ludwig. "βασιλεία." *TDNT* 1:579–93.

Schnider, Franz, and Werner Stenger. *Studien zum neutestamentlichen Briefformular*. NTTS 11. Leiden: Brill, 1987.

Schniewind, J. "Diktate zum Römerbrief." Unpublished manuscript, 1937.
Scrivener, Frederick H. *An Exact Transcript of the Codex Augiensis to Which Is Added a Full Collation of Fifty Manuscripts*. Cambridge: Deighton & Bell, 1859.

———, ed. *Η ΚΑΙΝΗ ΔΙΑΘΗΚΗ*. Cambridge: Deighton & Bell, 1873.

Sieffert, Friedrich. *Brief an die Galater: Das Neue Testament Griechisch*. 9th ed. Göttingen: Vandenhoeck & Ruprecht, 1899.

Slichtingius de Bukowiec, Jonas. *J. Slichtingius de Bukowiec Commentaria posthuma in plerosque Novi Testamenti libros*. Amsterdam: Philalethius, 1656–1865.

Soden, Hermann von, ed. *Die Schriften des Neuen Testaments in ihrer ältesten erreichbaren Textgestalt*. 4 vols. Göttingen: Vandenhoeck & Ruprecht, 1911–1913.

Souter, Alexander. *Novum Testamentum Graece*. 2nd ed. Oxford: Clarendon, 1950. Repr., 1962.

Stuiber, Alfred. "Amen." *JAC* 1 (1958): 153–59.

———. "Doxologie." *RAC* 4:210–26.

Tischendorf, Constantin von, ed. *Novum Testamentum Graece: Ad antiquissimos testes denuo recensuit; Apparatum criticum omni studio perfectum apposuit commentationem isagogicam praetexuit Constantinus Tischendorf*. 8th ed. 3 vols. Leipzig: Giesecke & Devrient, 1894.

Tregelles, Samuel Prideaux, ed. *The Greek New Testament Edited from Ancient Authorities with the Latin Version of Jerome from the Codex Amiatinus*. London: Bagster, 1870.

Vielhauer, Philipp *Geschichte der urchristlichen Literatur*. Berlin: de Gruyter, 1975.

Vogels, Heinrich Josef, ed. *Novum Testamentum Graece et Latine*. 4th ed. Freiburg im Breisgau: Herder, 1955.

Weiss, Bernhard. *Textkritik der paulinischen Briefe*. TU 14.3. Leipzig: Hinrichs, 1896.

Weiss, Johannes. "Beiträge zur paulinischen Rhetorik." Pages 165–247 in *Theologische Studien Bernhard Weiss zu seinem 70. Geburtstage*. Göttingen: Vandenhoeck & Ruprecht, 1897.

———. *Das Urchristentum*. Göttingen: Vandenhoeck & Ruprecht, 1917.

Wendland, Paul. *Die hellenistisch-römische Kultur in ihren Beziehungen zum Judentum und Christentum: Urchristliche Literaturformen*. 2nd and 3rd ed. HNT 1.3. Tübingen: Mohr, 1912.

Werner, Eric. "The Doxology in Synagogue and Church: A Liturgico-musical Study." *HUCA* 19 (1945): 275–351.

Westcott, Brooke Foss, and Fenton John Anthony Hort, eds. *The New Testament in the Original Greek: Volume 1, Text; Volume 2, Introduction [and] Appendix*. Cambridge: Macmillan, 1881. 2nd ed., 1896.

Westermann, Claus. "הלל." *TLOT* 1:371–76.

Wettstein, Johann Jakob. *Novum Testamentum Graecum*. 2 vols. Amsterdam: Dommerian, 1752.

Wilckens, Ulrich. *Der Brief an die Römer*. 4th ed. EKKNT 6.2 Düsseldorf: Benziger; Neukirchen-Vluyn: Neukirchener Verlag, 2006.

Windisch, Hans. *Die Katholischen Briefe*. 3rd ed. HNT 15. Tübingen: Mohr, 1951.

Wrede, William. *Paulus*. 2nd ed. Tübingen: Mohr, 1907.

Zahn, Theodor, and Friedrich Hauck. *Der Brief des Paulus an die Römer*. 3rd ed. KNT 6. Leipzig, 1925.

5

The Editorial Account as a Commentary on the Constitution of Text and Apparatus in Editions of the Greek New Testament

Editors of new editions of the Greek New Testament tackle the task of recovering the original text of New Testament authors from the manuscript tradition, to establish it critically and to document this reconstruction in an apparatus.[1] No printed text of the New Testament follows any one

---

1. Complete editions: Bernhard Weiss, ed., *Das Neue Testament: Textkritische Untersuchungen und Textherstellung*, 3 vols. (Leipzig: Hinrichs, 1894–1900); Eberhard Nestle, ed., *Novum Testamentum Graece* (Stuttgart: Württembergische Bibelanstalt, 1898); Eberhard Nestle and Erwin Nestle, eds., *Novum Testamentum Graece*, 13th ed. (Stuttgart: Württembergische Bibelanstalt, 1927); Erwin Nestle and Kurt Aland, eds., *Novum Testamentum Graece*, 25th ed. (London: United Bible Societies, 1963); Barbara Aland et al., eds., *Novum Testamentum Graece*, 28th ed. (Stuttgart: Deutsche Bibelgesellschaft, 2012) [NA[28]]; Kurt Aland et al., eds., *The Greek New Testament* (London: United Bible Societies, 1966); Barbara Aland et al., eds., *The Greek New Testament*, 5th ed. (Stuttgart: Deutsche Bibelgesellschaft, 2014); Hermann von Soden, ed., *Die Schriften des Neuen Testaments in ihrer ältesten erreichbaren Textgestalt*, 4 vols. (Göttingen: Vandenhoeck & Ruprecht, 1911–1913); Heinrich Joseph Vogels, ed., *Novum Testamentum Graece* (Düsseldorf: Schwann, 1920); Vogels, ed., *Novum Testamentum Graece et Latine*, 4th ed. (Freiburg im Breisgau: Herder, 1955); August Merk, ed., *Novum Testamentum Graece et Latine* (Rome: Pontifical Biblical Institute, 1933); Merk, ed., *Novum Testamentum Graece et Latine*, 9th ed. (Rome: Pontifical Biblical Institute, 1964); José Maria Bover, ed., *Novi Testamenti Biblia Graeca et Latina* (Madrid: Consejo Superior de Investigaciones Cientificas, 1943); Bover, ed., *Novi Testamenti Biblia Graeca et Latina*, 5th ed. (Madrid: Consejo Superior de Investigaciones Cientificas, 1968); George Dunbar Kilpatrick, ed., *Η ΚΑΙΝΗ ΔΙΑΘΗΚΗ*, 2nd ed. (London: British and Foreign Bible Society, 1958); R. V. G. Tasker, ed., *The*

manuscript throughout, although of course today numerous editions of individual manuscripts are available.[2] Critical editions seek to justify eclectic texts, even if sometimes this term is used with reservation.[3] In New Testament scholarship there is an extensive discussion about how editors practice eclecticism.[4]

In a programmatic assessment in 1973 an American textual critic, who has taken part in this discussion with numerous contributions, Eldon J. Epp, declared that contemporary New Testament scholarship has no acceptable textual theory at its disposal.[5] On the other hand the Institut für neutesta-

---

Greek New Testament Being the Text Translated in the New English Bible 1961: Edited with Introduction, Textual Notes, and Appendix (Oxford: Oxford University Press; New York: Cambridge University Press, 1964); José Maria Bover and José O'Callaghan, eds., *Nuevo Testamento Trilingüe* (Madrid: Biblioteca de Autores Cristianos, 1977); Bover and O'Callaghan, eds., *Nuevo Testamento Trilingüe*, 2nd ed. (Madrid: Biblioteca de Autores Cristianos, 1988); Giofranco Nolli, ed., *Novum Testamentum Graece et Latine* (Città del Vaticano: Libreria Editrice Vaticana, 1981); Zane C. Hodges and Arthur L. Farstad, eds., *The Greek New Testament According to the Majority Text* (Nashville: Nelson, 1982); Michael W. Holmes, ed., *The Greek New Testament: SBL Edition* (Atlanta: Society of Biblical Literature; Bellingham, WA: Logos Bible Software, 2010).

2. J. Keith Elliott with the assistance of the Institut romand des sciences bibliques (IRSB), Université de Lausanne, gives a catalogue, *A Bibliography of Greek New Testament Manuscripts*, 3rd ed., NovTSup 160 (Leiden: Brill, 2014).

3. Kurt Aland et al., eds., *Novum Testamentum Graece*, 26th ed. (Stuttgart: Deutsche Bibelgesellschaft, 1979; rev. printing 1983), 5* = English pp. 42*–43* [= NA[26]].

4. See J. Neville Birdsall, "The New Testament Text," in *From the Beginnings to Jerome*, vol. 1 of *The Cambridge History of the Bible*, ed. P. R. Ackroyd et al. (Cambridge: Cambridge University Press, 1970): 308–77, esp. p. 376: "In establishing the text we need to resort to an informed and reasoned eclectic approach, since no one strand of tradition has preserved the autograph or its approximation." Eldon J. Epp, "The Eclectic Method in New Testament Textual Criticism: Solution or Symptom?" *HTR* 69 (1976): 211–57; David C. Parker, "The Development of Textual Criticism since B. H. Streeter," *NTS* 24 (1977): 149–62; David Alan Black, *Rethinking New Testament Textual Criticism* (Grand Rapids: Baker Academic, 2002); Bart D. Ehrman and Michael W. Holmes, eds., *The Text of the New Testament in Contemporary Research: Essays on the Status Quaestionis*, 2nd ed. (Leiden: Brill, 2013).

5. Eldon J. Epp. "The Twentieth Century Interlude in New Testament Textual Criticism," *JBL* 93 (1974): 386–414 (= W. P. Hatch Memorial Lecture at the

mentliche Textforschung in Münster has come onto the scene with its claim for construing the text: "From the perspective of our present knowledge ... the only one which meets the requirements of the New Testament textual tradition" is precisely "the local-genealogical method."[6] This statement appeared in an editorial report that was prefixed to the 1979 edition.

This difference in points of view is astonishing when one considers that initial steps for a critical edition of the New Testament go back to the beginning of the eighteenth century. One is reminded of the proposals of Richard Bentley in 1720[7] and of the first critical editions: Edward Wells (1709/1719), Daniel Mace (1729), and Johann Albrecht Bengel (1734).[8] Before them the Oratorian Richard Simon had laid the foundation for New Testament textual criticism with his *Histoire critique du texte du Nouveau Testament* (Rotterdam: Leers, 1689).[9]

I cannot at this time go into the history of what is now three hundred years of criticism and its present-day discussion.[10] Instead, I suggest that we concern ourselves with one of the more modest issues.

Annual Meeting of the Society of Biblical Literature, 11 November 1973, Chicago, IL). On this see Kurt Aland, "The Twentieth Century Interlude in New Testament Textual Criticism," in *Text and Interpretation: Studies in the New Testament Presented to Matthew Black*, ed. Robert M. Wilson and Ernest Best (Cambridge: Cambridge University Press, 1979), 1–14; and Eldon J. Epp, "A Continuing Interlude in New Testament Textual Criticism?," *HTR* 73 (1980): 131–51.

6. NA^{26}, 43*.

7. Richard Bentley, *Dr. Richard Bentley's Proposals for Printing a New Edition of the Greek Testament, and St. Hieronymos's Latin Version* (London: Knapton, 1721), reproduced in Constantin von Tischendorf, ed., *Novum Testamentum Graece: Ad antiquissimos testes denuo recensuit; Apparatum criticum omni studio perfectum apposuit commentationem isagogicam praetexuit Constantinus Tischendorf*, 8th ed. (Leipzig: Giesecke & Devrient, 1894), 3:231–40.

8. Bruce M. Metzger and Bart D. Ehrman, *The Text of the New Testament: Its Transmission, Corruption, and Restoration*, 4th ed. (Oxford: Oxford University Press, 2005), 155–60.

9. "The first scholar to make any use of all three classes of evidence for the text of the New Testament—that is, Greek manuscripts, the early versions, and quotations from the Fathers—was probably Francis Lucas of Bruges (Brugensis) in his *Notationes in sacra Biblia, quibus variantia ... discutiuntur* (Antwerp: Plantinus, 1583)" (Metzger and Ehrman *Text of the New Testament*, 204).

10. On this see Eldon J. Epp, "Textual Criticism," in Eldon J. Epp and George W. MacRae, eds., *The New Testament and Its Modern Interpreters*, SBLCP (Philadelphia: Fortress; Atlanta: Scholars Press, 1989), 72–126.

First, I pose the question as to what one can expect with justification from an editorial report in this discipline. Second, I point to the close connection between constructing the text and forming the apparatus. To state this more specifically: today the critical value of an edition of the New Testament rests on three pillars, the editorial report, the printed text, and primarily the form of the apparatus. I will conclude with a series of suggestions for the presentation of the apparatus and with a call for presenting the text at least in the apparatus, if one should not want to print it. If an investigator can object that an edition neither prints the reading that he or she takes to be the original text, nor names it in the apparatus, then that is a serious charge.[11]

---

11. As J. Keith Elliott asserts in following C. H. Turner, the Gospel of Mark displays throughout an older use of language that by using the genitive of the personal pronoun designates the μαθητής unambiguously as Jesus's disciple as distinct from other disciples, such as John's disciples. Copyists, who were familiar with the later terminology, have obscured this fact. See J. Keith Elliott, "An Eclectic Textual Commentary on the Greek Text of Mark's Gospel," in *New Testament Textual Criticism: Its Significance for Exegesis; Essays in Honour of Bruce M. Metzger*, ed. Eldon J. Epp and Gordon D. Fee (Oxford: Clarendon, 1981), 56–57; Elliott, "Mathētēs with a Possessive in the New Testament," *TZ* 35 (1979): 300–304; Elliott, "The United Bible Societies' Textual Commentary Evaluated," *NovT* 17 (1975): 140–41; C. H. Turner, "Markan Usage: Notes, Critical and Exegetical, on the Second Gospel, V," *JTS* 26 (1925): 235–37; repr., in *The Language and Style of the Gospel of Mark: An Edition of C. H. Turner's "Notes on Marcan Usage" Together with Other Comparable Studies*, ed. J. Keith Elliott, NovTSup 71 (Leiden: Brill, 1993). The essays mentioned contain numerous further examples. NA[26] is inclined to follow the manuscripts ℵ B. Accordingly the personal pronoun is put in brackets in 6:41 and is absent in 9:14; 10:10, 13, 24; 14:16. It is missing also in 8:1 where these two witnesses depart from each other. Albert Huck, ed., *Synopsis of the First Three Gospels with the Addition of the Johannine Parallels*, rev. Heinrich Greeven, 13th ed. (Tübingen: Mohr, 1981) [Huck-Greeven] reads like NA[26] in 8:1; 9:14; 10:10, 13, 24. Against NA[26] he has αὐτοῦ in 6:41 and 14:16.

It is incorrect for the apparatuses to provide the material only selectively. One does not see Mark's use of language in 9:14; 10:10, 13, 24 either in the apparatus of NA[26] or in Huck-Greeven's apparatus. If one searches for the variants, their occurrence in the apparatus of Kurt Aland, ed., *Synopsis Quattuor Evangeliorum*, 15th rev. ed. (Stuttgart: Deutsche Bibelgesellschaft, 1997) helps partially. For 9:14 on which other apparatuses are silent, one is dependent on von Soden's edition of the text. To date no edition has printed the correct text throughout. None of

1. The Editorial Report as Giving Account for the Reconstruction of the Text

The addition of an editorial report, as indispensable as it might appear to be for us, is not to be taken as a matter of course in editions of the New Testament. For instance, Karl Lachmann printed the editorial account for his 1831 edition in *Theologische Studien und Kritiken*.[12] Even so he was not spared sharp and invidious critique of his accomplishment. One editorial report of our day is indeed dated, but not signed. It derives from George D. Kilpatrick. The date is October 18, 1957.[13] A historical example of an anonymous report would be Daniel Mace in 1729.[14] But here one recognizes the reason for this anonymity. Mace was one of the first who published a critical text.[15] The edition of the Gospel of Luke, for which the International Greek New Testament Project is responsible, names no editor on the title page. This happens at this juncture for different rea-

---

the editions of the twentieth century referred to in n. 1 above, has printed the correct reading for the four passages named in the apparatus (apart from the edition of von Soden already referred to). Further examples are listed in my essay, Eberhard Güting "Amen, Eulogie, Doxologie: Eine textkritische Untersuchung," in *Begegnungen zwischen Christentum und Judentum in Antike und Mittelalter: Festschrift für Heinz Schreckenberg*, ed. Dietrich-Alex Koch and Hermann Lichtenberger, SIJD 1 (Göttingen: Vandenhoeck & Ruprecht, 1993), 131–62 [ch. 4 in this collection].

12. Karl Lachmann, "Rechenschaft über seine Ausgabe des Neuen Testaments von Professor Lachmann in Berlin," *TSK* 3 (1830): 817–45.

13. Kilpatrick's edition, which one associates with the catch phrase "radical eclecticism," is not identical with the publication indicated in n. 1 above. I have at my disposal a later series of installments, which were printed privately ("for private circulation only"): George Dunbar Kilpatrick, *Mark: A Greek-English Diglot for the Use of Translators* (London: British and Foreign Bible Society, 1958). On Kilpatrick's complete New Testament see Matthew Black and Robert Davidson, eds., *Constantin von Tischendorf and the Greek New Testament* (Glasgow: University of Glasgow Press, 1981), 31.

14. Daniel Mace, *The New Testament in Greek and English: Containing the Original Text Corrected from the Authority of the Most Authentic Manuscripts; And a New Version Form'd Agreeably to the Illustrations of the Most Learned Commentators and Critics; With Notes and Various Readings, and a Copious Alphabetical Index*, 2 vols. (London: Roberts, 1729).

15. Metzger and Ehrman, *Text of the New Testament*, 157–58.

sons. This edition was the publication of a committee.[16] As a rule, editors are named.

Although or because we have no generally accepted theory, just such a theory is missing in the most recent editorial reports. They are edited eclectically; but even this term is used with hesitation.[17] The local-genealogical method of the Münster Institut für neutestamentliche Textforschung can only give warrants for some of the decisions.[18] Not rarely taking account of this methodological point of view results in a different text from the one given in the Münster edition.[19] Apart from the eclectic method, which unites editors today, differences in text-critical judgment are apparent above all in the varying emphases on preference for certain witnesses and also in the varying preference for one of the great manuscript traditions, the so-called Western text, or the Alexandrian, or also the Byzantine text. The last, even if taken seriously, is, in view of the state of today's research, somewhat grotesque.[20] The text critic Heinrich Greeven, who died in 1990, developed an independent and formidable contribution. In numerous decisions Greeven based his approach on the examination of assimilation.[21] In the Synoptic Gospels one perceives the

---

16. *The New Testament in Greek: The Gospel according to St. Luke*, 2 vols. (Oxford: Clarendon, 1984-1987). See "Introduction," v.

17. Besides the introductory essays mentioned in n. 4 above, see Gordon D. Fee, "Rigorous or Reasoned Eclecticism—Which?" in *Studies in New Testament Language and Text: Essays in Honour of George Kilpatrick on the Occasion of His Sixty-Fifth Birthday*, ed. J. Keith Elliott, NovTSup 44 (Leiden: Brill, 1976): 174-97.

18. Kurt Aland and Barbara Aland, *The Text of the New Testament: An Introduction to the Critical Editions and to the Theory and Practice of Modern Textual Criticism*, 2nd ed. (Grand Rapids: Eerdmans; Leiden: Brill, 1989).

19. Cf. the dissenting vote of Bruce M. Metzger in Metzger, ed., *A Textual Commentary on the Greek New Testament: A Companion Volume to the United Bible Societies' Greek New Testament (Fourth Revised Edition)*, 2nd ed. (Stuttgart: Deutsche Bibelgesellschaft, 1994), 49, 70, 88, among others.

20. Gordon D. Fee, "The Majority Text and the Original Text of the New Testament," *BT* 31 (1980): 107-18.

21. Gordon D. Fee, "Modern Text Criticism and the Synoptic Problem," in *J. J. Griesbach: Synoptic and Text-Critical Studies 1776-1976*, ed. Bernard Orchard and Thomas R. W. Longstaff, SNTSMS 34 (Cambridge: Cambridge University Press, 1978), 154-69; Fee, "A Text-Critical Look at the Synoptic Problem," *NovT* 22 (1980): 12-28; J. Keith Elliott, "Textual Criticism, Assimilation and the Synoptic Gospels," *NTS* 26 (1980): 231-41. W. F. Wisselink, *Assimilation as a Criterion for*

phenomenon that in the course of the tradition the gospels texts interacted with one another. Preferences for certain manuscript traditions are substantiated in the editorial reports.[22]

The basic issue that every editorial report must confront lies in the enormous number of witnesses that have been preserved. The Greek witnesses alone encompass more than 5,000 and new ones are still discovered and published.[23] Up to the Carolingian Renaissance the Latin witnesses for the gospels alone number more than 450.[24] Alongside ancient translations citations in the fathers come into play as witnesses.[25]

The editorial report indicates which manuscripts were followed and must indicate whether these are thoroughly and reliably cited. In 1987 J. Keith Elliott produced in book form a critique of editorial achievements in this regard.[26] Only three editorial undertakings can claim that they go

---

the Establishment of the Text: A Comparative Study on the Basis of Passages from Matthew, Mark, and Luke (Kampen: Kok, 1989).

22. Controversial questions regarding texts from the early period are approached preferably by methodological investigations of citations from the fathers, cf., e.g., Gordon D. Fee, "Origen's Text of the New Testament and the Text of Egypt," NTS 28 (1982): 348–64; Larry Hurtado, Text-Critical Methodology and the Pre-Caesarean Text: Codex W in the Gospel of Mark (Grand Rapids: Eerdmans, 1981); Bart D. Ehrman, "Methodological Developments in the Analysis and Classification of New Testament Documentary Evidence," NovT 29 (1987): 22–45; David C. Parker, An Introduction to the New Testament Manuscripts and Their Texts (Cambridge: Cambridge University Press, 2008).

23. Bruce M. Metzger, Manuscripts of the Greek Bible: An Introduction to Greek Palaeography (New York: Oxford University Press, 1981), 5, enumerates 5,366. Kurt Aland and Barbara Aland, The Text of the New Testament, 2nd ed. (Stuttgart: Deutsche Bibelgesellschaft, 2006), 172, mentioned 2,280 lectionaries alongside 3,200 manuscripts of the text. See also Kurt Aland et al., Kurzgefasste Liste der griechischen Handschriften des Neuen Testaments, 2nd ed., ANTF 1 (Berlin: de Gruyter, 1994). Updates are found on the web: https://tinyurl.com/SBL7012b.

24. Bonafatius Fischer, ed., Die lateinischen Evangelien bis zum 10. Jahrhundert, IV: Varianten zu Johannes, AGLB 18 (Freiburg am Breisgau: Herder, 1991), 8*.

25. See n. 9 above. Gordon D. Fee, revised by Roderick L. Mullen, "The Use of the Greek Fathers for New Testament Textual Criticism," in Ehrman and Holmes, Text of the New Testament in Contemporary Research, 351–73.

26. J. Keith Elliott, A Survey of Manuscripts Used in Editions of the Greek New Testament, NovTSup 57 (Leiden: Brill, 1987), see also, Elliott, "The Citation of Manuscripts in Recent Printed Editions of the Greek New Testament," NovT 25 (1983): 97–132; Elliott, "Old Latin Manuscripts in Printed Editions of the Greek

back to their own collations of manuscripts.[27] Most editors work with published editions of individual manuscripts and rely on apparatuses from earlier editions. Since the older numeration of manuscripts by Caspar René Gregory was changed,[28] one finds in more recent editions incorrect numbers taken over from such sources, which by mistake have not been converted.[29] After all, incorrect citations of witnesses happen only in such undertakings, which themselves go back to collations, subject to criticism—and criticism was indeed raised.[30]

Naturally editions that work with their own collations cannot do this without relying on printed sources. The early translations into Latin, Coptic, Syriac, Armenian, and Georgian are just as indispensable as the citations from Greek, Latin, and Syriac in the fathers. The sources that are used are referred to in the editorial report.

Each edition works with sigla, systems of cross references, and abbreviations. The arrangement and form of the apparatuses need to be accounted

---

New Testament," *NovT* 26 (1984): 225–48; Elliott, "The Citation of Greek Manuscripts in Six Printed Texts of the New Testament," *RB* 92 (1985): 539–56.

27. NA^{26}, 2* and 10*; Birdsall and Elliott, *New Testament in Greek*, vi: "The evidence of all Greek manuscripts used is derived from new collations either of the manuscripts themselves or of microfilms or other reproductions." Strangely, O'Callaghan speaks of a collation of the Itala, when he takes over the readings of a printed edition: *Nuevo Testamento Trilingüe*, 1. xxiii.

Of course the primary editions of ancient translations were produced on the basis of manuscripts. For the editions of the Itala and the Vulgate the work of the Archabbey Beuron set the trend with their Vetus Latina undertaking. Numerous special investigations dedicate themselves to research on the manuscript tradition.

28. Concordances of sigla are found in Kurt Aland, *Kurzgefasste Liste der griechischen Handschriften des Neuen Testaments, I: Gesamtübersicht*, ANTF 1 (Berlin: de Gruyter, 1963), 321–71. An enlarged second edition has been printed: Aland et al., *Kurzgefasste Liste der griechischen Handschriften des Neuen Testaments, I: Gesamtübersicht*, 2nd ed. ANTF 1 (Berlin: de Gruyter, 1994).

29. E.g., in Huck-Greeven, Tischendorf's minuscule 254 on John 15:20 is cited on p. 75. The correct number is Gregory 238. The same mistake occurs on p. 157 in the apparatus for Luke 11:53.

30. Besides methodological deficiencies, Kurt Aland accused the International Greek New Testament Project of collation errors. See his review in *Gnomon* 56 (1984): 481–97, esp. 487–95. Collation errors in NA^{26} and in additional editions are mentioned in Stan Larson, "The 26th Edition of the Nestle-Aland *Novum Testamentum Graece*: A Limited Examination of Its Apparatus," *JSNT* 12 (1981): 53–68; and in Wisselink, *Assimilation as a Criterion*, 108–19.

for. In some cases introductory matters for the use of apparatuses obscure the text-critical problems that are latent in them. I turn now to this issue.

2. The Presentation of Variants as an Element of Text-Critical Work.

In 1 Cor 6:5 an addition to the text is mentioned. The NA²⁶ quotes in the apparatus the reading of several translations—(f), (g) (= *proximum et*), sy^p, bo^ms—for [retranslated back into Greek] και του αδελφου. None of the editions named in note 1 read the addition as the text.³¹

Günther Zuntz and Neville A. Birdsall have advocated the view that supposedly the printed text is corrupt.³² If this is, indeed, an old corruption, the presentation in the apparatus needs to be changed. The apparatus would then contain no addition, as the symbol ⊤ suggests. Rather, και του αδελφου would be the original text, which the entire Greek tradition would have lost due to homoioteleuton, and we would have to read: ανα μεσον του αδελφου και του αδελφου αυτου.

In Matt 4:17 old Syriac witnesses and an old Latin witness exhibit a shorter form of the text in contrast with the Greek manuscript tradition. k sy^s.c Justin Clement Origen Euseb Victor of Antioch leave out the words μετανοειτε and γαρ, and read: ηηγγικεν η βασιλεια των ουρανων. All editions, including *The Greek New Testament* (5th ed.) and NA²⁶ as well as NA²⁸ and Michael W. Holmes, *Greek New Testament: SBL Edition*, print the longer text: μετανοειτε, ηγγικεν γαρ η βασιλεια των ουρανων.³³ Bruce M. Metzger gives the grounds for the text-critical decision: "The unanimity of the Greek evidence, as well as the overwhelming testimony of the rest of the versional and patristic witnesses, seemed to the Committee to require that the words be retained in the text."³⁴ Metzger cites the opposite opinion that 4:17 was secondarily assimilated to 3:2. F. C. Burkitt had advocated this reading energetically: "What right [have we] to reject the oldest Syriac and oldest Latin when they agree?"³⁵ Birdsall also advocated this text. Brooke

---

31. NA²⁶, 448.
32. Günther Zuntz, *The Text of the Epistles: A Disquisition upon the Corpus Paulinum*, Schweich Lectures of the British Academy, 1953 (London: Cumberlege, 1953), 15; Birdsall "New Testament Text," 375.
33. NA²⁸, 8.
34. Metzger, *Textual Commentary*, 10.
35. F. C. Burkitt, "Introduction," in *The Biblical Text of Clement of Alexandria*

Foss Westcott and Fenton John Anthony Hort took the reading as weighty enough to acknowledge its status as an "alternative reading."[36]

If this shorter text is original, the identification of this reading in the apparatus as an omission would be incorrect. Instead, the text as printed by most editions would contain a secondary addition.

Among exegetes it is a controversial question whether the explanatory comment in John 4:9 goes back to a redaction of the original text of the gospel or whether we have to do here with an addition from a later transmission. The words ου γαρ συγχρωνται Ιουδαιοι Σαμαριταις are missing in the witnesses ℵ* D it^{abdej} cop^{fajj}. Birdsall paraphrases "Jews do not use the same vessels as Samaritans" and designates the text as an "expansion."[37] Alongside numerous other witnesses, the papyri P[63, 66, 75, 76] support the printed text, which at least would speak for the age of this potential "insertion." Tischendorf decided for the reading of Codex Sinaiticus ℵ; Westcott and Hort printed the text in brackets, whereby the variant is designated as an "alternative reading"; Nestle-Aland likewise put it in brackets, which indicated uncertainty about the originality of the text.[38]

In many cases an edition makes a decision quite unambiguous when it indicates in the apparatus that a witness changes the word order. Sometimes the question arises as to whether a manuscript or group of witnesses actually alters the arrangement. Is it not rather that the printed text is incorrect and needs to be corrected according to the manuscripts?

Birdsall discussed an impressive example of word order that is perhaps original as suggested by Burkitt. In Mark 10:11–12 we read Jesus's abrupt judgment about divorce. The parallel events of a divorce by the husband (ος αν απολυση) and a divorce by the wife (και εαν αυτη απολυσασα) are expressed in sequence. Both condemnations of divorce have the form of generally valid legal statements of casuistic law. A few old witnesses surprise the textual critic with a striking arrangement: εαν απολυση γυνη τον ανδρα αυτης και γαμηση αλλον μοιχαται. και εαν ανηρ απολυση την γυναικα

---

in the Four Gospels and the Acts of the Apostles, ed. P. Mordaunt Barnard, TS 5.5 (Cambridge: Cambridge University Press, 1899): xix.

36. Birdsall, "New Testament Text," 330; Brooke Foss Westcott and Fenton John Anthony Hort, eds., *The New Testament in the Original Greek*, vol. 2, *Introduction: Appendix* (Cambridge: Macmillan, 1881): 275.

37. Birdsall, "New Testament Text," 375.

38. Tischendorf, *Novum Testamentum Graece*, 772; Westcott and Hort, *New Testament in the Original Greek*, 2:291; NA[26], 6*.

μοιχαται W 1 sy^s. This seems to suggest an understanding of the text according to which Jesus does not want to engage in the discussion by his contemporaries about divorce. Birdsall interprets the statement rather as a clear reference to the behavior of the Tetrarch Herod Antipas, who had married the wife of his half-brother, and whose behavior John the Baptizer had criticized earlier. "For this criticism Jesus' forerunner John the Baptist had met his death. Jesus continues the attack, bringing home the point by this striking reversal of the normal 'order of precedence', and perhaps suggesting (as does the story of John the Baptist's execution) that Herodias was the stronger-willed of the two."[39]

One manuscript omits a verse, another has an insertion. If the editor has made the right judgment, his or her specification is correct. But if this is not the case, the text needs to be corrected according to the reading in the apparatus. In my opinion, if doubts are possible or appropriate, it would be more correct to express them in the apparatus: "Reading in the apparatus: perhaps original."

In New Testament scholarship tradition varies over how to indicate such possibly original readings in the apparatus.[40] A critic of NA[26] has severely criticized this edition, because it unjustifiably gave up this tradition.[41] Be that as it may, I think that an editor should consider this point carefully.

---

39. J. Neville Birdsall, "Textual Criticism and New Testament Studies: An Inaugural Lecture Delivered in the University of Birmingham on 10 May 1984," paper presented at Birmingham University, 10 May, 1984, 6.

40. Johann Albrecht Bengel, ed., *Η ΚΑΙΝΗ ΔΙΑΘΗΚΗ: Novum Testamentum Graecum* (Tübingen: Berger, 1734), title page verso; Johann Jacob Griesbach, ed., *Η ΚΑΙΝΗ ΔΙΑΘΗΚΗ: Novum Testamentum Graece*, 4 vols. (Leipzig: Göschen, 1803–1807), xix; Nestle and Nestle, *Novum Testamentum Graece*, 13th ed., 19*–22*. In the thirteenth through sixteenth editions, a symbol ◊ was used with which individual readings were marked. "Such readings and conjectures, which according to widespread opinion have special claim to originality, are distinguished by the symbol ◊ placed before it" (Nestle and Nestle, *Novum Testamentum Graece*, 16th ed., 8*). In the place of this the twentieth through twenty-fifth editions used the "!" symbol. Aland et al., *Greek New Testament*, xii–xiii, follow the tradition of Bengel and Griesbach. Here the subjective certainty of text-critical decisions can be measured with the use of an alphabetical system.

41. Rykle Borger, "NA[26] und die neutestamentliche Textkritik," *ThR* 52 (1987): 10.

3. The Design of the Apparatus Is Directly Dependent on the Reconstruction of the Text

At the beginning of the twentieth century the number of known New Testament variants was estimated to be around 150,000.[42] Nestle-Aland, 26th ed., conveys about 15,000 variants in the apparatus.[43] *The Greek New Testament*,[44] under the responsibility of the same editors, prints considerably more substantial lists of witnesses, but on the other hand deals with only about 1,440 variants.[45] In addition, the text-critical commentary accompanying this volume, which gives reasons for the decisions of the editors, discusses additionally about 600 variants.[46] Since the beginning of the twentieth century, the number of known variants has grown considerably.

How many known variants should be included in an apparatus?

(1) Of course all variants must appear that are claimed by other editors to be the original text.[47]

(2) Variants should definitely appear which are represented in the literature of the discipline as possibly original or that the editors themselves assess as possibly original.

(3) Readings that can contribute to the reasoning for decisions of the editors have to be included, especially when it becomes transparent thereby which reading stood at the beginning of the later development of the text.

(4) In any case, a significant selection of readings that do not come into question as the original text should be included. This serves the purpose of textual criticism. It is essential for the critic to be able to review the most important manuscripts reasonably, and this includes the possibility

---

42. E. Nestle, *Einführung in das griechische Neue Testament*, 3rd ed. (Göttingen: Vandenhoeck & Ruprecht, 1909), 17-18.

43. K. Aland, "Der neue 'Standard Text' in seinem Verhältnis zu den frühen Papyri und Majuskeln," in Epp and Fee, *New Testament Textual Criticism*, 257.

44. Aland, *Greek New Testament*, see above, 121 note 1.

45. J. Keith Elliott, "The Third Edition of the United Bible Societies' Greek New Testament," *NovT* 17 (1978): 242-77.

46. Elliott, "Textual Commentary Evaluated," 130; Metzger, *Textual Commentary*.

47. Huck-Greeven fulfilled this desideratum, Huck-Greeven, xi. Greeven used the symbol • for such readings.

of ascertaining the scope of their idiosyncrasies.⁴⁸ Obviously a knowledge of the tendencies in the development of individual streams of textual transmission is no longer possible if the apparatuses filter out too many of the variants or include them too seldom.

(5) The errors of the copyists should also appear in the apparatuses. The mistakes that are made are characteristic of certain regions and periods.⁴⁹ An essential part of New Testament textual criticism was curtailed by leaving errors out of the apparatuses, that is, what an older tradition, following Louis Havet, called *"critique verbale."*⁵⁰

Detailed apparatuses, such as are available in the volumes published by the International Greek New Testament Project⁵¹ or in the series Das Neue Testament auf Papyrus of the Institut für neutestamentliche Textforschung,⁵² are indispensable for an adequate preservation of the standards of research. In addition they serve directly the project of an Editio critica maior Novi Testamenti, which has not been implemented to date.⁵³

As we have seen, an edited text and variant apparatuses provide together a context for interpretation to be considered methodologically. What recommendations result from this understanding for the design of the apparatuses?

---

48. Ernest C. Colwell formulated principles for eliminating variants, *Studies in Methodology in Textual Criticism of the New Testament*, NTTS 9 (Leiden: Brill, 1969), 96–105.

49. Cf. Colwell, *Studies in Methodology*, 106–24. Francis Thomas Gignac, "Phonological Phenomena in the Greek Papyri Significant for the Text and Language of the New Testament," in *To Touch the Text: Biblical and Related Studies in Honor of Joseph A. Fitzmyer*, ed. Maurya P. Horgan and Paul J. Kobelski (New York: Crossroad, 1989), 33–46.

50. Léon Vaganay, *Initiation à la critique textuelle du Nouveau Testament*, rev. Christian-Bernard Amphoux, 2nd ed. (Paris: Cerf, 1986), 87–98.

51. Birdsall and Elliott, *New Testament in Greek*.

52. Winfried Grunewald and Klaus Junack, *Das Neue Testament auf Papyrus, I: Die Katholischen Briefe*, ANTF 6 (Berlin: de Gruyter, 1986); Klaus Junack et al., *Das Neue Testament auf Papyrus, II: Die paulinischen Briefe, Teil 1, Röm., 1 Kor., 2. Kor.*, ANTF 12 (Berlin: de Gruyter, 1989).

53. Aland and Aland, *Text of the New Testament*, 34. In the meantime the volumes of the Catholic Epistles (1st ed., 1997–2005; 2nd ed., 2013) and Acts (2017) have appeared.

Recommendation 1: To Designate Witnesses and Counterwitnesses

In including variants in the apparatus, it is expedient to convey not only the witnesses for these readings, but also the witnesses for the printed text. Only in this way is it possible to recognize to a sufficient degree which witnesses support the editor for his printed text. This methodologically important requirement is fulfilled throughout by the edition of the United Bible Societies.[54] Admittedly, as already stated, this edition documents only a relatively small number of the known variants.[55] What the adoption of this recommendation means may be illustrated by a text-critical work that has not yet been published. In order to be able to investigate text-critically and with statistical methods the language of the Pauline texts with respect to their usage of asyndeton, it was necessary in fifty-one cases to compile laboriously from individual editions of Greek manuscripts all the witnesses of the finally approved readings.[56]

Because the ancient church copied the gospels more frequently than the Pauline epistles, considerably more variants are referred to in the apparatuses of the Synoptic Gospels than in the apparatuses of other New Testament writings. However, it is not on the basis of the state of the sources that in NA[26] textual witnesses and counterwitnesses for the Synoptic Gospels are listed in more than 50 percent of all cases of variation, whereas by contrast in other New Testament writings counterwitnesses are printed in less than 25 percent of all cases. To this day text-critical research results in increased interest in the Synoptic Gospels to the neglect of other New Testament writings.

---

54. Aland, *Greek New Testament*. This important requirement goes back to the German New Testament Congress, Breslau 1926, cf. K. Aland, review of *Luke*, 494.

55. Elliott, "Third Edition"; Elliott, "Textual Commentary Evaluated"; Metzger, *Textual Commentary*.

56. "One important new development in the apparatus is that for the first time in a Nestle edition the manuscripts for and against the text are given." J. Keith Elliott, "An Examination of the Twenty-Sixth Edition of the Nestle-Aland *Novum Testamentum Graece*," *JTS* 32 (1981): 24. The text-critical work mentioned in the text above was published in the meantime: Eberhard W. Güting and David L. Mealand, *Asyndeton in Paul: A Text-Critical and Statistical Enquiry into Pauline Style*, SBEC 39 (Lewiston, NY: Mellen, 1998).

5. The Editorial Account as a Commentary

Recommendation 2: To Provide a Structure for Variants to Be Presented

In the history of New Testament editions, editing approaches may be recognized that separate important variants from those considered less important. In his edition of the text Hermann von Soden printed two apparatuses, one below the other, whereby the more weighty readings were collected in the upper apparatus.[57] The apparatus of the *Greek New Testament* of the United Bible Societies, already recommended, from the first sharply cut its variant matter. Only such readings that in the view of Bible translators and revision committees contained substantial alternatives are supplied with an apparatus—though these certainly are comprehensive. One can also interpret the abandonment of counterwitnesses in the apparatuses of NA[26] as such a choice. However, an apparatus composed in this way does not facilitate research.

A further procedure to emphasize substantial variants consists of a system of coded letters of the alphabet, which Johann Albrecht Bengel used early on and which today is used once again in *The Greek New Testament*.[58] Of course an edition that emphasizes weighty alternatives to the text exposes itself to criticism. But on account of the abundance of transmitted variants it is to be welcomed when work on the text is supported in this manner.[59]

Scrutiny of the transmission process is aided by distinguishing variants from subvariants. A series of publications of the Institut für neutestamentliche Textforschung in Münster organizes variants by means of a numerical system according to their proximity to what is considered to be the original text and arranges subvariants by letters of the alphabet appended to the main variants.[60]

Recommendation 3: To Avoid Separating Variants That Belong Together

Often two or more individual variants are found in combination with one another in such a way that a change in the text leads to further changes in

---

57. Von Soden, *Schriften des Neuen Testaments*.
58. See Aland, *Greek New Testament*, xii–xiii.
59. Elliott dismisses the evaluation system as useless, see "Third Edition," 274.
60. Kurt Aland, ed., *Text und Textwert der griechischen Handschriften des Neuen Testaments, I: Die katholischen Briefe*, 3 vols., ANTF 9–11 (Berlin: de Gruyter, 1987).

another closely related passage. From this the recommendation arises not to isolate variants that belong together but to present them in correlation with each other. In this way in numerous passages one can make clear which text was the starting point for generating the variants.

In 2 Cor 5:20, for instance, the apparatus of the NA^{26} links D* F G *add* ὅν and P^{46} D* F G b Origen *om* οὖν. Actually both readings have a relevant connection with each other. I am of the opinion that the οὖν is a secondary addition. Also witnesses that have removed the relative pronoun ὅν, which is original, do not provide οὖν. The οὖν required a certain amount of time until it made its way into texts in general. The form of the text that eventually became accepted in the manuscript tradition provides a more effective, quotable text with an independent main clause. It is an asset of this recommended edition that in numerous passages it emphasizes the connection of variants linked to one another.[61]

Recommendation 4: Not to Allow Individual Witnesses to Disappear in Sigla for Groups of Manuscripts

From the beginning of the twentieth century, especially through the work of Eberhard Nestle, the procedure for composing text-critical apparatuses has become established: not to refer to individual manuscripts as witnesses, but with the help of sigla representing associated manuscripts to cite large groups of manuscripts. This procedure seems obvious in view of the still-growing inventory of manuscripts. The space required is enormously reduced and the overview is made easier. Thus one can write "it"

---

61. "I want to follow to the best of my ability a very important suggestion of Schmiedel's, although I still do not see clearly how far it will be possible for me to do so. He finds that the readings that Tischendorf specified frequently are much shorter, 'truncated,' than is necessary and practical. His suggestion would be to formulate the readings as long as possible. The longest reading should come first, in order to facilitate an overview. One could compare this with the parliamentary procedure to bring to a vote the most extensive motion first. Longer readings have the advantage, sometimes at least, to simplify and abbreviate the details of the witnesses. Schmiedel gives as examples Gal 5:1 τῇ ἐλευθερίᾳ ἡμᾶς Χριστὸς ἠλευθέρωσεν. στήκετε οὖν as a reading and Matt 21:29–31 οὐ θέλω … ὁ πρῶτος as a reading. Further, often a longer reading prevents the user from connecting two short readings that are not to be accepted together." Caspar-René Grégory, *Vorschläge für eine kritische Ausgabe des griechischen Neuen Testaments* (Leipzig: Hinrichs, 1911), 28.

[Itala = Old Latin] instead of a list of Itala manuscripts or "sa" instead of a list of Sahidic manuscripts. Greeven further developed this procedure by introducing special brackets. The counterwitnesses, which fall outside their group because of a different text, are mentioned within inequality signs < >.[62]

This procedure in all its forms leads to considerable disadvantages for text-critical work. The most serious defect of this procedure stems from the fact that in many passages the great text types are split up. The Alexandrian tradition, just as the so-called Western text, but also the Byzantine koine disintegrate again and again in individual witnesses, sometimes in two equally strong converging groups. The use of signs such as 𝕳 𝔐 𝔎 in such places is misleading. The details of the dissident texts would often result in an extremely long list.

The NA[26], which works with only one such sign, 𝔐 [majority text], uses concurrently a system of constant witnesses. In passages where witnesses and counterwitnesses are specified, a number of the witnesses are no longer mentioned as long as they go along with the Byzantine type of text: they disappear under the sign 𝔐.[63] Unfortunately this also occurs with witnesses that have nothing to do with the majority text, such as the minuscule 1739. Witnesses that disappear in 𝔐 are difficult to keep an eye on. Thus, it is reasonable that in the apparatus of the synopsis alongside the sign 𝔐 a group of constant witnesses appears, which indeed only display the Byzantine text, but which for the sake of the overview in addition to the sign 𝔐 are listed in square brackets.[64]

For the rest, a clear trend toward reduction of the number of group signs is discernible. The twenty-sixth edition of Nestle-Aland abandoned the sign 𝕳 used in earlier editions. Indeed, the *Synopsis* of Marie-Emile Boismard and Arnaud Lamouille is based on the apparatuses of von Soden but does not use his sigla. Only the symbol Koinè is utilized.[65] Greeven in his synopsis used the sign 𝕳.[66]

---

62. Huck-Greeven, 15.
63. NA[26], 10*, English 47*.
64. NA[26], vi. These are E/07, F/09, G/011, H/013.
65. Marie-Emile Boismard and Arnaud Lamouille, *Synopsis Graeca quattuor evangeliorum* (Leuven: Peeters, 1986), 1, etc.
66. Huck-Greeven, xix.

Recommendation 5: To Designate Alternatives to the Text

In the Anglo-Saxon world a much celebrated and repeatedly printed text was edited by the Englishmen Westcott and Hort, first published in 1881.[67] This edition distinguished itself by means of a commentary volume that accompanied the text. The editors committed themselves, independently from one another and in writing, to decisions that as such went into the reconstruction of the text.

The text produced in this way and supported by a new theory of the text presents marginal readings that were to be regarded as equally valued alternatives to the text. These marginal readings are not only listed in reprints until today, but have also been cited as such up to the twenty-fifth edition of the Nestle-Aland and again in the SBL edition edited by Holmes (2010).

From the perspective of a critical apparatus, alternatives to the text are those readings that the editor holds to be so. They should be marked as such. The copious use of brackets [ ] in *The Greek New Testament* and in NA[26] is not the best way to identify these passages, because brackets are often used to designate secondary portions of the text.[68] By contrast one can recommend Greeven's procedure explained above, because he emphasized variants that other editors print as the text with the mark •.[69]

In a phase of New Testament scholarship in which the assessment of witnesses and the constitution of the text are weighed down by too many and too great uncertainties, it must become an absolute requirement that apparatuses are presented in a form which has been methodically well designed.

Addendum

On principle Epp did not want readings that appear only once to be included in apparatuses.[70] If this stipulation were to be taken seriously,

---

67. Brooke Foss Westcott and Fenton John Anthony Hort, eds., *The New Testament in the Original Greek: Vol. 1, Text* (Cambridge: Macmillan, 1881).

68. J. Keith Elliott, "The Use of Brackets in the Text of the United Bible Societies' Greek New Testament," *Bib* 60 (1979): 575–77.

69. Huck-Greeven, xi.

70. Elcon J. Epp, "Toward the Clarification of the Term 'Textual Variant,'" in *Studies in New Testament Language and Text: Essays in Honour of George Kilpatrick on the Occasion of His Sixty-Fifth Birthday*, ed. J. Keith Elliott, NovTSup 44

not just a few correct readings would be eliminated from apparatuses. The original conclusion of Galatians (without ἀμήν with G) and of Hebrews (ἡ χάρις μετὰ πάντων with P⁴⁶*) would then be lost for text-critical research. Readings that clarify the early history of the development of the text should, in my, opinion not be eliminated from apparatuses.

Bibliography

Aland, Barbara, Kurt Aland, Johannes Karavidopoulos, Carlo Maria Martini, and Bruce Metzger, eds. *The Greek New Testament*. 5th ed. Stuttgart: Deutsche Bibelgesellschaft; United Bible Societies, 2014. [UBS⁵]

———, eds. *Novum Testamentum Graece*. 28th ed. Stuttgart: Deutsche Bibelgesellschaft, 2012. [NA²⁸]

Aland, Kurt. *Kurzgefasste Liste der griechischen Handschriften des Neuen Testaments, I: Gesamtübersicht*. ANTF 1. Berlin: de Gruyter, 1963.

———. "Der neue 'Standard Text' in seinem Verhältnis zu den frühen Papyri und Majuskeln." Pages 257–75 in *New Testament Textual Criticism: Its Significance for Exegesis; Essays in Honour of Bruce M. Metzger*. Edited by Eldon J. Epp and Gordon D. Fee. Oxford: Clarendon, 1981.

———, ed., *Synopsis Quattuor Evangeliorum*. 15th rev. ed. Stuttgart: Deutsche Bibelgesellschaft, 1997.

———, ed., *Text und Textwert der griechischen Handschriften des Neuen Testaments, I: Die katholischen Briefe*. 3 vols. ANTF 9–11. Berlin: de Gruyter, 1987.

———. "The Twentieth Century Interlude in New Testament Textual Criticism." Pages 1–14 in *Text and Interpretation: Studies in the New Testament Presented to Matthew Black*. Edited by Robert M. Wilson and Ernest Best. Cambridge: Cambridge University Press, 1979.

———. Review of *Luke*, the International Greek New Testament Project. *Gnomon* 56 (1984): 481–97.

(Leiden: Brill, 1976), 173: "When is a 'reading' a 'variant'? When the reading is a 'significant' reading by virtue of its appropriateness as a possibly original reading. And how is a variant thus fit and appropriate? By virtue of its character as a reading that makes sense, that is not an undisputably demonstrable scribal error, that is not a mere orthographic difference, and that is not a singular reading." Philip W. Comfort follows him ("The Greek Text of the Gospel of John According to the Early Papyri," *NTS* 36 [1990]: 626).

Aland, Kurt, and Barbara Aland. *The Text of the New Testament: An Introduction to the Critical Editions and to the Theory and Practice of Modern Textual Criticism*. 2nd ed. Grand Rapids: Eerdmans; Leiden: Brill, 1989.

———. *The Text of the New Testament*. 2nd ed. Stuttgart: Deutsche Bibelgesellschaft, 2006.

Aland, Kurt, Matthew Black, Carlo Maria Martini, Bruce M. Metzger, Allen Wikgren, eds. *Novum Testamentum Graece*. 26th ed. Stuttgart: Deutsche Bibelgesellschaft, 1979; rev. printing 1983. [NA^{26}]

Aland, Kurt, with Michael Welte, Beate Köster, and Klaus Junack. *Kurzgefasste Liste der griechischen Handschriften des Neuen Testaments*. 2nd ed. ANTF 1. Berlin: de Gruyter, 1994.

Bengel, Johann Albrecht, ed. *Η ΚΑΙΝΗ ΔΙΑΘΗΚΗ: Novum Testamentum Graecum*. Tübingen: Berger, 1734.

Bentley, Richard. *Dr. Richard Bentley's Proposals for Printing a New Edition of the Greek Testament, and St. Hieronymos's Latin Version*. London: Knapton, 1721.

Birdsall, J. Neville. "The New Testament Text." Pages 308–77 in *From the Beginnings to Jerome*. Vol. 1 of *The Cambridge History of the Bible*. Edited by P. R. Ackroyd, C. F. Evans, G. W. H. Lampe, and S. L. Greenslade. Cambridge: Cambridge University Press, 1970.

———. "Textual Criticism and New Testament Studies: An Inaugural Lecture Delivered in the University of Birmingham on 10 May 1984." Paper presented at Birmingham University, 10 May, 1984.

Black, David Alan. *Rethinking New Testament Textual Criticism*. Grand Rapids: Baker Academic, 2002.

Black, Matthew, and Robert Davidson, eds. *Constantin von Tischendorf and the Greek New Testament*. Glasgow: University of Glasgow Press, 1981.

Boismard, Marie-Emile, and Arnaud Lamouille. *Synopsis Graeca quattuor evangeliorum*. Leuven: Peeters, 1986.

Borger, Rykle. "NA^{26} und die neutestamentliche Textkritik." *ThR* 52 (1987): 1–58.

Bover, José Maria, ed. *Novi Testamenti Biblia Graeca et Latina*. 5th ed. Madrid: Consejo Superior de Investigaciones Cientificas, 1968.

———. *Novi Testamenti Biblia Graeca et Latina*. Madrid: Consejo Superior de Investigaciones Cientificas, 1943.

Bover, José Maria, and José O'Callaghan, eds. *Nuevo Testamento Trilingüe*. Madrid: Biblioteca de Autores Cristianos, 1977.

———, eds., *Nuevo Testamento Trilingüe*. 2nd ed. Madrid: Biblioteca de Autores Cristianos, 1988.
Burkitt, F. C. "Introduction." In *The Biblical Text of Clement of Alexandria in the Four Gospels and the Acts of the Apostles*. Edited by P. Mordaunt Barnard. TS 5.5. Cambridge: Cambridge University Press, 1899.
Colwell, Ernest C. *Studies in Methodology in Textual Criticism of the New Testament*. NTTS 9. Leiden: Brill, 1969.
Comfort, Philip W. "The Greek Text of the Gospel of John According to the Early Papyri." *NTS* 36 (1990): 625–29.
Ehrman, Bart D. " Methodological Developments in the Analysis and Classification of New Testament Documentary Evidence." *NovT* 29 (1987): 22–45.
Ehrman, Bart D., and Michael W. Holmes, eds. *The Text of the New Testament in Contemporary Research: Essays on the Status Quaestionis*. 2nd ed. NTTS 42. Leiden: Brill, 2013.
Elliott, J. Keith. *A Bibliography of Greek New Testament Manuscripts*. 3rd ed. NovTSup 160. Leiden: Brill, 2014.
———. "The Citation of Greek Manuscripts in Six Printed Texts of the New Testament." *RB* 92 (1985): 539–56.
———. "The Citation of Manuscripts in Recent Printed Editions of the Greek New Testament." *NovT* 25 (1983): 97–132.
———. "An Eclectic Textual Commentary on the Greek Text of Mark's Gospel." Pages 47–60 in *New Testament Textual Criticism: Its Significance for Exegesis; Essays in Honour of Bruce M. Metzger*. Edited by Eldon J. Epp and Gordon D. Fee. Oxford: Clarendon, 1981. Repr., pages 159–70 in *Essays and Studies in New Testament Textual Criticism*. Edited by J. Keith Elliott. EFNT 3. Cordoba: El Almendro, 1992.
———. "An Examination of the Twenty-Sixth Edition of the Nestle-Aland *Novum Testamentum Graece*." *JTS* 32 (1981): 19–49.
———. "Mathētēs with a Possessive in the New Testament." *TZ* 35 (1979): 300–304.
———. "Old Latin Manuscripts in Printed Editions of the Greek New Testament." *NovT* 26 (1984): 225–48.
———. *A Survey of Manuscripts Used in Editions of the Greek New Testament*. NovTSup 57. Leiden: Brill, 1987.
———. "Textual Criticism, Assimilation and the Synoptic Gospels." *NTS* 26 (1980): 231–41.
———. "The Third Edition of the United Bible Societies' Greek New Testament," *NovT* 17 (1978): 242–77.

———. "The United Bible Societies' Textual Commentary Evaluated." *NovT* 17 (1975): 130–50.

———. "The Use of Brackets in the Text of the United Bible Societies' Greek New Testament." *Bib* 60 (1979): 575–77.

Epp, Eldon J. "A Continuing Interlude in New Testament Textual Criticism?" *HTR* 73 (1980): 131–51.

———. "The Eclectic Method in New Testament Textual Criticism: Solution or Symptom?" *HTR* 69 (1976): 211–57. Repr., pages 141–73 in *Studies in the Theory and Method of New Testament Textual Criticism*. Edited by Eldon J. Epp and Gordon D. Fee. SD 45. Grand Rapids: Eerdmans, 1993.

———. "Textual Criticism." Pages 72–126 in *The New Testament and Its Modern Interpreters*. Edited by Eldon J. Epp and George W. MacRae. SBLCP. Philadelphia: Fortress; Atlanta: Scholars Press, 1989.

———. "Toward the Clarification of the Term 'Textual Variant.'" Pages 153–73 in *Studies in New Testament Language and Text: Essays in Honour of George Kilpatrick on the Occasion of His Sixty-Fifth Birthday*. Edited by J. Keith Elliott. NovTSup 44. Leiden: Brill, 1976. Repr., pages 47–61 in *Studies in the Theory and Method of New Testament Textual Criticism*. Edited by Eldon J. Epp and Gordon D. Fee. SD 45. Grand Rapids: Eerdmans, 1993.

———. "The Twentieth Century Interlude in New Testament Textual Criticism." *JBL* 93 (1974): 386–414.

Fee, Gordon D. "The Majority Text and the Original Text of the New Testament." *BT* 31 (1980): 107–18.

———. "Modern Text Criticism and the Synoptic Problem." Pages 154–69 in *J. J. Griesbach: Synoptic and Text-Critical Studies 1776–1976*. Edited by Bernard Orchard and Thomas R. W. Longstaff. SNTSMS 34. Cambridge: Cambridge University Press, 1978.

———. "Origen's Text of the New Testament and the Text of Egypt." *NTS* 28 (1982): 348–64.

———. "Rigorous or Reasoned Eclecticism—Which?" Pages 174–97 in *Studies in New Testament Language and Text: Essays in Honour of George Kilpatrick on the Occasion of His Sixty-Fifth Birthday*. Edited by J. Keith Elliott. NovTSup 44. Leiden: Brill, 1976.

———. "A Text-Critical Look at the Synoptic Problem." *NovT* 22 (1980): 12–28.

Fee, Gordon D., revised by Roderic L. Mullen. "The Use of the Greek Fathers for New Testament Textual Criticism." Pages 351–73 in *The*

Text of the New Testament in Contemporary Research: Essays on the Status Quaestionis. Edited by Bart D. Ehrman and Michael W. Holmes. 2nd ed. NTTS 42. Leiden, Boston: Brill, 2013.

Fischer, Bonafatius, ed., *Die lateinischen Evangelien bis zum 10. Jahrhundert, IV: Varianten zu Johannes.* AGLB 18. Freiburg im Breisgau: Herder, 1991.

Gignac, Francis Thomas. "Phonological Phenomena in the Greek Papyri Significant for the Text and Language of the New Testament." Pages 33–46 in *To Touch the Text: Biblical and Related Studies in Honor of Joseph A. Fitzmyer.* Edited by Maurya P. Horgan and Paul J. Kobelski. New York: Crossroad, 1989.

Grégory, Caspar-René. *Vorschläge für eine kritische Ausgabe des griechischen Neuen Testaments.* Leipzig: Hinrichs, 1911.

Griesbach, Johann Jacob, ed., *Η ΚΑΙΝΗ ΔΙΑΘΗΚΗ: Novum Testamentum Graece.* 4 vols. Leipzig: Göschen, 1803–1807.

Grunewald, Winfried, and Klaus Junack. *Das Neue Testament auf Papyrus, I: Die Katholischen Briefe.* ANTF 6. Berlin: de Gruyter, 1986.

Güting, Eberhard W. "Amen, Eulogie, Doxologie: Eine textkritische Untersuchung." Pages 131–62 in *Begegnungen zwischen Christentum und Judentum in Antike und Mittelalter: Festschrift für Heinz Schreckenberg.* Edited by Dietrich-Alex Koch and Hermann Lichtenberger. SIJD 1. Göttingen: Vandenhoeck & Ruprecht, 1993. [Ch. 4 in this collection.]

Güting, Eberhard W., and David L. Mealand. *Asyndeton in Paul: A Text-Critical and Statistical Enquiry into Pauline Style.* SBEC 39. Lewiston, NY: Mellen, 1998.

Hodges, Zane C., and Arthur L. Farstad, eds. *The Greek New Testament According to the Majority Text.* Nashville: Nelson, 1982.

Holmes, Michael W., ed. *The Greek New Testament: SBL Edition.* Atlanta: Society of Biblical Literature; Bellingham, WA: Logos Bible Software, 2010.

Huck, Albert, ed. *Synopsis of the First Three Gospels with the Addition of the Johannine Parallels.* Rev. by Heinrich Greeven. 13th ed. Tübingen: Mohr, 1981.

Hurtado, Larry. *Text-Critical Methodology and the Pre-Caesarean Text: Codex W in the Gospel of Mark.* Grand Rapids: Eerdmans, 1981.

Junack, Klaus, Eberhard Güting, Ulrich Nimtz, and Klaus Witte. *Das Neue Testament auf Papyrus, II: Die paulinischen Briefe, Teil 1, Röm., 1 Kor., 2. Kor.* ANTF 12 Berlin: de Gruyter, 1989.

Kilpatrick, George Dunbar, ed. *Η ΚΑΙΝΗ ΔΙΑΘΗΚΗ*. 2nd ed. London: British and Foreign Bible Society, 1958.

———. *Mark: A Greek-English Diglot for the Use of Translators*. London: British and Foreign Bible Society, 1958.

Lachmann, Karl. "Rechenschaft über seine Ausgabe des Neuen Testaments von Professor Lachmann in Berlin." *TSK* 3 (1830): 817–45.

Larson, Stan. "The 26th Edition of the Nestle-Aland *Novum Testamentum Graece*: A Limited Examination of Its Apparatus." *JSNT* 12 (1981): 53–68.

Mace, Daniel. *The New Testament in Greek and English: Containing the Original Text Corrected from the Authority of the Most Authentic Manuscripts; And a New Version Form'd Agreeably to the Illustrations of the Most Learned Commentators and Critics; With Notes and Various Readings, and a Copious Alphabetical Index*. 2 vols. London: Roberts, 1729.

Merk, August, ed. *Novum Testamentum Graece et Latine*. Rome: Pontifical Biblical Institute, 1933.

———, ed. *Novum Testamentum Graece et Latine*. 9th ed. Rome: Pontifical Biblical Institute, 1964.

Metzger, Bruce M. *Manuscripts of the Greek Bible: An Introduction to Greek Palaeography*. New York: Oxford University Press, 1981.

———. *A Textual Commentary on the Greek New Testament: A Companion Volume to the United Bible Societies' Greek New Testament (Fourth Revised Edition)*. 2nd ed. Stuttgart: Deutsche Bibelgesellschaft, 1994.

Metzger, Bruce M., and Bart D. Ehrman, eds. *The Text of the New Testament: Its Transmission, Corruption, and Restoration*. 4th ed. Oxford: Oxford University Press, 2005.

Nestle, Eberhard. *Einführung in das griechische Neue Testament*. 3rd ed. Göttingen: Vandenhoeck & Ruprecht, 1909.

———, ed., *Novum Testamentum Graece*. Stuttgart: Württembergische Bibelanstalt, 1898.

Nestle, Eberhard, and Erwin Nestle, eds. *Novum Testamentum Graece*. 13th ed. Stuttgart: Württembergische Bibelanstalt, 1927.

Nestle, Erwin, and Kurt Aland, eds. *Novum Testamentum Graece*. 25th ed. London: United Bible Societies, 1963.

The New Testament in Greek: The Gospel according to St. Luke. 2 vols. Oxford: Clarendon, 1984–1987.

Nolli, Giofranco, ed. *Novum Testamentum Graece et Latine*. Città del Vaticano: Libreria Editrice Vaticana, 1981.

Parker, David C. "The Development of Textual Criticism since B. H. Streeter." *NTS* 24 (1977): 149–62.

———. *An Introduction to the New Testament Manuscripts and Their Texts*. Cambridge: Cambridge University Press, 2008.

Simon, Richard. *Histoire critique du texte du Nouveau Testament*. Rotterdam: Leers, 1689.

Soden, Hermann von, ed. *Die Schriften des Neuen Testaments in ihrer ältesten erreichbaren Textgestalt*. 4 vols. Göttingen: Vandenhoeck & Ruprecht, 1911–1913.

Tasker, R. V. G., ed. *The Greek New Testament Being the Text Translated in the New English Bible 1961: Edited with Introduction, Textual Notes, and Appendix*. Oxford: Oxford University Press; New York: Cambridge University Press, 1964.

Tischendorf, Constantin von, ed. *Novum Testamentum Graece: Ad antiquissimos testes denuo recensuit; Apparatum criticum omni studio perfectum apposuit; Commentationem Isagogicam praetexuit Constantinus Tischendorf*. 8th ed. 3 vols. Leipzig: Giesecke & Devrient, 1869–1894.

Turner, C. H. "Markan Usage: Notes, Critical and Exegetical, on the Second Gospel, V." *JTS* 26 (1925): 225–40. Repr., in *The Language and Style of the Gospel of Mark: An Edition of C. H. Turner's "Notes on Marcan Usage" Together with Other Comparable Studies*. Edited by J. Keith Elliott. NovTSup 71. Leiden: Brill, 1993.

Vaganay, Léon. *Initiation à la critique textuelle du Nouveau Testament*. Rev. by Christian-Bernard Amphoux. 2nd ed. Paris: Cerf, 1986.

Vogels, Heinrich Josef, ed. *Novum Testamentum Graece*. Düsseldorf: Schwann, 1920.

———, ed. *Novum Testamentum Graece et Latine*. 4th ed. Freiburg im Breisgau: Herder, 1955.

Weiss, Bernhard, ed. *Das Neue Testament: Textkritische Untersuchungen und Textherstellung*. 3 vols. Leipzig: Hinrichs, 1894–1900.

Westcott, Brooke Foss, and Fenton John Anthony Hort, eds. *The New Testament in the Original Greek: Volume 1, Text; Volume 2, Introduction [and] Appendix*. Cambridge: Macmillan, 1881. 2nd ed., 1896.

Wisselink, W. F. *Assimilation as a Criterion for the Establishment of the Text: A Comparative Study on the Basis of Passages from Matthew, Mark, and Luke*. Kampen: Kok, 1989.

Zuntz, Günther. *The Text of the Epistles: A Disquisition upon the Corpus Paulinum*. Schweich Lectures of the British Academy 1946. London: Oxford University Press, 1953.

6
Weakly Attested Original Readings of the Manuscript D 05 in Mark

Any reader who opens a Greek Synopsis or glances at the apparatus of a New Testament will notice before long that numerous readings of Codex Bezae and its relatives are absent from the text of Mark and are not named in its apparatus. Readings that have been recommended by notable textual critics are thus no longer discussed in our commentaries. Today I intend to concentrate on such readings of D that in my opinion have a claim to represent the original text of the author. I shall discuss only a few of the more numerous secondary readings of D, since in most cases there is no dispute among textual critics about these. Using such a procedure I do not join the partisans of D.

1. *Ars critica ad elocutionem auctoris refert*

An apt example may be found in Mark 10:1. Here D offers οχλος in the singular joined to a verb in the same number. While Matthew and Luke give reports of the gathering of crowds in singular and in plural, Mark in such contexts uses the singular of οχλος at least thirty-seven times. If the printed text of the majority of our editions were correct here, we would have to accept the sole exception to the use of οχλος in Mark's gospel. Yet the singular is found in D Θ 565, συνερχεται παλιν ο οχλος, and also (with a different verb) in W fam[13] k b c ff² i r¹ sy^s. C. H. Turner convincingly argued the originality of this reading: "Marcan usage shews conclusively that οχλος is right against οχλοι, and I have no doubt that συνερχεται παλιν ο οχλος should be read with D 565 syr-sin a b c ff i k (*conuenit turba*)."[1] George Dunbar Kilpatrick was alone in printing it.[2]

---

1. C. H. Turner, "Marcan Usage: Notes, Critical and Exegetical, on the Second

It has been known for a long time that Mark uses the connecting particles sparingly. His text abounds in asyndeta.³ Turner listed passages in which the D-tradition preserved them.⁴ This and other lists show that in the text of Mark there are far more asyndeta than the ordinary reader of an ordinary New Testament will notice. In 1:22 for instance, καὶ² is not original; D Θ e b c ff² preserve asyndeton. In 2:26 πως is an addition; B D 2427 r¹ t have asyndeton. In 7:28 ναι is secondary; it is omitted by P⁴⁵ D W Θ fam¹³ 565 700 *l* 751 *l* 890 b c d ff² i sy^s arm geo².⁵ In 10:9 ουν is an addition; here we follow D k* Clement. In 12:37 D, in company with many other manuscripts, supports asyndetic αυτος Δαυειδ λεγει αυτον κυριον; we follow ℵ B D L W Δ Θ Ψ 28 565 1342 2427 k e a c ff² i q r¹ sa.⁶ In 13:8 likewise D, in company with ℵ B L W Ψ 28 124 2427 sa, backs an asyndetic εσονται σεισμοι.⁷ Turner compared the reliability of manuscripts in preserving asyndeton.⁸ Statistically B and the Old Latin k outpass Codex Bezae in this respect. In one passage, however, D and k (together with

---

Gospel, IX," *JTS* 29 (1928): 289; repr. in *The Language and Style of the Gospel of Mark: An Edition of C. H. Turner's "Notes on Marcan Usage" Together with Other Comparable Studies*, ed. J. Keith Elliott, NovTSup 71 (Leiden: Brill, 1993), 118.

2. George Dunbar Kilpatrick, ed., *Mark: A Greek-English Diglot for the Use of Translators* (London: British and Foreign Bible Society, 1958), 25; Kilpatrick, "Πορευεσθαι and Its Compounds," *JTS* 48 (1946–1947): 63, repr. in *The Principles and Practice of New Testament Textual Criticism: Collected Essays of G. D. Kilpatrick*, ed. J. Keith Elliott, BETL 96 (Leuven: Leuven University Press, 1990), 24; J. Keith Elliott, "The United Bible Societies' Textual Commentary Evaluated," *NovT* 17 (1975): 141; Elliott, "The Relevance of Textual Criticism to the Synoptic Problem," in *The Interrelations of the Gospels*, ed. David L. Dungan, BETL 95 (Leuven: Leuven University Press, 1990), 355; repr., *Essays and Studies in New Testament Textual Criticism*, ed. J. Keith Elliott, EFNT 3 (Cordoba: El Almendro, 1992), 153–54.

3. John C. Hawkins, *Horae Synopticae: Contributions to the Study of the Synoptic Problem*, 2nd ed. (Oxford: Clarendon, 1909), 109, 137–38.

4. C. H. Turner, "Marcan Usage: Notes, Critical and Exegetical, on the Second Gospel, VII," *JTS* 28 (1926): 15–19; repr., Elliott, *Language and Style*, 74–78.

5. Heinrich Greeven and Eberhard Güting, *Textkritik des Markusevangeliums*, Theologie, Forschung und Wissenschaft 11 (Münster: LIT, 2005), 389–90; Michael W. Holmes, *The Greek New Testament: SBL Edition* (Atlanta: Society of Biblical Literature; Bellingham, WA: Logos Bible Software, 2010), 87.

6. Holmes, *Greek New Testament*, 103.

7. Greeven and Güting, *Textkritik des Markusevangeliums*, 621–22.

8. Turner, "Marcan Usage VII," 19 (=Elliott, *Language and Style*, 78).

Clement) are alone in supporting an original asyndeton: we follow them in 10:9.[9]

Turner defended the asyndeton in Mark 1:22.[10] He is so convinced of the correctness of his verdict that he uses this instance among others to demonstrate the value of D and its tradition.[11] Matthew Black also gave a list of instances where D is almost alone in presenting asyndeton.[12] I leave the question open as to whether we have to consider these readings as original: 6:26, D sa^ms (Gonzalo Aranda Perez quotes 8 13 74 114 T99); 10:41, D 64 b c ff² i r¹; 13:17, D sa^ms (Gonzalo Aranda Perez quotes 73). For in 6:26 we lack the testimony of the Afra and in 10:41 and 13:17 the African witness k casts its ballot against the asyndeton, as it does in 11:14. In 11:14, however, the originality of the asyndeton may be defended; witnesses are D 565 a q sy^s Origen.

Mark is an accomplished narrator. He is impulsive. He likes parentheses and supplementary notes. While telling tales his style is concise. His mastery in choosing tense and aspect are generally acknowledged. Not generally acknowledged is the extent of the loss that befell the transmission of his imperfects. Constatin von Tischendorf, indeed, notified those whom it might concern of this blemish of our tradition.[13] This had little effect. Whenever Mark uses ακολουθειν to describe followers and following, he does not intend to speak metaphorically. His aim is vivid impression. In 10:52, in telling of a blind man healed, he says και ευθυς ανεβλεψεν και ηκολουθει αυτω εν τω οδω. The author regularly uses the imperfect when using this verb. Tradition introduced the aorist instead in every single instance. D^gr is also among the manuscripts that transmit faulty text here (for instance, 15:41).

To demonstrate that an imperfect is original is not always easy, as in 6:12. Here, too, we read against D. Luke's text is dependent upon Mark's

---

9. G. D. Kilpatrick, in J. K. Elliott, *Language*, 184.

10. C. H. Turner, "A Textual Commentary on Mark I," *JTS* 28 (1926–1927): 153–54.

11. Turner, "Textual Commentary," 149.

12. Matthew Black, *An Aramaic Approach to the Gospels and Acts*, 3rd ed. (Oxford: Clarendon, 1968), 40–41.

13. Constantin von Tischendorf, ed., *Novum Testamentum Graece: Ad antiquissimos testes denuo recensuit; Apparatum criticum omni studio perfectum apposuit commentationem isagogicam praetexuit Constantinus Tischendorf*, 8th ed. (Leipzig: Giesecke & Devrient, 1869), 1:389, referring to Mark 15:4.

and uses διηρχοντο in 9:6 (cf. Matt 10:7). I endeavor to show that εθαυμαζεν is original in 6:6. This imperfect is not weakly attested. But ℵ D B* 565 579 2427 transmit εθαυμασεν. This form I consider to be secondary. Bernhard Weiss assumed that εθαυμαζεν is secondary here, but he did not present an argument for his view. Nor did other exegetes.[14]

Since text-critical decisions regarding this variant reading have rarely, if ever, been argued, the argumentation of Weiss is of interest to us. In his *Textkritik der vier Evangelien*, Weiss gathers instances in which a secondary tradition has replaced an original imperfect with an aorist form. This apparently occurred more than once, in order to assimilate differing forms with one another. The following imperfects are regarded as original by Weiss: 1:18, ηκολουθουν; 2:15, ηκολουθουν; 3:6, εδιδουν; 6:16, ελεγεν; 7:24, ηθελεν; 8:24, ελεγεν; 8:25, ενεβλεπεν; 9:38, ηκολουθει; 10:10, επηρωτων; 14:35, επιπτεν; 14:72, εκλαιεν; 15:12, παλιν αποκριθεις ελεγεν.

In examining these decisions we keep in mind that unfounded "minor agreements" of Matthew and Luke against Mark ought not to be accepted.[15] There are none. We follow a so-called Western reading in Luke 22:62 supported by 0171^vid e a b ff² i l r¹.[16]

---

14. Bernhard Weiss, *Textkritik der vier Evangelien*, TU 19.2 (Leipzig: Hinrichs, 1899), 62; Weiss, *Die Evangelien des Markus und Lukas*, 9th ed. (Göttingen: Vandenhoeck & Ruprecht, 1901), 90f, n. *; Marie-Joseph Lagrange, *Évangile selon Saint Marc*, 4th ed., EB (Paris: Gabalda, 1929), 148; Vincent Taylor, *The Gospel According to St. Mark: The Greek Text with Introduction, Notes and Indexes*, 2nd ed. (London: Macmillan, 1966), 301; Greeven and Güting, *Textkritik des Markusevangeliums*, 307–9. Willoughby C. Allen, however, in support of the reading of A C D L Θ 0133 fam¹ fam¹³ sy^h, called attention to the frequent imperfects in Mark, see Allen, *The Gospel According to Saint Mark* (London: Rivingtons, 1915), 47.

15. Weiss, *Textkritik der vier Evangelien*, 60–62.

16. Weiss, *Textkritik der vier Evangelien*, 60–62. On Luke 22:62 see P. L. Hedley, "The Egyptian Texts of the Gospels and Acts," *CQR* 118 (1934): 193; and Kurt Aland, "Alter und Entstehung des D-Textes im Neuen Testament: Betrachtungen zu P⁶⁹ und 0171," in *Miscellania Papirologica Ramon Roca-Puig*, ed. Sebastià Janeras (Barcelona: Fundacio Salvador Vives Casajuana, 1987), 37–61. Bruce M. Metzger, in his *A Textual Commentary on the Greek New Testament: A Companion Volume to the United Bible Societies' Greek New Testament (Fourth Revised Edition)*, 2nd ed. (Stuttgart: Deutsche Bibelgesellschaft, 1994), 151, argues for the original status of the verse Luke 22:62. In view of its attestation I am not convinced by his argument.

We disagree with Weiss in 2:14, in 9:38 (reading ος ουκ ακολουθει μεθ ημων και εκωλυομεν αυτον with D k a b c ff² Augustine), and in 10:2.[17] In 10:2 the reference to Pharisees is a secondary intrusion.[18] The assumption that in these three passages we come across assimilation within the context is unfounded.[19]

We do not argue on the supposition that in cases of diverging tradition the imperfect is always to be preferred. There are occasions where it is secondary, as Weiss is able to show in 6:56, in 14:49, and in 15:13.[20] Other passages quoted by Weiss possibly require decisions different from his verdict. For each reading we examine the attestation. Witnesses that support the imperfect forms differ from one another. But in support of original readings again and again we come across combinations that deserve a certain amount of confidence. Among them are manuscripts that in more than one passage preserve original readings, even if almost alone. Let us enlarge, then, the list of Weiss and supply the attestation:

1:18	ηκολουθουν	B 892 2427
2:14	ηκολουθει	C* W 892 fam¹
2:15	ηκολουθουν	P⁸⁸ ℵ B L Wᶜ Δ 0130 565 l r² z bo arm
3:6	εδιδουν	B L fam¹³ 28 565 700 892* 2427 2542 e b c d ff² i l q r¹ z bo^mss
6:6	εθαυμαζεν	A C D L W Θ Π fam¹ fam¹³ 33 a b c d f ff² i q r¹ z sy^s sy^h
6:12	εκηρυσσον	A W Θ fam¹ fam¹³ 33 1006 1506 a b d f ff² i l q r¹ z sy^s sy^h
6:16	ελεγεν	P⁴⁵vid ℵ B C L Δ Θ 33 892 1342 2427 f bo
6:35	ελεγον	ℵ B L Δ Θ 33 579 892 1342 2427
7:24	ηθελεν	A B D L N X Γ Θ Π c q sa sy^p
8:24	ελεγεν	ℵᶜ A B L X Γ Δ Π fam¹ 2427 sa sy^p
8:25	ενεβλεπεν	ℵᶜ B L Δ 13 28 69 346
9:13	ηθελον	ℵ B C* D L k

---

17. Weiss, *Textkritik der vier Evangelien*, 60 and 61 n. 2.

18. Greeven and Güting, *Textkritik des Markusevangeliums*, 488–89; Holmes, *Greek New Testament*, 94.

19. In the passage quoted (Weiss is apparently thinking of 2:14) D does not preserve the original text, but has a secondary reading; Weiss, *Textkritik der vier Evangelien*, 60 and 61 n. 2.

20. Weiss, *Textkritik der vier Evangelien*, 60 and 61 n. 2.

9:38	εκωλυομεν	ℵ B C* D L M Δ fam¹ k
10:2	επηρωτων	ℵ B C D L M Δ Θ k a c d f ff² l r¹ z
10:10	επηρωτων	ℵ B C L Δ Θ
14:35	επιπτεν	ℵ B L 0112
14:54	ηκολουθει	G W Θ Ψ fam¹ fam¹³ 205 565 700 2542ˢ k c d ff² q r¹ z
14:72	εκλαιεν	ℵᶜ Aᶜ B L W Ψ 0250 0276 fam¹ fam¹³ 28 33 157 180 597 700 892 1006 1424 1506 2427 syʰ
15:12	ελεγεν	ℵ B C 1342 2427 syʰ

Three passages in my list show readings supported neither by B nor by ℵ.[21] Yet I am willing to defend these readings even against these witnesses. One of these passages is 2:14. Here the decision is supported by the observation that manuscripts are inclined to take over ηκολουθησεν from a synoptic parallel. This is the case in 1:20 and in 14:54.

The second passage, 6:6, contains the form εθαυμαζεν, a verb appropriate within its context, and we notice that Mark uses the imperfect of θαυμαζειν elsewhere, too (5:20; 15:44).[22] If this observation is correct, a faulty sigma was taken from the immediate vicinity (6:5 εθεραπευσεν). We read εθαυμαζεν.

In our third passage, in 14:54, the following observations support the reading ηκολουθει. Imperfects are not common in Matthew, since Matthew normally alters Markan imperfects. If Matthew uses the imperfect of ακολουθειν, he reproduces Markan idiom (Matt 9:9 = Mark 2:14 = Luke 5:28; Matt 9:19 = Mark 5:24; Matt 26:58 = Mark 14:54 = Luke 22:54). It is unlikely that in this one case he should introduce Markan idiom against Mark.

We argued our decision concerning one detail of Mark's style, his use of the imperfect. One could similarly develop arguments based on other aspects of his language. We saw that D kept original asyndeta. D preserves another aspect of Mark's speech, his habit of describing action without identifying the agent. Here other manuscripts add ο δε Ιησους and the like,

---

21. Another passage (6:12) presents us with the first member of a chain of four imperfects. These protected each other; least protected were numbers one and two, as Tischendorf revealed. Scribes noticed that the imperfect was correct in this sequence of verbs and desisted from a consequent introduction of aorists, but—alas!—they neglected to reconstitute the correct text.

22. Against Weiss, *Textkritik der vier Evangelien*, 60 and 61 n. 2.

while D follows the author.²³ D in many places has a monotonous και where other manuscripts prefer variation and introduce δε. D is not the only one to excel in this detail. B also often preserves the less elegant readings of Mark against a combination of witnesses. Weiss, Turner, Lagrange—to mention just these textual critics—have listed many examples.

2. *Fontem lectionum quaerimus*

Apart from the appeal to an author's style, one of the most effective arguments is the identification of one of several readings as the source of the others. This method of arguing is prominent in the "local-genealogical" method of the Münster Institute for New Testament Textual Research.²⁴ To qualify for such a role, we require a reading to be suitable as a starting point for all readings found in the textual history of the transmitted passage. All of them ought to be understandable as corrections, improvements, expansions, and transformations of this source.

A well-developed tree of variants may be studied in Mark 8:26. Brooke Foss Westcott and Fenton John Anthony Hort saw that our Antiochene manuscripts show the conflation of two older stages of the text, namely, of the Alexandrian reading μηδε εις την κωμην εισελθης (B L fam¹ sy^s sa geo^Adysh) and of the African reading μηδενι ειπης εις την κωμην (k).²⁵ It is

---

23. See 1:25, 41; 2:19; 5:40; 9:19; 14:22; 15:34. D supports a secondary text in 2:4; 3:23; 5:13, 19; 6:31, 34; 8:17; 12:41; 15:4. According to J. Keith Elliott ονοματι Ιαειρος in 5:22 is to be deleted, as the testimony of D e a ff² i suggests. See Elliott, "An Eclectic Textual Commentary on the Greek Text of Mark's Gospel," in *New Testament Textual Criticism: Its Significance for Exegesis; Essays in Honour of B. M. Metzger*, ed. Eldon J. Epp and Gordon D. Fee (Oxford: Clarendon, 1981), 47–60, esp. 53–54 (repr., Elliott, *Essays and Studies*, 165). See also Eberhard Nestle, *Philologia sacra: Bemerkungen über die Urgestalt der Evangelien und der Apostelgeschichte* (Berlin: Reuther & Reichard, 1896), 20.

24. Kurt Aland and Barbara Aland, *The Text of the New Testament: An Introduction to the Critical Editions and to the Theory and Practice of Modern Textual Criticism*, 2nd ed. (Grand Rapids: Eerdmans; Leiden: Brill, 1989).

25. Brooke Foss Westcott and Fenton John Anthony Hort, eds., *The New Testament in the Original Greek: Volume 1, Text; Volume 2, Introduction [and] Appendix* (Cambridge: Macmillan, 1881; 2nd ed., 1896), 2:99–100; C. H. Turner, "Marcan Usage: Notes, Critical and Exegetical, on the Second Gospel, II," *JTS* 26 (1924): 14–20; Turner, "Western Readings in the Second Half of Mark's Gospel," *JTS* 29 (1927/1928): 2; Turner, "The Textual Criticism of the New Testament," in

clear that in the process of conflation of these two texts the more ancient μηδενι was changed to μηδε. D, too, has the reading of k, but it adds υπαγε εις τον οικον σου και. Hort decided in favor of the Alexandrian text. But this decision does not explain the development of the text from its original form to later stages. Indeed the Alexandrian reading is an effort to correct, for it seeks to get rid of an imprecise εις that copyists sensed to be a provincialism of Mark. Turner realized that the reading of k is the source of various secondary developments.[26]

Turner raised the question whether in Mark 10:29 η πατερα is an element of the author's text.[27] It must be decided whether η μητερα η πατερα is original, or whether the omission of η πατερα in D k a ff² vg¹ makes sense. Turner argued, and I am willing to argue, that D almost alone apart from a few Old Latin witnesses preserved the original text. They testify to a "Western noninterpolation," a meaningful reading which we recognize as the source of all changes. η μητερα is a striking reading and cannot be interpreted as a correction of an older text.

3. Ardua librariis auctori non ardua

As is well known, it was Albrecht Bengel who introduced the term "harder reading" into our critical methodology. It is not easy to handle this criterion correctly. In a meaningful sense it presupposes that the textual critic is able to ascertain which reading presented a real obstacle from the viewpoint of the copyist.

I take an example of a difficult reading from the Inaugural Lecture of J. Neville Birdsall.[28] Birdsall defends the reading of ℵ B D L Δ Θ 33 565 700 892 1342 2427 a b c ff² i n l r¹ sa^mss in Mark 7:31, ηλθεν δια Σιδωνος. This reading does not seem to make sense. Traveling from Tyrus to the Lake of Tiberias by way of Sidon would prolong a journey unnecessarily. Contrariwise, a well-attested reading that rearranges the sentence with its

---

A New Commentary on Holy Scripture Including the Apocrypha, ed. Charles Gore, Henry Leighton Goudge, and Alfred Guillaume, 3 vols. (London: SPCK, 1929), 3:718–29, cf. 728.

26. Greeven and Güting, *Textkritik des Markusevangeliums*, 420–23.
27. Turner, "Western Readings," 6.
28. J. Neville Birdsall, "Textual Criticism and New Testament Studies: An Inaugural Lecture Delivered in the University of Birmingham on May 10, 1984," paper presented at Birmingham University, 10 May, 1984, 5.

verb appears to be in harmony with a known pattern of reference to both coastal cities. It reads: εξελθων εκ των οριων Τυρου και Σιδωνος ηλθεν.

Evidently in 1:6 δερριν (D a) as describing the garment of the Baptist was objected to by scribes.[29] Also in 1:6 εσθων (ℵ B L* Δ 33) was an unusual word which invited alteration to εσθιων.[30] There was a difficulty regarding context, not language, in οργισθεις Mark 1:41 (D a ff² r¹ Ephraem).[31] In 9:18, ρασσει (D 565) was possibly a difficult word for scribes.[32] A difficulty was felt with the word that Mark uses in the narrative of the request by Joseph of Arimathaea, namely, πτωμα in Mark 15:43 (D k sy^s) and 15:45 (πτωμα ℵ B L Θ 565; πτωμα αυτου D sy^s).[33] Everywhere in these examples we find D among the witnesses that preserve the ancient text.

4. *Assimilationem textuum cave*

Scribes show the tendency to assimilate texts with one another. Once doubt is raised as to the correctness of a word, a copyist is likely to check the context in order to ascertain correct words and spellings. Or the copyist makes the point even before the author intended to make it. Second, variants from synoptic parallels are taken over into the texts either deliberately or

---

29. Ernst von Dobschütz, *Eberhard Nestle's Einführung in das griechische Neue Testament*, 4th ed. (Göttingen: Vandenhoeck & Ruprecht, 1923), 7; Turner, "Textual Criticism," 3:728.

30. BDF §101 n. 23.

31. Kirsopp Lake, "ΕΜΒΡΙΜΗΣΑΜΕΝΟΣ and ΟΡΓΙΣΘΕΙΣ: Mark 1:40–43," *HTR* 16 (1923): 197; Turner, "Textual Commentary," 151; Turner, "Textual Criticism," 3:728; Gustav Stählin, "ὀργή," *TDNT* 5:427 n. 326; R. V. G. Tasker, *The Greek New Testament Being the Text Translated in the New English Bible 1961: Edited with Introduction, Textual Notes, and Appendix* (Oxford: Oxford University Press; New York: Cambridge University Press, 1964), 414; J. M. Ross, "The United Bible Societies Greek New Testament," *JBL* 95 (1975): 119; E. J. Pryke, *Redactional Style in the Marcan Gospel*, SNTSMS 33 (Cambridge: Cambridge University Press, 1978), 122, 149, 153; Werner George Kümmel, review of NA²⁶, *ThR* 45 (1980): 87; Harald Riesenfeld, "Sind Konjekturen bei einer Übersetzung des Neuen Testaments notwendig?" in *Text, Wort, Glaube: Studien zur Überlieferung, Interpretation und Autorisierung biblischer Texte Kurt Aland gewidmet*, ed. Martin Brecht, AKG 50 (Berlin: de Gruyter, 1980), 40–46; Greeven and Güting, *Textkritik des Markusevangeliums*, 120–22.

32. Turner, "Western Readings," 3.

33. Turner, "Western Readings," 13; Holmes, *Greek New Testament*, 113.

unintentionally. Third, in addition to assimilation within the context and to loans from synoptic parallels, there are various assimilations with patterns of biblical language.

As an example of assimilation within the context I name the reading εξηραμμενην in Mark 3:3. Here D is among the manuscripts that assimilate an original ξηραν with the text of Mark 3:1.[34] Mark 10:19, like its synoptic parallels Matt 11:18–19 and Luke 18:20, presents a list of prohibitions that follows closely its Old Testament patterns in Exod 20:12–17 and Deut 5:17–21. Matthew in his sequence of prohibitions and in his language depends on the text of the Septuagint. Luke's arrangement of the commandments gives the text that B has in Deut 5:17–21. Both texts have influenced the Markan tradition: μη αποστερησης, originally present in 10:19, is deleted in numerous witnesses, but not in ℵ A C D Θ 0274 13 565 892 2427 k a aur b c d f ff² l q sy ˢ·ʰ sa bo Irenaeus ˡᵃᵗ. The Lukan word order μη μοιχευσης μη φονευσης is found in most Markan manuscripts, but not in D k Irenaeus. These present μη μοιχευσης μη πορνευσης, but no μη φονευσης.

Turner took the view that this text, which differs from Matthew and Luke, shows the original word order. Here an interpretation is added to two commandments, μη πορνευσης to μη μοιχευσης, and μη αποστερησης to μη ψευδομαρτυρησης. The denial of the receipt of a *depositum* was apparently more common an offense than murder was.[35] If this interpretation is correct, we have to follow here Codex Bezae and the African witness k.[36]

In the Gethsemane passage we find a striking correspondence between the Matthean text and the Markan model. Matthew has τον αυτον λογον ειπων in Matt 26:44; Mark writes the same clause in Mark 14:39. But in Mark the words are lacking in D k a b c d ff². Since Mark's gospel does not explicitly tell of a threefold prayer, and thus has no reason to give the content of a third prayer, we conclude that this clause is not original to its text. Kilpatrick argued the originality of the omission by referring to a linguistic observation: "ο αυτος seems to be going out of use in ordinary Greek at this time. Apart from this passage it does not occur in the four works which

---

34. George Dunbar Kilpatrick defends the participle: "Some Notes on Marcan Usage," *BT* 7 (1956): 2–9; repr., Elliott, *Principles and Practice*, 266; repr., Elliott, *Language and Style*, 164); Greeven and Güting, *Textkritik des Markusevangeliums*, 178–80.

35. Turner, "Western Readings," 5–6.

36. Greeven and Güting, *Textkritik des Markusevangeliums*, 504–6.

belong to the lowest level of Greek in the New Testament, Mark, John, Revelation, and the Pastoral Epistles."[37]

5. Divide lectiones et impera

An examination of the Greek witnesses to Mark 10:2 reveals a considerable amount of disorder. The witnesses disagree as to whether we have to read Φαρισαιοι or οι Φαρισαιοι, on the position of προσελθοντες, likewise whether και or δε is to be preferred, and also whether a conjunction is needed here. Finally, Codex Bezae merely transmits και, with k a b d r¹ sy^s geo^Adysh, the Sahidic manuscript P. Palau Ribes (= sa 1) and another Sahidic manuscript quoted as sah 21 (= sa 123) by Horner. There is one Greek witness that supports D: Origen.[38] Origen does not mention Pharisees.

It is evident that και επηρωτων is the original variant reading.[39] What may be said for it?

1. A conspicuous disorder in the transmission.
2. The evidence: D, Origen, and the ancient translations carry considerable weight.

---

37. George Dunbar Kilpatrick, *Literary Fashions and the Transmission of Texts in the Graeco-Roman World*, Center for Hermeneutical Studies in Hellenistic and Modern Culture; Protocol Series of Colloquies 19 (Berkeley: University of California, 1976), 1–8.

38. Tischendorf, *Novum Testamentum Graece*, 1:318 (Origen, *Comm. Matt.* 3.636 at Matt 19:3).

39. Westcott and Hort, *New Testament in the Original Greek*, 176; F. C. Burkitt, ed., *Evangelion da-Mepharreshe: The Curetonian Version of the Four Gospels, with the Readings of the Sinai Palimpsest* (Cambridge: Clarendon, 1904), 98; Adalbert Merx, *Die vier kanonischen Evangelien nach ihrem ältesten bekannten Texte* (Berlin: Reimer, 1905), 2.2:112–13; Julius Wellhausen, *Das Evangelium Marci*, 2nd ed. (Berlin: Reimer, 1909), 77; C. H. Turner, "Marcan Usage: Notes, Critical and Exegetical, on the Second Gospel," *JTS* 25 (1924): 382; repr., Elliott, *Language and Style*, 8; Turner, "Western Readings," 5; Marie-Joseph Lagrange, *Critique Textuelle, II: La Critique Rationnelle*, 2nd ed. (Paris: Gabalda, 1935), 70; George Dunbar Kilpatrick, "Western Text and Original Text in the Gospels and Acts," *JTS* 44 (1943): 31; Tasker, *Greek New Testament*, 415; Metzger, *Textual Commentary*, 104 (minority vote of Metzger and Wikgren); Elliott, "Eclectic Textual Commentary," 58–59; Holmes, *Greek New Testament*, 94.

3. The correct reading restores a peculiarity of Mark's style, namely, a predicate used without a subject.[40]
4. Another argument is rarely, if ever, mentioned in the discussion of our present passage. Mark 10:2 opens an old lection. For this practical reason και is deleted as superfluous from the text of some lectionaries.[41] The needs of public reading are probably the cause of all the changes listed. The supplement to the text was taken from Matt 19:3.
5. Numerous manuscripts that do not support the original text are divided among themselves as to the text that ought to be supported. That there are several variants in word order in a short segment of the text confirms our decision. This aspect of our critical procedure may be called the assurance of *divide lectiones et impera.*

Mark 1:11 may serve as a second example of proceeding on the principle *divide lectiones et impera.* We have three variants to choose from: εγενετο εκ των ουρανων is found in ℵ² A B K L Δ Π fam¹ fam¹³ 33 700 892, in many additional minuscules, in numerous lectionaries, and in sy ᴾ and our Coptic versions. In Θ 28 565 *l*2211 geo^Adysh we read εκ των ουρανων ηκουσθη. Since εκ των ουρανων without any verbal predicate is also transmitted (by ℵ* D d ff² t *l*184 Diatessaron), εγενετο and ηκουσθη are evidently secondary additions. ℵ* D and their companions have the original text.[42]

6. *An brevis lectio potior sit an longa argumentis eget*

On many passages there is debate as to whether a longer or a shorter reading is to be preferred. Not a few passages lost part of their texts owing to the inadvertence of scribes. A scribe is more likely to add than to omit. It is not difficult to furnish proof for this by statistics. But in a given case this observation is of little avail. Which text is original?

Griesbach put forward the proposition that in most cases a shorter variant is to be preferred. This is the first of his fifteen *canones.* His reasoning is knowledgeable and circumspect.[43] Westcott and Hort reserved a prominent

---

40. Turner, "Marcan Usage," 377–86.
41. B. Aland et al., eds., *The Greek New Testament*, 5th revised ed. (Stuttgart: Deutsche Bibelgesellschaft; United Bible Societies, 2014), 158.
42. Greeven and Güting, *Textkritik des Markusevangeliums*, 62–64.
43. See Metzger, *Textual Commentary*, 120; and Eldon J. Epp, "The Eclectic

place for the shorter readings of the D-text. Their observation that the D-text preserves old "noninterpolations" is, despite much criticism, correct.

Westcott and Hort found Western noninterpolations in the Gospel of Luke, but were uncertain as to whether this phenomenon could be established elsewhere. They mentioned Mark 2:22, 10:2, and 14:39.[44] Today opinion is no longer divided regarding 2:22; the omission of text in this passage is considered as a fault caused by one of the typically Markan parentheses. The words put in brackets by Westcott and Hort belong in the text: αλλα οινον νεον εις ασκους καινους. Here, then, we decide against the shorter reading of D 2427 a b d ff² i r¹ t.[45] Our result is confirmed by a synoptic comparison. Matthew and Luke follow Mark's text and by adhering to their model reveal its structure.

Wherever a synoptic comparison leads to a definite result, we may move safely (see on 10:2 and 14:39 above). For example, in Mark 3:32 και αι αδελφαι σου is to be deleted as a supplement; here we decide against D.[46] In Mark 14:65 the clause και περικαλυπτειν αυτου το προσωπον is not original; here we follow D and are supported by a sy^s bo^{mss}.[47] Similarly in Mark 16:1 a synoptic comparison causes us to delete διαγενομενου του σαββατου Μαρια η Μαγδαληνη και Μαρια η Ιακωβου και Σαλωμη;[48] here we read the text of D and are supported by Old Latin k and a.[49]

Wherever synoptic comparisons are not available or yield no results, decisions will be more difficult. The same will be true, if the longer text

---

Method in New Testament Textual Criticism: Solution or Symptom?," *HTR* 69 (1976): 211–57, esp. 225–29; repr., *Studies in the Theory and Method of New Testament Textual Criticism*, ed. Eldon J Epp and Gordon D. Fee, SD 45 (Grand Rapids: Eerdmans, 1993), 141–73.

44. Westcott and Hort, *New Testament in the Original Greek*, 176.

45. C. H. Turner, "Marcan Usage: Notes, Critical and Exegetical, on the Second Gospel, IV," *JTS* 26 (1925): 147; repr., Elliott, *Language and Style*, 25–26; Metzger, *Textual Commentary*, 79.

46. See Westcott and Hort, *New Testament in the Original Greek*, "Notes on Select Readings," 24; Wellhausen, *Evangelium Marci*, 28; Metzger, *Textual Commentary*, 82 (minority vote); Greeven and Güting, *Textkritik des Markusevangeliums*, 215–18.

47. Turner, "Western Readings," 10–11; Turner, "Textual Criticism," 3:728.

48. Turner, "Western Readings," 13–14; Greeven and Güting, *Textkritik des Markusevangeliums*, 736–37.

49. Turner, "Western Readings," 6; Taylor, *St. Mark*, 471.

is in no way conspicuous in its language or even corresponds to Markan stylistic habits.

In some passages we expect from the context to meet obvious additions. Detail presupposed from the narrative is made explicit by the scribe. On the other hand, in such passages the impression may be gained that somewhere in the process of transmission one of Mark's redundant phrases was skipped over and ought to be restored. Cases in which such considerations are in conflict need careful examination of the evidence. Before we proceed with the argument that a particular seeming imperfection of Mark's style was improved upon by scribes we have to check whether comparable passages show evidence of similar corrections. Stylistic blemishes may after all be due to scribes. We expect certain types of corrections to be almost universal. Other types we remember to have met in but few Alexandrian witnesses. The urge to correct was different in different areas. If our assumptions seem to be in conflict with the witnesses that support us, we may have to decide against our assumptions.

In Mark 11:31 we find τι ειπωμεν in D Θ Φ fam¹ 28 565 700 k a b c r¹. Turner regarded this phrase as an example of Mark's well-known redundancy.[50] I take this phrase to be an obvious completion intended to clarify Mark's vivid narrative.[51]

Turner likewise in 12:23 regarded οταν αναστωσιν, which is added to εν αναστασει by some manuscripts, as an example of Markan redundancy.[52] Among the many variations in this verse, the conjunction ουν is met with in various positions in the text and is consequently to be deemed secondary. The phrase οταν αναστωσιν also changes its position in witnesses of fam¹³. Other observations need to be considered. Among the witnesses that support Turner's text there are very few majuscules[53] and only one Old Latin manuscript, namely, q. The variant εν τη αναστασει alone is found in the African witness k and also in ℵ B C* L Δ Ψ 1342 2427 slav. And though our synoptic parallels follow the Markan text closely, the presence of οταν αναστωσιν in Mark leads to a "minor agreement" of the parallels against their source. We have learned to distrust such a result: οταν αναστωσιν arose from conflation within the context. Its source is Mark 12:25.[54]

---

50. Turner, "Western Readings," 9; Taylor, *St. Mark*, 512.
51. Greeven and Güting, *Textkritik des Markusevangeliums*, 562–63.
52. Turner, "Western Readings," 8.
53. The apparatus of UBS³ lists only X; the apparatus of UBS⁵ lists E F H.
54. Greeven and Güting, *Textkritik des Markusevangeliums*, 586–87.

On the other hand, one could argue that our evidence could be understood as supporting the view that a correction of Mark's redundancy is found here. The claim that Alexandrian scholars introduced corrections must, however, be demonstrated in a sufficient number of cases before it can be accepted.

7. Accipe regulam Friderici Blasii

On the eve of our century Friedrich Blass set down a rule that should not disappear from our memory. This rule is to be credited to a century strongly devoted to the case of justice:

> My critical procedure is based upon the principle that in order to distribute evenly what is found in the text to author and scribes alike, one should allot as much as possible of stupidity and absent-mindedness to the latter. For an author writes down what he has to tell with consciousness and from his own experience, unless he is a compiler, which Mark is not. A copyist, however, puts his eye and his memory to work, not his mind or his phantasy.[55]

Two last examples I will give in order to illustrate how this rule works.

In Mark 1:29 it is clear, in my view, that the phrase μετα Ιακωβου και Ιωαννου presupposes a singular in the predicate of that sentence. Witnesses differ as to the presence of ευθυς, as to the position of the prepositional phrase εκ της συναγωγης, and on the suitability of the conjunctions και or δε. These differences hint at the presence of early corrections. The phrase εξελθοντες ηλθον was indeed accepted by many critics, but it is intolerable in this context.[56] Karl Ludwig Schmidt regarded this plural as original, but he also found the reading "curious."[57] Turner, Lagrange, and Metzger defended the plural verb.[58]

---

55. Friedrich Blass, *Textkritische Bemerkungen zu Markus*, BFCT 3 (Gütersloh: Bertelsmann, 1899), 56.

56. Wellhausen, *Evangelium Marci*, 11.

57. Karl Ludwig Schmidt, *Der Rahmen der Geschichte Jesu: Literarkritische Untersuchungen zur ältesten Jesusüberlieferung* (Berlin: Trowitzsch, 1919), 55 and 56 n. 1.

58. C. H. Turner, "Marcan Usage: Notes, Critical and Exegetical, on the Second Gospel, V," *JTS* 26 (1925): 228; repr., Elliott, *Language and Style*, 39; Turner, "Textual Commentary," 155; Lagrange, *Critique Textuelle*, 48; Metzger, *Textual Commentary*, 64; Pryke, *Redactional Style*, 109 n. 2.

It is clear, of course, that ευθυς (in D W e aur c d ff² r¹ sy^{s.p}) is to be deleted as an addition. Among the witnesses for the singular of the predicate are B fam¹ fam¹³ 565 579 700 1342 2427 and (with slightly varied position of the prepositional phrase) D Θ e aur b c f ff² q r¹ bo arm, and also (adding a secondary δε) W; sy^s renders και εξηλθεν εκ της συναγωγης και ηλθον εις τον οικον Σιμωνος Κηφα και Ανδρεου. A singular suits the long series of singulars in chapter 1. Matthew 8:14 and Luke 4:38 have a singular and therefore support a singular in Mark's text. Referring to the rule of Blass, I consider the singular as original.[59]

In my second example, taken from Mark 10:7, the context supports a disputed segment of the text. It reveals the omission (read by א B Ψ 892* sy^s) to be secondary. J. Keith Elliott argued that we have to follow D and that the omission of και προσκολληθησεται προς την γυναικα αυτου is an error. If we decided to omit these words, the result would be nonsense. The two who according to our text shall be one remain incomplete: therefore, the statement loses its reference.[60]

In this paper I have not given opinions, but reasoning. The reasons are introduced as *éléments d'une critique rationnelle*. Reasons step onto the stage and with them original readings of Mark. They knock and ask to be admitted into our New Testaments.

And now the rule of Blass in Latin:

Participes operis sunt scriptor et auctor aperte.
Auctor habet sensum, somnia scriptor habet.[61]

Bibliography

Aland, Barbara, Kurt Aland, Johannes Karavidopoulos, Carlo M. Martini, and Bruce M. Metzger, eds. *The Greek New Testament*. 5th ed. Stuttgart: Deutsche Bibelgesellschaft; United Bible Societies, 2014.

Aland, Barbara, Kurt Aland, Johannes Karavidopoulos, Carlo M. Martini, and Bruce M. Metzger, eds., *Novum Testamentum Graece*. 27th ed. Stuttgart: Deutsche Bibelgesellschaft, 2001.

---

59. Greeven and Güting, *Textkritik des Markusevangeliums*, 96–98.

60. J. Keith Elliott, "The Use of Brackets in the Text of the United Bible Societies' Greek New Testament," *Bib* 60 (1979): 575; Greeven and Güting, *Textkritik des Markusevangeliums*, 493–95.

61. The epigram I owe to my friend Alfons Weische of Münster.

Aland, Kurt. "Alter und Entstehung des D-Textes im Neuen Testament: Betrachtungen zu P^{69} und 0171." Pages 37–61 in *Miscellania Papirologica Ramon Roca-Puig*. Edited by Sebastià Janeras. Barcelona: Fundacio Salvador Vives Casajuana, 1987.

Aland, Kurt, and Barbara Aland. *The Text of the New Testament: An Introduction to the Critical Editions and to the Theory and Practice of Modern Textual Criticism*. 2nd ed. Grand Rapids: Eerdmans; Leiden: Brill, 1989.

Allen, Willoughby C. *The Gospel According to Saint Mark*. London: Rivingtons, 1915.

Birdsall, J. Neville. "Textual Criticism and New Testament Studies: An Inaugural Lecture Delivered in the University of Birmingham on 10 May 1984." Paper presented at Birmingham University, 10 May, 1984.

Black, Matthew. *An Aramaic Approach to the Gospels and Acts*. 3rd ed. Oxford: Clarendon, 1968.

Blass, Friedrich. *Textkritische Bemerkungen zu Markus*. BFCT 3. Gütersloh: Bertelsmann, 1899.

Burkitt, F. C., ed. *Evangelion da-Mepharreshe: The Curetonian Version of the Four Gospels, with the Readings of the Sinai Palimpsest*. Cambridge: Clarendon, 1904.

Dobschütz, Ernst von. *Eberhard Nestle's Einführung in das griechische Neue Testament*. 4th ed. Göttingen: Vandenhoeck & Ruprecht, 1923.

Elliott, J. Keith. "An Eclectic Textual Commentary on the Greek Text of Mark's Gospel." Pages 47–60 in *New Testament Textual Criticism: Its Significance for Exegesis; Essays in Honour of Bruce M. Metzger*. Edited by Eldon J. Epp and Gordon D. Fee. Oxford: Clarendon, 1981. Repr., pages 159–70 in *Essays and Studies in New Testament Textual Criticism*. Edited by J. Keith Elliott. EFNT 3. Cordoba: El Almendro, 1992.

———. "The Relevance of Textual Criticism to the Synoptic Problem." Pages 348–59 in *The Interrelations of the Gospels*. Edited by David L. Dungan. BETL 95. Leuven: Leuven University Press, 1990. Repr., pages 147–58 in *Essays and Studies in New Testament Textual Criticism*. Edited by J. Keith Elliott. EFNT 3. Cordoba: El Almendro, 1992.

———. "The United Bible Societies' Textual Commentary Evaluated." *NovT* 17 (1975): 130–50.

———. "The Use of Brackets in the Text of the United Bible Societies' Greek New Testament." *Bib* 60 (1979): 575–77.

Epp, Eldon J. "The Eclectic Method in New Testament Textual Criticism: Solution or Symptom?" *HTR* 69 (1976): 211–57. Repr., pages 141–73 in *Studies in the Theory and Method of New Testament Textual Criticism*. Edited by Eldon J. Epp and Gordon D. Fee. SD 45. Grand Rapids: Eerdmans, 1993.

Greeven, Heinrich, and Eberhard Güting. *Textkritik des Markusevangeliums*. Theologie, Forschung und Wissenschaft 11. Münster: LIT, 2005.

Hawkins, John C. *Horae Synopticae: Contributions to the Study of the Synoptic Problem*. 2nd ed. Oxford: Clarendon, 1909.

Hedley, P. L. "The Egyptian Texts of the Gospels and Acts." *CQR* 118 (1934): 188–230.

Holmes, Michael W., ed. *The Greek New Testament: SBL Edition*. Atlanta: Society of Biblical Literature; Bellingham, WA: Logos Bible Software, 2010.

Kilpatrick, George Dunbar. *Literary Fashions and the Transmission of Texts in the Graeco-Roman World*. Center for Hermeneutical Studies in Hellenistic and Modern Culture; Protocol Series of the Colloquies 19. Berkeley: University of California, 1976.

———, ed., *Mark: A Greek-English Diglot for the Use of Translators*. London: British and Foreign Bible Society, 1958.

———. "Πορευεσθαι and Its Compounds." *JTS* 48 (1946/1947): 61–63. Repr. in *The Principles and Practice of New Testament Textual Criticism: Collected Essays of G. D. Kilpatrick*. Edited by J. Keith Elliott. BETL 96. Leuven: Leuven University Press, 1990.

———. "Some Notes on Marcan Usage." *BT* 7 (1956): 2–9. Repr. as pages 261–69 in *The Principles and Practice of New Testament Textual Criticism: Collected Essays of G. D. Kilpatrick*. Edited by J. Keith Elliott. BETL 96. Leuven: Leuven University Press, 1990. Repr. as pages 159–65 in *The Language and Style of the Gospel of Mark: An Edition of C. H. Turner's "Notes on Marcan Usage" Together with Other Comparable Studies*. Edited by J. Keith Elliott. NovTSup 71. Leiden: Brill, 1993.

———. "Western Text and Original Text in the Gospels and Acts." *JTS* 44 (1943): 24–36.

Kümmel, Werner Georg. Review of NA[26]. *ThR* 45 (1980): 88.

Lagrange, Marie-Joseph. *Critique Textuelle, II: La Critique Rationnelle*. 2nd ed. Paris: Gabalda, 1935.

———. *Évangile selon Saint Marc*. 4th ed. EB. Paris: Gabalda, 1929.

Lake, Kirsopp. "ΕΜΒΡΙΜΗΣΑΜΕΝΟΣ and ΟΡΓΙΣΘΕΙΣ: Mark 1:40–43." *HTR* 16 (1923): 197–98.

Merx, Adalbert. *Die vier kanonischen Evangelien nach ihrem ältesten bekannten Texte*. Berlin: Reimer, 1905.

Metzger, Bruce M. *A Textual Commentary on the Greek New Testament: A Companion Volume to the United Bible Societies' Greek New Testament (Fourth Revised Edition)*. 2nd ed. Stuttgart: Deutsche Bibelgesellschaft, 1994.
Nestle, Eberhard. *Philologia sacra: Bemerkungen über die Urgestalt der Evangelien und der Apostelgeschichte*. Berlin: Reuther & Reichard, 1896.
Pryke, E. J. *Redactional Style in the Marcan Gospel: A Study of Syntax and Vocabulary as Guides to Redaction in Mark*. SNTSMS 33. Cambridge: Cambridge University Press, 1978.
Riesenfeld, Harald. "Sind Konjekturen bei einer Übersetzung des Neuen Testaments notwendig?" Pages 40–46 in *Text, Wort, Glaube: Studien zur Überlieferung, Interpretation und Autorisierung biblischer Texte Kurt Aland gewidmet*. Edited by Martin Brecht. AKG 50. Berlin: de Gruyter, 1980.
Ross, J. M. "The United Bible Societies Greek New Testament." *JBL* 95 (1975): 112–21.
Schmidt, Karl Ludwig. *Der Rahmen der Geschichte Jesu: Literarkritische Untersuchungen zur ältesten Jesusüberlieferung*. Berlin: Trowitzsch, 1919.
Stählin, Gustav. "ὀργή." *TDNT* 5:422–47.
Tasker, R. V. G., ed. *The Greek New Testament Being the Text Translated in the New English Bible 1961: Edited with Introduction, Textual Notes, and Appendix*. Oxford: Oxford University Press; New York: Cambridge University Press, 1964.
Taylor, Vincent. *The Gospel according to St. Mark: The Greek Text with Introduction, Notes and Indexes*. 2nd ed. London: Macmillan, 1966.
Tischendorf, Constantin von, ed., *Novum Testamentum Graece: Ad antiquissimos testes denuo recensuit; Apparatum criticum omni studio perfectum apposuit commentationem isagogicam praetexuit Constantinus Tischendorf*. 8th ed. 3 vols. Leipzig: Giesecke & Devrient, 1869–1894.
Turner, C. H. "Marcan Usage: Notes, Critical and Exegetical, on the Second Gospel." *JTS* 25 (1924): 377–86. Repr. in *The Language and Style of the Gospel of Mark: An Edition of C. H. Turner's "Notes on Marcan Usage" Together with Other Comparable Studies*. Edited by J. Keith Elliott. NovTSup 71. Leiden: Brill, 1993.
———. "Marcan Usage: Notes, Critical and Exegetical, on the Second Gospel, II." *JTS* 26 (1924): 14–20.

---. "Marcan Usage: Notes, Critical and Exegetical, on the Second Gospel, IV." *JTS* 26 (1925): 145–56. Repr., pages 23–35 in *The Language and Style of the Gospel of Mark: An Edition of C. H. Turner's "Notes on Marcan Usage" Together with Other Comparable Studies*. Edited by J. Keith Elliott. NovTSup 71. Leiden: Brill, 1993.

---. "Marcan Usage: Notes, Critical and Exegetical, on the Second Gospel, IX." *JTS* 29 (1928): 275–89. Repr., pages 104–19 in *The Language and Style of the Gospel of Mark: An Edition of C. H. Turner's "Notes on Marcan Usage" Together with Other Comparable Studies*. Edited by J. Keith Elliott. NovTSup 71. Leiden: Brill, 1993.

---. "Marcan Usage: Notes, Critical and Exegetical, on the Second Gospel, V." *JTS* 26 (1925): 225–40. Repr. in *The Language and Style of the Gospel of Mark: An Edition of C. H. Turner's "Notes on Marcan Usage" Together with Other Comparable Studies*. Edited by J. Keith Elliott. NovTSup 71. Leiden: Brill, 1993.

---. "Marcan Usage: Notes, Critical and Exegetical, on the Second Gospel, VII." *JTS* 28 (1926): 9–30. Repr., in *The Language and Style of the Gospel of Mark: An Edition of C. H. Turner's "Notes on Marcan Usage" Together with Other Comparable Studies*. Edited by J. Keith Elliott. NovTSup 71. Leiden: Brill, 1993.

---. "A Textual Commentary on Mark I." *JTS* 28 (1926–1927): 145–58.

---. "The Textual Criticism of the New Testament." Pages 718–29 in vol. 3 of *A New Commentary on Holy Scripture Including the Apocrypha*. Edited by Charles Gore, Henry Leighton Goudge, and Alfred Guillaume. 3 vols. London: SPCK, 1929.

---. "Western Readings in the Second Half of Mark's Gospel." *JTS* 29 (1927/1928): 1–16.

Weiss, Bernhard. *Die Evangelien des Markus und Lukas*. 9th ed. Göttingen: Vandenhoeck & Ruprecht, 1901.

---. *Textkritik der vier Evangelien*. TU 19.2. Leipzig: Hinrichs, 1899.

Wellhausen, Julius. *Das Evangelium Marci*. 2nd ed. Berlin: Reimer, 1909.

Westcott, Brooke Foss, and Fenton John Anthony Hort, eds. *The New Testament in the Original Greek: Volume 1, Text; Volume 2, Introduction [and] Appendix*. Cambridge: Macmillan, 1881. 2nd ed., 1896.

7

The Relevance of Literary Criticism for the Text of the New Testament: A Study of Mark's Traditions on John the Baptist

1. Introduction

Textual criticism looks back upon a long tradition of painstaking work.[1] Wherever variation became evident, manuscripts have been studied, ancient translations have been compared, the testimony of the fathers has been gathered. The apparatuses of our editions are improving, but let us admit that they are still far from satisfactory.[2] With satisfaction, however,

---

1. I wish to thank Professor Christopher M. Tuckett for valuable remarks on a draft of this essay.

2. The presentation of evidence in editions needs careful consideration. As units of variation are defined and witnesses are listed, by implication the text-critical evaluation of the material presented is regularly imposed on this material. In my article "Der editorische Bericht als Kommentar zur Textkonstitution und zum Apparat in Editionen des Neuen Testaments," *Editio* 7 (1993): 94–108 (ch. 5 in this collection), I have named some standards an editor ought to meet when listing the data that support or fail to support his text-critical decisions. Other authors, too, are discussing the methodological issues involved in selecting or ignoring variants and witnesses: Tjitze Baarda, "What Kind of Critical Apparatus for the New Testament Do We Need? The Case of Luke 23:48," in *New Testament Textual Criticism, Exegesis and Church History: A Discussion of Methods*, ed. Barbara Aland and Joël Delobel, CBET 7 (Kampen: Kok Pharos, 1994), 37–97; Ernest C. Colwell, with Ernest W. Tune, "Method in Classifying and Evaluating Variant Readings," in *Studies in Methodology in Textual Criticism of the New Testament*, ed. Ernest C. Colwell, NTTS 9 (Leiden: Brill, 1969), 96–105; J. Keith Elliott, "The International Project to Establish a Critical Apparatus to Luke's Gospel," *NTS* 29 (1983): 531–38; Elliott, "The Purpose and Construction of a Critical Apparatus to a Greek New Testa-

we see that work on the testimony of the church fathers and also of several heretics is being taken up with enthusiasm. Our methodology for using this testimony is being refined.³ In New Testament exegesis we have been aware for a long time that New Testament texts are not absolutely devoid of secondary accretions, of glosses, of additions. Some of our exegetes have been reluctant to admit the facts whenever manuscript testimony to corruption in our Greek texts is lacking. Let us be clear about this: I regard it as a deficiency of an edition, if *cruces interpretum* are not marked within its edited text. A user of such an edition would have to conclude either that the editor considers his edited text to be free from corruption, or else that he was failing in one of his responsibilities, the task of *recensio*.

Today I wish to open discussion on two apparent glosses in the Gospel of Mark, namely, Mark 1:2-3 and Mark 9:12b. Manuscript evidence to

---

ment," in *Studien zum Text und zur Ethik des Neuen Testaments: Festschrift zum 80. Geburtstag von Heinrich Greeven*, ed. W. Schrage, BZNW 47 (Berlin: de Gruyter, 1986), 125-43; Elliott, *A Survey of Manuscripts Used in Editions of the Greek New Testament*, NovTSup 57 (Leiden: Brill, 1987); William J. Elliott, "The Need for an Accurate and Comprehensive Collation of All Known Greek NT Manuscripts with Their Individual Variants Noted *in pleno*," in *Studies in New Testament Language and Text: Essays in Honour of George D. Kilpatrick on the Occasion of His Sixty-Fifth Birthday*, ed. J. Keith Elliott, NovTSup 44 (Leiden: Brill, 1976), 137-43; Eldon J. Epp, "Toward the Clarification of the Term 'Textual Variant,'" in Elliott, *Studies in New Testament Language*, 153-73; repr., in *Studies in the Theory and Method of Textual Criticism*, ed. Eldon J. Epp and Gordon D. Fee, SD 45 (Grand Rapids: Eerdmans, 1993), 47-61; Moisés Silva, "Modern Critical Editions and Apparatuses of the Greek New Testament," in *The Text of the New Testament in Contemporary Research: Essays on the Status Quaestionis; A Volume in Honor of Bruce M. Metzger*, ed. Bart D. Ehrman and Michael W. Holmes, SD 46 (Grand Rapids: Eerdmans, 1995), 283-96; Martin L. West, *Textual Criticism and Editorial Technique: Applicable to Greek and Latin Texts* (Stuttgart: Teubner, 1973).

3. See my review of *Marcion und sein Apostolos: Rekonstruktion und historische Einordnung der marcionitischen* Paulusbriefausgabe, by Ulrich Schmid, *NovT* 42 (1997): 396-405; and Bart D. Ehrman, "Heracleon and the 'Western' Textual Tradition," *NTS* 40 (1994): 161-79. See also the surveys of Gordon D. Fee, "The Use of the Greek Fathers for New Testament Textual Criticism," in Ehrman and Holmes, *Status Quaestionis*, 191-207; J. Lionel North, "The Use of the Latin Fathers for New Testament Textual Criticism," in Ehrman and Holmes, *Status Quaestionis*, 208-23; and Sebastian P. Brock, "The Use of the Syriac Fathers for New Testament Textual Criticism," in Ehrman and Holmes, *Status Quaestionis*, 224-36.

support my view is not at hand in the case of 9:12b. In the case of 1:2-3 it is not unequivocal. Hence the author who set out to write his book is our decisive witness.[4]

2. A Gloss in Mark 9:12b

καὶ πῶς γέγραπται ἐπὶ τὸν υἱὸν τοῦ ἀνθρώπου, ἵνα πολλὰ πάθῃ καὶ ἐξουδενηθῇ;

The passage Mark 9:11-13 is considered a redactional text. It was not merely inherited by Mark, he wrote it. Rudolf Bultmann argued that verse 11 refers to 9:1. Robert H. Lightfoot agreed.[5] In this passage the disciples are privileged to receive instruction from Jesus. The question regarding the teaching of the scribes takes up a theme vital for a Jewish-Christian community. If Elijah needs to appear before the consummation of the age, how can Christian claims be upheld? Jesus supplies the answer. But the

---

4. There is evidence that the present text of Mark is marred by further glosses not generally recognized as secondary texts. One of these is to be found in Mark 10:32. Nigel Turner called attention to an irregular δέ in this verse: "οἱ δέ does not mark a change of subject" (Turner, *Syntax*, vol. 3 of *A Grammar of New Testament Greek*, James Hope Moulton [Edinburgh: T&T Clark, 1978], 37). His suggestion that καί be accepted here is not acceptable, though. There is a wide selection of variant readings, which indicates a disturbed text. It is preferable to follow the testimony of D K fam[13] 28 700 1010 a b. Mark's καὶ ἐθαμβοῦντο was glossed in various ways. Several textual critics have recognized corruption here and have made suggestions to heal it. Günther Zuntz proposed omitting καὶ ἐθαμβοῦντο, of which our gloss is a fuller and simpler version. C. H. Turner suggested the conjecture ἐθαμβεῖτο. See Zuntz, "Ein Heide las das Markusevangelium," in *Markus-Philologie: Historische, literargeschichtliche und stilistische Untersuchungen zum zweiten Evangelium*, ed. Hubert Cancik, WUNT 33 (Tübingen: Mohr, 1984), 215; C. H. Turner, *The Study of the New Testament 1883 and 1920*, 3rd ed. (Oxford: Clarendon, 1926), 62. The paper presented here discusses readings that lack the specific evidence used in the traditional text-critical procedures.

5. Rudolf Bultmann, *Geschichte der synoptischen Tradition*, 2nd ed. FRLANT 29 (Göttingen: Vandenhoeck & Ruprecht, 1931), 132 and n. 1; Bultmann, *Geschichte der synoptischen Tradition: Ergänzungsheft*, ed. Gerd Theissen and Philipp Vielhauer, 5th ed., FRLANT 29.2 (Göttingen: Vandenhoeck & Ruprecht, 1979), 51; Robert H. Lightfoot, *History and Interpretation in the Gospels* (London: Hodder & Stoughton, 1935), 92.

meaning of this saying does not lie at its surface. "But I say unto you: Elijah has come and they did to him as they wished, as it is written with regard to him." The thoughtful reader is expected to gather that John the Baptist is the *Elijah redivivus* alluded to. Matthew, who copies this saying, also expands it to make it even more impressive. Under such circumstances the view is unacceptable that Mark should have inserted the gloss himself. I refer to Johannes Weiss, Bultmann, Ernst Lohmeyer, Norman Perrin, and Gerd Theissen.[6]

Or is there a convincing interpretation of this passage? Taken as a gloss its meaning would be: How is it possible to find a Scriptural reference stating that the Son of Man must suffer much and be reduced to nothing? An answer surely cannot refer to the central passage that Mark has in mind. For this quotation is carefully prepared by the text of the first announcement of the passion (Mark 8:31). Its ἀπεδοκίμασαν (12:10-11) is forceful and well placed at the climax of a parable with fatal momentum. Does the context of Mark 9:12b give clues to a commentator?

Rudolf Pesch considered this passage to be part of a pre-Marcan passion narrative. Motives are merged.[7] The question in Mark 9:12b, according to Pesch, has the function of associating the two men in their

---

6. Bultmann, *Geschichte der synoptischen Tradition*. See also Johannes Weiss, *Das älteste Evangelium: Ein Beitrag zum Verständnis des Markus-Evangeliums und der ältesten evangelischen Überlieferung* (Göttingen: Vandenhoeck & Ruprecht, 1903), 233; Alex Pallis, *Notes on St. Mark and St. Matthew*, 2nd ed. (London: Milford, 1932), 31; Ernst Lohmeyer, *Das Evangelium des Markus*, 10th ed. KEK 1.2 (Göttingen: Vandenhoeck & Ruprecht, 1937), 183 n. 1; Norman Perrin, "The Christology of Mark: A Study in Methodology," *JR* 51 (1971): 173-87, repr., *The Interpretation of Mark*, ed. William R. Telford (Edinburgh: T&T Clark, 1995), 125-40, esp. p. 135.

7. Rudolf Pesch, *Das Markusevangelium, 2: Kommentar zu Kap. 8,27-16,20*, HThKNT 2.2 (Freiburg: Herder, 1991), 71. The view that Mark is merely the redactor of a pre-Marcan *Grundschrift* has been criticized. There seems to be wide agreement on Mark's use of pre-Marcan material, but also a growing recognition of a distinct measure of creativity channeled by the theological aims of this author. "Mark is a composite text which displays considerable awkwardness at pericope level but considerable sophistication when viewed holistically" (William R. Telford, "The Pre-Marcan Tradition in Recent Research," in *The Four Gospels: Festschrift Frans Neirynck*, ed. F. van Segbroeck et al., BETL 100 [Leuven: Leuven University Press, 1992]: 2:711).

common destiny.[8] The verb ἐξουδενηθῇ refers to the text of Psalm 89:39 (LXX 88:38) καὶ ἐξουδένωσας ... τὸν χριστόν σου. By taking up the imagery of the suffering Righteous One the destiny of both men is brought into focus.

Since, however, the question in 9:12b remains unanswered, we must find out who asked it. Werner H. Kelber approached our passage from a less traditional viewpoint. In describing the narrative design of Mark he focused his interest upon the hermeneutical and theological consequences recognizable in a stage of deliberate literary transformation of received oral materials.[9] Kelber called attention to the function of scripture references within the specific context of Mark's passion narrative. Reporting on an article of Howard C. Kee[10] he states: "The author proceeded from the observation that 'the number of quotations from and allusions to scripture increases sharply' at the point where the narrative moves toward death. In Mark 11–16, Kee tabulated 57 scriptural quotations, approximately 160 allusions to scripture and 60 scriptural influences."[11] This reliance on the authority of Scripture to give his passion narrative the desired emphasis is paralleled, as Kelber says, by the use of scriptural allusions in some Marcan Son of Man sayings. "In Mark 9:11–13 the passion of the Son of Man is linked by divine necessity (*dei elthein prooton*) with that of Elijah, and both deaths are in accord with Scripture (9:12 *poos gegraptai*; 9:13 *kathoos gegraptai*)."[12] Accordingly the text of 9:12b is meaningful within Mark's design, if we follow this author here. We do not, and perhaps I will be permitted to repeat the statement that Mark does not give his scriptural reference at this early juncture of his narrative. In fact, no scriptural reference is required, as far as Mark is concerned.

---

8. Pesch, *Markusevangelium 2*, 79.

9. Werner H. Kelber, *The Oral and the Written Gospel: The Hermeneutics of Speaking and Writing in the Synoptic Tradition, Mark, Paul, and Q* (Philadelphia: Fortress, 1983).

10. Howard C. Kee, "The Function of Scriptural Quotations and Allusions in Mark 11–16," in *Jesus und Paulus: Festschrift für Werner Georg Kümmel zum 70. Geburtstag*, ed. E. Earle Ellis and Erich Grässer (Göttingen: Vandenhoeck & Ruprecht, 1975), 165–88.

11. Kelber, *Oral and the Written Gospel*, 196–97.

12. Kelber, *Oral and the Written Gospel*, 196.

3. Glosses in Mark 1:2–3

καθὼς γέγραπται ἐν τῷ Ἠσαΐᾳ τῷ προφήτῃ· ἰδοὺ ἀποστέλλω τὸν ἄγγελόν μου πρὸ προσώπου σου ὃς κατασκευάσει τὴν ὁδόν σου. φωνὴ βοῶντος ἐν τῇ ἐρήμῳ· ἑτοιμάσατε τὴν ὁδὸν κυρίου, εὐθείας ποιεῖτε τὰς τρίβους αὐτοῦ.

The beginning of the Gospel of Mark is by no means void of textual alterations. A carefully phrased proem like the one written by the author of the Gospel of Luke apparently commands some respect on the part of scribes. They resist the impulse to make improvements. As a consequence, alterations in Luke 1:1–4 are less numerous and less momentous than the ones to be studied in Mark. The apparatus of Nestle-Aland lists one variant only that involves Luke 1:3.[13]

Greek manuscripts, ancient versions, and early fathers are divided in their testimony regarding the phrase υἱοῦ θεοῦ in Mark 1:1. Many church fathers are listed among the witnesses to the omission, among them Irenaeus and Origen.[14]

Some authors, indeed, were reluctant to consider υἱοῦ θεοῦ or, as several witnesses testify, υἱοῦ τοῦ θεοῦ, as a gloss. The editors of UBS[4] enclosed one form of the addition within square brackets. Their hesitation was explained by the strong testimony for the addition, among them B D and

---

13. Barbara Aland et al., eds., *Novum Testamentum Graece,* 27th ed., 8th printing corrected and extended to Papyri 99–116 (Stuttgart: Deutsche Bibelgesellschaft, 2001).

14. Origen, *Comm. Jo.* 1.13.81 (Preuschen, 18); I. 24.128 and 129 (Preuschen, 134); Origen, *Cels.* II.4 (Koetschau, 131); Basil, *Contra Eunomium* II.15.15 (Sesboüé, de Durand. and L. Doutreleau, 58). The late character of the insertion is underscored by the observation that in Irenaeus it is transmitted with the obviously corrected reading "*in prophetis*," see III.16.3 and III.10.6. Adalbert Merx had already called attention to this text-critical observation in 1905; see Merx, *Die vier kanonischen Evangelien nach ihrem ältesten bekannten Texte* (Berlin: Reimer, 1905), 2:3, n. 1. In the Greek text of Irenaeus, *Haer.* III.11.8 (Sagnard, 198), we find Ἀρχὴ τοῦ εὐαγγελίου ... ὡς γέγραπται ἐν Ἠσαΐᾳ τῷ προφήτῃ. In a note Sagnard adds: "Ἰησου Χριστοῦ add. edd., quae voces desunt in Barocciani 206 ut in lat" (p. 198). In Joseph M. Alexanian, "The Armenian Version of the New Testament," in Ehrman and Holmes, *Status Quaestionis,* 159, attention is called to the fact that the evidence of the Armenian version in support of the omission is not correctly rendered in UBS[3] (p. 118). It is correctly given, however, in UBS[4] (p. 117).

W, and also by the consideration that υἱοῦ θεοῦ could have been omitted through oversight.[15] There are strong arguments, however, to support the view that we meet an ancient gloss here.

One of these is based on the observation that this unit of variation is transmitted in three forms. Rather than assuming that some scribes replaced υἱοῦ θεοῦ by υἱοῦ τοῦ θεοῦ we take the differing forms of the apposition together with an early and widespread testimony for an omission as an indication that an addition was inserted on more than one occasion or more than one place of origin.

A second argument is based on the observation that this verse is not the only one in Mark to transmit such an addition. As is well known, two similar additions to the text of Mark are found in Mark 8:29, namely, ὁ υἱὸς τοῦ θεοῦ or ὁ υἱὸς τοῦ θεοῦ τοῦ ζῶντος. Scribes, then, were eager to insert such phrases in appropriate places.

There is a third argument for this text-critical decision based on a consideration proper to this paper. The admission of this gloss into the text of Mark implies a modern disregard for the care with which this author introduces concepts and referential matter into the context of his narrative. A heavenly voice, unheard by onlookers, imparts this item of information in a narrative unit often referred to as prologue. As Frank J. Matera and others pointed out, this voice gives privileged information to the reader, information that is withheld from the dramatis personae, save the person addressed.[16]

Not a few authors defended the original status of υἱοῦ θεοῦ by stating that an omission by oversight is easily explained where a series of *nomina sacra* is involved.[17] In a text-critical study Bart D. Ehrman sought a fresh observation to meet the fallacy of such an argument within this debate:

---

15. Bruce M. Metzger, *A Textual Commentary on the Greek New Testament: A Companion Volume to the United Bible Societies' Greek New Testament (Fourth Revised Edition)*, 2nd ed. (Stuttgart: Deutsche Bibelgesellschaft, 1994), 62.

16. Frank J. Matera, "The Prologue as the Interpretative Key to Mark's Gospel," *JSNT* 34 (1988): 3–20; repr. in Telford, *Interpretation of Mark*, 289–306. The value of this fascinating interpretation is not impaired by the circumstance that this author failed to realize that υἱοῦ θεοῦ is not part of Mark's text, see pp. 4 and 6 (290 and 292).

17. Rudolf Pesch, *Das Markusevangelium, 1: Einleitung und Kommentar zu Kap. 1,1–8,26*, 5th ed., HThKNT 2.1 (Freiburg: Herder, 1989), 74, n. a.

In further support of this view is a practical consideration that until quite recently has been entirely overlooked. It should strike us as somewhat odd that the kind of careless mistake alleged to have occurred here, the omission of two rather important words should have happened precisely where it does—within the first six words of the beginning of a book ... I should note that recent manuscript analyses have indeed demonstrated that scribes were more conscientious transcribers at the beginning of a document.[18]

Υἱοῦ θεοῦ, of course, is a secondary addition to complete the list of references to this important concept of Mark (cf. 1:11; 3:11; 5:7; 9:7; 12:6; 13:32; 14:61; 15:39).[19]

Critical editions inform us that the series of verses inserted between verses 1 and 4 show three forms. Some witnesses have verse 3 and omit the text of the quotation blended from two sources, Exod 23:20 and Mal 3:1. Other witnesses merge the text of this blend of quotations to the text of verse 3, a slightly adapted quotation from Isa 40:3.

Two witnesses add further verses taken from Luke. Both add to the quotation from Isa 40:3, but they do not exactly follow either the text of their Lukan source, as far as we can gather, or the text of Isa 40:4–8. The text of Old Latin c and of W may be taken from the apparatuses of Constantin von Tischendorf and Hermann von Soden, or from the respective

---

18. Bart D. Ehrman, *The Orthodox Corruption of Scripture: The Effect of Early Christological Controversies on the Text of the New Testament* (Oxford: Oxford University Press, 1993), 73; Ehrman, "The Text of Mark in the Hands of the Orthodox," *LQ* 5 (1991): 150–51; Peter M. Head, "A Text-Critical Study of Mark 1:1: The Beginning of the Gospel of Jesus Christ," *NTS* 37 (1991): 629.

19. "In no other passage in the Gospels is there any evidence that 'Son of God' was ever omitted from the text" (Peter M. Head, "Christology and Textual Transmission: Reverential Alterations in the Synoptic Gospels," *NovT* 35 [1993]: 115); Head, "Text-Critical Study," 627. Among the authors who defended the shorter text are the following exegetes: Julius Wellhausen, *Das Evangelium Marci*, 2nd ed. (Berlin: Reimer, 1909), 3; Gustav Wohlenberg, *Das Evangelium des Markus*, 3rd ed., KNT 2 (Leipzig: Deichert, 1930), 36; Joseph Sickenberger, *Die Geschichte des Neuen Testamentes*, 4th ed. (Bonn: Hanstein, 1934), 32; Jan Slomp, "Are the Words 'Son of God' in Mark 1:1 Original?," *BT* 28 (1977): 146, 150; Adela Yarbro Collins, "Establishing the Text: Mark 1:1," in *Texts and Contexts: Biblical Texts in their Textual and Situational Contexts; Essays in Honor of Lars Hartman*, ed. Tord Fornberg and David Hellholm (Oslo: Scandinavian University Press, 1955), 111–27.

editions of Henry A. Sanders and of Walter Matzkow-Kurt Aland.[20] Since the texts of the two manuscripts differ from each other and do not find the support of any other known manuscript tradition, it is obvious that these additions were added much later than the ones we have to consider.

For our purpose, it is not necessary to discuss the text of the Washington Gospels and the Colbertinus in detail. These manuscripts bear witness to a desire of early scribes to augment the scriptural base of Mark's references to John the Baptist. If 1:2b could be proved to be secondary, this would lengthen the list of such insertions.

In addition to the disorders listed, according to Tischendorf there is indication of patristic testimony to the effect that 1:2b is not uniformly supported by this branch of our tradition. In his *Novum Testamentum Graece*, Tischendorf names three fathers who according to him did not read 1:2b in the context of a quotation: Basil the Great, Epiphanius, and Victorinus.[21]

It is doubtful, however, whether this conclusion bears scrutiny. It is true, two of these references may be taken to support Tischendorf's conclusion. Basil writes: Ἀρχὴ τοῦ εὐαγγελίου Ἰησοῦ Χριστοῦ καθὼς γέγραπται ἐν τῷ Ἡσαΐᾳ τῷ προφήτῃ· φωνὴ βοῶντος.[22] Comparing the beginnings of the four gospels, Basil praises the theological approach of the Gospel of John as a climax of this genre. The incipit of John is quoted verbatim, the incipit of Matthew and Mark, likewise. The beginning of Luke is not quoted, but is characterized briefly instead.

Basil's text of Mark as quoted above is augmented by C V and numerous later (or inferior) witnesses with the insertion of εν τη ερημω. If this is the younger text, as the editor seems to assume, we find here an inclination to elucidate similar to the one observed in the gospel manuscripts c and W mentioned above. But Basil's quotation of Mark does not prove beyond doubt that Basil read exactly what he quoted. Basil may well have

---

20. Henry A. Sanders, *Facsimile of the Washington Manuscript of the Four Gospels in the Freer Collection* (Ann Arbor: The University of Michigan, 1912); Adolf Jülicher, ed., *Itala: Das Neue Testament in altlateinischer Überlieferung, nach den Handschriften herausgegeben von Adolf Jülicher, durchgesehen und zum Druck besorgt von Walter Matzkow und Kurt Aland*, II. Markusevangelium, 2nd ed. (Berlin: de Gruyter, 1970).

21. Constantin von Tischendorf, *Novum Testamentum Graece* (Leipzig: Giesecke & Devrient, 1869), 1:217.

22. *Contra Eunomium*, II.15.15 (Sesboüé, de Durand, and Doutreleau, 58).

shortened his text in order to improve the structure of his argument. At any rate, we cannot exclude this possibility.

The reference of Epiphanius to Mark may be seen in a similar way. Μᾶρκος ... ἀλλὰ ἀπὸ τῆς ἐν τῷ Ἰορδάνῃ πραγματείας ποιεῖται τὴν εἰσαγωγὴν τοῦ εὐαγγελίου καί φησιν, ἀρχὴ τοῦ εὐαγγελίου ὡς γέγραπται ἐν Ἡσαΐᾳ τῷ προφήτῃ, φωνὴ βοῶντος ἐν τῇ ἐρήμῳ, κτλ.[23] The characterization of the narrative design of Mark's incipit in another passage by this author asserts that Mark quoted the law and the prophets. We read: πῶς τε ὁ Μᾶρκος περὶ τῶν ἐν τῷ κόσμῳ πεπραγματευένων <διηγήσατο> καὶ φωνῆς βοώσης ἐν τῇ ἐρήμῳ περί <τε> τοῦ κυρίου τοῦ διὰ προφητῶν πεπροφητευμένου καὶ νόμου.[24] But it is not clear which quotation he found in his manuscript. If this τοῦ διὰ προφητῶν πεπροφητευμένου καὶ νόμου refers to a transmitted reading ἐν τοῖς προφήταις (1:2a), this would be an indication of a late form of Mark's incipit as found by Epiphanius. In quoting he drops at least Ἰησοῦ Χριστοῦ. The text of the manuscript he quoted is not clear.

The text of Victorinus in his *Commentarii in Apocalypsin* is too short to support the view of Tischendorf. He writes: "Marcus incipit sic: initium evangelii Iesu Christi sicut scriptum est in Esaia."[25] What follows is attributed to Hieronymus by Johannes Haussleiter.[26]

On the other hand, there is no doubt that Origen found both quotations in his Gospel of Mark. His testimony to this effect is impressive. Not only does he quote in extenso, he adds that the author altered the wording of both quotations in a characteristic way. For he replaced τὰς τρίβους τοῦ θεοῦ ἡμῶν of Mal 3:1 by τὰς τρίβους αὐτοῦ and he omits

---

23. Epiphanius, *Pan.*, LI.6.4 (Holl, 255).

24. Epiphanius, *Pan.*, LXIX.22.4 (Dummer, 173). Insertions into the reconstructed text are insertions of Karl Holl.

25. Victorinus, *Comm. in Apocalypsin*, IV.4 (Haussleiter, 52).

26. Alexander Globe stated that Irenaeus is one of the authors who testify to the omission of verse 1:2b from the text of Mark. Collins pointed out: "He is correct in stating that Irenaeus cited only vss 1 and 3 from John 1 and only vss 1 and 18 from Matthew 1. The paraphrase of Luke 1, however, must include at least vs 8, as well as vs 5, because only vs 8 mentions Zachary's offering sacrifice to God. Globe's statement that Irenaeus omits the quotation from Malachi in Mark 1:2 is misleading, because it implies that the following quotation from Isaiah is cited. It is not. In fact, the quotations of Irenaeus are selections, not 'contractions'" (Collins, "Establishing the Text," 113). See Globe, "The Caesarean Omission of the Phrase 'Son of God' in Mark 1:1," *HTR* 75 (1982): 209–18.

ἐμπροσθέν μου from the text of Isa 40:3 οὐ παρέθετο τὸ προσκείμενον τὸ "'Ἐμπροσθέν μου.'"[27]

4. Lachmann's Critique of the Traditional Insertion of Verses 2 and 3 into the Text of Mark

As early as 1830 Karl Lachmann voiced the opinion that Mark 1:2–3 is not part of the original text of the author. This opinion falls into line with the observation that the state of preservation of the Gospel of Mark is far from excellent. "Often where our traditions fluctuate considerably this may contribute to reaching a decision. The abundance of fluctuating readings in the Gospel of Mark leads everyone to the conviction that its transmission was hardly careful and that certainly in a number of passages it is corrupted."[28]

In passing Lachmann gives his position on the synoptic question. He has not found evidence to support the view that Mark knows the text of either of the other Synoptic Gospels[29] or, to be more specific, that he abstracts Old Testament quotations from one of the Synoptic Gospels in order to use them in a different function or context.[30]

Here we already find an argument that we read also in his second edition of the Greek New Testament. "Mark never uses a passage of the Old Testament except in direct speech."[31] In addition to this argument, which appeals to a literary reading of Mark's narrative, Lachmann takes exception to two specific shortcomings of the Received Text.

(1) A quotation to give legitimation to the forerunner quoted in the name of the evangelist himself is out of harmony with the evident purpose of his introduction. "If indeed the author designed to do something extraordinary in the beginning of the book, something he did not do again, certainly a testimony of Holy Scripture on behalf of Christ was needed rather than one on behalf of the forerunner."[32]

(2) The quotation disrupts the easy flow of the narrative and obstructs

---

27. Origen, *Comm. Jo.*, I. 24.131 and I.26.137 (Preuschen 135, 136).
28. Karl Lachmann, "Rechenschaft über seine Ausgabe des Neuen Testaments," *TSK* 3 (1830): 841.
29. Lachmann, "Rechenschaft über seine Ausgabe," 843.
30. Lachmann, "Rechenschaft über seine Ausgabe," 844.
31. Lachmann, "Rechenschaft über seine Ausgabe," 843.
32. Lachmann, "Rechenschaft über seine Ausgabe," 844.

the understanding of an important point the author wishes to make. "What is more, these words interrupt the progression of speech, make it totally incomprehensible, speech which is–without them–simple and smooth: ἀρχὴ τοῦ εὐαγγελίου Ἰησοῦ Χριστοῦ υἱοῦ θεοῦ ἐγένετο Ἰωάννης, βαπτίζων ἐν τῇ ἐρήμῳ καὶ κηρύσσων βάπτισμα μετανοίας εἰς ἄφεσιν ἁμαρτιῶν."[33]

Lachmann summarized his critique of these glosses in the *Praefatio* to the second volume of his Greek New Testament of 1850:

> Mark 1:1.4 Ἀρχὴ τοῦ εὐαγγελίου Ἰησοῦ Χηριστοῦ υἱοῦ θεοῦ ἐγένετο Ἰωάννης βαπτίζων ἐν τῇ ἐρήμῳ. These words were singled out by Origen 4:15 e: "For how can John be a beginning of a gospel?" Nor can these words, ἐγένετο Ἰωάννης βαπτίζων ἐν τῇ ἐρήμῳ, be understood in any reasonable way if separated from the preceding words, unless you allow the matter to have been told unexpectedly and without plan, this "John made his appearance baptizing in the desert ..." But in the beginning of Mark the interjection subverts the true interpretation. It is an annotation by pious readers, if I am not mistaken, in contrast to the practice of this evangelist who does not use the words of Old Testament authors unless they come from the lips of those whom he causes to speak. Therefore, when one of these readers had added what usually was placed here, ὡς γέγραπται ἐν τῷ Ἡσαΐᾳ τῷ προφητῇ φωνὴ βοῶντος ἐν τῷ ἐρήμῳ, ἑτοιμάσατε τὴν ὁδὸν κυρίου, εὐθείας ποιεῖτε τὰς τρίβους αὐτοῦ, another reader succeeded him who decided what Matthew and Luke had put somewhere else ought to be inserted here, ἰδοὺ ἀποστέλλω τὸν ἄγγελόν μου πρὸ προσώπου σου, ὃς κατασκευάσει τὴν ὁδόν σου. Because the name Isaias did not suit these words, they had to write what others have, namely, ἐν τοῖς προφήταις. In conflict with the same practice of Mark, which I have stated to have been observed by him in quoting testimonies of Scripture, is what we read in 15:28 and what is omitted by many and the best manuscripts καὶ ἐπληρώθη ἡ γραφὴ ἡ λέγουσα καὶ μετὰ ἀνόμων ἐλογίσθη, a text Luke gives at a far distant passage in a speech of Christ, 22:37.[34]

Lachmann argued that none of the passages quoted in Mark 1:1–3 were supplied by the author but were inserted by certain readers, pious individuals, as he surmised. I wish to underscore a few points in this argument.

---

33. Lachmann, "Rechenschaft über seine Ausgabe," 844.

34. Karl Lachmann, ed. *Novum Testamentum Graece et Latine*, 2nd ed. (Berlin: Reimer, 1850), 2:vi–vii; cf. Westcott and Hort, *New Testament in the Original Greek, Appendix*, 27.

Lachmann refers his readers to a literary reading of Mark's text. He expects them to observe that Mark as the author of a gospel disclaims any argument from Scripture in his own name. Lachmann, too, is convinced that the approach of this author to his narrative was not perfunctory, but that he proceeded with care. Clouds may overshadow the figures of a scene, but to surprise the reader by an ill-chosen series of quotes is not to be expected of an accomplished narrator. Lachmann, the distinguished editor of *Der Nibelunge Not mit der Klage*, of the *Iwein*, of *Lucretius*, refers to the argument from context adding only necessary detail. He asks Origen to state what he himself wishes to say.

In concluding, Lachmann quotes another example of an inappropriate interjection. Both force the author to forego his role as a narrator and make him a teacher. Lachmann's example parallels two closely related arguments, an argument from the style, supported by excellent witnesses and an argument from the style supported by no witness at all. Both lead to the recommendation of a shorter text on the authority and experience of a literary critic and editor, one of the finest in the history of our discipline.[35]

5. The Syntax of the First Sentence of Mark's Gospel

Lachmann's arguments force us to consider whether the beginning of Mark's Gospel has been handed down to us in its original wording. There are evident insertions, namely, the appositions υἱοῦ θεοῦ and υἱοῦ τοῦ θεοῦ, and also in some traditions additional verses. There is at least one scribal correction, namely, the variant reading ἐν τοῖς προφήταις, so A W fam[13]

---

35. Lachmann's view was endorsed by Christian Hermann Weisse, *Die evangelische Geschichte kritisch und philosophisch bearbeitet* (Leipzig: Breitkopf & Härtel, 1838), 1:258; Wellhausen, *Evangelium Marci*, 3–4; Wellhausen, *Einleitung in die ersten drei Evangelien*, 2nd ed. (Berlin: Reimer, 1911), 44, n. 1; Alfred F. Loisy, *L' Évangile selon Marc* (Paris: Nourry, 1912), 55–56: "Celle-ci est d'ailleurs un cas unique dans le second Évangile, ou le narrateur n' allègue jamais de l'Ancien Testament; elle vient en surcharge et ne se lie pas au récit, qu'elle glosse par anticipation." Willi Marxsen called attention to the fact that the passage quoted presents the only *Reflexionszitat* used by this author. He did not discuss the critical position developed by Lachmann (Marxsen, *Der Evangelist Markus: Studien zur Redaktionsgeschichte des Evangeliums*, 2nd ed., FRLANT 49 [Göttingen: Vandenhoeck & Ruprecht, 1959], 18 n. 4).

vg^ms sy^h Irenaeus^lat.³⁶ Textual criticism enables us to gain from the transmitted variants the more original form.

Is this evidently more original form of the text Mark's text? If stylistic anomalies are visible against the background of Mark's Greek, this may cast doubt on the transmitted text and may give additional support to Lachmann's observation of an ancient corruption. If there are no anomalies in the first verses of Mark, it ought to be possible to reconstruct its syntax in a convincing way.³⁷

A number of exegetes argued that the prologue proper of Mark began with the conjunction καθώς. This implies that Mark placed a subordinate clause at the beginning of his prologue and also that the words ἀρχὴ τοῦ εὐαγγέλιου Ἰησοῦ Χηριστοῦ are meant to be a superscription.³⁸ It is widely conceded that Mark, when using εὐαγγέλιον, refers to some oral proclamation of his time and not to a written gospel in its later technical sense.³⁹ The view that ἀρχὴ τοῦ εὐαγγέλιου Ἰησοῦ Χηριστοῦ refers to the first part of Mark's text, or is meant to introduce the whole gospel in a solemn manner, would tend to lead to the assumption that this part of Mark's Gospel was added at a time when its text needed revision. This conclusion, however, is hardly ever suggested.⁴⁰

---

36. See §3 above.

37. In his analysis of Mark 1:1, M. Eugene Boring presented a concise review of the options discussed in the exegetical literature, see Boring, "Mark 1:1–15 and the Beginning of the Gospel," *Semeia* 52 (1990): 43–81.

38. Hort championed that view and defended the separateness of verse 1 (Westcott and Hort, *New Testament in the Original Greek*, Appendix, 23). This view was taken up by, among others, Wellhausen, *Evangelium Marci*, 3; Marie-Joseph Lagrange, *Évangile selon Saint Marc*, 4th ed., EB (Paris: Gabalda, 1929), 1; Vincent Taylor, *The Gospel according to St. Mark*, 2nd ed. (London: Macmillan, 1966), 152; Pesch, *Markusevangelium*, 1:74.

39. "Im NT ist εὐαγγέλιον die mündliche Predigt, nie werden die Briefe oder die Evangelien εὐαγγελίον genannt" (Gerhard Friedrich, "εὐαγγελίον," *TDNT* 2:735. In the context of the Sayings Gospel Q the term εὐαγγελίζεσθαι is discussed by James M. Robinson ("The Sayings Gospel Q," in *The Four Gospels 1992: Festschrift Frans Neirynck*, ed. F. van Segbroeck et al., 3 vols., BETL 100 [Leuven: Leuven University Press, 1992], 1:370–72).

40. This suggestion is proposed by Friedrich, "εὐαγγελίον," 2:727 n. 52 with a reference to Tatian and the Evangeliarium Hierosolymitanum (i.e., the Palestinian Syriac Gospel lectionary). I will seek to show below that this proposition is based on a misunderstanding of Mark's narrative design.

There are authors who do not accept this view. Gerhard Arnold, for instance, argued that a quotation introduced by καθὼς γέγραπται is never, in any of the instances he lists, construed with what follows. "All quotations introduced in this way refer to an immediately preceding context."[41] Similarly J. Keith Elliott stated: "In Mark (8 instances) and Matthew (21:6, 26:24, 27:10 v.l., 28:6) the καθώς clause follows the main clause. The only instance where this rule is in question is at Mark 1:2."[42] Arnold's conclusion, therefore, is that 1:2-3 must be construed with what precedes and that 1:4 is the beginning of a second sentence. Arnold compared opening remarks in numerous Hellenistic and Classical writings and considered 1:1-3 to be an example of such opening remarks. While this view is hardly convincing here,[43] what Arnold writes on καθώς cannot easily be brushed aside. Parallels for this καθώς in Mark as presented by Vincent Taylor[44] are not quite to the point.[45]

If ἀρχή is not an element of a traditional topos of an opening paragraph, it may not refer to the beginning of a book, which Mark is about to write. On the other hand, I agree with the view of Arnold that alleged parallels for a superscription ἀρχὴ τοῦ εὐαγγελίου Ἰησοῦ Χηριστοῦ do not really support this interpretation. In particular the introduction in Hos. 1:2-3, ἀρχὴ λόγου κυρίου πρὸς Ωσηε, is not a superscription.[46]

Several authors paid attention to the specific ways in which Mark introduces explanatory and referential matter in the form of a parenthe-

---

41. Gerhard Arnold, "Mk 1.1 und Eröffnungswendungen in griechischen und lateinischen Schriften," *ZNW* 68 (1977): 123.

42. J. Keith Elliott, "καθως and ωσπερ in the New Testament," *FNT* 4 (1991): 55. Similarly Robert A. Guelich, "The Beginning of the Gospel: Mark 1:1-15," *BR* 27 (1982): 6.

43. The prologue of Mark shows little contact with the conventions of ancient προοίμια, πρόλογοι, or the less formal incipits; see Dennis E. Smith, "Narrative Beginnings in Ancient Literature and Theory," *Semeia* 52 (1990): 1-9, and Robert C. Tannehill, "Beginning to Study 'How Gospels Begin,'" *Semeia* 52 (1990): 185-91.

44. Vincent Taylor, *The Gospel according to St. Mark*, 2nd ed. (Grand Rapids: Baker, 1981), 153.

45. Mark lacks the sequence καθὼς ... οὕτως in our passage. In 1 Cor 2:9 ἀλλά refers to matter already discussed; see Arnold, "Mk 1.1 und Eröffnungswendungen," 124.

46. The superscription of Hosea is found in verse 1:1 of the book; cf. Arnold, "Mk 1.1 und Eröffnungswendungen," 123.

sis.⁴⁷ The manner in which this material is embedded into narrative units occasionally engenders misunderstanding. C. H. Turner recommended an interpretation of Mark 1:1-4 in which Mark 1:2-3 appears as a parenthesis. Heinrich J. Holtzmann argued that a text comprising only 2a-3 could be accepted as a parenthesis more easily than the traditional text could.⁴⁸ We ought to notice, however, that the stylistic anomaly of Mark's καθὼς γέγραπται is not dealt with in a convincing way on the basis of such an interpretation. Nor is it admissible to use an argumentum ad hominem here, as Boring does.⁴⁹ The view that an author ending on Mark 16:8 could have done almost anything is not acceptable.

Another anomaly is noticeable in the series of quotations allegedly assembled by the author of this gospel. On comparing ἐν τοῖς προφήταις with the reading ἐν τῷ Ἠσαΐᾳ τῷ προφήτῃ we decided that the former looks like a scribal correction of the latter text. And the list of witnesses representing both readings seemed to support our decision. But there is a third variant to be considered at this point of the transmitted text, namely, the reading of D Θ fam¹ 700 *l*844 *l*2211 Irenaeus Origen *partim* Epiphanius: ἐν Ἠσαΐᾳ τῷ προφήτῃ.

If we compare this text with the preferred reading of ℵ B L Δ 33 565 892 1241 2427 sy^p hmg copt Origen *partim* ἐν τῷ Ἠσαΐᾳ τῷ προφήτῃ, we are inclined to regard it as another scribal correction dependent upon the preferred text. The article is certainly awkward, for we know that Mark

---

47. C. H. Turner, "Marcan Usage: Notes, Critical and Exegetical, on the Second Gospel, IV," *JTS* 26 (1926): 145-56; repr., *The Language and Style of the Gospel of Mark: An Edition of Turner's 'Notes on Marcan Usage' Together with Other Comparable Studies*, ed. J. Keith Elliott, NovTSup 71 (Leiden: Brill, 1993), 23-35; Max Zerwick, *Untersuchungen zum Markus-Stil: Ein Beitrag zur stilistischen Durcharbeitung des Neuen Testaments* (Rome: Pontifical Biblical Institute, 1937), 130-38.

48. Heinrich J. Holtzmann, *Das Evangelium nach Marcus*, vol. 2 of *Die Synoptiker: Hand-Commentar zum Neuen Testament*, 3rd ed. (Tübingen: Mohr, 1901), 111-12. The view that 1:1b is a secondary gloss added to Mark's text is defended by, among others, Marie-Joseph Lagrange, *Évangile selon Saint Marc*, 9th ed. (Paris: Gabalda, 1966), 4; Sickenberger, *Geschichte des Neuen Testamentes*, 33; A. E. J. Rawlinson, *The Gospel according to St. Mark* (London: Methuen, 1949), 6; Taylor, *Gospel according to St. Mark*, 153.

49. Boring, "Mark 1:1-15 and the Beginning of the Gospel," 50. Boring criticizes Mary Ann Tolbert, *Sowing the Gospel: Mark's World in Literary-Historical Perspective* (Minneapolis: Augsburg Fortress, 1989), 341-46.

is particular about his articles when introducing characters for the first time. Is it safe to assume that the article goes back to the author here? Among the quotations from the fathers that I have noted I have only once seen a text that took up this article. All other quotations had ἐν Ἠσαΐᾳ τῷ προφήτῃ.⁵⁰

This text, which apparently is considered acceptable by the authors quoting it, may in part lead back to manuscripts that had this corrected reading. In other instances obviously the fathers put down what they considered correct: ἐν Ἠσαΐᾳ τῷ προφήτῃ. If so many of them are positive about this stylistic feature, how can we assume that the author himself was inattentive right at the beginning of a gospel? When introducing John, when introducing Jesus, Mark is careful to use the anarthrous form of the names.⁵¹ Evidently the assumption is to be preferred that καθὼς γέγραπται ἐν τῷ Ἠσαΐᾳ τῷ προφήτῃ was supplied by some later hand, not by the author.

C. H. Turner acted as a spokesman of ancient exegetes, of Origen, of Basil, of Victor of Antioch. He considered 1:2–3 as one of the characteristic parentheses of this author and argued that the syntax of 1:1 must be seen as connected with 1:4. "The beginning of the proclamation of good news about Jesus as Messiah and Son of God, was John the Baptizer's preaching in the wilderness a baptism of repentance for remission of sins."⁵²

I prefer to accept the argument of Lachmann and consider it possible that in some passages of our gospels corruption occurred, even if manuscript evidence for the original text is missing. Corruption normally leaves

---

50. Irenaeus, *Haer.* 3.11.8 (Sagnard, 198); Origen, *Comm. Jo* 1.13.81 (Preuschen, 18); Origen, *Cels.* 2.4 (Koetschau, 131); Basil, *Contra Eunomium* 2.15.15 (Sesboüé, de Durand, and Doutreleau, 58); Epiphanius, *Pan.* 51.5.4 (Holl, 255); Victorinus 4.4 (Haussleiter, 52). It is true that there is one passage in Origen that has Ἀρχὴ τοῦ εὐαγγελίου Ἰησοῦ Χριστοῦ καθὼς γέγραπται ἐν [τῷ] Ἠσαΐᾳ τῷ προφήτῃ· ἰδοὺ ἐγὼ ἀποστέλλω τὸν ἄγγελόν μου πρὸ προσώπου σου, namely, Origen, *Comm. Jo.* 1.24.128 and 129 (Preuschen, 134) and the manuscripts seem to support the article. But the editor of Origen, Preuschen, prefers the form of text quoted in *Cels.* and remarks: "τω fehlt in S. 17,32 u[nd] C. Cels. II.4 [I.131.14 Koetschau] u. ist wohl mit D.1.22 alii Iren. zu str.[eichen]" (134).

51. C. H. Turner in dealing with Markan usage apparently does not notice the reason for his omission of the article in 1:9. His respect for the evidence, however, leads him in both instances he discussed to decisions that are, at least in my opinion, correct. See Turner, "Marcan Usage, IV," 137.

52. "Marcan Usage, IV," 146 (repr., Elliott, *Language and Style*, 24).

traces and I have dealt with some of these. I am not willing to consider this possibility as a serious deficiency in a literary analysis of our sources.[53]

I summarize as follows these considerations regarding Mark's text: Ἀρχὴ τοῦ εὐαγγελίου Ἰησοῦ Χηριστοῦ ἐγένετο Ἰωάννης ὁ βαπτίζων ἐν τῇ ἐρήμῳ κηρύσσων βάπτισμα μετανοίας εἰς ἄφεσιν ἁμαρτιῶν.

1. This sentence states the close association of the public appearance of John with what later was styled the gospel of Jesus Christ.
2. The form of this sentence can be characterized as a summary such as Mark usually places at the beginning of a major section of his narrative.
3. This sentence is pregnant in its conciseness, and it avoids unnecessary articles in order to give the beginning of the book dignity: ἐν τῇ ἐρήμῳ κηρύσσων βάπτισμα μετανοίας εἰς ἄφεσιν ἁμαρτιῶν.
4. The first word of this sentence is predicative. For this reason the anarthrous ἀρχή is correct; it conforms to Colwell's rule.
5. The decision to place a predicate at the beginning of a book is perfectly admissible. An author who speaks an Aramaic dialect, as we assume Mark to have done, will normally tend to use such word order for various purposes. Here we see the author deliberately using dignified speech. His keynote requires further comment in a section that will follow.[54]

---

53. Recently Christopher M. Tuckett argued for a balanced consideration of source-critical and text-critical data with special reference to the much-discussed problem of the "minor agreements" in triple-tradition material. Some decades ago Frederick M. Grant argued that there is necessarily a certain degree of overlap involving form-critical and text-critical considerations. See Tuckett, "The Minor Agreements and Textual Criticism," in *Minor Agreements: Symposion Göttingen 1991*, ed. Georg Strecker, GTA 50 (Göttingen: Vandenhoeck & Ruprecht, 1993), 138, 142; Grant, "Where Form Criticism and Textual Criticism Overlap," *JBL* 59 (1940): 11–21.

54. See §7 below.

6. The Contribution of Q Studies to
Our Understanding of Mark's Narrative

A number of authors have endeavored to explain the purpose and function of scriptural quotations in Mark's Gospel.[55] They have analyzed these texts in the context of Mark's redactional work or, more recently, they have analyzed this evidence in an effort to understand Mark's literary and narrative techniques. These authors did not consider the alternative that Mark 1:2–3 was added in order to meet a later need.[56]

First we must emphasize that Q-texts with their polished rhetorical structures form a distinct contrast to Mark's narrative techniques. Q develops speech and dialogue in a way that integrates parallelism and numerical patterning, catchwords and lexical patterning, repetition and climax. Q presents his universal theological outlook in speech; Mark tells tales. On the other hand Mark could use Q-materials. He endeavored to integrate them into his own narrative. Overlap texts reveal his use of Q, as for instance in his quotation of the divine voice on the occasion of Christ's baptism (Mark 1:11).[57] Some studies on the text of Q maintain that the use of Scripture references is not a common element in Q. Sections incorporating Scripture quotations are ascribed to later editorial stages in the production of this source.[58]

We find explicit references to Scriptures in the temptation narrative (Q 4:4, 8, 10–11) and in Q 7:27. We need to be aware, though, that the

---

55. David S. New, *Old Testament Quotations in the Synoptic Gospels and the Two Document Hypothesis*, SCS 37 (Atlanta: Scholars Press, 1993); W. S. Vorster, "The Function of the Use of the Old Testament in Mark," *Neot* 14 (1981): 62–72; Kee, "Function of Scriptural Quotations," 165–88; Alfred Suhl, *Die Funktion der alttestamentlichen Zitate und Anspielungen im Markusevangelium* (Gütersloh: Mohn, 1965).

56. Harry T. Fleddermann (*Q: A Reconstruction and Commentary*, BTS 1 [Leuven: Peeters, 2005], 75) cites Mark 1:2 as an element of Mark's narrative.

57. Fleddermann, *Q: A Reconstruction and Commentary*, discusses problems of the overlap between Mark and Q (75–77).

58. Arland D. Jacobson states, "There are several signs of lateness in the temptation pericope: The use of the title, "Son of God," the use of the LXX and, indeed, of the only explicit quotations in the whole of Q; the apparently late literary form; and the use of the name for the Evil One, which is attested nowhere else in Q." (Jacobson, *The First Gospel: An Introduction to Q* [Sonoma, CA: Polebridge, 1992]: 90–91).

interpretation of Q is complicated by the high number of difficult issues, issues that are being studied intensively in the scholarly community.[59]

James M. Robinson, in an analysis of "conscious organizing intentions" in Q,[60] found traces of a formative stage in the theology of the Q community in which reasons for the ascription of the "Son of God" title were still discussed, and in which also the title ὁ ἐρχόμενος in its specific context within Q had not yet become a formally fixed element. A cento of clauses from Isaiah in Q 7:22 "serves to define Jesus's Inaugural Sermon and his healing of the centurion's boy as validating the ascription to him of the title ὁ ἐρχόμενος."[61] The inclusio Q 7:18–35 does not yet presuppose the text of Luke 4:1–10 that apparently was formed at a later stage to give substance to some of the positions of the Q community in confrontation with their opponents.

> However, the distinctiveness of the role of the Son of God title in the Temptation must be seen more sharply: Christological titles are almost never derived or justified in the canonical texts themselves, but are rather presupposed and used as commonly known and accepted. But here the Temptation is built primarily (in two of the three temptations) around defining and defending that title. Jesus rejects the devil's inferences from that title, and validates himself as conforming to the true meaning of the title, in that he knows and observes Torah faithfully (He quotes Deut. 8,3; 6,16; 6,13 with the quotation formula, γέγραπται, found elsewhere in Q only at 7.27).[62]

Robinson concluded that the baptism of Jesus was included in the "narrative preface of Q":

> If the Baptism of Jesus with the heavenly voice identifying him as ὁ υἱός μου ὁ ἀγαπητός, is to be included in Q, then the temptation (Q 4.1–13) would be the authoritative Christian interpretation, similar to the role of Q 7.19-22 in Christianizing the title John had used, ὁ ερχόμενος (Q 3.16). These two instances of the formation of Christology are rather unique

---

59. Ronald A. Piper, "In Quest of Q: The Direction of Q Studies," in *The Gospel Behind the Gospels: Current Studies in Q*, ed. Ronald A. Piper, NovTSup 75 (Leiden: Brill, 1995), 1–18.

60. Robinson, "Sayings Gospel Q," 361–88.

61. Robinson, "Sayings Gospel Q," 365.

62. Robinson, "Sayings Gospel Q," 384.

in the New Testament, perhaps indicative of the archaic traditions preserved in Q.[63]

We must bear in mind that the Gospel of Mark is an early literary venture and that its presentation of scriptural evidence necessarily exposes early phases of a process of research that sought to augment this evidence in the course of a number of years. Christian scribes who were engaged in this type of research had to overcome various difficulties. Not the least of these difficulties was the problem of gaining access to handwritten copies of prophetic and other Scriptures.

Insight into this problem of early Christian authors may be gained from a later source, from the Gospel of Matthew. While the evangelist was able to consult the text of Isaiah, there are data that lead to the inference that Matthew did not have access to a copy of the Dodekapropheton, or to a scroll of Jeremiah, an author who for other reasons is only rarely cited in early Christian texts.[64] Matthew uses scriptural quotations from Q and also texts quoted by Mark. To these he adds further traditions to shape his formula quotations.

In comparing this approach of Q to a current problem of its time with the design of Mark's narrative gospel, we observe characteristic differences. While Q uses Scripture to introduce claims concerning christological titles such as ὁ ἐρχόμενος and ὁ υἱὸς τοῦ θεοῦ, Mark with a similar aim designs narrative. Mark relies on authoritative voices. One of them is the answer of Christ in Mark 9:13. Another voice is reported in 1:7, ἔρχεται ὁ ἰσχυρότερός μου.

Similarly the first use of the "Son of God" title in Mark is ascribed to the divine voice in Mark 1:11. This settles it for Mark, while for Luke in a

---

63. Robinson, "Sayings Gospel Q," 385. The introduction of the Sayings Gospel Q cannot be reconstructed from our materials. See Fleddermann, *Q: A Reconstruction and Commentary*, 210; F. Neirynck, "The Minor Agreements and Q," in Piper, *Gospel Behind the Gospels*, 65 ("All we can possibly retain ... is the assumption that the Q introduction had the disciples as the audience of the Sermon").

64. Ulrich Luz, *Das Evangelium nach Matthäus, 1: Mt 1–7*, EKKNT 1.1 (Zurich: Benziger; Neukirchen: Neukirchener Verlag, 1985), 135 with nn. 6 and 7. I refer here to results of a study by Dietrich-Alexander Koch, *Die Schrift als Zeuge des Evangeliums: Untersuchungen zur Verwendung und zum Verständnis der Schrift bei Paulus*, BHT 69 (Tübingen: Mohr, 1986), 45–46.

later phase of gospel production a scriptural quotation is considered suited to such an occasion.[65]

Whether scribes who copied Mark relied on the tradition of Q for the insertion of 1:2b, or whether they cited either Matt 11:10 or Luke 7:27, cannot be ascertained. But the form of the quoted text makes it unlikely that there is an independent origin for the quotation in Q. The Marcan text omits ἔμπροσθέν σου and is, therefore, secondary to a form that exhibits a full parallelism as found in Q.

If Mark 1: 2a–3 is not Markan, it could have been taken from Q, which we reconstruct on the evidence of minor agreements.[66] Occasionally the view has been expressed that the quotation of Isa 40:3 in Matt 3:3 and Luke 3:4 in these authors could be traced to Q.[67]

---

65. Several authors consider the quotation of Ps 2:7 in Luke 3:22 to be the original text. Ehrman defended this reading: Ehrman, *Orthodox Corruption of Scripture*, 62–77; Ehrman, "The Text of the Gospels at the End of the Second Century," in *Codex Bezae: Studies from the Lunel Colloquium June 1994*, ed. David C. Parker and Christian-B. Amphoux, NTTS 22 (Leiden: Brill, 1996), 106. Greeven and Boismard/Lamouille in their synopses printed it. I am not quite convinced that Robinson's suggestion of a "narrative preface" of Q is warranted. The form of the introduction, which must have included elements such as Ναζαρα, or πασα ἡ περιχωρος του Ιορδανου, and at least the fact of Jesus's baptism, is a problem not yet solved. I refer my readers to an analysis of Robinson's argument by Risto Uro, "John the Baptist and the Jesus Movement: What Does Q Tell Us?," in Piper, *Gospel Behind the Gospels*, 237–39.

66. Recent endeavors to prove the acquaintance of Mark with a written text of the Sayings Gospel Q, as argued by Fleddermann, and also by David C. Catchpole and J. Lambrecht, have been questioned on methodological grounds by Frans Neirynck and Ismo Dunderberg. See Neirynck, "Assessment," in *Mark and Q: A Study of the Overlap Texts*, ed. Harry T. Fleddermann, BETL 122 (Leuven: Leuven University Press, 1995), 261–307; Dunderberg, "Q and the Beginning of Mark," *NTS* 41 (1995): 501–11.

67. "Again in all three gospels John's preaching is introduced by the quotation from Isaiah φωνὴ βοῶντος κτλ. Seeing that in no other case does the editor of Mark himself introduce a quotation or reference to the Old Testament it is probable that this occurred also in Q" (B. H. Streeter, "St. Mark's Knowledge and Use of Q," in *Studies in the Synoptic Problem, by Members of the University of Oxford*, ed. W. Sanday [Oxford: Clarendon, 1911], 168).

7. Final Control: A Gloss Impairs Mark's Narrative Design

At the beginning of this essay evidence of secondary influences was presented, which have a bearing upon the transmission of Mark's opening sentence. An anomaly visible against the background of Mark's role as author of a narrative gospel was forcefully argued by Lachmann. I considered his argument in extenso. Exegetical work concentrated upon the interpretation of Mark's first sentence reveals obvious difficulties. The position of καθώς within the transmitted text poses problems and therefore gives rise to objections that support the view that this portion was grafted onto the original text. Finally, the division of witnesses over an article in the enlarged text-form was considered to be an indication of its secondary origin: ἐν τῷ Ἠσαΐᾳ does not conform to Mark's style (cf. 7:6; 12:36).

Mark introduces his narrative without introducing himself. Even his prologue is a narrative text. I suggest a final control: an effort to interpret 1:1–13 as an original entity designed to enlighten the reader for what he has to expect.

Mark shares privileged information, as Matera has stated. He introduces characters. At the same time he is careful to raise expectations and to spread elements of indistinctiveness likely to raise questions. Let us consider his design.

Almost everywhere in his gospel in speaking of people Mark uses arthrous forms. This is not in conflict with standards of Koine Greek. He never does this, however, when introducing a new figure. Here the anarthrous form is in sole use: ἐγένετο Ἰωάννης, ... ἦλθεν Ἰησοῦς. All this proves that the author is fully aware of what is involved in his task of introducing characters, preparing scenes, selecting his terms. Mark does not introduce John with the obvious term of his contemporary Flavius Josephus (*Ant.* 18.116–119). Instead of ὁ βαπτιστής, a term he knows, he writes ὁ βαπτίζων.

Mark introduces two prominent figures. For our investigation it is important to see how he accentuates the difference between them. Several passages throw light upon this theme. To begin with, the work of both figures is placed within a common local frame (1:5; 3:7–8), but it involves temporal difference (1:14). At an important juncture the author implies that a common task joins both men. Yet it is not Mark as a narrator who takes responsibility for this statement, but one of his figures: "The baptism of John, was heaven its origin or men?" (11:30). No attention is paid to the hometown of John nor to his parents. The desert as the place of his activities is set in relief. Since the arid area called desert borders on the Jordan River, we find no contradiction in this concept.

For the introduction of the second figure, Jesus, Mark guards the narrative unity of location. This also serves to unite the figures. But there is no cooperation. Jesus is baptized in the Jordan as it is described. It is understood that the recipients of John's baptism immersed themselves. The account is short. There is no explicit reference to the meeting of the two men. The reader may even gain the impression that the Baptist was unaware of who it was that he baptized. The heavenly sign is revealed to Jesus, the heavenly voice remains unknown to anyone, except to the readers of this account. It is possible to read the privilege of a heavenly voice as a commission, the victorious encounter with Satan as an initiation. All this is told not with reference to John, but to Jesus.

John is depicted in the midst of streams of visitors. The whole of Jerusalem and all of Judea crowd together. They confess their sins. In comparison Jesus appears to be alone. His place of origin, Nazareth in Galilee, is mentioned. Nothing is said about other Galileans. His work has not yet begun. Yet his activity is being described as led by the Spirit. Mark does not use an adjective. This word is introduced not at this point of Mark's narrative, but earlier in a saying of John: the stronger one baptizes with the Holy Spirit.

Jesus overcomes Satan, and angels serve him where beasts of the desert roam. He, of whom great things are said, is never himself described.

It is telling, I think, how sparingly abstract terms appear in this account. The first sentence mentions τὸ εὐαγγελίον, but there is no explanation. The first sentence speaks of Jesus Christ, but no further remark is added in clarification. The "Vorgeschichte" explicitly states the origin of the ἐξουσία of Jesus, but this word is not yet used. Never in the whole text of his gospel does the narrator call him the "Son." Never does he make use of the title "Son of Man." It is reserved for the speech of Jesus regarding himself. And the word κύριος, used in several scenes, conveys the impression that the author is wholly unfamiliar with this aspect of Christian terminology, which he is not.

If we are asked which "Textsorte" we read here, the answer must be unequivocal. Mark enters as a narrator, he does not come as a teacher. Whenever he speaks himself, he is telling a tale—unless he explains or establishes contact with a listener.

The whole prologue (i.e., vv. 1+4–13, as I am arguing) is replete with elements of narrative climax. The first verb (ἐγένετο, v. 4) makes a statement (as 1:14–15 do), after which the narrative has begun: καὶ ἐξεπορεύετο ... καὶ ἐβαπτίζοντο ... καὶ ἦν ... καὶ ἐκήρυσσεν (vv. 5–7). After this the narrative continues with aorists: καὶ ἐγένετο ἐν ἐκείναις ταῖς ἡμέραις ἦλθεν ... καὶ ἐβαπτίσθη ... καὶ ... εἶδεν ... καὶ φωνὴ ἐγένετο (vv. 9–11). Twice in this second part of the "Vorgeschichte" the familiar dramatic εὐθύς of our author makes its appearance (vv. 10, 12). We know that he does not use ἰδού in narrative. Finally, another dramatic expedient appears, Mark's historic present (v. 12).

Fittingly, as we expected in this accomplished narrative, tension is then relaxed. Three imperfects linger on our minds (v. 13). To discover a series of Scripture verses (i.e., vv. 2–3) in this sequence amounts to discovering disorder.

8. Summary

For a long time, literary criticism has been an established procedure for the student of the New Testament. Its present discussion is integrating new aspects, but its value and function within the continuing interplay of methods have not been challenged. Insights into the meaning of literary genres; into the communicative structures operating in the relation of an audience and its author, especially as studied within the frame of reference of Greco-Roman antiquity; and insights into literary devices and their contributions to form gained from modern and from classical literatures have all led to a refinement in its approaches. Yet still it is the task of literary criticism to clarify purpose and occasion in the production of a literary work, to delimit the date and circumstances of its publication, to define its genre, to ascertain its integrity and state of transmission, and to analyze, if at all possible, stages of its genesis.

In contemporary contributions to the textual criticism of the New Testament it is not always perceived to what degree the perspectives and results of literary criticism are a basic element of editorial procedure. For textual criticism itself, however, as well as for all other areas of New Testament studies, it is essential that unity and coherence of all procedures are discussed and consciously maintained.

In the course of a study of Mark's traditions on John the Baptist, evidence has been adduced to show that textual criticism is methodologically dependent upon the results and perspectives of literary criticism. The scope and experience of literary analysis are apt to lead textual criticism into new strategies of analysis and argumentation.

With regard to the text of Mark it is argued that the transmitted text received glosses in 1:2–3 and 9:12b.

Bibliography

Aland, Barbara, Kurt Aland, Johannes Karavidopoulos, Carlo M. Martini, and Bruce M. Metzger, eds., *Novum Testamentum Graece*. 27th ed. 8th printing corrected and extended to Papyri 99–116. Stuttgart: Deutsche Bibelgesellschaft, 2001.

Alexanian, Joseph M. "The Armenian Version of the New Testament." Pages 157–72 in *The Text of the New Testament in Contemporary Research: Essays on the Status Quaestionis; A Volume in Honour of Bruce M. Metzger*. Edited by Bart D. Ehrman and Michael W. Holmes. SD 46. Grand Rapids: Eerdmans, 1995.

Arnold, Gerhard. "Mk 1.1 und Eröffnungswendungen in griechischen und lateinischen Schriften." *ZNW* 68 (1977): 123–27.

Baarda, Tjitze. "What Kind of Critical Apparatus for the New Testament Do We Need? The Case of Luke 23:48." Pages 37–97 in *New Testament Textual Criticism, Exegesis and Church History: A Discussion of Methods*. Edited by Barbara Aland and Joël Delobel. CBET 7. Kampen: Kok Pharos, 1994.

Basil. *Contre Eunome suivi de Eunome Apologie*. Edited by Bernard Sesboüé, George Matthieu de Durand, and Louis Doutreleau. SC 299, 305. Paris: Editions du Cerf, 1982–1983.

Boring, M. Eugene. "Mark 1:1–15 and the Beginning of the Gospel." *Semeia* 52 (1990): 43–81.

Brock, Sebastian P. "The Use of the Syriac Fathers for New Testament Textual Criticism." Pages 224–36 in *The Text of the New Testament in Contemporary Research: Essays on the Status Quaestionis; A Volume in Honor of Bruce M. Metzger*. Edited by Bart D. Ehrman and Michael W. Holmes. SD 46. Grand Rapids: Eerdmans, 1995.

Bultmann, Rudolf. *Geschichte der synoptischen Tradition*. 2nd ed. FRLANT 29. Göttingen: Vandenhoeck & Ruprecht, 1931.

———. *Geschichte der synoptischen Tradition: Ergänzungsheft*. Edited by Gerd Theissen and Philipp Vielhauer. 5th ed. FRLANT 29.2. Göttingen: Vandenhoeck & Ruprecht, 1979.

Collins, Adela Yarbro. "Establishing the Text: Mark 1:1." Pages 111–27 in *Texts and Contexts: Biblical Texts in their Textual and Situational Con-*

texts; Essays in Honor of Lars Hartman. Edited by Tord Fornberg and David Hellholm. Oslo: Scandinavian University Press, 1955.

Colwell, Ernest C., with Ernest W. Tune. "Method in Classifying and Evaluating Variant Readings." Pages 96–105 in *Studies in Methodology in Textual Criticism of the New Testament.* Edited by Ernest C. Colwell. NTTS 9. Leiden: Brill, 1969.

Dunderberg, Ismo. "Q and the Beginning of Mark." *NTS* 41 (1995): 501–11.

Ehrman, Bart D. "Heracleon and the 'Western' Textual Tradition." *NTS* 40 (1994): 161–79.

———. *The Orthodox Corruption of Scripture: The Effect of Early Christological Controversies on the Text of the New Testament.* Oxford: Oxford University Press, 1993.

———. "The Text of Mark in the Hands of the Orthodox." *LQ* 5 (1991): 143–56.

———. "The Text of the Gospels at the End of the Second Century." Pages 95–122 in *Codex Bezae: Studies from the Lunel Colloquium June 1994.* Edited by David C. Parker and Christian-B. Amphoux. NTTS 22. Leiden: Brill, 1996.

Elliott, J. Keith. "The International Project to Establish a Critical Apparatus to Luke's Gospel." *NTS* 29 (1983): 531–38.

———. "καθως and ωσπερ in the New Testament." *FNT* 4 (1991): 55–81.

———. "The Purpose and Construction of a Critical Apparatus to a Greek New Testament." Pages 125–43 in *Studien zum Text und zur Ethik des Neuen Testaments: Festschrift zum 80. Geburtstag von Heinrich Greeven.* Edited by W. Schrage. BZNW 47. Berlin: de Gruyter, 1986.

———. *A Survey of Manuscripts Used in Editions of the Greek New Testament.* NovTSup 57. Leiden: Brill, 1987.

Elliott, William J. "The Need for an Accurate and Comprehensive Collation of All Known Greek NT Manuscripts with Their Individual Variants Noted *in pleno*." Pages 137–43 in *Studies in New Testament Language and Text: Essays in Honour of George D. Kilpatrick on the Occasion of His Sixty-Fifth Birthday.* Edited by J. Keith Elliott. NovTSup 44. Leiden: Brill, 1976.

Epiphanius. *Panarion, Haer. 34–64.* Edited by Karl Holl. GCS 31. Leipzig: Hinrichs, 1922.

———. *Panarion, Haer. 65–80.* Edited by Jürgen Dummer. 2nd ed. GCS 37. Berlin: Akademie, 1985.

Epp, Eldon J. "Toward the Clarification of the Term 'Textual Variant.'" Pages 153–73 in *Studies in New Testament Language and Text: Essays in Honour of George D. Kilpatrick on the Occasion of His Sixty-Fifth Birthday*. Edited by J. Keith Elliott. NovTSup 44. Leiden: Brill, 1976. Repr. as pages 47–61 in *Studies in the Theory and Method of New Testament Textual Criticism*. Edited by Eldon J. Epp and Gordon D. Fee. SD 45. Grand Rapids: Eerdmans, 1993.

Fee, Gordon D. "The Use of the Greek Fathers for New Testament Textual Criticism." Pages 191–207 in *The Text of the New Testament in Contemporary Research: Essays on the Status Quaestionis; A Volume in Honor of Bruce M. Metzger*. Edited by Bart D. Ehrman and Michael W. Holmes. SD 46. Grand Rapids: Eerdmans, 1995.

Fleddermann, Harry T. *Q: A Reconstruction and Commentary*. BTS 1. Leuven: Peeters, 2005.

Friedrich, Gerhard. "εὐαγγέλιον." *TDNT* 2:721–36.

Globe, Alexander. "The Caesarean Omission of the Phrase 'Son of God' in Mark 1:1." *HTR* 75 (1982): 209–18.

Grant, Frederick C. "Where Form Criticism and Textual Criticism Overlap." *JBL* 59 (1940): 11–21.

Guelich, Robert A. "The Beginning of the Gospel: Mark 1:1–15." *BR* 27 (1982): 5–15.

Güting, Eberhard. "Der editorische Bericht als Kommentar zur Textkonstitution und zum Apparat in Editionen des Neuen Testaments" *Editio* 7 (1993): 94–108. [= chapter 5 in this collection]

———. Review of *Marcion und sein Apostolos: Rekonstruktion und historische Einordnung der marcionitischen Paulusbriefausgabe*, by Ulrich Schmid. *NovT* 42 (1997): 396–405.

Head, Peter M. "Christology and Textual Transmission: Reverential Alterations in the Synoptic Gospels." *NovT* 35 (1993): 105–29.

———. "A Text-Critical Study of Mark 1:1: The Beginning of the Gospel of Jesus Christ." *NTS* 37 (1991): 621–29.

Holtzmann, Heinrich J. *Das Evangelium nach Marcus*. Vol. 2 of *Die Synoptiker: Hand-Commentar zum Neuen Testament*. 3rd ed. Tübingen,: Mohr, 1901.

Irenaeus. *Contre les Hérésies, Livre III*. Edited by François Louis Marie Matthieu Sagnard. SC 34. Paris: Editions du Cerf, 1952.

Jacobson, Arland D. *The First Gospel: An Introduction to Q*. Sonoma, CA: Polebridge, 1992.

Jülicher, Adolf, ed. *Itala: Das Neue Testament in altlateinischer Überlieferung, nach den Handschriften herausgegeben von Adolf Jülicher, durchgesehen und zum Druck besorgt von Walter Matzkow und Kurt Aland, II: Markusevangelium*. 2nd ed. Berlin: de Gruyter, 1970.

Kee, Howard C. "The Function of Scriptural Quotations and Allusions in Mark 11–16." Pages 165–88 in *Jesus und Paulus: Festschrift für Werner Georg Kümmel zum 70. Geburtstag*. Edited by E. Earle Ellis and Erich Grässer. Göttingen: Vandenhoeck & Ruprecht, 1975.

Kelber, Werner H. *The Oral and the Written Gospel: The Hermeneutics of Speaking and Writing in the Synoptic Tradition, Mark, Paul, and Q*. Philadelphia: Fortress, 1983.

Koch, Dietrich-Alexander. *Die Schrift als Zeuge des Evangeliums: Untersuchungen zur Verwendung und zum Verständnis der Schrift bei Paulus*. BHT 69. Tübingen: Mohr, 1986.

Lachmann, Karl, ed., *Novum Testamentum Graece et Latine*. 2nd ed. 2 vols. Berlin: Reimer, 1842–1850.

———. "Rechenschaft über seine Ausgabe des Neuen Testaments." *TSK* 3 (1830): 817–45.

Lagrange, Marie-Joseph. *Évangile selon Saint Marc*. 4th ed. EB. Paris: Gabalda, 1929.

———. *Évangile selon Saint Marc*. 9th ed. EB. Paris: Gabalda, 1966.

Lightfoot, Robert H. *History and Interpretation in the Gospels*. London: Hodder & Stoughton, 1935.

Lohmeyer, Ernst. *Das Evangelium des Markus*. 10th ed. KEK 1.2. Göttingen: Vandenhoeck & Ruprecht, 1937.

Loisy, Alfred. *L' Évangile selon Marc*. Paris: Nourry, 1912.

Luz, Ulrich. *Das Evangelium nach Matthäus, 1: Mt 1–7*. EKKNT 1.1. Zurich: Benziger; Neukirchen: Neukirchener Verlag, 1985.

Marxsen, Willi. *Der Evangelist Markus: Studien zur Redaktionsgeschichte des Evangeliums*. 2nd ed. FRLANT 49. Göttingen: Vandenhoeck & Ruprecht, 1959.

Matera, Frank J. "The Prologue as the Interpretative Key to Mark's Gospel." *JSNT* 34 (1988): 3–20. Repr., pages 289–306 in *The Interpretation of Mark*. Edited by William R. Telford. Edinburgh: T&T Clark, 1995.

Merx, Adalbert. *Die vier kanonischen Evangelien nach ihrem ältesten bekannten Texte*. 2 vols. Berlin: Reimer, 1905.

Metzger, Bruce M. *A Textual Commentary on the Greek New Testament: A Companion Volume to the United Bible Societies' Greek New Testament*

(Fourth Revised Edition). 2nd ed. Stuttgart: Deutsche Bibelgesellschaft, 1994.

Moulton, James Hope, with W. F. Howard and Nigel Turner. *A Grammar of New Testament Greek*. 4 vols. Edinburgh: T&T Clark, 1908–1976.

Neirynck, Frans. "Assessment." Pages 261–307 in *Mark and Q: A Study of the Overlap Texts*. Edited by Harry T. Fleddermann. BETL 122. Leuven: Leuven University Press, 1995.

———. "The Minor Agreements and Q." Pages 49–72 in *The Gospel Behind the Gospels: Current Studies in Q*. Edited by Ronald A. Piper. NovTSup 75. Leiden: Brill, 1995.

New, David S. *Old Testament Quotations in the Synoptic Gospels and the Two Document Hypothesis*. SCS 37 Atlanta: Scholars Press, 1993.

North, J. Lionel. "The Use of the Latin Fathers for New Testament Textual Criticism." Pages 208–23 in *The Text of the New Testament in Contemporary Research: Essays on the Status Quaestionis; A Volume in Honor of Bruce M. Metzger*. Edited by Bart D. Ehrman and Michael W. Holmes. SD 46. Grand Rapids: Eerdmans, 1995.

Origen. *Der Johanneskommentar*. Edited by Erwin Preuschen. GCS 10. Leipzig : Hinrichs, 1903.

———. *Schriften vom Martyrium: Buch I–IV, Gegen Celsus*. Edited by Paul Koetschau. GCS 1. Leipzig: Hinrichs, 1899.

Pallis, Alex. *Notes on St. Mark and St. Matthew*. 2nd ed. London: Milford, 1932.

Perrin, Norman. "The Christology of Mark: A Study in Methodology." *JR* 51 (1971): 173–87. Repr., in *The Interpretation of Mark*. Edited by William R. Telford. Edinburgh: T&T Clark, 1995.

Pesch, Rudolf. *Das Markusevangelium, 1: Einleitung und Kommentar zu Kap. 1,1–8,26*. HThKNT 2.1. 5th ed. Freiburg: Herder, 1989.

———. *Das Markusevangelium, 2: Kommentar zu Kap. 8,27–16,20*. HThKNT 2.2. Freiburg: Herder, 1991.

Piper, Ronald A. "In Quest of Q: The Direction of Q Studies." Pages 1–18 in *The Gospel Behind the Gospels: Current Studies in Q*. Edited by Ronald A. Piper. NovTSup 75. Leiden: Brill, 1995.

Rawlinson, A. E. J. *The Gospel according to St. Mark*. London: Methuen, 1949.

Robinson, James M. "The Sayings Gospel Q." Pages 361–88 in vol. 1 of *The Four Gospels 1992: Festschrift Frans Neirynck*. Edited by F. van Segbroeck, C. M. Tuckett, G. Van Belle, and J. Verheyden. 3 vols. BETL 100. Leuven: Leuven University Press, 1992.

Sanders, Henry A. *Facsimile of the Washington Manuscript of the Four Gospels in the Freer Collection*. Ann Arbor, The University of Michigan, 1912.
Sickenberger, Joseph. *Die Geschichte des Neuen Testamentes*. 4th ed. Bonn: Hanstein, 1934.
Silva, Moisés. "Modern Critical Editions and Apparatuses of the Greek New Testament." Pages 283–96 in *The Text of the New Testament in Contemporary Research: Essays on the Status Quaestionis; A Volume in Honor of Bruce M. Metzger*. Edited by Bart D. Ehrman and Michael W. Holmes. SD 46. Grand Rapids: Eerdmans, 1995.
Slomp, Jan. "Are the Words 'Son of God' in Mark 1:1 Original?" BT 28 (1977): 143–50.
Smith, Dennis E. "Narrative Beginnings in Ancient Literature and Theory." *Semeia* 52 (1990): 1–9.
Streeter, B. H. "St. Mark's Knowledge and Use of Q." Pages 165–83 in *Studies in the Synoptic Problem, by Members of the University of Oxford*. Edited by W. Sanday. Oxford: Clarendon, 1911.
Suhl, Alfred. *Die Funktion der alttestamentlichen Zitate und Anspielungen im Markusevangelium*. Gütersloh: Mohn, 1965.
Tannehill, Robert C. "Beginning to Study 'How Gospels Begin.'" *Semeia* 52 (1990): 185–91.
Taylor, Vincent. *The Gospel According to St. Mark: The Greek Text with Introduction, Notes and Indexes*. 2nd ed. London: Macmillan, 1966.
———. *The Gospel According to St. Mark: The Greek Text with Introduction, Notes and Indexes*. 2nd ed. Grand Rapids: Baker, 1981.
Telford, William R. "The Pre-Marcan Tradition in Recent Research." Pages 695–723 in vol. 2 of *The Four Gospels: Festschrift Frans Neirynck*. Edited by F. van Segbroeck, C. M. Tuckett, G. van Belle, and J. Verheyden. 3 vols. BETL 100. Leuven: Leuven University Press, 1992.
Tischendorf, Constantin von, ed., *Novum Testamentum Graece: Ad antiquissimos testes denuo recensuit; Apparatum criticum omni studio perfectum apposuit commentationem isagogicam praetexuit Constantinus Tischendorf*. 8th ed. 3 vols. Leipzig: Giesecke & Devrient, 1869–1894.
Tolbert, Mary Ann. *Sowing the Gospel: Mark's World in Literary-Historical Perspective*. Minneapolis: Augsburg Fortress, 1989.
Tuckett, Christopher M. "The Minor Agreements and Textual Criticism." Pages 119–42 in *Minor Agreements: Symposium Göttingen 1991*.

Edited by Georg Strecker. GTA 50. Göttingen: Vandenhoeck & Ruprecht, 1993.

Turner, C. H. "Marcan Usage: Notes, Critical and Exegetical, on the Second Gospel, IV." *JTS* 26 (1925): 145–56. Repr., pages 23–35 in *The Language and Style of the Gospel of Mark: An Edition of C. H. Turner's "Notes on Marcan Usage" Together with Other Comparable Studies*. Edited by J. Keith Elliott. NovTSup 71. Leiden: Brill, 1993.

———. *The Study of the New Testament 1883 and 1920*. 3rd ed. Oxford: Clarendon, 1926.

Uro, Risto. "John the Baptist and the Jesus Movement: What Does Q Tell Us?" Pages 231–57 in *The Gospel Behind the Gospels: Current Studies in Q*. Edited by Ronald A. Piper. NovTSup 75. Leiden: Brill, 1995.

Victorinus. *Victorini episcopi Petavionensis Opera*. Edited by Johannes Haussleiter. CSEL 49. Vienna: Tempsky, 1916.

Vorster, W. S. "The Function of the Use of the Old Testament in Mark." *Neot* 14 (1981): 62–72.

Weiss, Johannes. *Das älteste Evangelium: Ein Beitrag zum Verständnis des Markus-Evangeliums und der ältesten evangelischen Überlieferung*. 2 vols. Göttingen: Vandenhoeck & Ruprecht, 1903.

Weisse, Christian Hermann. *Die evangelische Geschichte kritisch und philosophisch bearbeitet*. 2 vols. Leipzig: Breitkopf & Härtel, 1838.

Wellhausen, Julius. *Einleitung in die ersten drei Evangelien*. 2nd ed. Berlin: Reimer, 1911.

———. *Das Evangelium Marci*. 2nd ed. Berlin: Reimer, 1909.

West, Martin L. *Textual Criticism and Editorial Technique: Applicable to Greek and Latin Texts*. Stuttgart: Teubner, 1973.

Westcott, Brooke Foss, and Fenton John Anthony Hort, eds. *The New Testament in the Original Greek: Volume 1, Text; Volume 2, Introduction [and] Appendix*. Cambridge: Macmillan, 1881. 2nd ed., 1896.

Wohlenberg, Gustav. *Das Evangelium des Markus*. 3rd ed. KNT 2. Leipzig: Deichert, 1930.

Zerwick, Max. *Untersuchungen zum Markus-Stil: Ein Beitrag zur stilistischen Durcharbeitung des Neuen Testaments*. Rome: Pontifical Biblical Institute, 1937.

Zuntz, Günther. "Ein Heide las das Markusevangelium." Pages 205–22 in *Markus-Philologie: Historische, literargeschichtliche und stilistische Untersuchungen zum zweiten Evangelium*. Edited by Hubert Cancik. WUNT 33. Tübingen: Mohr, 1984.

8
Open Questions in the Discussion of New Testament Text-Critical Methodology

One of the generally accepted procedures of New Testament textual criticism is the analysis of grammar and style of Hellenistic Greek authors, and specifically of New Testament authors. Several critics have called attention to the fact that scribes sometimes observe stylistic habits of authors and are inclined to introduce these even into passages where their authors did not show them. This observation, of course, adds to the difficulty of properly handling the criterion of the author's style.

In view of these debates some *monenda* are apposite:
1. It is regrettably true that important critical decisions that were argued generations ago have been accepted by New Testament commentators but not by editors.
2. It is regrettably true that even the best conjectures of critics of the past hardly ever received due recognition in editions of the New Testament.
3. It is regrettably true that the latest edition that annotated known corruptions of New Testament passages ("cruces interpretum") was an edition of the nineteenth century.
4. Exegetes have identified secondary glosses in the text of several New Testament writings. Editors have ignored this discussion; they have ignored these findings.

The distinguished American textual critic Eldon J. Epp published an essay on the theme of this article.[1] In the small volume *Rethinking New*

---

1. The following are suitable as introductions to New Testament textual criticism: Eberhard W. Güting, "An Introduction to the Textual Criticism of the New Testament," pp. 1–24 in this volume; Bart D. Ehrman and Michael W. Holmes, *The Text of the New Testament in Contemporary Research: Essays on the Status*

Testament Textual Criticism, he deals with contemporary controversies of New Testament textual criticism, more precisely not its controversies but its "issues."[2] He states the theme of his essay as "Issues in New Testament Textual Criticism." The sixty pages of his knowledgeable report take up some questions that I have posed. Germanists will, I think, take note with interest that Epp detects two epochal changes. In Epps's opinion first the epoch of the textus receptus comes to an end with Karl Lachmann, that is, the epoch of the prescientific New Testament text. And second, in our time, according to Epp, the classical period of New Testament textual criticism comes to an end, that is, the formation of a variety of methodological approaches that all pursue one goal, to construct the original text, the text of the author.

What tasks thereafter New Testament textual criticism has to tackle remains to be resolved. In order to gain empathy with his readers, Epp relates a story. For many years he had a small card, as was quite common in the previous century, on which a distich was printed, a couplet from the English

---

Quaestionis, 2nd ed. (Leiden: Brill, 2013); Barbara Aland, "Text Criticism of the Bible. II. New Testament," *RPP* 12:576–78; David C. Parker, *An Introduction to the New Testament Manuscripts and Their Texts* (Cambridge: Cambridge University Press, 2008); James R. Royse, *Scribal Habits in Early Greek New Testament Papyri*, NTTS 36 (Leiden: Brill, 2008); Bruce M. Metzger, *The Text of the New Testament: Its Transmission, Corruption, and Restoration*, 3rd ed. (Oxford: Oxford University Press, 1992); Metzger and Ehrman, *The Text of the New Testament: Its Transmission, Corruption, and Restoration*, 4th ed. (Oxford: Oxford University Press, 2005); Barbara Aland, "Textgeschichte/Textkritik der Bibel, II. Neues Testament," *TRE* 33:155–68; Larry W. Hurtado, "Beyond the Interlude? Developments and Directions in New Testament Criticism," in *Studies in the Early Text of the Gospels and Acts: The Papers of the First Birmingham Colloquium on the Textual Criticism of the New Testament*, ed. David G. K. Taylor, Texts and Studies 3/1 (Birmingham: University of Birmingham Press, 1999), 26–48; Léon Vaganay, *Initiation à la Critique Textuelle du Nouveau Testament*, 2nd ed. rev. Christian-Bernard Amphoux (Paris: Cerf, 1986); Vaganay, *An Introduction to New Testament Textual Criticism*, 2nd ed., rev. and updated by Christian-Bernard Amphoux and Jenny Heimerdinger, trans. Jenny Heimerdinger (Cambridge: Cambridge University Press, 1991); Kurt Aland and Barbara Aland, *The Text of the New Testament: An Introduction to the Critical Editions and the Theory and Practice of Modern Textual Criticism*, 2nd ed. (Grand Rapids: Eerdmans; Leiden: Brill, 1989).

2. Eldon J. Epp, "Issues in New Testament Textual Criticism," in *Rethinking New Testament Textual Criticism*, ed. David Alan Black (Grand Rapids: Baker, 2002), 17–76.

poet Alexander Pope (1688–1744): "Exegetes who major issues shun / and hold their farthing candles to the sun." As a conscientious writer Epp looked up the source of the quotation before he incorporated it into his lecture. The concordance for Pope's works, however, did not contain the couplet. What was he to do? A friend who had a preliminary draft of the essay—without the source of the citation—promptly sent him an email that resolved the issue. Edward Young, an author of the same period (1683–1765) had stated: "How commentators each dark passage shun / And hold their farthing candles to the sun." It will not strike text critics as difficult to prefer the more powerful text of the established author over the weaker text transmitted orally. Oral tradition alters. (Of course this does not mean that not all versions of an altered song in particular cases may be of interest for cultural history.)

Modern scholars who cite a published author are responsible for the accuracy of what is quoted, at least when they do not document the cited edition. However, if they name the editor, then they thereby pass on the responsibility. In this case the editor takes responsibility and becomes the authority for the authorial text. As we know, this is not always an enviable responsibility.

On an earlier occasion I have pointed out the responsibility that is connected with the composition of a critical apparatus.[3] In that essay I set forth five suggestions for structuring a critical apparatus. The present article about the discussion of methods among New Testament textual critics does not address Germanists directly, nor historians of philosophy, nor music scholars, nor editors of medieval literature. However, by referring to questions that are discussed in a related discipline, I would like to present some suggestions concerning problems encountered in editorial work in general.

1. The Aporia of the Original Text

When Lachmann with the aid of carefully collated manuscripts published a critically edited New Testament (1831), he was, apart from Edward Wells and Daniel Mace, the first who ventured to break away from the textus receptus of early modern times.[4]

---

3. Eberhard Güting, "Der editorische Bericht als Kommentar zur Textkonstitution und zum Apparat in Editionen des Neuen Testaments," in *Editio* 7 (1993): 94–108 [ch. 5 in this collection].

4. Karl Lachmann, ed., *Novum Testamentum Graece et Latine*, 2 vols. (Berlin: Reimer, 1831). See also Lachmann, "Rechenschaft über seine Ausgabe

A new period began in 1831, when for the first time a text was constructed directly from the ancient documents without the intervention of any printed edition, and when the first systematic attempt was made to substitute scientific method for arbitrary choice in the discrimination of various readings. In both respects the editor, Lachmann, rejoiced to declare that he was carrying out the principles and unfulfilled intentions of Bentley, as set forth in 1716 and 1720.[5]

Lachmann did not believe that he was able to produce the original text of New Testament authors. However, he undertook to approach "the manuscripts that the fourth century read" on the basis of the agreements between the Old Latin witnesses, the Vulgate tradition, and the oldest surviving Greek witnesses.[6] The splendid edition of Brooke Foss Westcott and Fenton John Anthony Hort was the first to claim to have published the New Testament in its original Greek wording. In order to be fair one must add, however, that all editions of the nineteenth century modestly qualified their editorial achievement. This holds for Lachmann, Samuel Prideaux Tregelles, Constantin von Tischendorf, Westcott and Hort. The twentieth century also tended toward restraint. The claim of Westcott and Hort to have produced "The New Testament in the Original Greek" was not accepted anywhere; and the presently leading edition of Nestle-Aland stated until recently: "But it is not yet possible to formulate a comprehensive theory of the textual tradition that would accommodate all the results of recent textual research."[7]

Nevertheless right up until the present, New Testament textual crit-

---

des Neuen Testaments," *TSK* 3 (1830): 817–45. On Wells, see Metzger, *Text of the New Testament*, 108–9 [= 4th ed., 155]; Egert Pöhlmann, *Einführung in die Überlieferungsgeschichte und in die Textkritik der antiken Literatur* (Darmstadt: Wissenschaftliche Buchgesellschaft, 1994–2003), 2:137. On Mace, see Metzger, *Text of the New Testament*, 110–11 [= 4th ed., 157–58].

5. Brooke Foss Westcott and Fenton John Anthony Hort, eds., *The New Testament in the Original Greek* (Cambridge: Macmillan, 1881), 2:13.

6. Metzger, *Text of the New Testament*, 125 [= 4th ed., 170]; Pöhlmann, *Einführung in die Überlieferungsgeschichte*, 139–42.

7. Barbara Aland et al., eds., *Novum Testamentum Graece*, 28th ed. (Stuttgart: Deutsche Bibelgesellschaft, 2012), 49*. The quotation is taken from the 27th ed. (Aland et al., eds., *Novum Testamentum Graece*, 27th ed., 8th printing corrected and extended to Papyri 99–116 [Stuttgart: Deutsche Bibelgesellschaft, 2001]), see English introduction, 7*.

ics saw their true task to be the production of the original text of New Testament authors. Kurt and Barbara Aland, for example, assumed that in their *Greek New Testament* a major part of all units of variation that they had decided upon reproduced the original wording.[8] The textual critic Christian-Bernard Amphoux on the other hand, following Léon Vaganay, sought this original text preferably in the Western rather than in the Alexandrian tradition.[9] Günther Zuntz, the distinguished classical scholar among New Testament textual critics, stated: "The purpose and goal of textual criticism is the recovery, within the limits of possibility, of the original text."[10] Paul Maas saw things no differently for the entire field of classical philology: "The task of textual criticism is the recovery of a text (*constitutio textus*) that approximates the autograph (original) as nearly as possible. A revised dictation by the author is equivalent with a transcription in his own hand."[11]

However, a shadow fell over this confident and resolute work when in a paper in 1994 the American patristic scholar William L. Petersen began to speak. Petersen raised a series of unsettling questions and intensified them by means of disquieting statements. "What Text Can New Testament Textual Criticism Ultimately Reach?" read the title of his lecture at a conference in Münster.[12] This conference and its consequences were followed with great interest.[13]

---

8. "If a set of variations in the *Greek New Testament* is designated with A, this means that the editors were certain that the text replicated in the text above means the original wording and that none of the variations reproduced in the apparatus represent an authentic rival" (Aland and Aland, *Text of the New Testament*, 54).

9. Vaganay, *Initiation à la critique textuelle*, 12.

10. Günther Zuntz, *The Text of the Epistles: A Disquisition upon the Corpus Paulinum*, Schweich Lectures of the British Academy 1946 (London: Oxford University Press, 1953), 1.

11. Paul Maas, *Textual Criticism* (Oxford, Clarendon, 1958), 5.

12. William L. Petersen, "What Text Can New Testament Textual Criticism Ultimately Reach?," in *New Testament Textual Criticism, Exegesis and Church History: A Discussion of Methods*, ed. Barbara Aland and Joël Delobel, CBET 7 (Kampen: Kok Pharos, 1994), 136–52.

13. "Recently B. Aland has explicitly stated that the original text reflected in the manuscript tradition is something quite different from the autographs" (Jacobus H. Petzer, "The History of the New Testament Text: Its Reconstruction, Significance and Use in New Testament Textual Criticism," in Aland and Delobel, *New Testament Textual Criticism*, 36 n. 94).

Earlier in a conference at Notre Dame University (1988) the exegete Helmut Koester had already put his finger on our ignorance of the text of the gospels of the second century.[14]

Petersen found evidence in the oldest patristic citations of New Testament passages that these were known in a form different from what we read in our canonical gospels. Thus, for example, in Tatian's *Diatessaron* the phrase εἷς ἐστιν ὁ ἀγαθός from Matthew (19:17) took the form: *ḥad hw lam ṭābā' 'abbā' dᵉbashmajjā'*. In Latin this reads: *Unus est bonus, pater, qui in coelo.*[15] Petersen considers our Matthean text to be corrected on theological grounds, that is, it is an abbreviated text.[16]

In Luke 24:39 the disciples encounter the Risen One. They take him to be a πνεῦμα and are afraid. Petersen notes that Ignatius of Antioch (d. 107) cites the passage in his letter to Smyrna (3.1.2): "Touch me and see that I am not a bodiless phantom [δαιμόνιον ἀσώματον]." We find this δαιμόνιον ἀσώματον likewise in Origen, Eusebius, and Jerome, as well as modified into φάντασμα in Tertullian in *Marc.* 4.43.6. Bruce M. Metzger reports that according to Tertullian this φάντασμα derives from Marcion's Gospel; according to Petersen it modifies the oldest transmission of Luke's text. According to him the word πνεῦμα in Luke 24:39 is secondary.[17]

Petersen gives a third example in Matt 22:37 with its Synoptic parallels (Mark 12:30; Luke 10:27). The passage cited quotes the Shema, the Jewish confession of the one God. Petersen can show that Justin cites a two-part confession three times, invariably with the same wording: ἀγαπήσεις κύριον τὸν θεόν σου ἐξ ὅλης τῆς καρδίας σου καὶ ἐξ ὅλης τῆς ἰσχύος σου (*Dial.* 93.2, 3; *1 Apol.* 16.6). In Mark's text Petersen is able to cite an important witness from the time around 400, the Afra recension of k from Bobbio, that likewise attests this wording. In the Lukan text (10:27) Petersen points out the fact that the Cureton Syriac actually attests a four-part wording that,

---

14. Helmut Koester, "The Text of the Synoptic Gospels in the Second Century," in *Gospel Tradition in the Second Century: Origins, Recensions, Text, and Transmission*, ed. William L. Petersen, CJAn 3 (Notre Dame, IN: University of Notre Dame Press, 1989), 19–37.

15. Petersen, "What Text," 142.

16. Petersen, "What Text," 143–44.

17. Bruce M. Metzger, *A Textual Commentary on the Greek New Testament: A Companion Volume to the United Bible Societies' Greek New Testament (Fourth Revised Edition)*, 2nd ed. (Stuttgart: Deutsche Bibelgesellschaft, 1994), 160; Petersen, "What Text," 144–45.

8. Open Questions in the Discussion of Text-Critical Methodology 205

however, in the first two parts likewise renders the text of Justin. According to Petersen this is the original text of Mark, deleted in our editions.[18] Petersen also points out that before him Arthur Vööbus, Eberhard Nestle, and Westcott advocated this view.[19]

The question posed here for New Testament textual criticism is as follows: Is it possible that important aspects of the oldest, original texts have completely disappeared from our editions? Petersen has raised this question. I am prepared to answer in the affirmative without hesitation. Nevertheless, I would like to qualify the statement by adding that a general mistrust of the attainability of an original text intended by this author is in fact inappropriate. The data and the patterns of argumentation used by this author correspond to what is customary in New Testament textual criticism.

Certainly one aspect of this discussion is unsettling. The view is not new that the oldest text, the authorial text, in places is not preserved in our editions and, what is more disconcerting, cannot be reclaimed. It is found in numerous comments of distinguished exegetes, but at the same time finds no place among the conclusions that have been incorporated into textbooks.

If it is true that the original conclusion of the Gospel of Mark is no longer preserved in the tradition, there is no means of reproducing it. If it is true that in the editorial work on the Gospel of John original parts of the text were eliminated, we have no real chance of doing anything further about this evidence. The fact that the Gospel of John was revised is one of the acknowledged results of Johannine research, even if details of the results are often debated.[20]

Martin Dibelius, hardly unknown in New Testament scholarship, published during World War II contributions to textual criticism, to style, and to literary criticism in Acts. With good reason he advocated the view that the early transmission of the text of Acts marred the text of the author to a considerable degree.[21] In Acts 2, for instance, an outpouring of the Spirit on Pentecost is reported that leads to a language miracle. The Galileans

---

18. Petersen, "What Text," 146–47.
19. Petersen, "What Text," 147.
20. Matthias Rissi, "'Die Juden' im Johannesevangelium," *ANRW* 26.3:2099–141.
21. Martin Dibelius, *Aufsätze zur Apostelgeschichte*, ed. Heinrich Greeven, 5th ed., FRLANT 42 (Göttingen: Vandenhoeck & Ruprecht, 1968).

filled with the Spirit spoke to the astonishment of the people of Jerusalem in the languages of Parthians, Medes, and Elamites, and many other languages, among them also the language of Judea. Even in antiquity readers considered this word in this list to be erroneous. Dibelius and many other authors followed this opinion.[22]

For instance, in view of the successful healings through the apostles in Acts 5:17 a trial scene and an outbreak of anger from the high priest and his entourage is reported. According to our printed text the high priest with his associates arose and laid his hands on the apostles. Anyone who views this scene with the eyes of antiquity has reason to be disconcerted. High-ranking persons who arise in order to act in such a manner are difficult to imagine. Friedrich Blass, the classical philologist, saw this and instead of the word ἀναστάς in the source conjectured the personal name Ἅννας. Later likewise the name Hannas was found in Middle Egyptian tradition.[23] This was an illustrious confirmation of a modern conjecture.

Acts 4:25 exhibits an overloaded sentence: ὁ τοῦ πατρὸς ἡμῶν διὰ πνεύματος ἁγίου στόματος Δαυὶδ παιδός σου εἰπών. The text can hardly be in order. We agree with Dibelius in this.[24] Dibelius notices a similarly incongruous phrase in Acts 1:2 and attributes both to an interpolator, who wished to insert a "theology of the Holy Spirit."[25] He himself conjectured the deletion of the terms πνευματος αγιου "and possibly also του πατρος ημων."[26] Dibelius declared:

> I have not by a long shot mentioned all passages in which uncertainties exist. With this brief overview, I would only like to show (1) that textual criticism of Acts ought not be confined to the assessment of the Western text; (2) that exegesis of Acts should not set itself the goal of explain-

---

22. Martin Dibelius, "Der Text der Apostelgeschichte," in Dibelius, *Aufsätze zur Apostelgeschichte*, 82; Bruce M. Metzger, *New Testament Studies: Philological, Versional, and Patristic*, NTTS 10 (Leiden: Brill, 1980), 46–56; Eberhard Güting, "Der geographische Horizont der sogenannten Völkerliste des Lukas (Acta 2:9–11)," *ZNW* 66 (1975): 149–69 (ch. 2 in this collection).

23. It is found also in the Itala witness p from the twelfth century. See NA[27], 333. The conjecture of Blass was accepted by Preuschen, Wellhausen, Loisy, and Dibelius; see Ernst Haenchen, *Die Apostelgeschichte*, 5th ed., KEK 3 (Göttingen: Vandenhoeck & Ruprecht, 1965), 203 n. 2.

24. Dibelius, *Aufsätze zur Apostelgeschichte*, 81.

25. Dibelius, *Aufsätze zur Apostelgeschichte*, 82.

26. Dibelius, *Aufsätze zur Apostelgeschichte*, 81.

ing all impossibilities of the text, but should preferably strive for the enhancement of the text; (3) that the history of the book before its inclusion in the New Testament gives us the right to make such conjectures.[27]

Indeed, since then various authors are inclined to agree with this assessment.

Various critics are asking whether the vigorously sought after goal of textual criticism, the reconstruction of the original text of an author, is desirable anyway. Eldon J. Epp asks in a well-informed, equally provocative essay: "Which 'original' or 'originals' ought we to seek? Or, to anticipate a more radical question, ought textual critics to seek or emphasize the search for an 'original' at all?"[28] The textual critic David C. Parker saw in the early development of multiple text forms that deviated from each other a positive event that as such deserves attention and scholarly interest.[29] This question has already generated fruitful and fascinating results in a recent publication.[30]

2. The Aporia of Conjecture

Philological work on the acclaimed principles of the method of Lachmann and Maas that takes place in three stages ranks high in the editing of classical Greek and Latin literature. The *recensio* assesses whether for an author the text derives from an open or from a closed transmission, that is, whether this goes back to one or several archetypes. The *examinatio* considers whether what has been transmitted as the oldest text withstands a philological analysis or perhaps in places is to be identified as corrupt. In this last case the *emendatio*, if at all possible, is imperative. New Testament textual criticism of course adopts these methods. Nevertheless, it

---

27. Dibelius, *Aufsätze zur Apostelgeschichte*, 83. This essay has continued to have a powerful effect. In a recently published work on the textual criticism of Acts, Dibelius is repeatedly cited: *The Book of Acts as Church History/Apostelgeschichte als Kirchengeschichte: Text, Textual Traditions, and Ancient Interpretations/Text, Texttraditionen und antike Auslegungen*, ed. Tobias Nicklas and Michael Tilly, BZNW 120 (Berlin: de Gruyter, 2003), 120.

28. Eldon J. Epp, "The Multivalence of the Term 'Original Text' in New Testament Textual Criticism," *HTR* 92 (1999): 263.

29. David C. Parker, *The Living Text of the Gospels* (Cambridge: Cambridge University Press, 1997).

30. Nicklas and Tilly, *Book of Acts as Church History*.

is admitted that the wide dissemination of contaminated witnesses creates considerable difficulties. Nevertheless, in his epoch making work on the Pauline tradition, Zuntz has shown that original tradition is verifiable in all regional texts, and therefore Johann Jakob Griesbach's assumptions about the character of the text in the Byzantine tradition need to be corrected. Something more definite about this will be discussed in the third section below.

However, first it must be said that in broad areas of New Testament textual criticism the need to emend corrupted passages is conceded with considerable reticence. Metzger, for instance, states:

> Before a conjecture can be regarded as even probable, it must satisfy the two primary tests that are customarily applied in evaluating variant readings in manuscripts: (1) it must be intrinsically suitable and (2) it must account for the corrupt reading or readings in the transmitted text. There is, however, an important difference between the method of applying these tests to a conjectural emendation and that of applying them to variants in manuscripts. We accept the variant that best satisfies the tests; but we require of a successful conjecture that it shall satisfy them absolutely well.[31]

The well-known textbook by Kurt Aland and Barbara Aland, *Der Text des Neuen Testaments* (2nd ed.; Stuttgart: Deutsche Bibelgesellschaft, 1989), names twelve principles for text-critical work. Rule 1 states peremptorily: "The solution of difficulties in the text by means of a conjecture or the identification of glosses, interpolations, etc., in passages where the transmission of the text displays no disruptions should not be allowed; it means a capitulation in face of the problems or rather a violation of the text."[32] The problem of conjectures is presented in the textbook of the French textual critic Amphoux with considerable reticence, but judiciously: "Donc, en principe, on ne saurait prohiber d'une façon absolue les conjectures."[33] The author recommends placing convincing conjectures in the apparatus.[34] Whereas the American scholar John Strugnell published "A Plea for Conjectural Emendation in the New Testament" in *Catholic Biblical Quarterly*

---

31. Metzger, *Text of the New Testament*, 182–83 [= 4th ed., 227].
32. Aland and Aland, *Text of the New Testament*, 284.
33. Vaganay, *Initiation à la critique textuelle*, 129.
34. Vaganay, *Initiation à la critique textuelle*, 129.

in 1974,³⁵ on the other hand the critic George D. Kilpatrick insisted on his sweepingly stark rejection of such emendation: "We may assume as a rule of thumb that at each point the true text has survived somewhere or other among our manuscripts.... I am able to sustain my contention because basically I think conjecture in the NT a dubious enterprise, but a reasonable resort in the LXX."³⁶

Yet it must be stated that numerous editors, exegetes, and critics have acknowledged the need to emend corrupt passages also in the New Testament. Zuntz writes: "That *emendatio* has no scope in the criticism of the New Testament is an unverifiable *petitio principii*."³⁷ Lachmann, Tregelles, Tischendorf, and Bernhard Weiss published their own emendations.³⁸ The important conjectures of Jean Leclerc, Richard Bentley, and Carel Cobet³⁹ have been discussed in New Testament exegesis and in part have been preferred to the transmitted readings. Zuntz described some readings as ancient conjectures and accepted them.⁴⁰ Today conjectures are also put

---

35. John Strugnell, "A Plea for Conjectural Emendation in the New Testament, with a Coda on 1 Cor 4:6," *CBQ* 36 (1974): 543–58.

36. George D. Kilpatrick, "Conjectural Emendation in the New Testament," in *New Testament Textual Criticism: Its Significance for Exegesis; Essays in Honor of Bruce M. Metzger*, ed. Eldon J. Epp and Gordon D. Fee (Oxford: Clarendon, 1981), 349 and 360.

37. Zuntz, *Text of the Epistles*, 12, see also p. 226.

38. Metzger, *Text of the New Testament*, 184 [= 4th ed., 229–30]. I have discussed a conjecture of Lachmann based on a literary approach to the Gospel of Mark (Eberhard Güting, "The Relevance of Literary Criticism for the Text of the New Testament: A Study of Mark's Traditions on John the Baptist," in Taylor, *Studies in the Early Text of the Gospels and Acts*, 142–67 [ch. 7 in this collection]).

39. On Leclerc, see n. 42 below. On Bentley, see my remarks in §6 below. Zuntz commended Cobet's conjecture ΗΔΕΙΟΝΑ in place of the transmitted ΠΛΕΙΟΝΑ in Heb 11:4. He justifiably called it a brilliant conjecture. See Zuntz, *Text of the Epistles*, 16.

40. Zuntz, *Text of the Epistles*, 120. Thus this author considers the reading εαυτον rather than εαυτους transmitted in Heb 12:3 as an ancient correction—evidently necessary and therefore correct. In 1 Cor 6:5 Zuntz verifies an ancient mistake in the text by homoioarcton, namely, the omission of αναμεσον αδελφου και. Zuntz considers the restoration of the correct αναμεσον αδελφου και αναμεσον αδελφου αυτου by means of the Peshitta to be an ancient correction of this Syriac translation or of its Greek source (see Zuntz, *Text of the Epistles*, 15). Zuntz explains the common reading in P⁴⁶ and in the minuscule manuscript 1518 in Heb 10:2 ἐπεὶ κἄν as follows: "The upshot, so far, of our examination of the text

forward by exegetes and are debated. David Alan Black, who in an essay discusses and in part rejects seventeen new conjectures in the Gospel of Matthew, still makes it clear that he himself does not in principle reject conjectures.[41]

Finally, in spite of all theoretical warnings regarding passages with a corrupt text, conjectures have been taken over into editions of the New Testament. This happened for the first time in an edition of the *Greek New Testament* in 1966. In Acts 16:12 this edition read ἥτις ἐστὶν πρώτης μερίδος τῆς Μακεδωνίας πόλις, κολωνία. The apparatus designates this reading as a conjecture, but along with this, indicates three Vulgate manuscripts as witnesses for this reading as well as "Provençal" and "Old German"[42] In the second installment of the Epistles of Peter edited within the *Editio Critica Maior* a text was printed that could not present any Greek attestation. The reading οὐχ εὑρεθήσεται in 2 Pet 3:10 is attested merely in the Coptic tradition of the Dialect V and within the Old Syriac tradition in one witness of the Philoxenian. The editors consider it possible that this text transmits an ancient conjecture.[43] They print this in their leading line.[44] After this hap-

---

of P[46] is a twofold *caveat*. On the one hand, it has been found to be beset with a great number of scribal slips; on the other, it preserves at least some very ancient conjectural alterations of the original wording. It is worth marking both these facts as noteworthy features of the early history of the text. They suggest, among other things, that readings attested by P[46] alone should never be accepted unless their intrinsic quality can stand the severest test; they also suggest that scribal slips must be discarded in assessing the basic quality of this most ancient witness." (p. 23). See also the index, "Conjectures in N.T."

41. David Alan Black, "Conjectural Emendations in the Gospel of Matthew," *NT* 31 (1989): 14.

42. *The Greek New Testament*, ed. Kurt Aland et al. (London: United Bible Societies, 1966). This decision was explicitly defended by one of the editors: Allen P. Wikgren, "The Problem in Acts 16:12," in Epp and Fee, *New Testament Textual Criticism*, 171–78. Wikgren attributed the conjecture to Jean Leclerc (Clericus).

43. *Novum Testamentum Graecum: Editio Critica Maior; Edited by the Institute for New Testament Textual Research; IV. Catholic Letters/Die Katholischen Briefe; Part 1, Text; Die Petrusbriefe*, ed. Barbara Aland et al. (Stuttgart: Deutsche Bibelgesellschaft, 2000), 21* and 252.

44. The textual critic J. Keith Elliott criticized this decision and called for not taking up conjectures into apparatuses of editions ("The *Editio Critica Maior*: One Reader's Reactions," in *Recent Developments in Textual Criticism: New Testament*,

pened, one ought to wonder what further conjectures will find their way into an edited text.[45]

3. The Aporia of Regional Texts

The differentiation of manuscript witnesses according to their geographical provenance was introduced into New Testament textual criticism by J. Albrecht Bengel. Griesbach used the differentiation of provenance as a criterion in the assessment of readings. B. H. Streeter and Zuntz refined the definition of this criterion.[46]

If formerly a distinction was only made between Asian and Egyptian manuscripts, we now generally speak today of three transmission traditions—the Alexandrian, the Byzantine, and the so-called Western tradition.[47] The identification of a fourth, the so-called Caesarean text form, is contested.[48] The claim is not disputed that in its entirety the Alexandrian textual attestation belongs to the most eminent witnesses of the transmission of the New Testament. In effect the Byzantine transmission is the least pure tradition that is preserved. However, Zuntz produced important evidence that the Byzantine transmission also contains independent tradition witnessing to variants that are otherwise lost.[49] In Heb 2:8, for instance, our printed texts contain a solecism. It is hardly imaginable that an author such as the creator of Hebrews, with his thoroughgoing refined style, could have introduced an incorrect word order here. Only the papyrus P[46] along with a few Byzantine witnesses has the correct word

---

Other Early Christian and Jewish Literature, ed. Wim Weren and Dietrich-Alex Koch, STAR 8 [Assen: Royal Van Gorcum, 2003], 133 n.10).

45. Almost a half century earlier at the instigation of the Zurich New Testament scholar Wilhelm Schmiedel, numerous conjectures were added to the apparatus information of the Nestle text; see Eberhard Nestle and Erwin Nestle, *Novum Testamentum Graece*, 13th ed. (Stuttgart: Württembergische Bibelanstalt, 1927), preface.

46. David C. Parker reported on this methodological advance: "The Development of Textual Criticism since B. H. Streeter," in *NTS* 24 (1977): 149–62.

47. Metzger, *Text of the New Testament*, 211–19 [= 4th ed., 305–15].

48. Metzger, *Text of the New Testament*, 214–15, 290 [= 4th. ed., 310–12]; B. Aland, "Text Criticism of the Bible," 165.

49. Zuntz, *Text of the Epistles*, 49–57.

order ἐν γὰρ τῷ ὑποτάξαι, a word order that is in line with other passages in Hebrews.[50]

Today one sees more clearly that the so-called Western text (one should speak of Western texts or Western readings) was in no way confined to the western part of the Roman Empire; on the contrary one detects its origin in the East. In Egypt evidently throughout several centuries Western and Alexandrian text witnesses were circulated and copied. Zuntz goes so far as to designate the Western text as the older stream of tradition that largely determined the texts of the second century. By means of philology and by utilizing ancient manuscripts Alexandrian scholars, according to his view, created a text form that surpassed the texts of their predecessors in accuracy.[51]

The assessment of Western readings and Western witnesses is controversially debated. Westcott and Hort displayed a divided attitude. On the one hand they recognized that Western witnesses do not contain a series of Alexandrian interpolations—they spoke of "Western noninterpolations." On the other hand they rejected numerous Western readings. Their reasoning was brief and gives the impression that the mere designation of a reading as "Western" amounts to an assessment. However, individual Western readings have been identified and defended by distinguished critics as components of the original text. I will give an example.

The uncial W (032/Washingtonianus), supported by two minuscules (1 and 2542), by the oldest Syriac translation (sy^s), and by the oldest Georgian translation (geo^{adysh}), attests a very noteworthy wording of a saying of Jesus about divorce. The text of Mark 10:11–12 first uses the word "woman," then the word "man." I translate: "If a woman dismisses her husband and marries another, she commits adultery. And if a man dismisses his wife, he commits adultery." Without some interpretation this remains very enigmatic. Dismissing one's wife was in Jewish marriage law the right of the man, and it required a divorce decree in proper form. To be sure,

---

50. Zuntz, *Text of the Epistles*, 50–51. Zuntz names numerous other examples in which this ancient papyrus, supported by a few Byzantine witnesses attests the original correct reading.

51. Zuntz, *Text of the Epistles*, 271–72: "The Alexandrian work on the text of the Scriptures was a long process rather than a single act.... The final result was the survival of a text far superior to that of the second century, even though the revisers, being fallible humans, rejected some of its correct readings and introduced some faults of their own."

in Babylonian and Egyptian law there was also the possibility of a divorce by the woman.[52] In Jewish law, however, as a rule this was not possible. Numerous exegetes accept a Western reading here, because they are of the opinion that this odd saying of Jesus is very susceptible to interpretation. Jesus alluded to the scandalous behavior of Herodias toward her husband Herod Boethos that had been made public. She had sent her husband a divorce decree. Jesus's statement takes up public criticism and conveys: If what the wife does makes adulterers of her present and her future husbands, what is the situation, if the husband orders a divorce decree? This text form advocated by F. C. Burkitt, Birdsall, and other exegetes is admittedly exegetically disputed.[53] Here, indeed, I accept that the Alexandrian transmission has accommodated the text to the common perceptions and inverted the word order.

In 1 Cor 5:6 only Western witnesses display δολοῖ instead of the otherwise transmitted ζυμοῖ. Here an expression from the gospel (Matt 13:33; Luke 13:21) influenced the Pauline text. Irenaeus (4.27.4) and Jerome (he mentions "*codices nostri*") support the correct reading of the manuscript D/06: Οὐκ οἴδατε ὅτι μικρὰ ζύμη ὅλον τὸ φύραμα δολοῖ; "Do you not know that a little yeast spoils the whole dough?"[54]

In 1 Cor 15:10 Zuntz prefers a reading that has exclusively Western attestation: D* F G Ambrosius, Ambrosiaster, Pelagius, and Orosius (this in the Gothic tradition) attest πτωχή instead of κενή.[55] In Mark 1:22 the Western witnesses D Θ e preserve an original asyndeton that the remaining tradition has smoothed out with a καί.[56]

---

52. Ernst Bammel, "Markus 10:11f. und das jüdische Eherecht," *ZNW* 61 (1970): 95–101.

53. J. Neville Birdsall, "Textual Criticism and New Testament Studies: An Inaugural Lecture Delivered in the University of Birmingham on 10 May 1984" (paper presented at Birmingham University, 10 May, 1984), 5–6. See also on this reading Heinrich Greeven and Eberhard Güting, *Textkritik des Markusevangeliums*, Theologie, Forschung und Wissenschaft 11 (Münster: LIT, 2005), 496–98. Herodias reproached her husband Herod Boethos for his political inactiveness and persuaded his half-brother Antipas to dismiss his Nabatean wife and to marry her. The faulty word Φιλίππου in Mark 6:17 is not supported by the text of Matthew: D, the Afra k, and numerous Old Latin manuscripts support the elision of Φιλίππου in Matt 14:3.

54. Zuntz, *Text of the Epistles*, 114–15.

55. Zuntz, *Text of the Epistles*, 89–90.

56. Greeven and Güting, *Textkritik des Markusevangeliums*, 80–81.

Finally, the Old African Tradition of the Afra manuscript k provides a secondary short ending to Mark and thereby attests in its own way to the secondary character of the so-called long ending to Mark.[57] A complete list of original textual readings attested in the Western tradition cannot be given here.

Some authors go so far as to search for the original text form first of all in the Western text and designate the corresponding Alexandrian readings as secondary. In the recent past the exegete Joël Delobel takes the credit for having forcefully called attention to the problem of the Western text.[58]

In one area in which this question is still considered controversial—the area of research on Acts—it appears to me that the situation is now becoming clearer through a series of recent works. Where the Western text augments, rephrases, and paraphrases, the texts of Alexandrian witnesses prove their quality to a remarkable degree. The old thesis that Luke the author published two editions of Acts is also no longer advocated.[59]

In my opinion on this issue, one can gain no balanced assessment if one shows distrust toward the Western text as a whole or if one gives it preference to a great extent. The cautious opinion of Carlo M. Martini, of which Metzger also approved, counts on occasional correct readings of the Western tradition.[60] A recent opinion of the New Testament scholar Heike Omerzu states the prevalent consensus: "On the basis of the unequivocal tendency of the variations the majority of research certainly considers the Alexandrian version generally as more closely related to the original text, whereas the 'Western' tradition in individual cases can also have preserved original readings."[61] *The Greek New Testament* of the United Bible Societies

---

57. NA[27], 147; Barbara Aland et al, eds., *The Greek New Testament*, 5th ed. (Stuttgart: Deutsche Bibelgesellschaft, 2014), 188.

58. Joël Delobel, "The Text of Luke-Acts: A Confrontation of Recent Theories," in *The Unity of Luke-Acts*, ed. Joseph Verheyden, BETL 142 (Leuven: Leuven University Press, 1999), 83–107.

59. Nicklas and Tilly, *Book of Acts as Church History*.

60. Metzger, *Text of the New Testament*, 293 [= 4th ed., 308] states: "Most scholars date the emergence of the 'Western' text to the mid-second century, or shortly thereafter, but they also, as Martini has put it, 'leave the door open to an appreciation of the presence of particular readings in which D or other "Western" witnesses have, perhaps, preserved the most ancient reading.'"

61. Heike Omerzu, "Die Darstellung der Römer in der Textüberlieferung der Apostelgeschichte," in Nicklas and Tilly, *Book of Acts as Church History*, 150.

and the Nestle-Aland text have wrongly rejected a large number of Western readings, although these have been advocated in text-critical literature and by exegetes with substantial reasons.[62]

4. The Aporia of a Text-Critical Analysis of Style

In its efforts to come to assured results New Testament textual criticism has, as we have seen, refined its grasp of the enormous quantity of data. Whereas earlier, some had relied on the oldest and best witnesses, later in the nineteenth century it was generally accepted that even the best witnesses also contain errors. Some critics inquired into the geographical dissemination of variants and sought among them those that could have been written during the early stages of development, from which other readings are explicable as improvements, clarifications, copyist errors, corrections of style, and/or factual alterations.

Lexicographers researched the literature of Hellenistic times. With that the publication of nonliterary papyri acquired considerable importance. Grammars worked with the same material and refined the understanding of Koine Greek. Investigations of style in Paul, in the Synoptic Gospels, and in particular New Testament writings appeared and advanced textual criticism.

The textual critic C. H. Turner based his analyses on a thorough investigation of Mark's style.[63] Zuntz achieved noteworthy text-critical decisions from observing stylistic customs of Paul and the author of Hebrews. At the same time the question is occasionally raised whether the consistency of style of an author is really reliable. B. Aland asked: "Why should an author not have differed on some occasion from what we think we know from observing his or her style?"[64] The South African textual critic Jacobus H. Petzer stated: "It cannot be expected or presupposed that the language employed in the New Testament documents will of necessity

---

62. This holds for the text Mark 10:11–12 (considered above), 1 Cor 5:6, 15:10, and Mark 1:22.

63. J. Keith Elliott published Turner's work of the 1920s as a reprint (Elliott, ed., *The Language and Style of the Gospel of Mark: An Edition of C. H. Turner's Notes on "Markan Usage" Together with Other Comparable Studies*, NovTSup 71 [Leiden: Brill, 1993]).

64. B. Aland, "Text Criticism of the Bible," 163.

be consistent."[65] The American Epp pointed out that occasionally a reading that may explain the development of an extant tradition stands over against another that blends in quite well with the author's style—such as in Matt 6:33.[66] Actually both explanations were propounded by members of the circle of editors, as Metzger's *A Textual Commentary* reports.[67] For this reason they came to a split decision—wrongly, because the attestation of the Afra witness k and Clement carry considerable weight. I translate: "Seek first the kingdom and its righteousness and all this will come to you."

Finally, a caveat—the frequently observed custom of copyists to insert a stylistic peculiarity secondarily into the text of an author in no way facilitates our dealing with the criterion of authorial style. I give as an example an attestation that makes the analysis presented nearly certain. When Mark names John the Baptist, he uses the expression ὁ βαπτιστής (Mark 6:25; 8:28), a term frequently used in the New Testament. He also uses ὁ βαπτίζων (Mark 1:4; 6:14, 24). Copyists have occasionally introduced the participle ὁ βαπτίζων in other passages in the text of Mark, where the author had used the common expression ὁ βαπτιστής ("the baptizer").[68]

5. The Question of the Validity of Text-critical Decisions

At this point in what I want to say a series of *monenda* needs to be formulated. I have presented questions in New Testament textual criticism that are unresolved and often controversial. Now, however, I intend to raise an unfamiliar question. Whereas Germanist editors in general set their own standards for their proposals, in New Testament scholarship there are two authorities for editorial standards. On the one hand we have practicing editors who sometimes, but by no means always, give justification for their procedure. On the other hand, we have textual critics who do not themselves edit but by their research set standards for editors. Are editors obliged to make allowance for conclusions that can be assessed as in part not persuasive, in part contestable, in part as elements of inconclusive debates? In this dispute one has to be on one's guard not to call for anything unreasonable.

---

65. Jacobus H. Petzer, "Author's Style and the Textual Criticism of the New Testament," *Neot* 24 (1990): 186.
66. Epp, "Issues in New Testament Textual Criticism," 32.
67. Metzger, *Textual Commentary*, 15–16.
68. Greeven and Güting, *Textkritik des Markusevangeliums*, 50–53.

8. Open Questions in the Discussion of Text-Critical Methodology 217

Can New Testament textual criticism put forward conclusions that have to be considered by future editors? It is understandable that an editor who is engaged in collating, collecting, and reviewing witnesses cannot at the same time survey text-critical scholarship in its entire breadth. However, a basic minimum of attention is called for.

Can New Testament textual criticism point out results? Let us inquire into the results of the prestigious textual critic Zuntz. Zuntz is not listed in the comprehensive bibliography of the third, fourth, and fifth editions of the *Greek New Testament*. His name appears in the list of abbreviations in *A Textual Commentary on the Greek New Testament* (1st ed., 1971; 2nd ed., 1994). Zuntz has thoroughly investigated two New Testament writings, Paul's 1 Corinthians and Hebrews. In addition, his epoch-making book contains text-critical decisions on numerous passages in other New Testament books. The editorial committee of the Nestle-Aland and of the *Greek New Testament* considered the scholarly results of Zuntz only in a restricted way. In part the committee drew on his arguments without naming him. Sometimes they mentioned him, but defended a different decision. His outstanding philological method, his thorough attention to all aspects of linguistic variation, and his well-considered assessment of all classes of evidence cause his book to stand out among other works of New Testament textual criticism. Zuntz is cited by name in five passages in 1 Corinthians and four passages in Hebrews.[69]

I have checked a selection of passages among the more than one hundred that should have been considered, that is, such passages in which *A Textual Commentary on the Greek New Testament* provided justification for a decision that differs from Zuntz. There are fifteen passages in Hebrews. In none of these passages are Metzger's arguments able to persuade readers.[70] The commentary does indeed contain many correct decisions, but

---

69. Metzger, *Textual Commentary*, 482 on 1 Cor 3:2; p. 485 on 1 Cor 5:5; pp. 486–87 on 1 Cor 6:14; pp. 495–96 on 1 Cor 11:15; pp. 498–99 on 1 Cor 13:4; p. 597 on Heb 7:21; p. 602 on Heb 11:11; pp. 603–4 on Heb 11:37; and p. 606 on Heb 13:21.

70. Zuntz, *Text of the Epistles*, 43 on Heb 1:3 correctly advocates instead of αυτου: δι εαυτου; p. 64 on Heb 1:8 recommends αυτου for the text, because σου is an adaptation of the Septuagint; pp. 32–33 on Heb 2:8 [αυτω] is to be deleted; pp. 34–35 on Heb 2:9 χωρις is to be read along with Harnack; p. 65 on Heb 3:2 [ολω] is to be deleted—Zuntz indicates doubt "+?"; p. 93 on Heb 3:6 ος is the logically correct, and the "more difficult" reading (*lectio ardua*); p. 118 on Heb 4:3 [την] is

this aspect of its critical accomplishment is evidence of inadequacy. It is evidence of inadequacy for an edition.

On an earlier occasion I myself have listed text-critical results that can be expected to improve the text of the Nestle-Aland.[71] Among these is the deletion of Rom 7:25a, recommended on the basis of text-critical standards.

6. The Question of the Validity of Evident Conjectures

In Philemon, a short piece that is deemed very personal, Paul the author makes reference to himself. Which designation he uses for himself is controversially debated among textual critics. The prominent classical philologist of the eighteenth century, Bentley (1662–1742), conjectured that in verse 9 πρεσβευτής should be read, and thus the Pauline sentence would say: "For the sake of *Agape* I would rather speak to you as the *envoy* and now also as the prisoner of Christ Jesus."[72] Instead of πρεσβευτής, the transmitted text has the noun πρεσβύτης, and this would be translated as "old man." Prominent exegetes and critics have given both the pros and cons.

The passage makes good sense with either word in question. The eminent exegete Robert B. Lightfoot advocated the conjecture and suggested that copyists of various Septuagint passages had discernibly confused the two words.[73] The pronunciation of the two words was only slightly different.

---

to be deleted; pp. 93–94 on Heb 6:2 instead of διδαχης, διδαχην is to be read; pp. 209–210 on Heb 9:1 [και] is to be deleted; pp. 54–55 on Heb 9:19 [και των τραγων] is to be deleted; p. 170 on Heb 11:11 στειρα is a gloss and is to be deleted; p. 16 n. 4 and p. 165 n. 4 on Heb 11:11 και αυτη Σαρρα is to be deleted; pp. 25–29 on Heb 12:1, it is carefully substantiated that ευπερισπαστον is to be read; p. 192 on Heb 13:15 the [οὖν] is to be inserted into the text without brackets; pp. 102–121 on Heb 13:2 [των αιωνων] is to be deleted; it is secondary.

71. Eberhard Güting and David L. Mealand, *Asyndeton in Paul: A Text-critical and Statistical Enquiry into Pauline Style*, SBEC 39 (Lewiston: Mellen, 1998), 172.

72. Richard Bentley, *Bentleii Critica sacra: Notes on the Greek and Latin Text of the New Testament, Extracted from the Bentley MSS in Trinity College Library*, ed. Arthur Ayres Ellis (Cambridge: Deighton, Bell, 1862), 73.

73. Robert B. Lightfoot, *Saint Paul's Epistles to the Colossians and to Philemon: A Revised Text with Introductions, Notes, and Dissertations* (London: Macmillan, 1879), 336–37.

Exegetes debate the applicability of each word more extensively than I can here. However, I wish to indicate what for me is the decisive point. "Envoy and prisoner of Christ Jesus" presents a persuasive conceptual pair. "Old man and now also a prisoner of Christ Jesus" is a less persuasive, virtually random association. In the context Paul foregoes throwing his authority for his request on the scales. He foregoes simply giving a command. However, the second term ("prisoner") indicates that this is meant to strengthen his request. This speaks for the validity of the conjecture. But the validity of the conjecture is also confirmed by the position of these two terms in the vocabulary of the copyists. Both words were familiar to copyists of the Septuagint. They occur quite frequently. For New Testament copyists by contrast, πρεσβύτης with its entire semantic field was an extremely obvious concept that occurred frequently. Over against this in the entire New Testament πρεσβευτής has no parallel apart from the occurrence of the corresponding verb in Paul.

The conjecture was recommended by George Benson,[74] Lightfoot (already mentioned), and Hort.[75] It underpins recent English and American Bible translations, among which is the prestigious Revised Standard Version (1946).[76] The New Testament scholar Ulrich Wilckens also took the reading as the basis of his translation with commentary.[77]

It was rejected by the textual critics Metzger and Neville J. Birdsall. The decisive point for Metzger is that in the judgment of various exegetes the word πρεσβευτης ("envoy") is inappropriate in the context.[78] Birdsall based his extensively reasoned rejection of the conjecture on two issues. First, in the numerous discussions of the life stages of people in Hellenistic authors no indication is found that the term πρεσβύτης appears to be inappropriate. Second, investigations of the phonology of the word in question with the aid of inscriptions and papyri do not verify that the confusion of ΕΥ and Υ was likely. This assessment is confirmed by the fact that in the

---

74. George Benson, *A Paraphrase and Notes on Six of the Epistles of St. Paul*, 2nd ed. (London: Waugh, 1752), 357.

75. Westcott and Hort, *New Testament in the Original Greek*, 2:136.

76. Erroll F. Rhodes, "Conjectural Emendations in Modern Translations," in Epp and Fee, *New Testament Textual Criticism*, 369.

77. Ulrich Wilckens, *Das Neue Testament: Übersetzt und kommentiert*, 5th ed. (Gütersloh: Mohn; Zurich: Benziger, 1977), 773.

78. Metzger, *Textual Commentary*, 588.

entire transmission the understanding did not vary. The transmitted text is unanimously transmitted.[79]

Over against these arguments I would place an undeniable fact—in the New Testament transmission there are textual errors that up until the end of the tradition of the Middle Ages remained unchanged. I commend the conjecture and take it to be a desideratum that editors of the New Testament put it into print.

7. The Question of the Validity of Philological *Examinatio*

The *examinatio* of a text transmitted from antiquity certainly amounts to a considerable challenge for the philological skills of a modern author. Not all New Testament scholars command a basic competence in classical philology. In their analyses, some of the best textual critics have been in the position of employing literary-critical criteria with confidence. I name here Julius Wellhausen, Eduard Schwartz, Adolf von Harnack, Dibelius, and Rudolf Bultmann.

Before World War I literary criticism wielded by important researchers aimed at interpreting linguistic and factual inconsistencies at sites of fracture in the characteristic style of a running text in order to separate the authorial text from editorial embellishment and alterations.[80] In this way it becomes clear that text-critical and literary-critical analyses frequently interact in a fruitful relationship.

A good example of this fruitful relationship can be found in John 4:1. Here the editorial committee of *The Greek New Testament* faced the task of deciding for the transmitted reading ο κυριος (= "the Lord") or for the reading ο Ιησους that likewise has been transmitted.

Ο κυριος in a narrative text in the Gospel of John is a rather rare phenomenon. Ιησους or ο Ιησους is the considerably more frequent mode of expression in the Fourth Gospel. Notably good witnesses speak for each reading. The argument that was decisive for the editors was the consideration that a copyist would hardly have changed an original ο κυριος to ο Ιησους.[81] This name occurs twice in the context. It seemed more probable for these editors that Ιησους repeated three times appeared stylistically

---

79. J. Neville Birdsall, "Πρεσβυτης in Philemon 9: A Study in Conjectural Emendation," *NTS* 39 (1993): 625–30.

80. Otto Merk, "Literarkritik II. Neues Testament," *TRE* 21:222–33.

81. Metzger, *Textual Commentary*, 176.

awkward to copyists and that they consequently wanted to give the text some variation that was preferable. Westcott and Hort supposed that the passage is corrupt and contains an old mistake.[82]

It so happens that a well-known exegete, Bultmann, analyzed the passage in his commentary. The passage deals with the stir that arose when Jesus made numerous disciples and baptized them. Bultmann as well as Charles Harold Dodd took 4:2 to be a redactional gloss, especially since the introductory καίτοιγε is not otherwise attested in the New Testament. Bultmann also took the phrase εγνω ο κυριος οτι (= "the Lord recognized") as a rather clumsy gloss, because in this gloss the title ο κυριος (= "the Lord") that occurs otherwise in redactional passages of the Gospel of John contradicts the author, and is foreign to his narrative.[83] Thus, in distinction from the assessment of the committee, ο κυριος appears to be original to the gloss and not ο Ιησους. I associate myself here with Rudolf Bultmann's interpretation, an interpretation that the editorial committee did not know of or did not consider: "ο Ιησους is a correction to match Johannine usage."[84] An edition should print the authorial text when possible, but here the UBS committee prints the authorial text in part and in part a redactional gloss in the amended form that copyists gave it.

Examinatio aims at the diagnosis of corrupt transmission, of a corruption in which the simple choice among transmitted variants is insufficient. In the nineteenth century numerous such passages were recognized. Westcott and Hort named more than sixty passages in their edition and designated them in their apparatus by a conspicuous symbol (†) as "*cruces interpretationis*."[85] Lachmann discussed such passages in the *Praefatio* of both volumes. Interpreters of the twentieth century likewise frequently entered the diagnosis of such a "crux."

Editors, by contrast, have hesitated conspicuously in this issue. I know of no edition of the twentieth century that identifies such passages for the user by a symbol or by the suggestion of a conjecture. Cruces need to be healed or to receive the suggestion of a conjecture. We have encountered examples of such corruption. What is methodologically unsettling is the

---

82. Westcott and Hort, *New Testament in the Original Greek*, 574.

83. John 6:23; 11:2; as well as regularly in the resurrection chapters John 20 and 21.

84. Rudolf Bultmann, *The Gospel of John: A Commentary* (Philadelphia: Westminster, 1971), 176 n. 2.

85. Westcott and Hort, *New Testament in the Original Greek*, 2:584–88.

fact that editors here shy away from clear assertions. Instead the view is defended that there are no corrupt passages in New Testament texts.

8. The Question of the Validity of the Findings of Literary Criticism

The example I gave in the previous section should show sufficiently that textual criticism that abandons literary criticism sometimes leads to erroneous analysis. Among New Testament scholars this fact is not universally recognized. Epp pointed specifically to the close relationship between literary-critical and text-critical inquiry. Quite clearly, then, such explorations of prior compositional levels in the Pauline letters and elsewhere in the New Testament have been regarded as legitimate text-critical enterprises by various scholars, whenever textual variants, manuscript marks, or other text-critical factors appear to reflect some kind of previous textual or literary layers or some textual disruption. My own judgment also is that such explorations remain within the proper domain of textual criticism.[86] I myself have published one literary critical analysis.[87]

However, it is clear that numerous essays in literary-critical investigation have led to dubious, often contentious results. Since literary criticism depends on the data available from textual criticism, and indeed takes its lead from these data, its task is certainly more difficult. Yet, there are in New Testament scholarship widely recognized literary-critical results, admittedly alongside others that are wrongly recognized.

Among the recognized results of a literary-critical approach is the knowledge that the concluding chapter of the Gospel of John is a redactional addendum. This judgment cannot be denied since chapter 20 ends with a typical conclusion for a book. I quote the conclusion in translation: "Jesus did many other signs in the presence of his disciples that are not

---

86. Epp "Multivalence of the Term," 267. I do not overlook the fact that in my affirmation of literary-critical investigations I go beyond the borders that this author establishes for literary inquiry; cf. Epp, "Multivalence of the Term," 268: "Any search for textual *preformulations* or *reformulations* of a literary nature, such as *prior* compositional levels, versions, or formulations, or *later* textual alteration, revision, division, combination, rearrangement, interpolation, or forming a collection of writings, legitimately falls within the sphere of text-critical activity *if such an exploration is initiated on the basis of some appropriate textual variation or other manuscript evidence*" (emphasis original).

87. Güting, "Relevance of Literary Criticism."

8. Open Questions in the Discussion of Text-Critical Methodology 223

written in this book. But these are written so that you may come to believe that Jesus is the Messiah, the Son of God, and that through believing you may have life in his name."[88]

Likewise, the case that 2 Corinthians is combined from several texts is widely recognized. These texts conceivably originated from an archive of the Corinthian congregation, and 2 Cor 10–13 and 2 Cor 8 and 9 are understood as separate entities.[89] Likewise the hypothesis of a sayings source Q in the gospel material of the Gospels of Matthew and Luke finds wide agreement.[90]

Whether the widely disseminated hypothesis of a signs source in the material of the Gospel of John is justified, must remain an open question. At any rate, my observations do not confirm Fortna's analysis.[91] For its part, Bultmann's brilliant exposition of the Gospel of John has attained agreement for this hypothesis.

The question arises whether an editor is justified in ignoring data of this type. Our present editions place the two spurious endings of Mark in double brackets.[92] They also put the secondary pericope John 7:53–8:11 in double brackets,[93] and likewise the interpolation in Luke 22:43–44.[94] Since a series of texts are generally considered either as discernible interpolations (discernible by textual criticism) or as redactional embellishments (discerned by literary criticism), double brackets might be added for further passages:

John 21:1–25
Rom 7:25a

---

88. NRSV. See Werner Georg Kümmel, *Einleitung in das Neue Testament*, 21st ed. (Heidelberg: Quelle & Meyer, 1983), 173; Kümmel took the acceptance of further redactionally inserted parts in the Gospel of John in a number of passages to be tenable (see pp. 174–75).

89. Georg Strecker, *Literaturgeschichte des Neuen Testaments* (Göttingen: Vandenhoeck & Ruprecht, 1992), 87: "Paul's Apologia;" p. 88: "The Collection Letters."

90. Strecker, *Literaturgeschichte des Neuen Testaments*, 161–70.

91. Robert T. Fortna, *The Gospel of Signs: A Reconstruction of the Narrative Source Underlying the Fourth Gospel*, SNTSMS 11 (Cambridge: Cambridge University Press, 1970).

92. NA^{28}, 175–76; UBS^5, 188–90.

93. NA^{28}, 322–23; UBS^5, 338–40.

94. NA^{28}, 278; UBS^5, 289.

Rom 16:25–27
1 Cor 14:34–36

Further, in case the evidence I have presented is accepted, the following may be added to the list:

Mark 1:2–3
Mark 9:12b
John 6:1–71[95]

Bibliography

Aland, Barbara. "Text Criticism of the Bible. II. New Testament." *RPP* 12:576–78.

———. "Textgeschichte/Textkritik der Bibel, II. Neues Testament." *TRE* 33:155–68.

Aland, Barbara, Kurt Aland, Gerd Mink, and Klaus Wachtel, eds., *Novum Testamentum Graecum: Editio Critica Maior; Edited by the Institute for New Testament Textual Research; Installment 2: The Letters of Peter; Part 1: Text; Part 2: Supplementary Material.* Stuttgart: Deutsche Bibelgesellschaft, 2000.

Aland, Barbara, Kurt Aland, Johannes Karavidopoulos, Carlo M. Martini, and Bruce M. Metzger. *The Greek New Testament.* 5th ed. Stuttgart: Deutsche Bibelgesellschaft, 2014.

———, eds., *Novum Testamentum Graece.* 27th ed. 8th printing corrected and extended to Papyri 99–116. Stuttgart: Deutsche Bibelgesellschaft, 2001.

———, eds. *Novum Testamentum Graece.* 28th ed. Stuttgart: Deutsche Bibelgesellschaft, 2012.

Aland, Kurt, and Barbara Aland. *Der Text des Neuen Testaments.* 2nd ed. Stuttgart: Deutsche Bibelgesellschaft, 1989.

———. *The Text of the New Testament: An Introduction to the Critical Editions and to the Theory and Practice of Modern Textual Criticism.* 2nd ed. Grand Rapids: Eerdmans; Leiden: Brill, 1989.

---

95. This essay was originally a lecture presented at the Internationale österreichisch-deutsche Tagung der Arbeitsgemeinschaft für germanistische Edition on the theme "Was ist Textkritik? Zur Geschichte und Relevanz eines Zentralbegriffs der Editionswissenschaft," Innsbruck, 25–28 February, 2004.

Aland, Kurt, Matthew Black, Bruce M. Metzger, and Allen Wikgren. *The Greek New Testament*. London: United Bible Societies, 1966.
Bammel, Ernst. "Markus 10:11f. und das jüdische Eherecht." *ZNW* 61 (1970): 95–101.
Benson, George. *A Paraphrase and Notes on Six of the Epistles of St. Paul*. 2nd ed. London: Waugh, 1752.
Bentley, Richard. *Bentleii Critica sacra: Notes on the Greek and Latin Text of the New Testament, Extracted from the Bentley MSS in Trinity College Library*. Edited by Arthur Ayres Ellis. Cambridge: Deighton, Bell, 1862.
Birdsall, J. Neville. "Πρεσβυτης in Philemon 9: A Study in Conjectural Emendation." *NTS* 39 (1993): 625–30.
———. "Textual Criticism and New Testament Studies: An Inaugural Lecture Delivered in the University of Birmingham on 10 May 1984." Paper presented at Birmingham University, 10 May 1984.
Black, David Alan. "Conjectural Emendations in the Gospel of Matthew." *NovT* 31 (1989): 1–15.
Bultmann, Rudolf. *The Gospel of John: A Commentary*. Philadelphia: Westminster, 1971.
Delobel, Joël. "The Text of Luke-Acts: A Confrontation of Recent Theories." Pages 83–107 in *The Unity of Luke-Acts*. Edited by Joseph Verheyden. BETL 142. Leuven: Leuven University Press, 1999.
Dibelius, Martin. *Aufsätze zur Apostelgeschichte*. Edited by Heinrich Greeven. 5th ed. FRLANT 42. Göttingen: Vandenhoeck & Ruprecht, 1968.
———. "Der Text der Apostelgeschichte." Pages 76–83 in *Aufsätze zur Apostelgeschichte*. Edited by Heinrich Greeven. 5th ed. FRLANT 42. Göttingen: Vandenhoeck & Ruprecht, 1968
Ehrman, Bart D., and Michael W. Holmes, eds. *The Text of the New Testament in Contemporary Research: Essays on the Status Quaestionis*. 2nd ed. NTTS 42. Leiden: Brill, 2013.
Elliott, J. Keith. "The *Editio Critica Maior*: One Reader's Reactions." Pages 129–49 in *Recent Developments in Textual Criticism: New Testament, Other Early Christian and Jewish Literature*. Edited by Wim Weren and Dietrich-Alex Koch. STAR 8. Assen: Van Gorcum, 2003.
———, ed. *The Language and Style of the Gospel of Mark: An Edition of C. H. Turner's "Notes on Marcan Usage" Together with Other Comparable Studies*. NovTSup 71. Leiden: Brill, 1993.

Epp, Eldon J. "Issues in New Testament Textual Criticism." Pages 17–26 in *Rethinking New Testament Textual Criticism*. Edited by David Alan Black. Grand Rapids: Baker, 2002.

———. "The Multivalence of the Term 'Original Text' in New Testament Textual Criticism." *HTR* 92 (1999): 245–81.

Fortna, Robert T. *The Gospel of Signs: A Reconstruction of the Narrative Source Underlying the Fourth Gospel*. SNTSMS 11. Cambridge: Cambridge University Press, 1970.

Greeven, Heinrich, and Eberhard Güting. *Textkritik des Markusevangeliums*. Theologie, Forschung und Wissenschaft 11. Münster: LIT, 2005.

Güting, Eberhard. "Der editorische Bericht als Kommentar zur Textkonstitution und zum Apparat in Editionen des Neuen Testaments." *Editio* 7 (1993): 94–108. [Ch. 5 in this collection.]

———. "Der geographische Horizont der sogenannten Völkerliste des Lukas (Acta 2:9–11)." *ZNW* 66 (1975): 149–69. [= chapter 2 in this collection]

———. "The Relevance of Literary Criticism for the Text of the New Testament: A Study of Mark's Traditions on John the Baptist." Pages 142–67 in *Studies in the Early Text of the Gospels and Acts: The Papers of the First Birmingham Colloquium on the Textual Criticism of the New Testament*. Edited by David G. K. Taylor. Texts and Studies 3/1. Birmingham: University of Birmingham Press, 1999. [= chapter 7 in this collection]

Güting, Eberhard, and David L. Mealand. *Asyndeton in Paul: A Text-Critical and Statistical Enquiry into Pauline Style*. SBEC 39. Lewiston, NY: Mellen, 1998.

Haenchen, Ernst. *Die Apostelgeschichte*. 5th ed. KEK 3. Göttingen: Vandenhoeck & Ruprecht, 1965.

Hurtado, Larry W. "Beyond the Interlude? Developments and Directions in New Testament Textual Criticism." Pages 26–48 in *Studies in the Early Text of the Gospels and Acts: The Papers of the First Birmingham Colloquium on the Textual Criticism of the New Testament*. Edited by David G. K. Taylor. Texts and Studies 3/1. Birmingham: University of Birmingham Press, 1999.

Kilpatrick, George D. "Conjectural Emendation in the New Testament." Pages 349–60 in *New Testament Textual Criticism: Its Significance for Exegesis; Essays in Honour of Bruce M. Metzger*. Edited by Eldon J. Epp and Gordon D. Fee. Oxford: Clarendon, 1981.

Koester, Helmut. "The Text of the Synoptic Gospels in the Second Century." Pages 19–37 in *Gospel Tradition in the Second Century: Origins, Recensions, Text, and Transmission*. Edited by William L. Petersen. CJAn 3. Notre Dame: University of Notre Dame Press, 1989.
Kümmel, Werner Georg. *Einleitung in das Neue Testament*. 21st ed. Heidelberg: Quelle & Meyer, 1983.
Lachmann, Karl, ed. *Novum Testamentum Graece et Latine*. 2nd ed. 2 vols. Berlin: Reimer, 1842–1850.
———. "Rechenschaft über seine Ausgabe des Neuen Testaments von Professor Lachmann in Berlin." *TSK* 3 (1830): 817–45.
Lightfoot, Robert B. *Saint Paul's Epistles to the Colossians and to Philemon: A Revised Text with Introductions, Notes, and Dissertations*. London: Macmillan, 1879.
Maas, Paul. *Textual Criticism*. Oxford, Clarendon, 1958.
Merk, Otto. "Literarkritik II. Neues Testament." *TRE* 21:222–33.
Metzger, Bruce M. *New Testament Studies: Philological, Versional, and Patristic*. NTTS 10. Leiden: Brill, 1980.
———. *The Text of the New Testament: Its Transmission, Corruption, and Restoration*. 3rd ed. Oxford: Oxford University Press, 1992.
———. *A Textual Commentary on the Greek New Testament: A Companion Volume to the United Bible Societies' Greek New Testament (Fourth Revised Edition)*. 2nd ed. Stuttgart: Deutsche Bibelgesellschaft, 1994.
Metzger, Bruce M., and Bart D. Ehrman. *The Text of the New Testament: Its Transmission, Corruption, and Restoration*. 4th ed. Oxford: Oxford University Press, 2005.
Nestle, Eberhard, and Erwin Nestle, eds. *Novum Testamentum Graece*. 13th ed. Stuttgart: Württembergische Bibelanstalt, 1927.
Nicklas, Tobias, and Michael Tilly, eds. *The Book of Acts as Church History/Apostelgeschichte als Kirchengeschichte: Text, Textual Traditions, and Ancient Interpretations/Text, Texttraditionen und antike Auslegungen*. BZNW 120. Berlin: de Gruyter, 2003.
Omerzu, Heike. "Die Darstellung der Römer in der Textüberlieferung der Apostelgeschichte." Pages 147–81 in *The Book of Acts as Church History/Apostelgeschichte als Kirchengeschichte: Text, Textual Traditions, and Ancient Interpretations/Text, Texttraditionen und antike Auslegungen*. Edited by Tobias Nicklas and Michael Tilly. BZNW 120. Berlin: de Gruyter, 2003.
Parker, David C. "The Development of Textual Criticism since B. H. Streeter." *NTS* 24 (1977): 149–62.

———. *An Introduction to the New Testament Manuscripts and Their Texts.* Cambridge: Cambridge University Press, 2008.

———. *The Living Text of the Gospels.* Cambridge: Cambridge University Press, 1997.

Petersen, William L. "What Text Can New Testament Textual Criticism Ultimately Reach?" Pages 136–52 in *New Testament Textual Criticism, Exegesis and Church History: A Discussion of Methods.* Edited by Barbara Aland and Joël Delobel. CBET 7. Kampen: Kok Pharos, 1994.

Petzer, Jacobus H. "Author's Style and the Textual Criticism of the New Testament." *Neot* 24 (1990): 185–97.

———. "The History of the New Testament Text: Its Reconstruction, Significance and Use in New Testament Textual Criticism." Pages 11–36 in *New Testament Textual Criticism, Exegesis and Church History: A Discussion of Methods.* Edited by Barbara Aland and Joël Delobel. CBET 7. Kampen: Kok Pharos, 1994.

Pöhlmann, Egert. *Einführung in die Überlieferungsgeschichte und in die Textkritik der antiken Literatur.* 2 vols. Darmstadt: Wissenschaftliche Buchgesellschaft, 1994–2003.

Rhodes, Erroll F. "Conjectural Emendations in Modern Translations." Pages 361–74 in *New Testament Textual Criticism: Its Significance for Exegesis; Essays in Honour of Bruce M. Metzger.* Edited by Eldon J. Epp and Gordon D. Fee. Oxford: Clarendon, 1981.

Rissi, Matthias. "'Die Juden' im Johannesevangelium." *ANRW* 26.3:2099–141.

Royse, James R. *Scribal Habits in Early Greek New Testament Papyri.* NTTS 36. Leiden: Brill, 2008.

Strecker, Georg. *Literaturgeschichte des Neuen Testaments.* Göttingen: Vandenhoeck & Ruprecht, 1992.

Strugnell, John. "A Plea for Conjectural Emendation in the New Testament, with a Coda on 1 Cor 4:6." *CBQ* 36 (1974): 543–58.

Vaganay, Léon. *Initiation à la critique textuelle du Nouveau Testament.* 2nd ed. Rev. by Christian-Bernard Amphoux. Paris: Cerf, 1986.

———. *An Introduction to New Testament Textual Criticism.* 2nd ed. Rev. and updated by Christian-Bernard Amphoux and Jenny Heimerdinger. Translated by Jenny Heimerdinger. Cambridge: Cambridge University Press, 1991.

Westcott, Brooke Foss, and Fenton John Anthony Hort, eds. *The New Testament in the Original Greek: Volume 1, Text; Volume 2, Introduction [and] Appendix.* Cambridge: Macmillan, 1881. 2nd ed., 1896.

Wikgren, Allen P. "The Problem in Acts 16:12." Pages 171–78 in *New Testament Textual Criticism: Its Significance for Exegesis; Essays in Honour of Bruce M. Metzger*. Edited by Eldon J. Epp and Gordon D. Fee. Oxford: Clarendon, 1981.

Wilckens, Ulrich. *Das Neue Testament: Übersetzt und kommentiert*. 5th ed. Gütersloh: Mohn; Zurich: Benziger, 1977.

Zuntz, Günther. *The Text of the Epistles: A Disquisition upon the Corpus Paulinum*. Schweich Lectures of the British Academy 1946. London: Oxford University Press, 1953.

9
The Standing of the Textual Critic Heinrich Greeven

A Celebratory Lecture in Commemoration of the One
Hundredth Anniversary of the Birth of the Founding Rector
and Scholar of the Ruhr-Universität Bochum, Professor
D. Dr. Heinrich Greeven, DD, Bochum, January 18, 2006

Anyone who is acquainted with the fascinating contributions of Heinrich Greeven to New Testament exegesis, social ethics, eschatology, the community structure of early Christianity, and not least, his contributions in church commissions and on university development boards, realizes how small in number Greeven's contributions to New Testament textual criticism are.[1]

It is hard to imagine how much arduous labor his personal collection of materials for his Synopsis must have caused him. I know from oral tradition that in 1965 he had already announced to his students the release of his *Synopsis*; it was published in 1981.[2] Greeven's judgments on the great textual critics, on the history of textual criticism, on the development of Synoptic theory since Johann Jacob Griesbach are well informed. When

---

1. Heinrich Greeven (October 4, 1906–June 7, 1990). Cf. Prof. Dr. Wolfgang Schrage's lecture on the occasion of the Academic Commemoration at the Ruhr-Universität Bochum on November 7, 1991, "Heinrich Greeven: Umrisse seines Lebens und Wirkens," *JWKG* 86 (1992): 275–90. The following Festschrift contains a bibliography of Heinrich Greeven: *Studien zum Text und zur Ethik des Neuen Testaments: Festschrift zum 80. Geburtstag von Heinrich Greeven*, ed. Wolfgang Schrage (Berlin: de Gruyter, 1986), 450–56.

2. Albert Huck, *Synopse der drei ersten Evangelien mit Beigabe der johanneischen Parallelstellen/Synopsis of the First Three Gospels with the Addition of the Johannine Parallels*, 13th ed., rev. Heinrich Greeven (Tübingen: Mohr, 1981).

he had to review a work on the testimony of lectionaries he spoke as a specialist.³ He consistently supported his opinions on individual readings, on individual manuscripts, or also on textual trajectories of specific geographical regions, by a comprehensive visual inspection of all available material. The entire transmission of the text he sought to understand as the history of the text. He directed his special interest and astute understanding toward the textual traditions of separate regions of the church. Here he did not shy away from any arduous research.⁴

It is well known that the distinguished textual critics and editors Brooke Foss Westcott and Fenton John Anthony Hort propagated the dictum: "Knowledge of the documents should precede final judgement upon readings."⁵ Someone like Greeven himself, who had to gather comprehensive materials, gradually in doing so attained more and more acquaintance with the copyists. His judgments about the Egyptian text or about the Old Georgian manuscripts matured in the course of many years.⁶

---

3. Heinrich Greeven, "Die Textgestalt der Evangelienlektionare," *ThLZ* 76 (1951): 513–22. Research on these is also presented in Bruce M. Metzger and Bart D. Ehrman, *The Text of the New Testament: Its Transmission, Corruption, and Restoration*, 4th ed. (Oxford: Oxford University Press, 2005), 49 n. 77.

4. Heinrich Greeven shared with his friends Professor J. Neville Birdsall and Professor Tjitze Baarda an interest in Diatessaron research, an interest that he pursued for a number of years in regular sessions and which led to a study of Syriac and Arabic versions of Tatian's traditions. See Tjitze Baarda, *The Calling of the Tax-Collector in the Eastern Diatessaron: Matthew—James—Levi; In Memory of J. Neville Birdsall (d. 1 July 2005), A Friend of Many Years* (Amsterdam: VU University Press, 2015), 7.

5. Brooke Foss Westcott and Fenton John Anthony Hort, eds., *The New Testament in the Original Greek, Vol. 2: Introduction [and] Appendix* (Cambridge: Macmillan, 1881), 2:31.

6. Along with the linguist Michael Job, Heinrich Greeven took on the task of translating the earliest Old Georgian manuscript of the four gospels into German. However, in the end only the first volume with the prolegomena was published. See Lamara Kadzaja, ed., *Die älteste georgische Vier-Evangelien-Handschrift: Aus dem Georgischen übersetzt von Heinrich Greeven und Michael Job* (Bochum: Brockmeyer, 1989). Anna Kharanauli deals with the beginnings of Georgian translation of the Bible. In her work the changing techniques of translation of later witnesses were characterized in the context of the Chanmeti texts and the methodological problems of the contemporary state of research were addressed. See Kharanauli, "Die Geschichte der Übersetzung der georgischen Bibel," *Phasis* 7 (2004): 58–68; Kharanauli, "Ein Chanmeti-Fragment der georgischen Übersetzung von Esra I:

It is a godsend that at his age Professor Greeven still succeeded in making his method of achieving text-critical decisions available in a textual critique of the Gospel of Mark. The volume appeared in the spring of 2005.[7] It has become evident thereby how many diverse points of view went into Greeven's decisions in each case. Today I have undertaken to make this diversity, often in competing points of view, a bit more obvious.

1. Collecting the Witnesses

According to Greeven, the grounds for a text-critical judgment should come from the individual passage.[8] However, what is an individual passage? Textual critics say, we should start with units of variation. All variants of a sentence that stand in connection with each other constitute a unit of variation and must be analyzed together. Accordingly modifications of the text that could occur independently or are independently plausible no longer belong to the particular unit of variation. On the basis of this fundamental

---

Fragen der Authentizität, Vorlage und Übersetzungstechnik," *Le Muséon* 116 (2003): 181–216; Kharanauli, "Das Chanmeti-Fragment aus Jeremia: Fragen seiner Entstehung und Übersetzungstechnik," *OrChr* 85 (2001): 204–36; Kharanauli, "Die Vorlage der georgischen Bibelübersetzungen und die methodischen Probleme" (paper presented at the tenth international colloquium of the Societas Caucasiologica Europaea, Munich, 2–5 August, 2000), 31; Kharanauli, "Einführung in die georgische Psalterübersetzung," in *Der Septuagintapsalter und seine Tochterübersetzungen: Symposium in Göttingen 1997*, ed. Anneli Aejmelaeus and Ulrich Quast, MSU 24 (Göttingen: Vandenhoeck & Ruprecht, 2000), 248–308; Bernard Outtier, "Les versions Géorgiennes de Marc: Recherches sur les versions du texte," *Mélanges de Science Religieuse* 56 (1999): 65–72. I know of three investigations by Neville J. Birdsall: "Georgian Studies and the New Testament," *NTS* 29 (1983): 306–420; Birdsall, "The Euthalian Material and Its Georgian Versions," *OrChr* 68 (1984): 170–95; Birdsall, "Introductory Remarks on the Pauline Epistles in Georgian," *StPatr* 18 (1974): 281–85. The following recent edition can be consulted: Jost Gippert, Zurab Sarjveladze, and Lamara Kadzaia, *The Old Georgian Palimpsest Codex Vindobonensis georgicus 2*, Monumenta Palaeographica Medii Aevi, Series Ibero-Caucasica, 1 (Turnhout: Brepols, 2007). I am grateful to Professor Dr. Winfried Boeder, Oldenburg University, for enlarging my bibliographic references. Works of R. Blake, Korneli Danelia, and R. Molitor are not noted.

7. Heinrich Greeven and Eberhard Güting, *Textkritik des Markusevangeliums*, Theologie, Forschung und Wissenschaft 11 (Münster: LIT, 2005).

8. Heinrich Greeven, "Text und Textkritik der Bibel, II: Neues Testament," *RGG* 6:723.

methodological improvement in the text-critical approach, I had to prepare collation sheets in the 1960s for a new edition of the Institute for New Testament Textual Research, Münster/Westphalia. The grounds for a text-critical judgment should be based on the individual passage. This is clear.

By way of contrast, for gathering material the procedure is different. In such a situation it is essential to address passages with appropriate questions. In Mark 15:1 we have to decide whether the article τῷ before the name Πιλάτῳ is original. It is present in A 0250 33 and in the Koine tradition. Here it is reasonable to ask whether the author Mark uses an article when referring to persons who have not been introduced before. When we have examined all names that occur, we discover that he does not. It is evident that in this respect Mark conforms to the prerequisites of a good style. Ὁ Πιλᾶτος is not used until further references to this prefect of Judea occur, and not the first time he is named. This is thus an anaphoric article. Greeven did not discuss this passage in his *Textkritik des Markusevangeliums*. Nevertheless, he left out the secondary article in the *Synopsis* that he edited.

In preparing his analysis, and, finally, in preparing his *Synopsis*, Greeven collected the attestation of ancient translations, first of all the Itala, but also the Old Syriac with its daughter translations, further the attestation of the Sahidic witnesses and of the Fayyumic and Bohairic, the attestation of Old Georgian, in addition to the attestation of further languages of translations. He devoted intensive study to the medieval transmission of Tatian. It is to be understood that he went back to published material wherever it was available. The introduction to his *Synopsis* provides precise information on this.

Text-critical work encounters gaps. If manuscripts are damaged or their attestation is omitted for other reasons, good editions provide corresponding lists. The limits of the translation languages must also be kept in mind. Greeven gave indications of this in his introduction. Before Greeven, Kurt Aland had listed in detail the relevant problems in volume five of Arbeiten zur neutestamentlichen Textforschung.[9]

The need to rely on citations runs into further difficulty. When the attestation of Greek, Latin, Syriac, and other fathers is consulted, those who work on textual criticism must check whether a critical edition concerning

---

9. Kurt Aland, ed., *Die alten Übersetzungen des Neuen Testaments, die Kirchenväterzitate und Lektionare*, ANTF 5 (Berlin: de Gruyter, 1972).

the text under consideration is available, or not.[10] The mere collection of citations, allusions, and reminiscences on the biblical text is insufficient. The textual critics Fee and Ehrman have studied this question in detail.[11]

Greeven also spoke out about this problem. Greeven refers to the fact that in the exposition of scriptural passages differences can be recognized between the text cited and the exposition, and these are indications that quoted texts were adapted to the established text. Sometimes one can reverse such adaptations with the help of critical editions and the manuscripts cited there.[12]

Reference should be made to an additional problem, for which I quote Greeven: "Furthermore quite often we are faced with the question whether the author wants to quote verbatim or wants only to make an allusion, whether the writer cites from memory or has 'looked it up.' In many cases investigations on the citation style of an author or work are therefore an indispensable requirement."[13]

Another difficulty, which however has notably dangerous consequences, is the fact that in many cases established editions document only a greatly reduced selection of readings in their apparatuses. With certain questions one is bound to consult Tischendorf and von Soden. Fortunately for the most part Greeven printed complete lists of variants. For other cases where only the attestation of the papyri need be considered, today one can rely on the edition of Philip W. Comfort and David J. Barrett. One

---

10. Greeven, "Text und Textkritik der Bibel," 721.

11. Gordon D. Fee revised by Roderic L. Mullen, "The Use of the Greek Fathers for New Testament Textual Criticism," in *The Text of the New Testament in Contemporary Research: Essays on the Status Quaestionis*, 2nd ed. (Leiden: Brill, 2013), 351–73; Amy M. Donaldson, "Explicit References to New Testament Variant Readings among Greek and Latin Church Fathers" (PhD diss., University of Notre Dame, 2009), https://tinyurl.com/sbl7012c. Eastern translations from antiquity and problems met with in quotations from these are discussed in Fee and Mullen, "Use of the Greek Fathers." See also Gordon D. Fee, "Method and Use of Patristic Evidence," in *Studies in the Theory and Method of New Testament Textual Criticism*, ed. Eldon J. Epp and Gordon D. Fee, SD 45 (Grand Rapids: Eerdmans, 1993), 299–359; Fee, "Origen's Text of the New Testament and the Text of Egypt," *NTS* 28 (1992): 348–64; Bart D. Ehrman, Gordon D. Fee, and Michael W. Holmes, eds., *The Text of the Fourth Gospel in the Writings of Origen*, vol. 1, NTGF 3 (Atlanta: Scholars Press, 1992).

12. Greeven, "Text und Textkritik der Bibel," 721.

13. Greeven, "Text und Textkritik der Bibel," 721.

should cite the second edition.[14] With the description of these ditches into which one can fall, I conclude this point on the collection of witnesses.

2. Inspecting the Witnesses

Before we invoke the available witnesses for a specific text-critical problem, we need to survey what is available. Even though Greeven took the individual passage as his starting point, and even though he was basically disposed to edit eclectically, he still decided often to investigate the author's entire use of language on a specific question. Even though the goal of inquiry was the language and text of an author, nevertheless the characteristics of the copyists constantly demanded an in-depth examination. First it was necessary to group the witnesses according to the time of their origin and their geographical provenance. The great age of a manuscript, of course, in no way precludes the transmission of a textual error. Even the best manuscripts transmit errors. Thus we speak of the character of the text of a manuscript or a group of manuscripts, and we attain this judgment through the analysis of the errors detected. Not infrequently manuscripts have errors that are found nowhere else. Often they are associated with other witnesses in a common error. If an error can be distinguished from other errors because of its peculiarity, this allows key errors to be identified. In some cases the witnesses under consideration reveal their common provenance by means of the key error.

Church provinces and geographical regions manifest characteristic errors that are associated with some widespread preferences of copyists. Thus clarification to make the text smoother, incorporation of differing readings from Synoptic parallels, and adaptation to the context are frequent everywhere. Also differing standards with regard to the accuracy of the requisite work become noticeable and lead to regional differences.

Greeven gave careful attention to the characteristic particularities of different regional traditions. To be sure, he recognized the frequently splendid quality of the Egyptian text and the Egyptian witnesses. However, Greeven exhibited at the same time a pronounced suspicion toward the readings of the Egyptian tradition. Frequently in his criticism he

---

14. Philip W. Comfort and David P. Barrett, eds., *The Text of the Earliest New Testament Greek Manuscripts: A Corrected and Enlarged Edition: New and Complete Transcriptions with Photographs* (Wheaton, IL: Tyndale, 2001).

polemicized against a "cult of the best manuscripts." By this he meant the fundamental preference of Egyptian readings in the textual criticism of Westcott and Hort and their critical followers.[15] Greeven is able to demonstrate that the manuscripts B and ℵ are occasionally linked in ancient errors that they have in common.

In Mark 15:6 Greeven diagnosed one such ancient error. ℵ B 2427 and A have here replaced the original ὅνπερ ᾐτοῦντο with its generalizing meaning by a verb that otherwise never appears in Mark: ὃν παρῃτοῦντο. Here the four witnesses are linked together in an ancient key error.[16]

A further example: Mark narrates skillfully. In order to set off the background of an incident from an actual event he uses the imperfect. Copyists have often replaced this with the aorist. Such an aorist is found in the manuscripts ℵ and B in Mark 6:6. With what was for him a characteristic expression, Greeven refers to the "inclination" [Gefälle] of the manuscript tradition. Imperfects are pushed aside.[17]

An impressive example for an undesirable "cult of the best manuscripts" is found in the text of Luke 19:38. The Nestle-Aland text here follows exclusively the witness of manuscript B. This is only rarely correct. B: Εὐλογημένος ὁ ἐρχόμενος ὁ βασιλεὺς ἐν ὀνόματι κυρίου. If one examines the variants, one recognizes the motive for altering the text. ὁ βασιλεύς was not present in the original text. However, copyists strove to assimilate the ὁ βασιλεύς of the Gospel of John (John 12:13). For these copyists Mark's phrase was less suitable: Εὐλογημένη ἡ ἐρχομένη βασιλεία τοῦ πατρὸς ἡμῶν Δαυίδ (Mark 11:10).[18]

A further example from the end of the Gospel of Mark: Mark 15:46 is speaking about the burial of Jesus. Joseph of Arimathea removes the corpse, wraps it in silk, and buries it. The Greek refers to this as ἔθηκεν ἐν μνημείῳ. But here ℵ and B are in conflict with this text with their reading ἐν μνήματι. Greeven is unable to detect any motive for replacing an

---

15. "The formation, e.g., of the Nestle text makes it the representative of the Egyptian text type rather than of the presumably original text" (Greeven, "Text und Textkritik der Bibel," 723).

16. Greeven and Güting, *Textkritik des Markusevangeliums*, 701.

17. Greeven and Güting, *Textkritik des Markusevangeliums*, 307.

18. Here Heinrich Greeven's text is admittedly not really better. The βασιλευς inserted in his text is supported above all by the witnesses *Rpl*.

original ἐν μνήματι later. Therefore, he takes the reading of the two most important Egyptian witnesses to be secondary.[19]

Greeven attributed the circulation of certain readings principally to an early influential recension. I do not wish to conceal that in this regard he occasionally overshot the target. One cannot always follow Greeven in the rejection of Egyptian readings. Also the assumption of authoritatively accepted intrusions into early texts is after the researches of Günther Zuntz and Carlo M. Martini no longer justified.[20] Nevertheless, his willingness to give preference to texts from non-Egyptian traditions remains categorically one of the great achievements of the textual critic Greeven.

In particular Greeven investigated readings of the so-called Western tradition intensively. Where this tradition is bolstered by witnesses from other regions, he was disposed to take their readings as original. In this regard he distanced himself clearly from Westcott and Hort. For these critics the finding "Western reading" had a thoroughly negative ring.

I will give some examples, but I want to emphasize that the establishment of a large number of such decisions is not required. Greeven's achievement is his methodological open-mindedness for different regional traditions and their claim to be considered as repositories of original readings.

For example, at the end of the Gospel of Mark among the Egyptian witnesses, the witnesses ℵ and B are almost alone with their omission of the spurious ending of Mark. Apart from the minuscule 304 only a few church fathers vouch for this reading. The Afra witness k indirectly supports this reading: it has its own addition. So a Western witness becomes an important partisan of our old Egyptians. Hence, for most textual critics the short ending of Mark holds as the original text of the author.

In Mark 9:38 Greeven edits a text that is attested almost exclusively by Western witnesses. These are Codex Bezae/05, all of the Itala witnesses with the exception of the manuscript from Brescia and Codex Aureus (f z), as well as and above all the Afra k. Only one other majuscule supports

---

19. Greeven and Güting, *Textkritik des Markusevangeliums*, 733.

20. Günther Zuntz, "The Text of the Epistles," in *Opuscula Selecta: Classica, Hellenistica, Christiana* (Totowa, NJ: Rowman & Littlefield; Manchester: Manchester University Press, 1972), 252–68; Zuntz, *The Ancestry of the Harclean New Testament*, British Academy Supplemental Papers 7 (London: Oxford University Press, 1945); Carlo M. Martini, *Il problema della recensionalità del codice B alla luce del papiro Bodmer XIV*, AnBib 26 (Rome: Pontifical Biblical Institute, 1966).

this text: W together with the minuscules 565 and 700 (W and 565 with the altered verb ουκ ηκολουθει). In addition, the Lake group and the Ferrar group testify with these.[21]

I do not wish to discuss this highly complicated variant here. This could only produce a glittering abridgement and simplification. But I will say what is for me the decisive argument: the analysis of the text of Luke and of the transmission of Luke—these give Greeven's assessment its conclusiveness.

The study of witnesses is principally an analysis of possible errors. For instance, the procedure of copyists in copying their exemplar constantly demands keen attention. Sometimes copyists are inattentive. They pass over an article, insert a conjunction, or give the subject of the sentence that is missing in the exemplar. They know the context and take information from it, which they occasionally use prematurely. They know other gospels or parts of their regional liturgy and take over phraseology from Synoptic parallels. They correct imperfections (such as, e.g., provincialisms in Mark's style), introduce something explanatory, or even enhance the dramatic art of the narrative. In the mouth of Judas, a doubled "Rabbi" sounds more impressive than a simple "Rabbi." In numerous places Greeven produced lists of variants in order to clarify typical mannerisms of copyists. By means of such lists of variants Greeven analyzed the so-called inclination of the tradition (Gefälle der Überlieferung).

For this the entire language of the Synoptics must constantly remain in view. In this way the analysis of Synoptic parallels is bound to become an essential tool. The Gospel of Luke influences the text of Mark. Even more frequently Greeven called attention to influences of the ecclesiastically influential text of Matthew on the tradition of Mark.[22] It is demanded of us that we distinguish the particularities of each of the Synoptic Gospels. Secondary readings that have infiltrated must be identified. Thereby it gradually becomes clear where copyists have encroached on the text; it

---

21. Barbara Aland, Kurt Aland, Johannes Karavidopoulos, Carlo M. Martini, and Bruce M. Metzger, eds., *The Greek New Testament*, 5th ed. (Stuttgart: Deutsche Bibelgesellschaft, 2014), 155.

22. Heinrich Greeven, "The Gospel Synopsis from 1776 to the Present Day," in *J. J. Griesbach: Synoptic and Text-Critical Studies 1776–1976*, ed. Bernard Orchard and Thomas R. W. Longstaff, SNTSMS 34 (Cambridge: Cambridge University Press, 1978), 23.

becomes conspicuous which language, which style, which kind of representation we can attribute to the individual Synoptic narrator.

Greeven speaks here of the circularity of the perception event, as others also do, for instance, the classical philologist Zuntz.[23] In the process of making the *tesserae* clearer, we draw near to the later composite view of the mosaic.

One can characterize text-critical work as being engaged with the text. The actual goal of the perception is the author as the source of a characteristic representation, as the conveyor of tradition, as the considered narrator.

Mark does not call Jesus the Son of God. Copyists have altered this (Mark 1:1; 8:29). Neither does Mark call Jesus "God's Holy One." A possessed person does (Mark 1:24). Jesus speaks of himself as the Son of Man (Mark 2:10, 28; 10:45, and frequently). Or in a metaphor he calls himself a prophet (Mark 6:4). His disciples address him as teacher (Mark 9:38), or also as the Christ (Mark 9:29).

Once the narrator reports a journey to Tyre, not a journey to Tyre and Sidon. The doubling in the designation of the region comes from the Gospel of Matthew (Matt 15:21).[24]

Mark the narrator possibly lived in Rome for many years. At any rate he loves concise sentences. Several generations of copyists have eliminated many asyndeta and have introduced connecting particles.

Mark has more precise statements about the religious parties of the time of Jesus than the other gospels. Twice he speaks of the Herodians (Mark 3:6; 12:13), and once of the Sadducees (Mark 12:18). In addition copyists increase the anti-Pharisaic statements of his gospel.

In the light of the extant variants little by little an assessment is gained of what truly is attested. Establishing an ancient tradition in no way implies a concurrent confirmation of originality for that text. This establishment

---

23. "The work is executed consequently in a theoretical circle of perception, in that at the same time it seeks to reconstitute the original text along with the outline of a history of the text, that is, a comprehensive view that convincingly explains the development of the manuscript transmission of texts of numerous manuscripts with multiple quite considerable divergences in succession, in parallel, and apart from each other." (Greeven, "Text und Textkritik der Bibel," 716); cf. Eberhard Güting, "The Methodological Contribution of Günther Zuntz to the Text of Hebrews," *NovT* 48 (2006): 6 [ch. 10 in this collection].

24. Greeven and Güting, *Textkritik des Markusevangeliums*, 381.

remains subject to the *examinatio*. I come now to the third aspect of the comprehensive method of Greeven.

3. The Justification of the Text-Critical Decision

As soon as a reading of a transmitted text is recognized as possibly the source of later, secondary readings, the actual work of the philologist begins, the *examinatio*. Philological *examinatio* investigates: Can this reading be the text of the author? Each reading has a context. The information it conveys, the form in which it is presented, and the possible implications are to be examined. How a statement in the Gospel of Mark has been assimilated and understood in Synoptic parallels is relevant. The investigation must take into account whether a reading fits the character of the passage to be analyzed and whether the statement is coherent with its location. It is just as important to consider whether the language of the evangelist and his way of presentation are harmonious with the reading. For this, grammars are to be consulted.

Usually internal criteria for the accuracy of a passage and external criteria of attestation are set over against each other. According to the style of a textual critic one sometimes decides on a preference for external or a preference for internal criteria. In his extensive justifications of text-critical decisions Greeven constantly gave equal space to both points of view.[25]

Greeven was not convinced that a text attested mainly by Egyptian witnesses always deserves preference. He reserved to himself the right to pass judgment on every tradition, including the Egyptian. This characterizes his standing as a textual critic. Greeven spoke of the circularity of the event of perception. It is worthwhile to say more about this aspect, which little by little produces a mosaic. Greeven occasionally discusses together variants that in the text of the gospel are found far removed from

---

25. Recently Chrys C. Caragounis has called attention to the fact that in the contexts of certain traditions the analysis of external attestation contributes almost nothing for attaining a text-critical assessment. This difficulty is due to our understanding of the traditions of pronunciation in Classical and Hellenistic Greek, which Caragounis interprets in close diachronic connection with the Neohellenistic pronunciation. In numerous passages that he presents, the textual critic must work almost exclusively with internal criteria. Quite evidently this information is of fundamental importance. See Caragounis, *The Development of Greek and the New Testament*, WUNT 167 (Tübingen: Mohr Siebeck, 2004), 475–564.

each other. I have shown how effective this is in Mark 1:1. Copyists have secondarily inserted the majestic title υιος θεου not only in Mark 1:1 but also in Mark 8:29. In this respect Mark the author pursues a literary objective, deferring such a central statement until the conclusion of his gospel. A gentile centurion expresses it: "Truly, this person was a Son of God!" (Mark 15:39).

For Mark 2:13 Greeven considers simultaneously textual variants from 3:7 and 7:31. This is occasioned by references to the Sea of Galilee in connection with prepositions. Greeven demonstrates that the prepositions εις/ επι/παρα την θαλασσαν are transmitted relatively consistently. Hence παρα in 2:13 and προς in 3:7 and εις in 7:31 should be considered as original. Here Greeven has identified the "inclination of the tradition" with the aid of extensive lists.[26]

In Mark 2:16 Greeven considers the syntactic pattern associated with verbs of sight. With οτι clauses, participial constructions appear frequently. Greeven shows that "seeing" in the strict sense (to see with one's own eyes) is predominantly construed with participles. By contrast οτι clauses appear if this seeing implies discovery, thus, for instance, in Mark 12:34, where Jesus sees the "prudent" answer of a scribe. Indeed it is easy to replace participial phrases by οτι clauses. However, for this in the light of transmitted variants only two passages come into question, Mark 2:16 and Mark 7:2. In both cases Greeven follows the old Egyptian witnesses: in both cases he votes against the participial form, although according to his view in both cases the meaning is "to see with one's own eyes." In 7:2 he even decides against his own Synopsis—correctly.[27]

On the basis of evidence Greeven was inclined even at an advanced age to reassess his own decisions. In his textual criticism of the Gospel of Mark he decided against the text of his own *Synopsis* in a number of passages. He took no part in creating a cult of established readings. So he remained what he was, a well-informed critic.

4. Open Questions in Greeven's Textual Criticism

What Greeven has accomplished for textual criticism of the Synoptic tradition, at least with Mark in mind, has become clear even if I have admittedly

---

26. Greeven and Güting, *Textkritik des Markusevangeliums*, 148–49.
27. Greeven and Güting, *Textkritik des Markusevangeliums*, 154–55, 353–54.

gone into rather too much detail. In this, however, something important has been left unsaid. Greeven's work sought to go beyond textual criticism to gather preliminary materials for the important and still open question with regard to literary relationships of the individual Synoptic Gospels to each other and to the sources that were taken over by them. He was of course aware that oral tradition has an impact on the texts, not only at the beginning of the writing of the gospels but also thereafter.

His own view of his work on the Synoptic Gospels as a preliminary stage is evident in his essay at the Griesbach Colloquium in Münster.[28] Greeven reports in detail on advances and regressions in the composition of synopses since the time of the Reformation and beyond. It is important for him that methods of textual criticism and literary criticism in their full sense are encountered as early as the scholarly work of Origen. He emphasizes that as early as 1809 Planck distinguished between the content and the form of Synoptic passages.[29] For him especially it was essential that his synopsis should not convey his own theory by its arrangement but provide space for the development of theories that might be possible. In this respect he praised the organization of Griesbach's synopsis.[30] To this day, it is an astonishingly open, controversially disputed question as to what relationship of dependence the Synoptic Gospels have with each other and with their sources.

Greeven's methodology leads on to a further frontier. Perhaps the considered and methodical analysis of ancient textual currents, as Greeven taught it, conceals this frontier somewhat. As much as we are able to say with regard to what is associated with older texts and what appears to be the result of secondary scribal activity, just as little can we specify what we have in our hands when it comes to the old texts.

Do we have the texts of the authors? Do we have the texts of ancient editors? Do we have the results of early revision? Zuntz was convinced that with the help of older manuscripts, scholars in the Alexandrian tradition revised and improved early traditions. Zuntz did not see, nor did he say that exemplary codices were designed, that editorial decisions were authoritatively established.

But yet we have unambiguous indications for early editorial activities.

---

28. Greeven, "Gospel Synopsis," 22–49.
29. Greeven, "Gospel Synopsis," 29.
30. Greeven, "Gospel Synopsis," 28.

We discern clearly traces of editors in Romans, in 1 Corinthians, in Ephesians, in the Gospel of John. Thus skepticism remains, here and in other passages, as to whether we can penetrate at all to the original text, the text of the author. Tasks remain, open questions remain.

Bibliography

Aland, Barbara, Kurt Aland, Johannes Karavidopoulos, Carlo M. Martini, and Bruce M. Metzger. *The Greek New Testament*. 5th ed. Stuttgart: Deutsche Bibelgesellschaft, 2014.

Aland, Kurt, ed. *Die alten Übersetzungen des Neuen Testaments, die Kirchenväterzitate und Lektionare*. ANTF 5. Berlin: de Gruyter, 1972.

Baarda, Tjitze. *The Calling of the Tax-Collector in the Eastern Diatessaron: Matthew—James—Levi; In Memory of J. Neville Birdsall (d. 1 July 2005), A Friend of Many Years*. Amsterdam: VU University Press, 2015.

Birdsall, Neville J. "The Euthalian Material and Its Georgian Versions." *OrChr* 68 (1984): 170–95.

———. "Georgian Studies and the New Testament." *NTS* 29 (1983): 306–420.

———. "Introductory Remarks on the Pauline Epistles in Georgian." *StPatr* 18 (1974): 281–85.

Caragounis, Chrys C. *The Development of Greek and the New Testament*. WUNT 167. Tübingen: Mohr Siebeck, 2004.

Comfort, Philip W., and David P. Barrett, eds. *The Text of the Earliest New Testament Greek Manuscripts: A Corrected and Enlarged Edition; New and Complete Transcriptions with Photographs*. Wheaton, IL: Tyndale, 2001.

Donaldson, Amy M. "Explicit References to New Testament Variant Readings among Greek and Latin Church Fathers." PhD diss., University of Notre Dame, 2009. https://tinyurl.com/sbl7012c.

Ehrman, Bart D., Gordon D. Fee, and Michael W. Holmes, eds. *The Text of the Fourth Gospel in the Writings of Origen*. 2 vols. NTGF 3. Atlanta: Scholars Press, 1992.

Fee, Gordon D. "Method and Use of Patristic Evidence." Pages 299–359 in *Studies in the Theory and Method of New Testament Textual Criticism*. Edited by Eldon J. Epp and Gordon D. Fee. SD 45. Grand Rapids: Eerdmans, 1993.

———. "Origen's Text of the New Testament and the Text of Egypt." *NTS* 28 (1992): 348–64.

Fee, Gordon D., revised by Roderic L. Mullen. "The Use of the Greek Fathers for New Testament Textual Criticism." Pages 351–73 in *The Text of the New Testament in Contemporary Research: Essays on the Status Quaestionis*. Edited by Bart D. Ehrman and Michael W. Holmes. 2nd ed. NTTS 42. Leiden, Boston: Brill, 2013.

Gippert, Jost, Zurab Sarjveladze, and Lamara Kadzaia. *The Old Georgian Palimpsest Codex Vindobonensis georgicus 2*. Monumenta Palaeographica Medii Aevi, Series Ibero-Caucasica 1. Turnhout: Brepols, 2007.

Greeven, Heinrich. "The Gospel Synopsis from 1776 to the Present Day." Pages 22–49 in *J. J. Griesbach: Synoptic and Text-Critical Studies 1776–1976*. Edited by Bernard Orchard and Thomas R. W. Longstaff. SNTSMS 34. Cambridge: Cambridge University Press, 1978.

———. "Die Textgestalt der Evangelienlektionare." *ThLZ* 76 (1951): 513–22.

———. "Text und Textkritik der Bibel, II: Neues Testament." *RGG* 6:716–25.

Greeven, Heinrich, and Eberhard Güting. *Textkritik des Markusevangeliums*. Theologie, Forschung und Wissenschaft 11. Münster: LIT, 2005.

Güting, Eberhard. "The Methodological Contribution of Günther Zuntz to the Text of Hebrews." *NovT* 48 (2006): 359–78. [Ch. 10 in this collection.]

Huck, Albert. *Synopse der drei ersten Evangelien mit Beigabe der johanneischen Parallelstellen/Synopsis of the First Three Gospels with the Addition of the Johannine Parallels*. 13th ed. Revised by Heinrich Greeven. Tübingen: Mohr, 1981.

Kadzaja, Lamara, ed. *Die älteste georgische Vier-Evangelien-Handschrift: Aus dem Georgischen übersetzt von Heinrich Greeven und Michael Job*. Bochum: Brockmeyer, 1989.

Kharanauli, Anna. "Das Chanmeti-Fragment aus Jeremia: Fragen seiner Entstehung und Übersetzungstechnik." *OrChr* 85 (2001): 204–36.

———. "Ein Chanmetifragment der georgischen Übersetzung von Esra I: Fragen der Authentizität, Vorlage und Übersetzungstechnik." *Le Muséon* 116 (2003): 181–216.

———. "Einführung in die georgische Psalterübersetzung." Pages 248–308 in *Der Septuaginta-Psalter und seine Tochterübersetzungen: Symposium in Göttingen 1997*. Edited by Anneli Aejmelaeus and Ulrich Quast. MSU 24. Göttingen: Vandenhoeck & Ruprecht, 2000.

———. "Die Geschichte der Übersetzung der georgischen Bibel." *Phasis* 7 (2004): 58–68.

———. "Die Vorlage der georgischen Bibelübersetzungen und die methodischen Probleme." Paper presented at the Tenth International Colloquium of the Societas Caucasiologica Europaea. Munich, 2–5 August, 2000.

Martini, Carlo M. *Il problema della recensionalità del codice B alla luce del papiro Bodmer XIV*. AnBib 26. Rome: Pontifical Biblical Institute, 1966.

Metzger, Bruce M., and Bart D. Ehrman. *The Text of the New Testament: Its Transmission, Corruption, and Restoration*. 4th ed. Oxford: Oxford University Press, 2005.

Outtier, Bernard. "Les versions Géorgiennes de Marc: Recherches sur les versions du texte." *Mélanges de Science Religieuse* 56 (1999): 65–72.

Schrage, Wolfgang. "Heinrich Greeven: Umrisse seines Lebens und Wirkens." *JWKG* 86 (1992): 275–90.

———. *Studien zum Text und zur Ethik des Neuen Testaments: Festschrift zum 80. Geburtstag von Heinrich Greeven*. BZNW 47. Berlin: de Gruyter, 1986.

Westcott, Brooke Foss, and Fenton John Anthony Hort, eds. *The New Testament in the Original Greek: Volume 1, Text; Volume 2, Introduction [and] Appendix*. Cambridge: Macmillan, 1881. 2nd ed., 1896.

Zuntz, Günther. *The Ancestry of the Harclean New Testament*. British Academy Supplemental Papers 7. London: Oxford University Press, 1945.

———. "The Text of the Epistles." Pages 252–665 in *Opuscula Selecta: Classica, Hellenistica, Christiana*. Totowa, NJ: Rowman & Littlefield; Manchester: Manchester University Press, 1972.

10
The Methodological Contribution of Günther Zuntz to the Text of Hebrews

Present studies in the field of textual criticism differ remarkably with regard to their goals. While numerous publications study the evidence with the explicit goal of identifying the original texts of authors, other publications concentrate their attention upon the contexts of scribes and their often meaningful secondary various readings.[1]

In view of these lines of research, which both deserve full critical appraisal, I wish to call attention to the rigorous standards of the textual criticism of Günther Zuntz and to its methodological results.

On January 7, 2000, the *Neue Osnabrücker Zeitung*, the Osnabrück newspaper, informed its readers that an unknown papyrus had become known and was due for publication by the Österreichische Nationalbibliothek, Vienna. This papyrus containing text from Heb 2:9–11 and 3:3–6 was assigned a date before 500 CE by the editor.[2] Nine papyri with text from Hebrews are known at present: P^{12} P^{13} P^{17} P^{46} P^{79} P^{89} P^{114} P^{116} P^{126}.

Those who have studied the text of Hebrews are aware that in 2:9 we find an important variant reading, a reading classified as original by Adolf von Harnack and many other exegetes, among them, notably,

---

1. See my article, "Offene Fragen in der Methodendiskussion der neutestamentlichen Textkritik," *Editio* 19 (2005): 77–98 (ch. 8 in this collection).

2. The editor, Professor Amphilochios Papathomas of Athens, suggested as its date the sixth or seventh century CE; see Papathomas, "A New Testimony to the Letter to the Hebrews," *JGRChJ* 1 (2001): 18–24. I refer, here, to the internet version of his article. The printed version, which appeared in the spring of 2003, specifies: "Palaeographical parallels allow us to date the papyrus to the fifth or possibly even to the sixth century." See Papathomas, "A New Testimony to the Letter to the Hebrews (2.9–11 and 3.3–6) (Tafel 6)," *Tyche* 16 (2001): 109.

Zuntz,[3] but which has not been admitted into any recent edition of the New Testament. As a consequence, it is accepted by commentators but not by editors. I had occasion to see the photographs of the papyrus on the internet. The result is negative: the papyrus is damaged in the passage in question, and the text cannot be restored.

Today the published materials on Hebrews allow a considerable advance beyond the texts available to Zuntz. We have the publications of the Institut für Neutestamentliche Textforschung in Münster: *Das Neue Testament auf Papyrus: Die paulinischen Briefe, Teil II*, ed. Barbara Aland, ANTF 22 (Berlin: de Gruyter 1994), the Nestle-Aland twenty-eighth edition of 2012, and the fifth edition of *The Greek New Testament* of 2014. The readings of the Vetus Latina from the Vetus Latina Institut at Beuron are invaluable for anyone who works on Hebrews. I shall refer to all of these materials.

The Task of Textual Criticism Defined

The one who asks, rather bluntly, precisely what task Zuntz had to tackle when writing his *Disquisition upon the Corpus Paulinum* will get the obvious answer: Zuntz had to define the textual character of the Chester Beatty Papyrus II, and he did exactly this. Probing into the text of the papyrus, one needs at the same time to pass judgment on the achievements and skills of the scribe, of the corrector, and to identify anything amiss. Zuntz describes his task by the terms of the classical philologist, namely, *recensio*, *examinatio*, and *emendatio*.[4] By no means is Zuntz willing to disown the tool of *emendatio*; he accepts, for instance, the splendid conjecture of Cobet with regard to Hebrews 11:4, ἡδίονα.[5]

---

3. "Günther Zuntz *28. Januar 1902 in Berlin †3. April 1992 in Cambridge. Scholar and musician"—These are the words engraved on his tombstone, according to the obituary—*bien recherché* and moving—of Professor Martin Hengel; see Günther Zuntz, *Lukian von Antiochien und der Text der Evangelien*. ed. Barbara Aland and Klaus Wachtel, AHAW.PH 2 (Heidelberg: Winter, 1995), 63–89; Zuntz, *The Text of the Epistles: A Disquisition upon the Corpus Paulinum*, Schweich Lectures of the British Academy 1946 (London: Oxford University Press, 1953), 34–35, 44.

4. Zuntz, *Text of the Epistles*, 8–14, referring (on 8–9) the reader to the first (1927) edition of the slim volume by Paul Maas: *Textkritik*, 3rd. ed. (Leipzig: Teubner, 1957); ET: Maas, *Textual Criticism* (Oxford: Clarendon, 1958).

5. Günther Zuntz, *Opuscula Selecta: Classica, Hellenistica, Christiana* (Totowa,

The considerable burden of his task, in the face of an enormous amount of accumulating evidence, becomes clear as the reader turns to the first chapter of his book. Zuntz reports on the situation of the textual criticism of the New Testament and on its agenda. Textual criticism, according to him, finds itself in a threefold dilemma.

Observing that our witnesses join one another in any imaginable combination,[6] we are driven to concede *contaminatio* as a disturbing element of our findings. To clarify the pedigree of manuscripts by forming *stemmata codicum* in Lachmann's manner is therefore simply impossible. Faced with this dilemma Zuntz proceeds with an analysis of *Leitfehler* ("indicative errors").[7] These secondary readings, which by the distinctive form of their corruption reveal a common archetype, are an indispensable instrument of the textual critic.

Second, Zuntz sets out to correct a consequential misconception of Johann Jacob Griesbach. This textual critic used the term "recension" as referring to three ancient types of edited text (Alexandrian, Western, Byzantine). Zuntz criticizes with care: "On this basis J. J. Griesbach, unsurpassed in carefulness, caution, and comprehensive knowledge, elaborated the classical system of three recensions."[8] Zuntz insists that a recension in the proper sense of the word is neither discernible in Alexandria, nor in the Western Text. The term Western Text, acccording to Zuntz, is to be used precisely. It is applicable only to readings with exclusively Western support. Accordingly, an alleged Western reading ceases to be Western as soon as, for instance, a testimony of Clement is found in its support.[9]

Zuntz, following Sir Frederic Kenyon, urges those who specialize in this field to see the second century, this period of uncontrolled transmission, as an age that predates all so-called recensions. He corrects, too, the erroneous judgments of Griesbach with regard to the Byzantine text: this

---

NJ: Rowman & Littlefield; Manchester: Manchester University Press, 1972), 254; Zuntz, *Text of the Epistles*, 16.

6. "There is in fact hardly any alinement [*sic*] of witnesses imaginable, right across the delimitation of the 'recensions', that does not actually occur" (Zuntz, *Text of the Epistles*, 6; see also p. 185).

7. See Maas, *Textkritik*, 27–31 (ET: 42–47).

8. Zuntz, *Text of the Epistles*, 5: "J. S. Semler (to whom besides we owe the misleading term 'recension')."

9. Zuntz, *Opuscula Selecta*, 254.

tradition does not depend on the West and, consequently, like the other sources of transmission preserves, on a limited scale, ancient readings of its own, readings that are genuine.[10]

Third, Zuntz obliges the textual critic to *examinatio* in the strict sense of the term. Textual criticism must examine each phrase, word, and letter. Here I must expose myself to the danger of clarifying what is clear. Let me state: lists of witnesses never decide text-critical alternatives.[11]

Zuntz is willing to inspect long lists of variants, for instance of Western readings, in order to single out the two readings that may claim an origin in the author's text and he finds σάρκινοι in 1 Cor. 3:3 supported by $D^{*,c}$ F G^{12} and δολοῖ in 1 Cor. 5:6 supported by D* and Ir^{lat} (corrumpit).[13]

---

10. "The rejection en bloc of the Byzantine text similarly tends to rob us of a most helpful instrument. This rejection is due to Griesbach, who, as we saw, considered the late text to derive from the two earlier 'recensions' combined. We shall see that this view is erroneous and thus gain another clue to the early history of the tradition" (Zuntz, *Text of the Epistles*, 12).

11. The knowledgeable attention to linguistic detail by this author tends to shift the balance between external and internal criteria in the latter direction, or as M.-E. Boismard states in a review, "le dernier mot revient en définitive à la critique interne"(review of *The Text of the Epistles*, by Günther Zuntz, *RB* 61 [1954]: 451–52).

12. Zuntz, *Text of the Epistles*, 99–100. Zuntz presents additional evidence in the testimony of Origen. The internal argument is decisive: Paul uses σάρκινος when speaking of human beings. I did not discover any editor who accepts these two occurrences of σάρκινοι in 1 Cor 3:3. Yet Griesbach considered the latter reading worthy of almost the same high esteem that the printed text rightfully receives; see Joseph Jacob Griesbach, ed., Η ΚΑΙΝΗ ΔΙΑΘΗΚΗ: *Novum Testamentum Graece* (Leipzig: Göschen, 1803–1807), 3:67 and p. xix: "Litera β notantur lectiones lectionibus in textum receptis paene aequiparandae."

13. Zuntz, *Text of the Epistles*, 114. Zuntz quotes the testimony of Irenaeus ("iv.27.4, referring to his *seniores* and confirmed by the Armenian version of the *c. Haereses*.") and of Jerome, who mentions *codices nostri*. The secondary variant reading "comes from εζυμωθη Mt. xiii.33 || Lk. xiii.21." I did not find any editor who would accept this correct reading. Griesbach held this reading in high esteem and accorded it his letter γ, see Griesbach, Η ΚΑΙΝΗ ΔΙΑΘΗΚΗ, 73, and xix: "Litera γ designantur eae, quae probabilitate inferiores quidem illis, non tamen aspernandae, sed ulteriore examine dignae videntur." Bruce M. Metzger attributed this reading to a "Western correction", see Metzger, *A Textual Commentary on the Greek New Testament: A Companion Volume to the United Bible Societies' Greek New Testament (Fourth Revised Edition)*, 2nd ed. (Stuttgart: Deutsche Bibelgesellschaft, 1994), 485.

10. The Methodological Contribution of Günther Zuntz   251

Zuntz is not willing, without further argument, to accept a reading on the sole authority of P[46].[14] He may accept a reading on the joint testimony of P[46] and B, if internal evidence, for instance, arguments from style and context, recommend that reading. In 1 Cor 3:2, for instance, P[46] and B (and 0185) omit ἔτι and this, according to Zuntz, "so greatly improves the style as to make the assumption of a mere scribal slip difficult".[15] The same witnesses are joined in "a palpable error" in Heb 7:2, reading παντός (witnesses

---

14. Zuntz, *Text of the Epistles*, 92.
15. Zuntz, *Text of the Epistles*, 40. Many years before Zuntz, Karl Lachmann objected to the particle as printed in the textus receptus: [ετι]. Brooke Foss Westcott and Fenton John Anthony Hort likewise put it in brackets. Bernhard Weiss was not willing to consider the omission a mere scribal slip (Weiss, *Textkritik der paulinischen Briefe* [Leipzig: Hinrichs, 1896], 102). Instead he surmised that ετι by anticipation had been transferred from 1 Cor 3:3. He deleted it in his edition: Weiss, *Die paulinischen Briefe im berichtigten Text* (Leipzig: Hinrichs, 1896), 142. Weiss mentions the text-critical decision of Lachmann and Westcott-Hort, a decision that was not taken up by the editors of the significantly revised 26th edition of the Nestle-Aland *Novum Testamentum Graece* (NA[26]; unchanged in the 27th [1996] and 28th [2012] editions), for it printed the faulty ετι (together with most other editions). It is something of a puzzle why well-known commentaries such as that by Hans Conzelmann (*Der erste Brief an die Korinther*, KEK 5 [Göttingen: Vandenhoeck & Ruprecht, 1969], 90) do not consider the text-critical judgment of Lachmann against ετι, nor the arguments of Weiss and Zuntz. Perhaps a mistaken interpretation of this particle convinced them, endorsed as it was by Luther, Debrunner, and Bauer: "auch jetzt noch nicht"; see Friedrich Blass and Albert Debrunner, *Grammatik des neutestamentlichen Griechisch*, 7th ed. (Göttingen: Vandenhoeck & Ruprecht, 1943), § 448.6; Walter Bauer, *Wörterbuch zu den Schriften des Neuen Testaments und der übrigen urchristlichen Literatur*, 5th ed. (Berlin: Töpelmann, 1963), s.vv. ετι (624) and νυν (1080). It is clear, indeed, that ουδε ετι και νυν must mean "even now no longer," which, however, does not suit the context and raises a suspicion not against the prospects of the sportsmen in Corinth, but rather against the logic of the presumed speaker. One is reminded here of Friedrich Blass's rule of textual criticism: "Participes operis sunt scriptor et auctor aperte / Auctor habet sensum, somnia scriptor habet." See my contribution to the Lunel Colloquium, "Weakly Attested Original Readings of the Manuscript D 05 in Mark," in *Codex Bezae: Studies from the Lunel Colloquium June 1994*, ed. David C. Parker and Christian-B. Amphoux, NTTS 22 (Leiden: Brill, 1996), 231 [ch. 6 in this collection].

are P[46] B sy[p]), and in the omission of τε in Heb 5:1, "which is against the style of the writer" (witnesses are P[46] B D[1] Ψ).[16]

He may accept a reading of P[46] and B in Heb 1:4, if it is supported by Clement of Rome[17] and is recommended by the known habits of the author: ἄγγελοι are mentioned without articles.[18] So much, at this point, for subsingular agreements.

Which reading may claim a place in the speech of the author? Which readings within the transmitted texts are ancient, and which, possibly, even original? Textual criticism must by no means halt at this barrier and fail to ask this question.

> The critic must choose between competing readings. If he refuses to do so, he renounces the very purpose of all his labours.... Textual criticism is not a branch of science. Its criteria are necessarily different from those sought by the scientist: they are not, for that reason, less exacting nor less definite. The convergence of arguments drawn from the distribution of the evidence, the dependence of one reading upon the other, the known habits and typical faults of scribes, the characteristic proclivities of interpolators, the development of the language, the stylistic peculiarities of the writer, the context of the passage in question—these, and still other factors combined can yield a certainty which is no whit inferior to that of the conclusions drawn from a Euclidean axiom.
>
> Every variant whose quality and origin has in this way been established must serve as a stone in the mosaic picture of the history of the tradition, for there is next to no other material from which it could be built up. At the same time the evaluation of individual readings depends to a large extent upon their place within this picture. This is another instance of that circle which is typical of the critical process; it is a fruitful and not a vicious circle. The critic may, indeed he must, aim at a comprehensive picture of the whole tradition; he reaches this goal by an untiring dedication to detail.[19]

The style of this written study that I have quoted reveals a surprising orality capable of establishing contact with the generation that Zuntz wished

---

16. Zuntz, *Text of the Epistles*, 40; Herbert Braun, *An die Hebräer*, HNT 14 (Tübingen: Mohr, 1984), 40.

17. 1 Clem. 36.2.

18. Zuntz, *Text of the Epistles*, 218. Braun, with due reserve, accepts this decision; see Braun, *An die Hebräer*, 34.

19. Zuntz, *Text of the Epistles*, 12–13.

to teach. My object here, however, is principally to describe how Zuntz proceeded with the task at hand.

Zuntz Analyzes 1 Corinthians and Hebrews

In his *The Text of the Epistles*, Zuntz presents an analysis of the transmission of the Corpus Paulinum. Zuntz quotes from Colossians, Ephesians, Philippians, Galatians, and from other Pauline letters, but his methodical approach is explicit. Its goal is a complete analysis of all units of variation in 1 Corinthians and in Hebrews. The language of this latter author and the language of Paul are the standards of reference against which the work of scribe and corrector are measured. Three sources of historical evidence, Byzantium, Alexandria, and the West of the empire, serve to reconstruct the language of Paul and the language of the author of Hebrews. Since the scribe has to devote his attention to two individual styles of writing, we must have ways of checking him. Are there any differences in the way certain language patterns are handled, and if so, what befell those books in the course of time? *Habent sua fata libelli*. Zuntz, indeed, is able to discover influences that left traces upon the book of Hebrews, influences from a period when Hebrews was not part of the Corpus.

Traces of an Early Editing of Hebrews

Is it possible to give a date for the Corpus Paulinum? Clement does not quote the Corpus. He quotes Romans and 1 Corinthians, apparently from an independent source. The Corpus, on the other hand, is known to Ignatius and Polycarp. These authors quote ten Pauline letters including Ephesians. The Corpus, then, is to be dated to about 100 CE and Zuntz adds to this conclusion: "2 Peter III.15 appears to refer to it."[20] Influences upon the text of Hebrews that predate the Corpus are evidently as early as the last decades of the first century. This sounds rather exciting. Are there such influences?

It was Harnack who observed that the Latin Vulgate is inclined to translate the word ἀπειθεῖν and its noun ἀπείθεια by the synonymous words corresponding to ἀπιστεῖν and ἀπιστία. In Hebrews this exchange is found

---

20. Zuntz, *Text of the Epistles*, 14.

in Heb 3:18; 4:6, 11; 11:31.[21] This tendency to replace ἀπειθεῖν and ἀπείθεια is a regular feature of this ancient version. The Vulgate prefers *increduli fuerunt, incredulitatem*, and so on. It is rather remarkable that the papyrus P[46] similarly introduces τοῖς ἀπιστήσασιν, δι' ἀπιστίαν, or τῆς ἀπιστίας in four passages of Hebrews whereas this witness does not do so in other parts of the Pauline Corpus. This phenomenon recurs exclusively in the four passages that use ἀπειθεῖν in this Epistle. It calls for an explanation.[22]

Zuntz presents this observation with a rather cautious question:

> But it remains a puzzle that P[46] should only in Hebrews (and not in the many instances in Romans and Ephesians) have introduced the synonym απιστειν; that, in Hebrews, it should have done so in all the four instances that could come into question; and that there should be other Greek evidence for two of them—such as there is not in the many other instances throughout the Pauline corpus. Perhaps this feature goes back to the time when Hebrews was still circulating separately?[23]

Zuntz argued that this observation could not establish any relationship between P[46] and the translator of the Vulgate. It could not be interpreted to establish a relation between old Western traditions and the text of this papyrus, since the older witnesses of the Western text regularly use *contumax, contumacia* to match ἀπειθής, ἀπείθεια. Since in the meantime the monks of the Beuron Institute edited their splendid edition of the Itala text of Hebrews, we can check this today. Quotations of Hebrews by Lucifer,

---

21. Adolf von Harnack, *Zur Revision der Prinzipien der neutestamentlichen Textkritik: Die Bedeutung der Vulgata für den Text der Katholischen Briefe und der Anteil des Hieronymus an dem Übersetzungswerk* (Leipzig: Hinrichs, 1916), 81; von Harnack, "Studien zur Vulgata des Hebräerbriefes," *SPAW* (1920): 181; repr. in *Studien zur Geschichte des Neuen Testaments und der alten Kirche* (Berlin: de Gruyter, 1931), 1:193.

22. Witnesses for απιστησασιν in 3:18 are P[46] lat sah; for απιστιαν in 4:6, P[46] ℵ lat sah boh arm; for απιστιας in 4:11, P[46] 104 1611 2005 lat sah sy[Ephraem] sy[h]; for απιστησασιν in 11:31, P[46] lat sah arm. In 3:18 Lucifer and Pseudo-Columbanus epistle 3 testify to *contumacibus*. In 4:6 Lucifer and Ambrose testify to *contumaciam*. In 4:11 Lucifer testifies to *contumaciae*.

23. Zuntz, *Text of the Epistles*, 124. Weiss took it for granted that Hebrews, from its earliest period of transmission, was part of the Pauline Corpus; see Hans Friedrich Weiss, *Der Brief an die Hebräer*, 15th ed., KEK 13 (Göttingen: Vandenhoeck & Ruprecht, 1991), 127.

Ambrosius, and an anonymous expositor of Hebrews support this judgment.[24] While old witnesses differing from the Vulgate have *contumax, contumacia*, the younger witnesses show *increduli, incredulitas*, and *infidelis*.

Evidently, then, this change in theological emphasis owes its origin to the East. Thus with due reserve, the assumption of Zuntz may be accepted. Hebrews suffered secondary alterations while not yet transmitted as a portion of the *Corpus Paulinum*. At this point let me add one caveat: Hebrews is no part of the earlier period of the Old Latin tradition.[25]

Zuntz Rehabilitates the Testimony of the Byzantine Text

Zuntz, as mentioned, criticizes Griesbach for neglecting the testimony of the Byzantine text. This tradition is valuable in spite of its many secondary accretions, for its testimony is independent from the West.

Since this point is important for Zuntz, he is careful to demonstrate the validity of his position. I consider this demonstration to be vital to the argument. This argument opposes the broad consensus of text-critical common sense. It observes agreements of the papyrus with a minority of Byzantine witnesses and seeks to establish that the majority, including most Egyptian uncials, transmits corruption in their texts. Zuntz argues that the minority readings were not restored by conjecture, but owe their correct text to a faithfully preserved tradition.[26]

Zuntz selects three passages to prove his point. First, 1 Cor 3:10. While the majority gives τὴν χάριν τοῦ θεοῦ, P[46] 0142 1611 1960 F (Latin) vulg[N.c.dem] arm read τὴν χάριν. The papyrus is accompanied by quotations from the fathers, namely, Clement, Theodoretus, Cyril, and Augustine.

---

24. Hermann Josef Frede, ed., *Vetus Latina: Die Reste der altlateinischen Bibel*, 25 Pars II, 5th fasc. (Freiburg im Breisgau: Herder, 1988), 1183 regarding 3:18; 1190 regarding 4:6; 1197 regarding 4:11; Frede, *Vetus Latina*, 9th fasc. (Freiburg im Breisgau: Herder, 1991), 1545 regarding 11:31.

25. Frede, *Vetus Latina*, 1st fasc. (Freiburg im Breisgau: Herder, 1975), 31. Manuscript 89 transmits the commentary of an Anonymus on the Epistles of Paul. "Die 397–405 entstandene Arbeit eines Anonymus macht von den griechischen Exegeten vor allem der antiochenischen Schule reichen Gebrauch und behandelt erstmals im lateinischen Westen auch den Hebräerbrief."

26. Zuntz, *Text of the Epistles*, 49 n. 2: "The 'Byzantine Text' is imperfectly known; it is not identical with that hybrid growth the *Textus Receptus* (see *J.T.S*. xliii, 1942, 25). The passages here discussed, however, raise no problem."

Zuntz notes *une finesse de language* of Paul. Since Paul does not introduce divine grace as a general concept, but refers to "a particular charisma with which that 'Grace of God' endows an individual," τὴν χάριν is appropriate as two parallel passages reveal: Rom 12:3 and Gal 2:9.[27]

Second, a passage from Heb 11:37: *om.* ἐπειράσθησαν P[46] 1241ˢ syᵖ sah Orᵖᵗ Eus.[28] Before the papyrus was published, the shorter reading was known from two minuscules only, namely, 2 and 327. Again this shorter reading finds support in the fathers and in some ancient versions. Zuntz mentions the Peshitta, Armenian, Sahidic, and Ethiopic versions together with Origen, Eusebius, Acacius, Socrates, and Theophylactus. Metzger's *Textual Commentary* adds 1984 ℓ[44] ℓ[53] Ephraem, Jerome, and Ps-Augustine.[29] Westcott and Hort had not mentioned this reading. The omission was accepted, however, into the text of Nestle-Aland (26th ed., 1983; 27th ed., 2001; 28th ed., 2012).

A third example for a weakly attested reading is to be found in Heb 2:6. Τίς is the text of the papyrus, whereas the majority reads τί. Zuntz calls attention to the fact that the author intends a slightly altered proposition as compared with the text of the Septuagint. He translates: "Who is the man (ἄνθρωπος) whom thou mindest?" ... "Truly (ἦ) the Son of Man, for him Thou visitest." The scribes almost everywhere succeed in restoring the Septuagint wording. The correct reading in this passage is supported by the uncials P[46] C* P, the minuscules 81 104 917 1288 1319 1834 1881 2127 2495, and also by d vulg^tol boh.[30]

Zuntz adds a number of further passages. In these P[46] is supported by the majority of Byzantine manuscripts. They include:

---

27. Zuntz, *Text of the Epistles*, 47. The majority of our text editions did not accept the text-critical decision of Zuntz. George Dunbar Kilpatrick, however, bracketed the secondary intrusion: [του θεου]; see Kilpatrick, ed., *Romans and 1 and 2 Corinthians: A Greek-English Diglot for the Use of Translators* (London: British and Foreign Bible Society, 1964), 34.

28. Zuntz, *Text of the Epistles*, 47.

29. Metzger, *Textual Commentary*, 604.

30. Zuntz, *Text of the Epistles*, 48. Braun, *An die Hebräer*, 53, accepts this decision. The textual critic Bernhard Weiss argued that τις is a fault caused by the following word ανθρωπος. The same mistake is found in the Septuagint wording of codex A; Weiss, *Textkritik der paulinischen Briefe*, 29. Editions of the New Testament do not accept the decision of Zuntz. Erich Grässer does not accept it either; see Grässer, *An die Hebräer*, EKKNT 17.1 (Zürich: Benziger; Neukirchen: Neukirchener Verlag, 1990), 116 n. 23.

Hebrews 2:8: ἐν τῷ γὰρ ὑποτάξαι, while printed by Nestle-Aland, is a corrupt word order, a solecism. The witnesses are ℵ B D 0243 Ψ 1739 [M] 1906. Zuntz argues that the correct reading (supported by the style of the author)[31] did not enter the Byzantine tradition by conjecture, but was present by tradition. The original text (ἐν γὰρ τῷ ὑποτάξαι) is supported by P46 A C K L P 056 075 0142 0150 0151 0278 33 1881. It was printed by Bengel and Griesbach.[32]

Hebrews 11:4: μαρτυροῦντος ... αὐτοῦ τοῦ θεοῦ is the correct wording supported by P13* P46 ℵ2 D1 Ψ 0285 1739 1881 lat sy boh Cl Or Chrys Theodoretus and the Byzantine witnesses. The faulty τῷ θεῷ is common to ℵ* A D* 33 326 1311 1834* 1836 arm eth.[33]

Hebrews 9:26: "The article before ἁμαρτίας is neither in P46 nor in the Byzantine text." Witnesses: P46 C D2 Ψ 0278 0285 1739 1881 pm. Zuntz refers to the argument from the style of the author: Hebrews speaks of ἁμαρτία without adding the article.[34] Here again the Old Uncials have a secondary article: ℵ A I P 33 81 104 365 630. Late witnesses preserve a genuine feature.

Internal considerations favor the Byzantine text in Heb 11:13. A standard phrase replaces a less standardized wording. κομισάμενοι τὰς ἐπαγγελίας ℵ* I P 33 81 326 365 436 1241S 2400 is found in many contexts;

---

31. Zuntz, *Text of the Epistles*, 50–51; cf. 10:15, μετὰ γὰρ τὸ προειρηκέναι, and 11:15, πρὸ γὰρ τῆς μεταθέσεως.

32. Johann Albrecht Bengel, ed., *Η ΚΑΙΝΗ ΔΙΑΘΗΚΗ: Novum Testamentum Graecum*, 2nd ed. (Tübingen: Berger, 1753), 415; Griesbach, *Η ΚΑΙΝΗ ΔΙΑΘΗΚΗ*, 3:280. The critical editions since Karl Lachmann are united in printing the corrupt reading, except for Heinrich Josef Vogels, who edited the correct εν γαρ τω; Vogels, *Novum Testamentum Graece et Latine, pars altera, Epistulae et Apocalypsis* (Freiburg im Breisgau: Herder, 1950), 671.

33. Zuntz, *Text of the Epistles*, 33, 51. The correct reading was printed by Bengel and Griesbach, but not by Lachmann and Tregelles. Weiss criticizes these authors for their unaccountable decision. He describes τω θεω as an adaptation of the same wording earlier in the verse, or as a copying mistake; see Weiss, *Textkritik der paulinischen Briefe*, 18.

34. Zuntz, *Text of the Epistles*, 52. While many critical editions accepted the secondary article, Tischendorf did not print it. This decision is remarkable, since it runs counter to Tischendorf's codex ℵ. Before him Griesbach did not print it; *Η ΚΑΙΝΗ ΔΙΑΘΗΚΗ*, 3:300. Braun recommended the reading, with reserve: Braun, *An die Hebräer*, 284; so Grässer, *An die Hebräer*, 196 n. 82. Nestle-Aland prints [της].

see 10:36; 11:39. The Papyrus is supported by the Byzantines, but now also by D: λαβόντες.³⁵ Witnesses are P⁴⁶ D ℵ² C 1739 1881 pm.³⁶

A superfluous article slightly alters the meaning of πολλοί in Heb 12:15. οἱ πολλοί is found in ℵ A 048 0150 33 1908 "with c. 12 other minn"³⁷ and also in Clement and Theodoretus, but πολλοί in this context is to be preferred, "many," so P⁴⁶ D H Ψ 1739 1881 pm.³⁸ Zuntz refers the reader to similar passages in Mark 6:2 and 9:26, where the secondary article alters the text. In one of these Nestle-Aland prints the correct decision, namely, in Mark 6:2.

The fact that in the last two instances D "joins the Byzantine bulk" means, according to Zuntz, "more than the accession of just one, old manuscript." "D may actually here be adding the whole weight of its whole group to the evidence for the Byzantine variant."³⁹

One last passage serves to illustrate the value of the Byzantine testimony. In Heb 9:19 Zuntz considers the list of witnesses as highly remarkable. His conclusion: the words καὶ τραγῶν or καὶ τῶν τραγῶν are an ancient interpolation into the text. It is found in more than one position, omitted by thirty Byzantine manuscripts from all subgroups of von Soden, omitted by the Peshitta, by the Harklean version, and by Chrysostom; the interpolation is lacking in P⁴⁶ and in ℵ² K L Ψ 0150 0151 0278 181 1241 1505 1739 1881 sy^{p.h.pal} Origen.⁴⁰

---

35. Zuntz, *Text of the Epistles*, 52–53.

36. Bengel, *Η ΚΑΙΝΗ ΔΙΑΘΗΚΗ*, 427, and Griesbach, *Η ΚΑΙΝΗ ΔΙΑΘΗΚΗ*, 3:306, print λαβοντες. Lachmann edited μη προσδεχαμενοι, but most of his sucessors edited μη κομισαμενοι. Weiss edited λαβοντες, and this was accepted in Nestle-Aland; see Weiss, *Paulinischen Briefe im berichtigten Text*, 582; Weiss, *Textkritik der paulinischen Briefe*, 29.

37. Zuntz, *Text of the Epistles*, 53 n. 2.

38. Bengel, *Η ΚΑΙΝΗ ΔΙΑΘΗΚΗ*, 429, and Griesbach, *Η ΚΑΙΝΗ ΔΙΑΘΗΚΗ*, 3:312, print πολλοι. The critical editions since Lachmann almost unanimously printed οι πολλοι; finally Kilpatrick and Nestle-Aland returned to the correct reading, πολλοι. See George Dunbar Kilpatrick, ed., *The Pastoral Letters and Hebrews: A Greek-English-Diglot for the Use of Translators* (London: British and Foreign Bible Society, 1963), 38.

39. Zuntz, *Text of the Epistles*, 54.

40. Zuntz, *Text of the Epistles*, 54–55. The interpolation, inherited from the textus receptus, has been an integral part of the critical texts until, finally, Nestle-Aland bracketed it "to indicate a certain doubt that they [i.e., these words] belong there" (Metzger, *Textual Commentary*, 599). Braun bracketed the words but indi-

Zuntz comments on these lists of witnesses.[41] He begins with patterns in which the papyrus is supported by an extremely small attestation. Its correct readings find support in F and G, in a few minuscules, in some church fathers, and also by great numbers of late manuscripts. I quote his conclusion: "The extant Old Uncials and their allies cannot be relied upon to furnish us with a complete picture of the textual material which the fourth and fifth centuries inherited from earlier times and handed on to the Middle Ages. P[46] has given us proof of that."[42]

Zuntz Rehabilitates the Western Text

To recommend Western readings, even today, requires some courage. Unsupported by evidence from non-Western sources these readings often resemble a puzzle. Westcott and Hort in their "Notes on Select Readings" regularly connect the term with a definite connotation of disapproval. Zuntz, however, endeavored to reinstate Western readings to their proper function. In this endeavor he was assisted by hundreds of variant readings found and published in P[46].

It is obvious that a proper use of this material needs some preparation. Zuntz in his day had only limited access to Old Latin witnesses. Since then work on the quotations from Latin fathers has greatly profited from the diligence of the editors at Beuron, in the Vetus Latina Institut. Similarly, collations of Old Latin manuscripts are readily accessible now, but they were not to the same extent for Zuntz; he had to make his own collations. Occasionally Zuntz speaks of the "scanty attestation of most of these variants."[43] He did use the publications of Hedley F. D. Sparks and of Carl Theodor Schaefer.[44]

According to Zuntz, there are three decisive witnesses in the West: (1) the Greek archetype of D FG, (2) Tertullian, and (3) the archetype of d

---

cated that they were interpolated into the text; see Braun, *An die Hebräer*, 276. Weiss defended the interpolation; see Weiss, *Brief an die Hebräer*, 481 n. 25.

41. Zuntz, *Text of the Epistles*, 55–57.
42. Zuntz, *Text of the Epistles*, 56.
43. Zuntz, *Text of the Epistles*, 122.
44. John Wordsworth, Henry J. White, Hedley F. D. Sparks, eds., *Novum Testamentum Domini nostri Iesu Christi latine secundum editionem S. Hieronymi*, 3 vols. (Oxford: Clarendon, 1889–1954); Carl Theodor Schaefer, *Untersuchungen zur Geschichte der lateinischen Übersetzung des Hebräerbriefs* (Freiburg im Breisgau: Herder, 1929).

and the non-Vulgate quotations in Latin fathers. The Vulgate is a Western witness, belonging to (3) only when it agrees with the decisive witnesses. Hence Jerome or individual scribes retained Old Latin features.

His own work on 1 Corinthians taught Zuntz that every other sample of Alexandrian and Western agreement he had tested, led to some type of "Western+" corruption. We need not rehearse his proceedings in detail. A considerable number of passages analyzed led, however, to results that on internal grounds and in view of their attestation could augment our grasp of Pauline style and argument.

This series of enquiries had an important methodical result that needs careful assessment. Zuntz came to the conclusion that none of the purely Western readings shared by P^{46} could be characterized as a common error. Seemingly common errors in each case turn out to be ancient survivals from two independent routes of transmission. I quote: "The absence of any striking special error common to the most outstanding Western manuscript and P^{46} (or its allies) is a first, definite hint that no direct relation exists between the 'Alexandrians' and the Western text."[45] This conclusion is reinforced by an analysis of two "purely Western"[46] readings from Hebrews that happen to recur in P^{46}.

In Heb 3:6 Zuntz defends ος as the logically correct reading.[47] He admits a possible argument against its reception, namely, "that this construction, so normal in Latin, is not easily paralleled in Greek."[48] Nevertheless, he is willing to attribute to this stylist the *lectio magis ardua*. The witnesses are: D* P^{46} 0243 6 88 424^c 1739 it$^{ar\ b\ d}$ vg Lucifer Theodore of Mopsuestia Ambrose.[49] The reading of the textus receptus is attested by P^{13} ℵ A B C D^1 I K P Ψ 0278 33 1881 it^v sy$^{p.h.pal}$ sah boh arm Jerome.

---

45. Zuntz, *Text of the Epistles*, 88.

46. Zuntz discusses in this section readings that, though Western in character, are supported by P^{46} and its allies. This terminology as used by Zuntz may appear somewhat misleading, see Zuntz, *Text of the Epistles*, 90.

47. Bengel and Griesbach gave attention to this reading. Bengel attributed his letter β to the alternative ος, and Griesbach attributed γ to the alternative reading; Bengel, *Η ΚΑΙΝΗ ΔΙΑΘΗΚΗ*, 416; Griesbach, *Η ΚΑΙΝΗ ΔΙΑΘΗΚΗ*, 3:282.

48. Zuntz, *Text of the Epistles*, 93.

49. Frede quotes Ambrose, *De Joseph* 49 (106.21, ed. Schenkl); Frede, *Vetus Latina*, 5:1171.

Because of its early and diversified attestation ου is preferred by Metzger, but not by Braun.[50]

In Heb 6:2 the genitive διδαχῆς is grammatically "inadmissible." In the midst of numerous genitives it disturbs the construction. "Διδαχή then must appear in the same case as θεμέλιον, the word to which it refers epexegetically."[51] Witnesses: P[46] B 0150 it[d.75].[52] The "inadmissible" reading is attested by ℵ A C D[gr] I K P 33 81 614 1739 pm. On account of its attestation Metzger decided differently (for the genitive), but not Braun.[53] The textual critic Bernhard Weiss listed two arguments in support of his decision: a scribal mistake, in view of the many genitives is a plausible assumption, and exegesis also casts its ballot for the better text, or, as I would prefer to recast the argument: The context supports this decision.[54]

To his eyes the material accessible in Hebrews yielded comparatively little, if analyzed in a similar way. Zuntz analyzed ten readings in Hebrews in which Eastern witnesses join their testimony with D. To check the results presented we should compare the lists of Zuntz with the fresh material from Beuron.

In Heb 12:27 the author interprets a prophetic utterance of Hag 2:6. The words ἔτι ἅπαξ ... σείσω mean that heaven and earth after one cosmic catastrophe will enter the perfect age, in Greek: τὸ δὲ ἔτι ἅπαξ δηλοῖ τῶν σαλευομένων μετάθεσιν. Nestle-Aland prints [τὴν] τῶν σαλευομένων μετάθεσιν.[55] Secondary articles are found in diverse forms in several sets

---

50. Metzger, *Textual Commentary*, 595; Braun, *An die Hebräer*, 83. Lachmann and his successors edited ου.

51. Zuntz, *Text of the Epistles*, 93.

52. Frede quotes the Itala manuscript 75: *doctrinam*, and, with due reserve, recommends both readings; Frede, *Vetus Latina*, 6th fasc. (Freiburg im Breisgau: Herder, 1989), 1262.

53. Metzger, *Textual Commentary*, 596; Braun, *An die Hebräer*, 160. The editors of the New Testament have been divided over the issue of this variant. Lachmann, Westcott-Hort, Nestle (5th ed., 1904), Weiss, and Kilpatrick preferred διδαχην; Tregelles, Tischendorf, Baljon, Vogels, Merk, Bover, and Nestle-Aland edited διδαχης.

54. Weiss, *Paulinischen Briefe im berichtigten Text*, 540; Weiss, *Textkritik der paulinischen Briefe*, 18.

55. Whereas Lachmann and most of his successors printed την των σαλευομενων μεταθεσιν, Westcott-Hort and Nestle-Aland edited [την] των σαλευομενων μεταθεσιν.

of witnesses, but they are lacking in D* P⁴⁶ 1739 [M] L 048 0243 323 arm.⁵⁶ Zuntz refers his audience to the style of the scholia on the classical writers and reminds us "that such word-exegesis is normally given without the article."⁵⁷ We are also reminded that articles applied to a new statement would be inappropriate.⁵⁸

In Heb 5:11 Zuntz defends the anarthrous phrase πολὺς λόγος on the authority of D* P⁴⁶* P 1319 arm. "What the author wants to say, and what the text without the article properly expresses, is: 'on this subject there is much to say, but it would be obscure.'"⁵⁹ Nestle-Aland still prints the incorrect article.⁶⁰

In Heb 12:3 Zuntz discusses the alternatives of a participial form. D* ᶜ P⁴⁶ P¹³ 2 1739 1881 and Euthymius testify to a perfect participle ἐκλελυμένοι. This would fall in line with verbal forms in the perfect tense in verses 5 and 13. Zuntz suggests that ἐκλυόμενοι was introduced by scribes to prepare the quotation of Prov 3:11, μὴ ἐκλύου, in v. 5.⁶¹ This is the only passage in this list that Zuntz decides with a measure of hesitation. He prints a question mark. It is remarkable, I think, that this variant is not discussed by Metzger and that Nestle-Aland rejects a reading against the testimony of D*·ᶜ P⁴⁶ P¹³ and 1739.

In Heb 4:3 the author is again expounding Ps 95. Zuntz remarks that the author freely refers to his text, for he omits the pronoun αὐτοῦ found in 3:18; 4:1; 4:10.⁶² The Vaticanus B adds its testimony to the witness of D* P⁴⁶ P¹³ᵛⁱᵈ and supports anarthrous κατάπαυσιν. The secondary article is caused by assimilation within the context, as Weiss pointed out.⁶³ The

---

56. Zuntz, *Text of the Epistles*, 117; NA²⁷, 585.

57. Zuntz, *Text of the Epistles*, 118.

58. Braun quotes Zuntz and adds that the variable position of την is an indication of its secondary origin; Braun, *An die Hebräer*, 444.

59. Zuntz, *Text of the Epistles*, 118, 257. Braun agrees with Zuntz; Braun, *An die Hebräer*, 150.

60. The editors since Lachmann are unanimous in editing περι ου πολυς ημιν ο λογος.

61. Zuntz, *Text of the Epistles*, 118. Braun, with due reserve, recommends the reading; Braun, *An die Hebräer*, 408.

62. Zuntz, *Text of the Epistles*, 118.

63. Weiss, *Textkritik der paulinischen Briefe*, 77. He was alone in printing this text, whereas Lachmann and many of his successors edited την καταπαυσιν. Tregelles, Westcott-Hort, and Nestle-Aland printed [την] καταπαυσιν. Braun is inclined to agree with Zuntz; Braun, *An die Hebräer*, 108.

anarthrous form is correct, a decision that should have been accepted by Nestle-Aland and Metzger.[64]

In Heb 13:9 a faulty participle περιπατήσαντες arose by adaptation to the aorist of the main verb. The correct form περιπατοῦντες is found in D* P[46] ℵ* A 1912 co. Zuntz refers to the present participle, *ambulantibus*, found in d z vulg.[65] Nestle-Aland gives the correct decision here.

In Heb 9:11 it was Westcott who correctly identified the origin of the disorder in the transmission of the text. The correct γενομένων ἀγαθῶν in deference to 10:1 was altered into μελλόντων ἀγαθῶν.[66] This explanation is generally accepted by commentators, for example, Metzger, Braun, Frede, Weiss.[67] Weiss argued that both participles in the phrases ἀρχιερεὺς τῶν γενομένων ἀγαθῶν and σκιὰν … τῶν μελλόντων ἀγαθῶν (10:1) have their specific suitability.[68] B is among the witnesses of the original text: D* d B P[46] 13 1611 1739 2005 sy[p.h.pal] Cyril-Jer Chrysostom Oecumenius.[69] The edition of Frede quotes for *bonorum factorum* the Old Latin manuscript 75.[70] The *Greek New Testament* cites the Georgian version for the correct reading.[71] Metzger's *Commentary* refers to its "superior attestation on the score of age and text type."[72]

In Heb 11:15 the context gives support to the present tense of the *lectio*

---

64. Metzger, *Textual Commentary*, 596.

65. Zuntz, *Text of the Epistles*, 118 n. 3. Braun agrees; Braun, *An die Hebräer*, 462. Frede lists numerous Old Latin manuscripts with *ambulantibus*, among them 65 75 89 109 and 61 51; Frede, *Vetus Latina*, 10th fasc. (Freiburg im Breisgau: Herder, 1991), 1635.

66. Brooke F. Westcott *The Epistle to the Hebrews* (London: Macmillan, 1889; repr., Grand Rapids: Eerdmans, 1965), 256. Similarly the textual critic Weiss argued for the correct reading, but he was, perhaps, not read. Weiss, *Textkritik der paulinischen Briefe*, 31.

67. Braun, *An die Hebräer*, 265; Frede, *Vetus Latina*, 7th fasc. (Freiburg im Breisgau: Herder, 1990), 1391; Weiss, *Brief an die Hebräer*, 464 n. 9; Metzger, *Textual Commentary*, 598. Braun, who argued for the correct reading, misconstrued the position of Zuntz and Westcott in their evaluation of this variant reading; see Braun, *An die Hebräer*, 265.

68. Weiss, *Brief an die Hebräer*, 464 n. 9.

69. Zuntz, *Text of the Epistles*, 119 and n. 2.

70. Frede, *Vetus Latina*, 7:1391.

71. Barbara Aland et al., eds., *The Greek New Testament*, 4th ed. (Stuttgart: Deutsche Bibelgesellschaft, 1993), 757.

72. Metzger, *Textual Commentary*, 598. The correct reading was edited by

ardua, μνημονεύουσιν. Present tenses are found in verses 14 and 16. Zuntz writes: "Here, as in ver. 22, μνημονεύειν means 'refer to.'"[73] The trouble arose when scribes understood "to remember." The correct reading is found in D* P[46] 1739* ℵ* Ψ and six minuscules,[74] also in Origen and Theodoretus. The Itala supports *meminissent*.[75] Nestle-Aland prints ἐμνημόνευον.[76]

In Heb 8:6 Zuntz argues on the basis of the attestation of the *lectio rarior*. Not τετύχηκεν but τέτυχεν is his choice. Τέτυχεν is read by D* P[46] ℵ* 075 A K L and nine minuscules, according to Zuntz. He lists 436 462 623 910 1610 1611 1888 1898 1912.[77] Nestle-Aland quotes three: 81 1242 2464, but knows *permultos*. The decision is correct in Nestle-Aland.[78]

In Heb 12:3 Zuntz recognizes a case where the best of our ancient witnesses testify to a corrupt text. "The singular [εἰς (ἑ)αυτον] is the only imaginable reading that fits the context, yet there is no ancient evidence for it."[79] If nowhere else, Zuntz is here willing to accept the view that the acceptable reading εἰς ἑαυτόν (A P 0150 ω vulg[B D al] Chrysostom) was intro-

---

Lachmann, Westcott-Hort, Weiss, Nestle (5th ed., 1904), Kilpatrick, and Nestle-Aland.

73. Zuntz, *Text of the Epistles*, 119.

74. Zuntz, *Text of the Epistles*, 119 n. 3; Barbara Aland, ed., *Das Neue Testament auf Papyrus: Die paulinischen Briefe, Teil 2*, ANTF 22 (Berlin: de Gruyter 1994), 330: *illeg*. D*. Braun (*An die Hebräer*, 366) lists 81 436 442 1739* 1834 1881 1908 2005.

75. Manuscripts 65 75 89 109 61, according to Frede, *Vetus Latina*, 9:1527.

76. The reading μνημονευουσιν was edited by Tregelles and Tischendorf. Most critical editions preferred εμνημονευον. Weiss argued that the present tense in v. 15 was adapted to the tenses in v. 14, εμφανιζουσιν and επιζητουσιν; Weiss, *Textkritik der paulinischen Briefe*, 43. Braun, quoting von Soden, likewise proposed this view; see *An die Hebräer*, 366.

77. Zuntz, *Text of the Epistles*, 119 n. 7. Zuntz argues on the base of the strong attestation: "The authority of the *lectio rarior* and the combined weight of almost all of the ancient witnesses is in favour of the reading of P[46]" (120). Blass-Debrunner notes that many Hellenistic authors are transmitted with the Ionian form τετευχε. Debrunner seems to favor this reading, and Weiss does, too. See Blass and Debrunner, *Grammatik des neutestamentlichen Griechisch*, §101 (ET: BDF, §101), and Weiss, *Textkritik der paulinischen Briefe*, 37.

78. Tregelles and Weiss adopted τετευχεν into their editions; Samuel Prideaux Tregelles, ed., *The Greek New Testament Edited from Ancient Authorities, with the Latin Version of Jerome, from the Codex Amiatinus* (London: Bagster, 1870), 887; Weiss, *Paulinischen Briefe im berichtigten Text*, 556.

79. Zuntz, *Text of the Epistles*, 120.

duced by conjecture. Witnesses for the corrupt text are: D* P⁴⁶ P¹³ ℵ Ψᶜ 048(?) 33 81 256 1288 1319 1739* 2127 z vulg^(A C al) pesh boh eth Ephraem.⁸⁰

The last reference in his list, Heb 13:21, shows variation as to the length of the formula εἰς τοὺς αἰῶνας, which in ℵ A (C*) K P 056 0150 0151 0243 0285 33 81 614 1739 [M] is given in the longer form εἰς τοὺς αἰῶνας τῶν αἰώνων. After inspecting two diverse types of text transmission in several Pauline and non-Pauline texts Zuntz decides that the shorter formula is to be preferred as the text of the author.⁸¹ The witnesses are: P⁴⁶ D C³ Ψ 6 104 365 1241ˢ 1505 syʰ sah arm Theodoretus.⁸² I consider it remarkable that Zuntz hesitates to give a similar decision for the short formula in 1:8. He writes: "One would confidently describe the shorter reading as 'Western', if Tertullian, *Adv. Prax.* 13 could be safely quoted for it; but I see no convincing argument against the assumption that he translated Ps. xl. 7, and translated it freely (he has *in aevum* only)."⁸³ Such critical care is to be acclaimed. Quotations from the fathers deserve care, indeed.

I am, however, inclined to call the full formula, as given by the Septuagint, a secondary restoration within the text of Hebrews.⁸⁴ I refer here to the criterion of author's style, to the known tendency to restore Septuagint texts, and to the attestation: B 33 it Tert Irenaeus.⁸⁵ Yet I agree that in this case the careful scholar may follow Zuntz.⁸⁶

Zuntz concentrates his attention with singular care upon single witnesses. His analysis of numerous items of textual variation results in recognition and disapproval, in recognition for the faithful preservation of ancient text and in disapproval for scribes who failed.

---

80. Metzger (*Textual Commentary*, 605) explains that this reading according to the Committee is "the least inadequately supported reading." Westcott-Hort accepted εις εαυτους into their edition.

81. Zuntz, *Text of the Epistles*, 121. Since the days of Lachmann critical editions have printed εις τους αιωνας των αιωνων, αμην.

82. Theodoretus and additional minuscules are listed in Aland, *Greek New Testament*, 772.

83. Zuntz, *Text of the Epistles*, 111.

84. Critical editions since Lachmann printed εις τον αιωνα του αιωνος. Westcott and Hort print εις τον αιωνα [του αιωνος]. Weiss suggested that a copying mistake was the cause of the shorter reading; Weiss, *Textkritik der paulinischen Briefe*, 89.

85. Frede, *Vetus Latina*, 4th fasc. (Freiburg im Breisgau: Herder, 1987), 1105: τ⁵⁶·⁷⁰ and Ireneaus 3.6.1 *sedes tua in aeternum virga directionis virga regni tui*.

86. Braun accepts the decision of Zuntz; Braun, *An die Hebräer*, 39.

In detail Zuntz identifies processes of transmission in which valuable items of more ancient text forms were lost. This leads to the notion of the "lesser Alexandrians," as opposed to the central group of proto-Alexandrian witnesses: P[46] B 1739. Zuntz is aware of the faults of each of these witnesses. He takes note of the more hasty moments of the professional work of the scribe of P[46], but Zuntz is also willing to identify the correspondence of two independent witnesses in ten cases of variation. Nine times D and the papyrus are absolutely right, and once they are joined in an ancient *Leitfehler*: εἰς ἑαυτούς.

Zuntz also studied the technical details of Harklean manuscripts, in the tradition of Pamphilus of Caesarea. Copies here transmit not only texts, but also pass on formulas of time-honored origin. Colophons on younger and on more ancient manuscripts reveal Caesarean editing techniques, but the edited texts are part of a tradition that is constantly in flux. Some Caesarean texts have, thus, little in common despite their common origin.

The famous Codex von der Goltz (1739), on the other hand, in numerous cases, surpasses the text of the lesser Alexandrians. We ought to understand that in an unknown number of passages its readings no longer preserve the text of its archetype. On account of the meticulous care of Zuntz, we now have some means of checking scribal performance. Of the ten approved readings 1739 follows suit only in four cases (9:11; 11:15; 12:3, 27). In these and not in all ten cases 1739 preserves the archetype. The codex does, however, preserve the reading of the archetype in the case of the corrupt ἑαυτούς in Heb 12:3.[87]

Let me close, finally, with some general remarks. What did we gain from an inspection of the specific procedure of Zuntz?

Zuntz introduces his procedure with a careful investigation of the methodical steps taken by his predecessors. He does not overlook the proposals of Richard Bentley.[88] Where recognition is due, his praise is noble.

---

87. Zuntz, *Text of the Epistles*, 120.

88. Richard Bentley, *Bentleii Critica sacra: Notes on the Greek and Latin text of the New Testament, extracted from the Bentley MSS in Trinity College Library*, ed. Arthur Ayres Ellis (Cambridge: Deighton, Bell, & Co., 1862), xvii–xix. The achievements of Bentley, Porson, and Housman in the field of textual criticism have been analyzed and discussed by numerous classical scholars. It is obvious that Bentley's *Proposals* gave strong impulses to Griesbach and to Lachmann. Charles O. Brink authored a well-reasoned account of Classical Studies in England: Charles O. Brink, *English Classical Scholarship: Reflections on Bentley,*

Where limitations have become visible in past work, he criticizes with care. Such restraint honors the critic.

Zuntz writes in a clear and vivid style. Time and again while reading his work I have been surprised by the freshness of his approach and by the multiplicity of aspects considered. His patient considerations on single units of variation are strictly to the point. Some of them leave the reader with an unforgettable impression. Let me mention the magisterial pleading for a subsingular reading of P[46] and 1739, for the reading εὐπερίσπαστον ἁμαρτίαν in Heb 12:1.[89] Let me mention also his calm assent to a reading proven ancient, mainly by the testimony of church fathers, namely, χωρὶς θεοῦ in Heb 2:9.[90] Camerarius and Bengel recommended this reading.[91] Harnack argued on its behalf.[92] Zuntz supports χωρὶς θεοῦ by referring to the style of the author. One uncial and two minuscules preserve the ancient reading: 0243 1739* 424c.[93] Many good commentators did accept it, but only one editor: Weiss.[94] Circumspection and care are the marks of this confidently handled method. Its eminence is shown by quotations in countless notes.

I did not gather pearls. He who reads Zuntz will find them. My attention was centered upon methodology. Not least visible are its merits in the points that Zuntz does not display. The corrector of P[46] found one mistake in ten.[95]

Zuntz shows that witnesses from the scriptoria come to us as survivors, and that collectively their transmission resembles streams. Zuntz shows that influences evade us, but that in spite of this evasion witnesses from three ancient regions are capable of testifying independently. Zuntz opened research on the achievements of the editors, on the methods of

---

Porson, and Housman (Cambridge: Clarke; New York: Oxford University Press, 1986); Brink, *Klassische Studien in England: Historische Reflexionen über Bentley, Porson und Housman* (Stuttgart: Teubner, 1997).

89. Zuntz, *Text of the Epistles*, 25–29.
90. Zuntz, *Text of the Epistles*, 34–35, 44, 285.
91. Bengel, *Η ΚΑΙΝΗ ΔΙΑΘΗΚΗ*, 415, accords to the reading his letter β. As to Camerarius see Friedrich Bleek, *Der Brief an die Hebräer* (Berlin: Dümmler, 1836), 2:278.
92. Zuntz, *Text of the Epistles*, 34.
93. Zuntz, *Text of the Epistles*, 34.
94. Weiss, *Paulinischen Briefe im berichtigten Text*, 520; Weiss, *Textkritik der paulinischen Briefe*, 54.
95. Zuntz, *Text of the Epistles*, 252.

ancient philologists, and on the traces correctors left in their work. I hope that I have succeeded in pointing out that Zuntz left much more than merely handfuls of inspirations. He left his questions and his method.

Bibliography

Aland, Barbara, ed. *Das Neue Testament auf Papyrus: Die paulinischen Briefe, Teil 2*. ANTF 22. Berlin: de Gruyter 1994.

Aland, Barbara, Kurt Aland, Johannes Karavidopoulos, Carlo M. Martini, and Bruce M. Metzger, eds. *The Greek New Testament*. 4th ed. Stuttgart: Deutsche Bibelgesellschaft, 1993.

———, eds. *Novum Testamentum Graece*. 27th ed., 8th printing corrected and extended to Papyri 99–116. Stuttgart: Deutsche Bibelgesellschaft, 2001.

———, eds. *Novum Testamentum Graece*. 28th ed. Stuttgart: Deutsche Bibelgesellschaft, 2012.

Aland, Kurt, Matthew Black, Carlo M. Martini, Bruce M. Metzger, and Allen Wikgren, eds. Nestle-Aland *Novum Testamentum Graece*. 26th ed. Stuttgart: Deutsche Bibelgesellschaft, 1979.

Bauer, Walter. *Griechisch-deutsches Wörterbuch zu den Schriften des Neuen Testaments und der übrigen urchristlichen Literatur*. 6th ed. Berlin: de Gruyter, 2012.

Bengel, Johann Albrecht, ed. *Η ΚΑΙΝΗ ΔΙΑΘΗΚΗ: Novum Testamentum Graecum*. 2nd ed. Tübingen: Berger, 1753.

Bentley, Richard. *Bentleii Critica sacra: Notes on the Greek and Latin text of the New Testament, extracted from the Bentley MSS in Trinity College Library*. Edited by Arthur Ayres Ellis. Cambridge: Deighton, Bell, & Co., 1862.

Blass, Friedrich, and Albert Debrunner. *Grammatik des neutestamentlichen Griechisch*. 7th ed. Göttingen: Vandenhoeck & Ruprecht, 1943.

———. *Grammatik des neutestamentlichen Griechisch*. Edited by Friedrich Rehkopf. 15th revised ed. Göttingen: Vandenhoeck & Ruprecht, 1979.

Bleek, Friedrich. *Der Brief an die Hebräer*. 3 vols. Berlin: Dümmler, 1828–1840.

Boismard, M.-E. Review of *The Text of the Epistles*, by Günther Zuntz. *RB* 61 (1954): 451–52.

Braun, Herbert. *An die Hebräer*. HNT 14. Tübingen: Mohr, 1984.

Brink, Charles O. *English Classical Scholarship: Reflections on Bentley, Porson, and Housman*. Cambridge: Clarke; New York: Oxford University Press, 1986.

———. *Klassische Studien in England: Historische Reflexionen über Bentley, Porson und Housman*. Stuttgart: Teubner, 1997.

Conzelmann, Hans. *Der erste Brief an die Korinther*. KEK 5. Göttingen: Vandenhoeck & Ruprecht, 1969.

Frede, Hermann Josef, ed. *Vetus Latina: Die Reste der altlateinischen Bibel, 25 Pars II*. Freiburg im Breisgau: Herder, 1975–1991.

Grässer, Erich. *An die Hebräer*. EKKNT 17.1. Zürich: Benziger; Neukirchen: Neukirchener Verlag, 1990.

Griesbach, Johann Jacob, ed. *Η ΚΑΙΝΗ ΔΙΑΘΗΚΗ: Novum Testamentum Graece*. 4 vols. Leipzig: Göschen, 1803–1807.

Güting, Eberhard. "Offene Fragen in der Methodendiskussion der neutestamentlichen Textkritik." *Editio* 19 (2005): 77–98. [Ch. 8 in this collection.]

———. "Weakly Attested Original Readings of the Manusccript D 05 in Mark." Pages 217–31 in *Codex Bezae: Studies from the Lunel Colloquium June 1994*. Edited by David C. Parker and Christian-Bernard Amphoux. NTTS 22. Leiden: Brill, 1996. [Ch. 6 in this collection.]

Harnack, Adolf von. "Studien zur Vulgata des Hebräerbriefes." *SPAW* (1920): 179–201. Repr. as pages 191–234 in vol. 1 of *Studien zur Geschichte des Neuen Testaments und der alten Kirche*. Berlin: de Gruyter, 1931.

———. *Zur Revision der Prinzipien der neutestamentlichen Textkritik: Die Bedeutung der Vulgata für den Text der Katholischen Briefe und der Anteil des Hieronymus an dem Übersetzungswerk*. Leipzig: Hinrichs, 1916.

Kilpatrick, George Dunbar, ed. *The Pastoral Letters and Hebrews: A Greek-English-Diglot for the Use of Translators*. London: British and Foreign Bible Society, 1963.

———, ed. *Romans and 1 and 2 Corinthians: A Greek-English Diglot for the Use of Translators*. London: British and Foreign Bible Society, 1964.

Maas, Paul. *Textkritik*. 3rd. ed. Leipzig: Teubner, 1957.

———. *Textual Criticism*. Translated from the German by Barbara Flower. Oxford: Clarendon, 1958.

Metzger, Bruce M. *A Textual Commentary on the Greek New Testament: A Companion Volume to the United Bible Societies' Greek New Testament*

(Fourth Revised Edition). 2nd ed. Stuttgart: Deutsche Bibelgesellschaft, 1994.

Papathomas, Amphilochios. "A New Testimony to the Letter to the Hebrews." *JBRChJ* 1 (2001): 18–24.

———. "A New Testimony to the Letter to the Hebrews (2.9–11 and 3.3–6) (Tafel 6)." *Tyche* 16 (2001): 107–10.

Schaefer, Karl Theodor. *Untersuchungen zur Geschichte der lateinischen Übersetzung des Hebräerbriefs*. Freiburg im Breisgau: Herder, 1929.

Tregelles, Samuel Prideaux, ed. *The Greek New Testament Edited from Ancient Authorities, with the Latin Version of Jerome, from the Codex Amiatinus*. London: Bagster, 1870.

Vogels, Heinrich Josef. *Novum Testamentum Graece et Latine, pars altera, Epistulae et Apocalypsis*. Freiburg im Breisgau: Herder, 1950.

Weiss, Bernhard. *Die paulinischen Briefe im berichtigten Text*. Leipzig: Hinrichs, 1896.

———. *Textkritik der paulinischen Briefe*. TU 14.3. Leipzig: Hinrichs, 1896.

Weiss, Hans Friedrich. *Der Brief an die Hebräer*. 15th ed. KEK 13. Göttingen: Vandenhoeck & Ruprecht, 1991.

Westcott, Brooke Foss. *The Epistle to the Hebrews*. London: Macmillan, 1889. Repr., Grand Rapids: Eerdmans, 1965.

Wordsworth, John, Henry J. White, and Hedley F. D. Sparks, eds. *Novum Testamentum Domini nostri Iesu Christi latine secundum editionem S. Hieronymi*, 3 vols. Oxford: Clarendon, 1889–1954.

Zuntz, Günther. *Lukian von Antiochien und der Text der Evangelien*. Edited by Barbara Aland and Klaus Wachtel. AHAW.PH 2. Heidelberg: Winter, 1995.

———. *Opuscula Selecta: Classica, Hellenistica, Christiana*. Totowa, NJ: Rowman & Littlefield; Manchester: Manchester University Press, 1972.

———. *The Text of the Epistles: A Disquisition upon the Corpus Paulinum*. Schweich Lectures of the British Academy 1946. London: Oxford University Press, 1953.

11

Texts of the First Hand and Texts of the Second Hand in the Textual Criticism of the New Testament

Introduction

Professional interpretation of New Testament texts maintains a high standard. Language, form, and content are open to investigation. Textual criticism in contrast seeks to establish the original form of early witnesses. In this process a multitude of material aspects requires full attention. Writing and copying, editing and correcting, adorning and binding, were crafts entrusted in antiquity to different artisans, artisans differing as to skills and training. Even in view of the refined techniques of present research, editors may still be confronted with difficulties.

Today text-critical work on the New Testament is confronted with a breathtaking challenge. Manuscripts and ancient translations, lectionaries, and citations in the church fathers are at our disposal and pose some distinct problems for interpreters. To reduce the abundant material to essential alternatives and to deliver philologically grounded judgments demands concentration and long years of experience.[1]

---

1. Bart D. Ehrman and Michael W. Holmes, eds., *The Text of the New Testament in Contemporary Research: Essays on the Status Quaestionis*, 2nd ed., NTTS 42 (Leiden: Brill, 2013); David C. Greetham, *Textual Scholarship: An Introduction* (Hoboken: Taylor & Francis, 2013); David C. Parker, *An Introduction to the New Testament Manuscripts and Their Texts* (Cambridge: Cambridge University Press, 2008); Larry W. Hurtado, "The New Testament in the Second Century: Text, Collections and Canon," in *Transmission and Reception: New Testament Text-Critical and Exegetical Studies*, ed. Jeff W. Childers and David C. Parker (Piscataway, NJ: Gorgias, 2006), 3–27; Eberhard Güting, "Offene Fragen in der Methodendiskussion der neutestamentlichen Textkritik," *Editio* 19 (2005): 77–98 (ch. 8 in this collection); Larry W. Hurtado, "Beyond the Interlude? Developments and Directions in

One can now retrieve witnesses on the internet and review manuscripts,[2] and one can access bibliographical resources in order to examine the research of earlier generations. Still the appraisal of Brooke Foss Westcott and Fenton John Anthony Hort remains: Judgments about readings cannot be achieved without the study of manuscripts.[3] Ancient scribes and their habits, ancient traditions and their destinies stand between the text of the author and the modern editor. The materiality of the writing substance and of the manuscripts and the technical organization of the working procedures present factors that ought not to be ignored.[4] They are an essential aspect for understanding the ancient work of editing.

1. The Hand of the Author: Autographs in the Transmission of Ancient Literature

In New Testament literature we encounter three kinds of texts: first, copies of ancient editions;[5] second, copies of such texts, which come

---

New Testament Textual Criticism," in *Studies in the Early Text of the Gospels and Acts: The Papers of the First Birmingham Colloquium on the Textual Criticism of the New Testament*, ed. David G. K. Taylor, Text and Studies 3/1 (Birmingham: University of Birmingham Press, 1999), 26–48; David C. Greetham, "Politics and Ideology in Current Anglo-American Textual Scholarship," *Editio* 4 (1990): 1–20.

2. Information about the "Digital Nestle-Aland" edition, "NT Transcripts," and the "Virtual Manuscript Room" is available at https://tinyurl.com/sbl7012d. In addition, transcriptions of very many of the oldest New Testament textual witnesses, along with color photographs and/or black and white photographs are available: see Karl Jaroš, ed., *Das Neue Testament nach den ältesten griechischen Handschriften: Die handschriftliche Überlieferung des Neuen Testaments vor Codex Sinaiticus und Codex Vaticanus* (Rupolding: Rutzen; Würzburg: Echter, 2006). [Updated edition: Karl Jaroš, ed., *Die ältesten griechischen Handschriften des Neuen Testaments* (Cologne: Böhlau, 2014).]

3. Brooke Foss Westcott and Fenton John Anthony Hort, eds., *The New Testament in the Original Greek: Introduction [and] Appendix* (Cambridge: Macmillan, 1881), 2:31: "Knowledge of documents should precede final judgement upon readings."

4. On the substance of writing materials one finds suggestive information in Egert Pöhlmann, *Einführung in die Überlieferungsgeschichte und in die Textkritik der antiken Literatur* (Darmstadt: Wissenschaftliche Buchgesellschaft, 1994), 1:1–9. See also Hans-Josef Klauck, *Ancient Letters and the New Testament: A Guide to Context and Exegesis* (Waco, TX: Baylor University Press, 2006).

5. The authors Reynolds and Wilson provide an introduction to the condition

about without the mediation of an editor; and third, modern editions of ancient texts, which rely on up-to-date editorial techniques and modern textual criticism. In the prologue to the Gospel of Luke, the author reveals that he sees himself in connection with an expansive production of Christian books; he names his noble benefactor, on whose help in publication he relies. One edition from the end of the first century is our Gospel of John: the editorial pointers are exceptionally clear.[6] Likewise the early form of our collection of Paul's letters is based on an edition at the end of the first century. Appropriate pointers, which one obtains by comparison of several later collections, are not entirely easy to interpret (see fig. 1).[7] Another collection, which is dated at the beginning of the second century, is an early edition of the four gospels.[8] At any rate, modern editions are not copies even if they edit a facsimile.[9]

---

of the libraries of Rome and of other cities and to the situation of editing ventures around the time of the end of the Republic. They set forth their results in the broad context of developments in the field of grammar, of linguistics, and of literary criticism. As early as 100 BCE the author Demetrius Lacon dealt with variants in the transmission of Epicurus's texts and was concerned with the correction of writing errors (P. Herc. 1012); see Leighton D. Reynolds and Nigel G. Wilson, *Scribes and Scholars: A Guide to the Transmission of Greek and Latin Literature*, 4th ed. (Oxford: Oxford University Press, 2013), 18.

6. Evidence is exhibited in the essay by Eberhard Güting, "Kritik an den Judäern in Jerusalem: Literarkritische Beiträge zu einem unabgeschlossenen Gespräch über den Evangelisten Johannes," in *Israel als Gegenüber: Vom Alten Orient bis in die Gegenwart; Studien zur Geschichte eines wechselvollen Zusammenlebens*, ed. Folker Siegert, SIJD 5 (Göttingen: Vandenhoeck & Ruprecht, 2000), 158–201.

7. Günther Zuntz has produced convincing arguments on the original form of the *Corpus Paulinum*, a collection of letters from about 100. See Zuntz, *The Text of the Epistles: A Disquisition upon the Corpus Paulinum*, Schweich Lectures of the British Academy 1946 (London: Oxford University Press, 1953), 14–17, 274–79. Zuntz names classical parallels for letters that, like Romans, went out to several recipients at the same time (p. 228 n. 1). Striking text lacunae, preserved in multiple old witnesses, become decisive indicators (Rom 1:7, 15; and Eph 1:1).

8. Graham Stanton, Martin Hengel, Theo Heckel, and others have sought to establish an early four-gospel canon; see Hurtado, "New Testament in the Second Century," 20–21.

9. New Testament criticism is founded upon facsimile editions to a considerable degree. Since the middle of the nineteenth century, photographic processes have been employed for the production of such editions. Apparently the earliest photographic edition of a portion of a New Testament manuscript appeared

Of course, inasmuch as New Testament research pursues history, it also deals with texts that were never destined for literary circulation: historical sources of all kinds, inscriptions, and archaeological findings, engravings on coins, official pieces of writing, documentary papyri from archives, private letters, talismans, magical papyri. After all, one can assume that all texts of the New Testament canon, even occasional letters, were destined for further distribution before they found entry into a canon.

All writings of the New Testament, inasmuch as they became literary texts, display the characteristics of ancient book production. Titles are named in subscripts, sometimes also the author, in older forms often only tersely. Yet there is a series of characteristics that are common to Christian books and that distinguish them from other Hellenistic and even Jewish writings. This can begin with the title. The names of the authors in the genitive and the title identified by the author in subscripts of Christian writings are not always the rule.[10] Peculiarities, such as the *nomina sacra*, which function as abbreviations and which can be traced back to public reading in worship, make Christian books quickly recognizable. It is less easy to recognize that the oldest manuscripts often display the hand of less practiced copyists, who only occasionally produce copies and do not have a cultivated book hand.[11] In the lively communication between Christian churches and regions there are manifold reasons for the occasional

---

as early as 1856: Frederic Madden, *Photographic Facsimiles of the Remains of the Epistles of Clement of Rome, Made from the Unique Copy Preserved in the Codex Alexandrinus* (London: British Museum, 1856). I owe this information to a statement by Frederick G. Kenyon in his facsimile edition: *British Museum: The Codex Alexandrinus (Royal MS 1 D V–VIII) in Reduced Photographic Facsimile: New Testament and Clementine Epistles* (London: British Museum, 1909), 6 n. 7. References to additional facsimiles are found in J. Keith Elliott, *A Bibliography of Greek New Testament Manuscripts*, 3rd ed., NovTSup 160 (Leiden: Brill, 2015).

10. Martin Hengel, *Die Evangelienüberschriften*, lecture presented 18 October 1981, SPAW.PH 1984/3. Heidelberg: Winter, 1984.

11. "What I think they all, in varying degrees, have in common is that, though the writing is far from unskilled, they are all the work of men not trained in calligraphy and so not accustomed to writing books.… In all of them there is a family resemblance; in none can be traced the work of the professional calligrapher or the rapid, informal hand of the private scholar" (Colin H. Roberts, *Manuscript, Society, and Belief in Early Christian Egypt*, Schweich Lectures of the British Academy 1977 [London: Oxford University Press, 1979], 14–15).

production of a copy.¹² All these products as copies have one thing in common: they lay claim to be literature, ordinary literature—*Kleinliteratur*, as Adolf Deissmann put it.

Of course, authors produced drafts of their writings, so-called ὑπομνήματα (notes). They were recorded on wax tablets or on sheets of parchment (2 Tim 4:13).¹³ Yet these are quite extraordinarily rare in ancient transmission. The epigrams of the poet Dioscorus of Aphrodito can be verified as autographs. This is due, however, only to the fact that this author of the sixth century was a notary and that public records from his office are preserved.¹⁴ By contrast, P.Lit.Lond. 165 (the so-called Anonymus Londinensis) apparently has to do with the work of a physician who works with his own texts of memoranda and reflects on them, as Tiziano Dorandi has shown.¹⁵ Normally prose texts were dictated by their authors and not written down in their own hand.¹⁶ In literary works in verse it happens routinely that authors worked on drafts in their own hand. But the completion of the work and the decision to publish it brought about the transition to dictation. The energetic plea of Quintilian for personal labors on literary works also in prose is indicative of a time in which this must have been very unusual.¹⁷ Occasionally authors sent letters written with their own hand. This was a sign of high appreciation and special

---

12. Hengel, *Die Evangelienüberschriften*, 33–47; Larry W. Hurtado, *The Earliest Christian Artifacts: Manuscripts and Christian Origins* (Grand Rapids: Eerdmans, 2006).

13. Carl Dziatzko, "Αὐτόγραφον," PW 2:2596–97.

14. Tiziano Dorandi, "Zwischen Autographie und Diktat: Momente der Textualität in der antiken Welt," in *Vermittlung und Tradierung von Wissen in der griechischen Kultur*, ed. Wolfgang Kullmann and Jochen Althoff (Tübingen: Narr, 1993), 79.

15. Dorandi, "Zwischen Autographie und Diktat," 73.

16. The deciphering of a large part of the charred library of Herculaneum in the Villa dei Papiri produced, among other things, instructive detail regarding the book production of the second century BCE. It is significant, as David Sider emphasizes, that the private library of the Epicurean philosopher Philodemos from the first century BCE contains no autograph of the philosopher. All preserved texts were produced, as Guglielmo Cavallo has shown, by professional scribes. See Sider, *The Library of the Villa dei Papiri at Herculaneum* (Los Angeles: Getty, 2005), 74; and Dorandi, "Zwischen Autographie und Diktat," 73.

17. Quintilian, *Inst.* 10.3.18–22.

honor.[18] Letters occasionally contained additions in one's own hand for authentication. In Galatians, Paul calls attention to the large letters with which he authenticates his letters (Gal 6:11).[19] Copies of Christian books of the fourth and fifth centuries were also frequently authenticated by subscriptions by the author. This certifies permission for publication.[20] The Jewish historian Flavius Josephus reports that in times of war, commanders of fortresses had instruction to accept commands from Aristobulos only in the form of autographs (*B.J.* 1.137).[21]

2. The Hand of the Copyist as the First Address of Textual Criticism

Ancient texts are only available for New Testament criticism as copies and as copies of copies. How many intermediate steps lie between an available copy and the original source underlying it is, in principle, impossible to ascertain. The philologist investigates whether the text at hand derives from an open or closed transmission, that is, whether all preserved copies can be demonstrated to go back to one single archetype. This is verifiable by identifying a characteristic error in all transmitted witnesses.[22]

---

18. Seneca, *Epistles* 40.1; Otto Roller, *Das Formular der paulinischen Briefe: Ein Beitrag zur Lehre vom antiken Briefe*, BWANT 58 (Stuttgart: Kohlhammer, 2010), 15.

19. One finds indications of authenticating passages "with my own hand" several times in Pauline letters (1 Cor 16:21; Gal 6:11; Phlm 19; Col 4:18). On the other hand, it is certain that Romans was dictated by Paul and not written with his own hand (Rom 16:22).

20. Oronzo Pecere, "La tradizione dei testi latini tra IV e V seculo attraverso i libri sottoscritti," in *Società romana e impero tardoantico IV: Tradizione dei classici, transformazioni della cultura*, ed. Andrea Guardina (Rome: Laterza, 1986), 19–81, 210–46, esp. 24–29 and 213–17 (cited according to Dorandi, "Zwischen Autographie und Diktat," 78).

21. If three brothers each attach an autograph to a contract about division of property rights, this allows recognition of a specific situation (Girolamo Vitelli, ed., *Papiri Greci e Latini* [Firenze: Le Monnier, 1927], vol. 8, no. 903 [47 CE], 52–54); for discussion, see Hans-Josef Klauck, *Ancient Letters and the New Testament: A Guide to Context and Exegesis* (Waco, TX: Baylor University Press, 2006), 57–58.

22. Instances of closed and of open traditions are presented by Egert Pöhlmann, "Textkritik und Texte im 19. und 20. Jh.," in Pöhlmann, *Einführung in die Überlieferungsgeschichte*, 2:137–209. (see also Michael W. Holmes, "Working with

Unfortunately in the course of the transmission of the New Testament, texts were rarely copied from one single exemplar. Because of comparison at an early stage with other manuscripts that often deviate with their readings, readings from several archetypes have infiltrated almost all witnesses. Thus one has to declare: "There is no cure against contamination in manuscripts."[23] Therefore New Testament textual criticism moves forward in a very eclectic manner. From point to point, which witness the editor wishes to prefer must constantly be tested.[24]

The hand of the scribe, the first hand, is the first address of New Testament textual criticism. It is usually clear whether we are dealing with an erudite scholar writing occasionally or instead the skilled hand of a professional scribe, as long as sufficient text is preserved.[25] Yet professional scribes differ a great deal. They differ in terms of agility, accuracy, and in professional skill. There are scribes who work absolutely consistently, who write volumes of four hundred pages without one noticing a new onset, or even a break. There are nervous scribes whose form of writing is always changing and whose work, as Alphonse Dain has shown, is mistakenly attributed to several scribes.[26] Occasionally scribes in the same scriptorium can be compared with one another.

The fact that for textual criticism the hand of the scribe is the first address holds true in several ways. If the one who copies leaves out a portion of the text, then we are initially unable to specify whether the error is

---

an Open Textual Tradition: Challenges in Theory and Practice," in *The Textual History of the Greek New Testament*, ed. Klaus Wachtel and Michael W. Holmes, TCSt 8 [Atlanta: Society of Biblical Literature, 2011], 65–78).

23. Paul Maas, *Textkritik*, 4th ed. (Leipzig: Teubner, 1960), 30; cf. 5–9 (ET of 3rd ed. [1957]: Maas, *Textual Criticism* [Oxford: Clarendon, 1958]).

24. One can recognize in an investigation on the Gospel of Mark how working textual criticism advances with an eclectic methodology: see Heinrich Greeven and Eberhard Güting, *Textkritik des Markusevangliums*, Theologie, Forschung und Wissenschaft 11 (Münster: LIT, 2005).

25. Standard paleographic works discuss distinctions between the writing style of professional scribes and, on the other hand, of the literarily educated, scholars, or higher government officials; see also Roller, *Formular der paulinischen Briefe*, 8–10 and n. 61.

26. Alphonse Dain, "Les manuscrits et le problème de la copie, I: L'aspect matériel du problème (1949/1964)," in *Griechische Kodikologie und Textüberlieferung*, ed. Dieter Harlfinger (Darmstadt, Wissenschaftliche Buchgesellschaft, 1980), 121.

to be attributed to the scribe or to his exemplar. If the scribe has influenced the language of the text or has misunderstood something, then it is also initially unclear whether his exemplar is perhaps responsible for it. But the readings of the scribe can be collected, analyzed, and investigated. The level of his orthography perhaps can be determined. The question can be raised regarding which text transmission his exemplar is to be ascribed: does he have to do with an Alexandrian text, with a Western text, or with a Byzantine tradition? The correctly transmitted components of the copy indicate a typical character against the foil of which one can search for the efficiency of the scribe.

Additions are then examined. Is the apparatus of Euthalius perhaps added? Are the pericopes perhaps enumerated according to two systems, as has occurred in Codex Vaticanus?

Biblical manuscripts that are designed to present the entire canonical text are sometimes conflated from quite different exemplars. Occasionally it was impossible to find an adequate exemplar in one's own monastery. Then it had to be procured from elsewhere. Such difficulties sometimes explain why in the middle of a biblical book the character of the text of a manuscript sometimes changes recognizably.

A well-investigated example of a manuscript, the text of which allows one to recognize quite different exemplars, is Codex Sinaiticus (א). In the three Synoptic Gospels this codex evidences an excellent Alexandrian text, which the editors Westcott and Hort would have called "neutral." By contrast, in the Pauline Epistles the quality of the transmission drops off considerably, so that the text critic Günther Zuntz assigns this text to the "lesser Alexandrians."[27] In Sinaiticus the text of the Revelation to John finally no longer belongs to the more valuable witnesses; C and A are clearly preferable to א. In the text of the Gospel of John the curious phenomenon was found that the first half (John 1:1–8:38) exhibits an explicitly Western tradition, but in contrast the remaining part features an Alexandrian text with a large share of Byzantine readings (John 8:39–21:25).[28]

---

27. Zuntz, *Text of the Epistles*, 107 and 131.

28. Gordon D. Fee, "Codex Sinaiticus in the Gospel of John: A Contribution to Methodology in Establishing Textual Relationships," *NTS* 15 (1968/1969): 23–44; repr., *Studies in the Theory and Method of New Testament Textual Criticism*, ed. Eldon J. Epp and Gordon D. Fee, SD 45 (Grand Rapids: Eerdmans, 1993), 221–43. This article gives further examples of changes in the character of the text within the text of a manuscript (see 221).

There are manuscripts the appearance of which clearly shows that the copyist found himself in a quandary. Codex Boernerianus, a bilingual Greek-Latin version, in several places leaves parts of the parchment empty. Initially it was not obviously clear what was to be inserted. Thus at the end of Romans space was left empty for a doxology. Does this doxology belong here or perhaps before chapter 15? This had to be clarified first of all.[29]

It sometimes happens that the text of a manuscript is written continuously, but simultaneously it is obvious that the scribe copied an exemplar arranged in lines of meaningful units. Repeated omissions in the length of such a line, as for example in Codex Vaticanus, or certain scribal errors, which Codex Boernerianus exhibits, are indications of such exemplars. Codex Bezae Cantabrigiensis, a bilingual Greek-Latin version, is divided in the text of the gospels into lines that represent units of meaning, a phenomenon that has been carefully analyzed. The reconstruction of the exemplar of this Greek-Latin tradition, divided into such lines, is one of the important results of this analysis.[30]

3. Corrections in the Original Hand: The Drawback of the Lost Reference

Not infrequently complex corrections are encountered in manuscripts, the origin of which is not simple to explain. It sometimes happens that the analyses lead different specialists to varying results. This is the case in a corrected passage of Codex Sinaiticus. The last verse of the Gospel of John, photographed in natural light, runs: "But there are also many other things that Jesus did. If every one of them were written down, I suppose that the world would not contain the books that would be written." Tischendorf assumed that the verse goes back to a second later scribe. Others disagreed with Tischendorf. However, since that time it can be shown on the basis of ultraviolet photographs that the first scribe washed away his own text

---

29. Open spaces in the text, damage to text borders, anomalies such as an irregular sequence of the skin surface and the flesh side in manuscripts in ancient and medieval traditions have often been observed and discussed; see Greetham, *Textual Scholarship*, 272–78.

30. David C. Parker, *Codex Bezae: An Early Christian Manuscript and Its Text* (Cambridge: Cambridge University Press, 1992), 73–76.

and inserted the noteworthy text himself.[31] One also finds in other manuscripts corrections that the scribe made after washing away the text.[32]

4. The Hand of the *Diorthōtēs*: The Profession of Corrector in Ancient Book Production

Correcting manuscripts was a profession for many ancient scribes. A very old example of the activity of a *diorthōtēs* was verified in one of the manuscripts from Herculaneum.[33] The bigger publishers of ancient Rome employed not only scribes but also correctors. Two notes in Codex Sinaiticus (at the end of Ezra and of Esther) report, with certain pride, that the text goes back to an exemplar of Origen's Hexapla that he himself corrected. Antoninus (the Martyr) collated (that is, dictated the exemplar anew), and the one doing the writing, Pamphilus (d. 309), made corrections in prison.[34] Both statements refer to the exemplar of ℵ. Normally correctors were less prominent. Yet the correcting of errors in copies of Christian books was often only carelessly carried out. In his foundational research on the Pauline manuscript P[46], Zuntz found that the official corrector had corrected only one in ten errors.[35]

When the Emperor Constantine, on the occasion of the founding of his new capital city Constantinople, ordered fifty Bible manuscripts in Caesarea for his new main churches, he brought the scriptorium there into dire straits. To produce fifty Bible manuscripts in a short period of time would have required a formidable number of scribes. So Eusebius decided, as he himself reports, to send a supply of three or four codices to Constantinople, perhaps in order not to fall into disfavor on account of his negligence.[36]

The English scholars Herbert J. M. Milne and Theodore C. Skeat have occupied themselves in extraordinary detail with two manuscripts, which

---

31. Herbert J. M. Milne and Theodore C. Skeat, *Scribes and Correctors of the Codex Sinaiticus* (London: British Museum, 1938), 12.

32. Parker, *Codex Bezae*, 76.

33. Tiziano Dorandi, "Den Autoren über die Schulter geschaut: Arbeitsweise und Autographie bei den antiken Schriftstellern," *ZPE* 87 (1991): 15–17.

34. Theodore C. Skeat, *The Collected Biblical Writings of Theodore C. Skeat*, ed. J. Keith Elliott, NovTSup 113 (Leiden: Brill, 2004), 17–18.

35. Zuntz, *Text of the Epistles*, 252–53.

36. Skeat, *Collected Biblical Writings*, 215–20.

evidently were produced at that time on the basis of the emperor's commission. This has to do with the renowned Codex Sinaiticus as well as the no less important Codex Vaticanus. Both scholars have examined them to no end and then analyzed them anew. Here it is of significance that the British Library has restored and smoothed out each individual folio of Codex Sinaiticus, which was acquired in 1933. Not until after this was done was each leaf examined with ultraviolet light.[37]

Paleographic evidence of emendations, such as the study of scholarly additions, the enumeration of layers and pericopes, and decorative elements make it possible to date Codex Sinaiticus in the decades between 330 and 350.[38] Milne and Skeat identify three scribes, who evidently worked simultaneously. Among the correctors both distinguish a contemporaneous corrector, who among other things corrected the entire New Testament. The details are of no interest to us here. Still it should be emphasized that the primary and earliest correction was carried out on the original exemplar.[39] One very remarkable event is indicative of the effectiveness of the corrector of that time. In one place in the Old Testament two passages occur out of order in such a way that in the middle of the text of 2 Esdras a text from 1 Chronicles abruptly appears. Neither scribe A nor scribe D, who correct other things here, notice the erroneous insertion.[40]

Scribal corrections are also occasionally overlooked by modern editors. In some cases this leads to the printing of a critically questionable text. Some twenty years ago at the Institut für Neutestamentliche Textforschung in Münster I called attention to a scribal correction at the end of the text of Hebrews. Thereafter an indication occurs in the

---

37. The procedure carried out by Douglas Cockerell was described in detail; see Milne and Skeat, *Scribes and Correctors*, 60–84. On the technical requirements of such restoration see, Peter Rück, ed., *Pergament: Geschichte, Struktur, Restaurierung, Herstellung*, Historische Wissenschaften 2 (Sigmaringen: Thorbecke, 1991), particularly the contributions on restoration, 229–337. [I am grateful to Richard Feldmann, the head of the manuscript department of the Universitäts- und Landesbibliothek, Münster, for his friendly advice.]

38. Milne and Skeat, *Scribes and Correctors*, 60–65.

39. Milne and Skeat, *Scribes and Correctors*, 2: "This, however, as Tischendorf acutely observed, merely proved that both revisers were collating the newly written manuscript with the exemplar."

40. Milne and Skeat, *Scribes and Correctors*, 2.

Nestle-Aland text, but not in the *Greek New Testament* from the same publisher.[41] The last word of Hebrews is missing in the original text of the witness P[46].[42] If one examines the passage in the facsimile edition of Frederick G. Kenyon, one recognizes without difficulty that a corrector has been at work on the verso of folio 38 (fig. 2).[43] Within the last three lines of the text of Hebrews this corrector conspicuously inserted another line. As is indicated by the same form of handwriting, the same corrector has added an additional word: ὑμων. He has thereby twice considerably changed the look of the writing: he has created an additional line, and he has made an insertion into the addition. One must tackle this finding thus: P[46*] om. και παντας τους αγιους, P[46 corr] habet; P[46*] om. ὑμων, P[46 corr] habet.

It is unclear whether the original text of Hebrews contained the inserted line. I know of no other witness for the omission. Thus the omission is arguably a scribal error. However, the fact that the last word does not belong in the original text can be seen as probable according to textual criticism. I am of the opinion that the text first written by the scribe repeats the original concluding blessing of the author: "Grace be with all." Two reasons support this opinion. First, the ὑμων, reminiscent of Pauline epistolary form, does not fit the text of a treatise, such as the one composed by the author of Hebrews. Second, an Old Latin witness attests the absence of ὑμων.[44] The author closes his treatise with "grace be with all," not with "grace be with you all." The Nestle-Aland text should give preference to the primary text of the author.

---

41. The volume contains the incorrect information that Papyrus 46 reads παντων υμων. This is the reading of the corrector. Cf. Barbara Aland et al., eds., *The Greek New Testament*, 5th ed. (Stuttgart: Deutsche Bibelgesellschaft, 2014), 749.

42. P[46*] om. ὑμων. Cf. Barbara Aland et al., eds., *Novum Testamentum Graece*, 28th ed. (Stuttgart: Deutsche Bibelgesellschaft, 2012), 684.

43. Frederick G. Kenyon, ed., *The Chester Beatty Biblical Papyri: Descriptions and Texts of Twelve Manuscripts on Papyrus of the Greek Bible*, fasc. 3, supplement: *Pauline Epistles: Plates* (London: Walker, 1937).

44. As the conclusion of the epistle to the Hebrews, the Anonymus Sangallensis transmits "*gratia cum omnibus amen*" (448); see Hermann Josef Frede, ed., *Vetus Latina: Die Reste der altlateinischen Bibel, 25 Pars II*, 11th fasc. (Freiburg im Breisgau: Herder, 1991), 209. The original hand D* also indirectly supports this text with its reading: Η χαρις μετα παντων των αγιων.

5. The Hand of Later Generations: The Reuse of Books in Palimpsests and in Bindings

One encounters relatively frequently in ancient transmission palimpsests—parchment codices whose original lettering was washed away for the purpose of new writing. Written pages were also used again for bindings. Parchment leaves were valuable—thus some medieval users of manuscripts did not shy away from cutting out unwritten pages from codices.[45] One such palimpsest is the renowned *Method of Mechanical Theorems* of Archimedes, which was lost for hundreds of years and which just a few years ago was auctioned for two million dollars.[46] The leaves are overwritten with medieval texts, with prayers. The reuse of the Archimedes Codex can be dated. It took place on April 14, 1229.[47] In the restoration and compilation of photographs, technical processes called "multispectral imaging" were applied.[48] When one considers that the physics of Galileo Galilei and later of Isaac Newton rested extensively on Archimedes, then an imminent edition of *Method of Mechanical Theorems* with the drawings of the mathematician as well as his writing about floating bodies, about spheres and cylinders, and further works is a sensation. The treatise just mentioned is dedicated to the renowned geographer Eratosthenes and begins with the words: Ἀρχιμήδης Ἐρατοσθένει χαίρειν.

---

45. Milne and Skeat, *Scribes and Correctors*, 13.

46. Reviel Netz and William Noel, *Der Kodex des Archimedes: Das berühmteste Palimpsest der Welt wird entschlüsselt* (Munich: Beck, 2007), 12.

47. Netz and Noel, *Kodex des Archimedes*, 182.

48. Netz and Noel, *Kodex des Archimedes*, 206–24. The process so named is also successfully applied to other ruined manuscripts, so also in the reconstruction of charred exemplars from Herculaneum. Sider, *Library of the Villa*, has reported on this in detail; see also Steven W. Booras and David R. Seely, "Multispectral Imaging of the Herculaneum Papyri," *Cronache Ercolanesi* 29 (1999): 95–100. David Sider has also referred to the application of computer programs in the reconstruction of severely damaged manuscripts by a Norwegian work group around Knut Kleve. See Knut Kleve, Espen S. Ore, and Ragnar Jensen, "Letteralogia: Computer e fotografia," *Cronache Ercolanesi* 17 (1987): 141–50. A special conference paid attention to procedures possible today for the comprehensive research on palimpsests; see *Rinascimento virtuale: Digitale Palimpsestforschung: Rediscovering Written Records of a Hidden European Cultural Heritage*, ed. Dieter Harlfinger (Bratislava, 2002).

There are at least sixty-three palimpsests among the preserved New Testament parchment manuscripts with the text in Greek.[49] One such palimpsest is Codex Ephraemi Syri Rescriptus, which today is in a deplorable condition. Constantin von Tischendorf published a two-volume edition of the Old and New Testament texts (1843, 1845).

Today, someone who goes into the manuscript section of the Bibliothèque Nationale in Paris to view Codex Ephraemi sees a manuscript that, due to treatment with chemical reagents, is almost illegible. At least two traditions are known about the employment of such chemicals at that time. The handbook of Kurt and Barbara Aland relates that the manuscript was deciphered by the Leipzig theology professor Fleck in 1834 and by Tischendorf in 1840–1841 by applying Gioberti tincture.[50] Caspar René Gregory relates that Fleck applied the tincture with the authorization of the librarian Karl Benedict Hase.[51] Gregory sought to exonerate Tischendorf from this investigation, which had such far-reaching consequences. Without exception today while one examines this manuscript, it is not allowed to be out of sight for a single moment. This goes without saying.

Concluding Remarks

Perhaps it is expedient in conclusion to assess technical resources and painstaking handwork in their interaction. To assemble complete manuscripts and manuscript indexes from thousands of fragments, which are at hand in precisely measured high gloss photographs, requires long years of patient manual work (fig. 3).[52] To discover a scribal error or a correction in

---

49. Kurt Aland and Barbara Aland, *Der Text des Neuen Testaments: Einführung in die wissenschaftlichen Ausgaben sowie in Theorie und Praxis der modernen Textkritik*, 2nd ed. (Stuttgart: Deutsche Bibelgesellschaft, 1989), 118 [ET: *The Text of the New Testament: An Introduction to the Critical Editions and to the Theory and Practice of Modern Textual Criticism*, 2nd ed. [Grand Rapids: Eerdmans; Leiden: Brill, 1989], 109). The classical philologist Egert Pöhlmann lists important ancient texts, which are transmitted on palimpsests; see Pöhlmann, *Einführung in die Überlieferungsgeschichte*, 8.

50. Aland and Aland, *Text des Neuen Testaments*, 118.

51. Caspar René Gregory, *Textkritik des Neuen Testamentes* (Leipzig: Hinrich, 1909), 1:42.

52. Franz-Jürgen Schmitz and Gerd Mink, *Liste der koptischen Handschriften des Neuen Testaments, I: Die sahidischen Handschriften der Evangelien*, ANTF 8, 13, 15 (Berlin: de Gruyter, 1986–1991). Franz-Jürgen Schmitz relates vividly what

a plain sequence of lines demands intense concentration. From the desolate sequence of darkened leaves of the manuscript *Ephraemi Syri Rescripti* there now exists an entire set of legible ultraviolet photographs. Nevertheless, it is always essential for the researcher to see the originals themselves. Even where technical procedures are available, it is not acceptable to do without the eye of the experienced editor.

Still another aptitude is essential, namely, the disposition to recognize the findings of earlier researchers and to test them. The working group that reconstructed the Archimedes palimpsest then discovered in a second phase of work that the older photographs and the older findings of Heiberg from the beginning of the twentieth century lent themselves to the correction of their own findings.[53] Editors should profit from what has been accomplished previously.

Bibliography

Aland, Barbara, Kurt Aland, Johannes Karavidopoulos, Carlo M. Martini, and Bruce M. Metzger, eds. *The Greek New Testament*. 5th ed. Stuttgart: Deutsche Bibelgesellschaft; United Bible Societies, 2014.

——, eds. *Novum Testamentum Graece*. 28th ed. Stuttgart: Deutsche Bibelgesellschaft, 2012. 5th corrected printing, 2016.

Aland, Kurt, and Barbara Aland. *Der Text des Neuen Testaments: Einführung in die wissenschaftlichen Ausgaben sowie in Theorie und Praxis der modernen Textkritik*. 2nd ed. Stuttgart: Deutsche Bibelgesellschaft, 1989.

——. *The Text of the New Testament: An Introduction to the Critical Editions and to the Theory and Practice of Modern Textual Criticism*. 2nd ed. Grand Rapids: Eerdmans; Leiden: Brill, 1989.

Booras, Steven W. and David R. Seely. "Multispectral Imaging of the Herculaneum Papyri." *Cronache Ercolanesi* 29 (1999): 95–100.

Dain, Alphonse. "Les manuscrits et le problème de la copie, I: L'aspect matériel du problème (1949/1964)." Pages 120–31 in *Griechische Kodikologie*

---

kind of arduous toil it takes to compile the fragments of many European libraries; see Schmitz, "Neue Fragmente zur bilinguen Majuskelhandschrift 070," in *Bericht der Hermann Kunst-Stiftung zur Förderung der neutestamentlichen Textforschung für die Jahre 1979 bis 1981* (Münster: Aschendorff, 1982), 71–92.

53. Netz and Noel, *Kodex des Archimedes*, 277.

und Textüberlieferung. Edited by Dieter Harlfinger. Darmstadt, Wissenschaftliche Buchgesellschaft, 1980.

Dorandi, Tiziano. "Den Autoren über die Schulter geschaut: Arbeitsweise und Autographie bei den antiken Schriftstellern." *ZPE* 87 (1991): 11–33.

———. "Zwischen Autographie und Diktat: Momente der Textualität in der antiken Welt." Pages 71–83 in *Vermittlung und Tradierung von Wissen in der griechischen Kultur*. Edited by Wolfgang Kullmann and Jochen Althoff. Tübingen: Narr, 1993.

Dziatzko, Carl. "Αὐτόγραφον." *PW* 2:2596–97.

Ehrman, Bart D., and Michael W. Holmes, eds. *The Text of the New Testament in Contemporary Research: Essays on the Status Quaestionis*. 2nd ed. NTTS 42. Leiden: Brill, 2013.

Elliott, J. Keith. *A Bibliography of Greek New Testament Manuscripts*. 3rd ed. NovTSup 160. Leiden: Brill, 2015.

Fee, Gordon D. "Codex Sinaiticus in the Gospel of John: A Contribution to Methodology in Establishing Textual Relationships." *NTS* 15 (1968/1969): 23–44. Repr., pages 221–43 in *Studies in the Theory and Method of New Testament Textual Criticism*. Edited by Eldon J. Epp and Gordon D. Fee. SD 45. Grand Rapids: Eerdmans, 1993.

Frede, Hermann Josef, ed. *Vetus Latina: Die Reste der altlateinischen Bibel, 25 Pars II*. Freiburg im Breisgau: Herder, 1975–1991.

Greetham, David C. "Politics and Ideology in Current Anglo-American Textual Scholarship." *Editio* 4 (1990): 1–20.

———. *Textual Scholarship: An Introduction*. Hoboken: Taylor & Francis, 2013.

Greeven, Heinrich, and Eberhard Güting. *Textkritik des Markusevangeliums*. Theologie, Forschung und Wissenschaft 11. Münster: LIT, 2005.

Gregory, Caspar René. *Textkritik des Neuen Testamentes*. 3 vols. Leipzig: Hinrich, 1900–1909.

Güting, Eberhard. "Kritik an den Judäern in Jerusalem: Literarkritische Beiträge zu einem unabgeschlossenen Gespräch über den Evangelisten Johannes." Pages 158–201 in *Israel als Gegenüber: Vom Alten Orient bis in die Gegenwart; Studien zur Geschichte eines wechselvollen Zusammenlebens*. Edited by Folker Siegert. SIJD 5. Göttingen: Vandenhoeck & Ruprecht, 2000.

———. "Offene Fragen in der Methodendiskussion der neutestamentlichen Textkritik." *Editio* 19 (2005): 77–98. [Ch. 8 in this collection.]

Harlfinger, Dieter, ed. *Rinascimento virtuale: Digitale Palimpsestforschung; Rediscovering Written Records of a Hidden European Cultural Heritage*. Bratislava, 2002.

Hengel, Martin. *Die Evangelienüberschriften*. Lecture presented 18 October 1981. SHAW.PH 1984.3. Heidelberg: Winter, 1984.

Holmes, Michael W. "Working with an Open Textual Tradition: Challenges in Theory and Practice." Pages 65–78 in *The Textual History of the Greek New Testament*. Edited by Klaus Wachtel and Michael W. Holmes. TCSt 8. Atlanta: Society of Biblical Literature, 2011.

Hurtado, Larry W. "Beyond the Interlude? Developments and Directions in New Testament Textual Criticism." Pages 26–48 in *Studies in the Early Text of the Gospels and Acts: The Papers of the First Birmingham Colloquium on the Textual Criticism of the New Testament*. Edited by David G. K. Taylor. Texts and Studies 3/1. Birmingham: University of Birmingham Press, 1999.

———. *The Earliest Christian Artifacts: Manuscripts and Christian Origins*. Grand Rapids: Eerdmans, 2006.

———. "The New Testament in the Second Century: Text, Collections and Canon." Pages 3–27 in *Transmission and Reception: New Testament Text-critical and Exegetical Studies*. Edited by Jeffrey Wayne Childers and David C. Parker. Piscataway, NJ: Gorgias, 2006.

Jaroš, Karl, ed., *Die ältesten griechischen Handschriften des Neuen Testaments*. Cologne: Böhlau, 2014.

———, ed. *Das Neue Testament nach den ältesten griechischen Handschriften: Die handschriftliche Überlieferung des Neuen Testaments vor Codex Sinaiticus und Codex Vaticanus*. Rupolding: Rutzen; Würzburg: Echter, 2006.

Kenyon, Frederick G. *The Chester Beatty Biblical Papyri: Descriptions and Texts of Twelve Manuscripts on Papyrus of the Greek Bible*. 8 vols. London: Walker, 1933–1941.

———. *The Codex Alexandrinus (Royal MS 1 D V–VIII) in Reduced Photographic Facsimile: New Testament and Clementine Epistles*. London: British Museum, 1909.

Klauck, Hans-Josef. *Ancient Letters and the New Testament: A Guide to Context and Exegesis*. Waco, TX: Baylor University Press, 2006.

Kleve, Knut, Espen S. Ore, and Ragnar Jensen. "Letteralogia: Computer e fotografia." *Cronache Ercolanesi* 17 (1987): 141–50.

Maas, Paul. *Textual Criticism*. Translated from the German by Barbara Flower. Oxford: Clarendon, 1958.

———. *Textkritik*. 4th ed. Leipzig: Teubner, 1960.
Madden, Frederic. *Photographic Facsimiles of the Remains of the Epistles of Clement of Rome, Made from the Unique Copy Preserved in the Codex Alexandrinus*. London: British Museum, 1856.
Milne, Herbert J. M., and Theodore C. Skeat. *Scribes and Correctors of the Codex Sinaiticus*. London: British Museum, 1938.
Netz, Reviel, and William Noel. *Der Kodex des Archimedes: Das berühmteste Palimpsest der Welt wird entschlüsselt*. Munich: Beck, 2007.
Parker, David C. *Codex Bezae: An Early Christian Manuscript and Its Text*. Cambridge: Cambridge University Press, 1992.
———. *An Introduction to the New Testament Manuscripts and Their Texts*. Cambridge: Cambridge University Press, 2008.
Pecere, Oronzo. "La tradizione dei testi latini tra IV e V secolo attraverso i libri sottoscritti." in *Società romana e impero tardoantico IV: Tradizione dei classici, transformazioni della cultura*. Edited by Andrea Guardina. Rome: Laterza, 1986.
Pöhlmann, Egert. *Einführung in die Überlieferungsgeschichte und in die Textkritik der antiken Literatur*. 2 vols. Darmstadt: Wissenschaftliche Buchgesellschaft, 1994.
———. "Textkritik und Texte im 19. und 20. Jh." Pages 137–209 in vol. 2 of *Einführung in die Überlieferungsgeschichte und in die Textkritik der antiken Literatur*. Darmstadt: Wissenschaftliche Buchgesellschaft, 2003.
Reynolds, Leighton D., and Nigel G. Wilson. *Scribes and Scholars: A Guide to the Transmission of Greek and Latin Literature*. 4th ed. Oxford: Oxford University Press, 2013.
Roberts, Colin H. *Manuscript, Society, and Belief in Early Christian Egypt*. Schweich Lectures of the British Academy 1977. London: Oxford University Press, 1979.
Roller, Otto. *Das Formular der paulinischen Briefe: Ein Beitrag zur Lehre vom antiken Briefe*. BWANT 58. Stuttgart: Kohlhammer, 2010.
Rück, Peter, ed. *Pergament: Geschichte, Struktur, Restaurierung, Herstellung*. Historische Wissenschaften 2. Sigmaringen: Thorbecke, 1991.
Schmitz, Franz-Jürgen. "Neue Fragmente zur bilinguen Majuskelhandschrift 070." Pages 71–92 in *Bericht der Hermann Kunst-Stiftung zur Förderung der neutestamentlichen Textforschung für die Jahre 1979 bis 1981*. Münster: Aschendorff, 1982.

Schmitz, Franz-Jürgen, and Gerd Mink., *Liste der koptischen Handschriften des Neuen Testaments, I: Die sahidischen Handschriften der Evangelien*. ANTF 8, 13, 15. Berlin: de Gruyter, 1986–1991.

Sider, David. *The Library of the Villa dei Papiri at Herculaneum*. Los Angeles: Getty, 2005.

Skeat, Theodore C. *The Collected Biblical Writings of Theodore C. Skeat*. Edited by J. Keith Elliott. NovTSup 113. Leiden: Brill, 2004.

Vitelli, Girolamo, ed. *Papiri Greci e Latini*. Vol. 8. Firenze: Le Monnier, 1927.

Westcott, Brooke Foss, and Fenton John Anthony Hort, eds. *The New Testament in the Original Greek: Volume 1, Text; Volume 2, Introduction [and] Appendix*. Cambridge: Macmillan, 1881. 2nd ed., 1896.

Zuntz, Günther. *The Text of the Epistles: A Disquisition upon the Corpus Paulinum*. Schweich Lectures of the British Academy 1946. London: Oxford University Press, 1953.

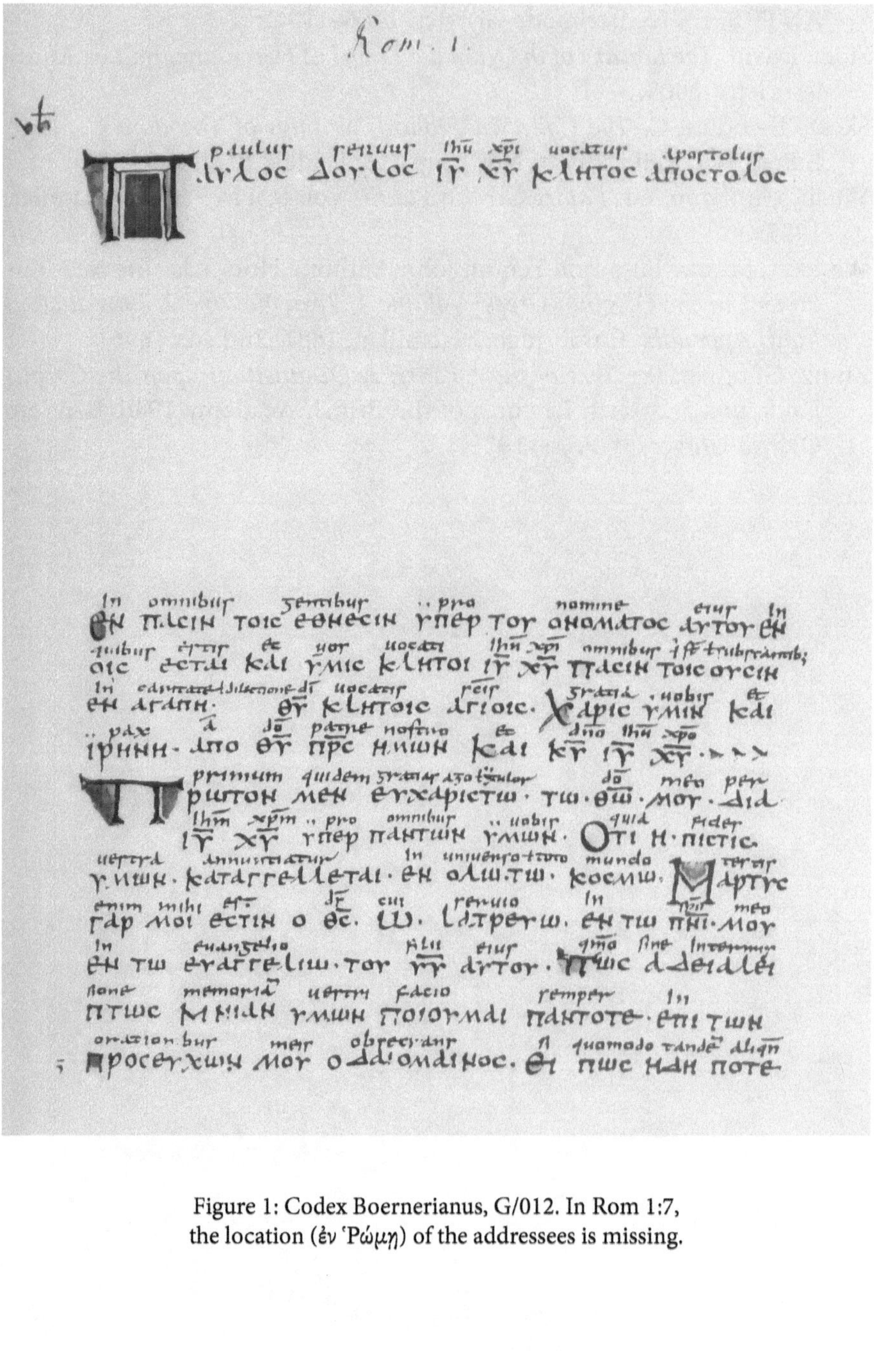

Figure 1: Codex Boernerianus, G/012. In Rom 1:7, the location (ἐν Ῥώμῃ) of the addressees is missing.

11. Texts of the First Hand and Texts of the Second Hand

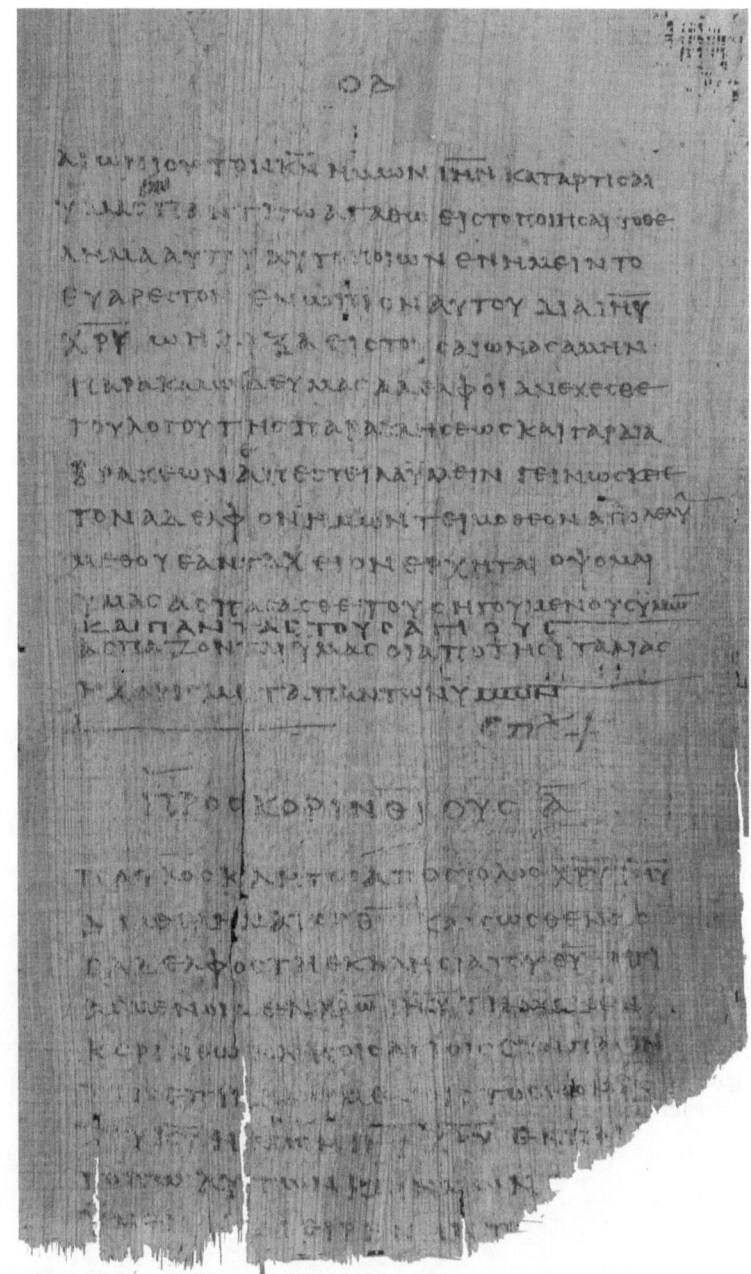

Figure 2: P⁴⁶, folio 38 verso (end of Hebrews, beginning of 1 Corinthians). In Heb 13:24, the first hand omitted και παντας τους αγιους; the corrector has written the missing words interlinearly, extending the final ς in αγιους as a line filler into the margin.

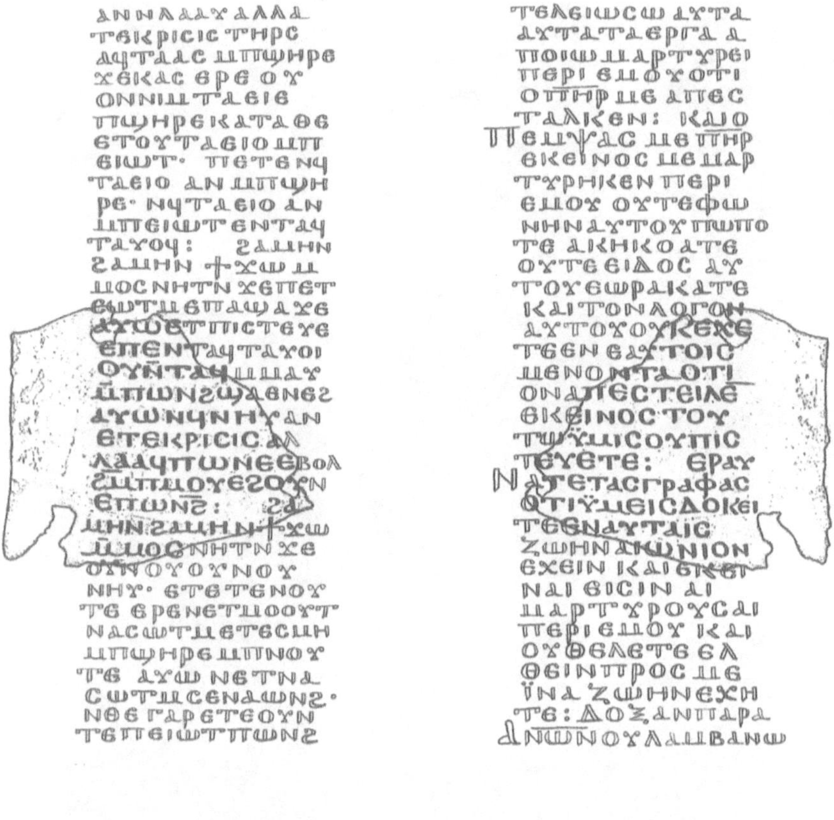

Figure 3: Fragment of the bilingual manuscript 070, supplemented by drawing. The Coptic text on the left and Greek text on the other side must be convincingly integrated into the column.

12
The International Status of New Testament Textual Criticism in Practice and in Theory since Karl Lachmann

Karl Lachmann is known as the first editor of a New Testament edited according to critical principles. His achievements in editing classical texts and his researches into Middle High German literature were pioneering features. In view of international recognition and later likewise of international criticism, it is necessary today to consider in detail the procedures adopted by this scholar. In his account written in German in 1830 the editor of the "strictly historically" edited New Testament[1] appears self-assured and not without acrimony. He acknowledges the achievement of his predecessor Johann Jakob Griesbach, but he also notes its limitations. "'Does reason exist to depart from the conventional reading?' was his question, whereas the normal question can only be, 'Does reason exist to deviate from the best attested reading?'"[2]

1. The Achievements of Karl Lachmann in the Area of New Testament Textual Criticism against the Background of What His Contemporaries Perceived

Lachmann is prepared to allow his method be called "mechanical." The time for internal criticism has not yet arrived. "In view of the devastating misuse of a suggestive criticism, he looked for criteria that would be

---

1. Winfried Ziegler, *Die "wahre strenghistorische Kritik": Leben und Werk Carl Lachmanns und sein Beitrag zur neutestamentlichen Wissenschaft* (Hamburg: Kovac, 2000).
2. Karl Lachmann,"Rechenschaft über seine Ausgabe des Neuen Testaments," *TSK* 3 (1830): 818.

objective and which one could follow rigorously. At times the rigor would be mechanical."[3] The language of the New Testament and of its authors cannot be investigated without clear editorial advances. Lachmann is not in a position to present even an approximation of the text of New Testament authors. All he can give are texts as they were verifiably in circulation in the oldest transmission of the fourth century. Arguments from internal criticism he rejected provisionally.[4]

Lachmann depends on the oldest citations of New Testament texts in patristic tradition,[5] on the oldest translations, especially the Old Latin, and on the work of Jerome.[6]

> The special critical significance of the Vulgate for Lachmann lay in its precisely determined date of composition, in the knowledge of its methodological approach, and in the ascertainability of its relationship to the earlier and simultaneous Greek and Latin texts. In particular where it deviates from the older Latin manuscripts, it supports the Eastern versions of the first four centuries, since the codices A, B, and C do indeed contain earlier materials.[7]

Together with Philip Buttmann, he collated the important Codex Fuldensis of the Vulgate.[8]

Lachmann intends to clear the way for criticism. But first criticism must be prepared to pay attention to tradition, even where it leads demonstrably to what is false.[9] The tradition, however, is encountered in two distinct forms: the Western and the Alexandrian. It goes without saying that where both traditions are consistent, neither is to be preferred. Where

---

3. Giorgio Pasquali, *Storia della tradizione e critica del testo*, 2nd ed. (Firenze: Le lettere, 2003), 4.

4. Lachmann, "Rechenschaft über seine Ausgabe," 819.

5. Lachmann, "Rechenschaft über seine Ausgabe," 833; cf. 836.

6. Lachmann, "Rechenschaft über seine Ausgabe," 824; Ziegler, "*Wahre strenghistorische Kritik,*" 177–78.

7. Ziegler, "*Wahre strenghistorische Kritik,*" 177–78. So earlier Friedrich Lücke, review of *Novum Testamentum Graece et Latine*, by Karl Lachmann," *GGA* (1843): 1333.

8. Ziegler, "*Wahre strenghistorische Kritik,*" 178; Martin Hertz, *Karl Lachmann: Eine Biographie* (Berlin: Hertz, 1851), 159.

9. Lachmann, "Rechenschaft über seine Ausgabe," 821.

one of the two is transmitted inconsistently, it strengthens the witness of the group of witnesses that is transmitted consistently.[10]

In his major edition of 1842–1850, Lachmann distinguished six levels of probability for evaluating witnesses.[11] This does not need to be presented here in detail.[12]

The readings transmitted only in the West, that is, readings that are absent in the East, are not taken over into the edited text. This is an axiomatic decision, based on what was still a quite limited knowledge of ancient manuscripts.[13] From today's perspective, this is no longer acceptable, because in the meantime Günther Zuntz has shown that all three streams of tradition from antiquity, the Western, the Alexandrian, and the Byzantine, have each preserved demonstrably original readings.[14]

Lachmann indicated precisely which works he was able to draw on in his edition, but also those on which he did not want to rely.[15] Lachmann's "mechanical" method predisposed him to take over "indisputably erroneous" readings into his edition, such as in Mark 9:23 (τὸ εἰ δύνῃ), and in Acts 20:4 (Θεσσαλονικέων δὲ Ἀρίσταρχος, κτλ). On the other hand, he is prepared to make emendations, such as in Rev 2:13 (Ἀντίπα rather than Ἀντίπας as in the tradition), or in 1 Cor 9:15 (νή instead of ἤ).[16] His criticism based in philology enables him without further ado to designate numerous additions as secondary.[17] Thus he also occasionally questions

---

10. Lachmann, "Rechenschaft über seine Ausgabe," 826–27.

11. Karl Lachmann, *Novum Testamentum Graece et Latine* (Berlin: Reimer, 1842); *Praefatio I*, pp. viii and xxxiii–xxxviii. *Tomus alter* (Berlin: Reimer, 1850).

12. On this see Ziegler, "*Wahre strenghistorische Kritik*," 187–91.

13. Lachmann, "Rechenschaft über seine Ausgabe," 827; cf. 827 and 835 note a. Irving Alan Sparks, "Lachmann, Karl (1793–1851)," *TRE* 20:368–70.

14. Eberhard Güting, "The Methodological Contribution of Günther Zuntz to the Text of Hebrews," *NovT* 48 (2006): 359–78 [ch. 10 in this collection].

15. Lachmann, "Rechenschaft über seine Ausgabe," 833–34.

16. The Nestle-Aland edition does not accept the last-named conjecture, but it lists it in its apparatus. See Barbara Aland et al., eds., *Novum Testamentum Graece*, 27th ed., 8th reprint, corrected and enlarged with reference to the papyri 99–116 (Stuttgart: Deutsche Bibelgesellschaft, 2001), 455. The 28th edition ceased to register modern emendations; see Barbara Aland et al., eds., *Novum Testamentum Graece*, 28th ed. (Stuttgart: Deutsche Bibelgesellschaft, 2012). In the second volume of his major edition Lachmann discussed in detail problems of emendation: see Lachmann, *Novum Testamentum*, iii–xiii.

17. Lachmann, "Rechenschaft über seine Ausgabe," 842. Caspar René Greg-

additions that still incorrectly appear in contemporary editions, as for example in Luke 24:12, 51, 52. With his three small stereotyped editions in 1831, 1837, and 1846, which still contained no apparatuses, Lachmann had already replaced the traditional textus receptus once and for all[18]— and this aspect of his achievement was immediately recognized by his contemporaries.[19] The major critical edition contained further advancements.[20] Lachmann emphasized explicitly the part that Buttmann had played in the completion of the major edition. In the meantime Lachmann had improved his approach, increased his understanding of the Latin tradition, and strengthened his evaluation of the early transmission process. The major edition is also the result of consistent *recensio*. Lachmann maintains that *emendatio* may follow but must not for the time being enter into the result.[21]

Lachmann took a great deal of care with the identification of witnesses worth being relied on. In a number of cases his investigations resulted in his rejection of manuscript editions and of collations. He had to do the collation himself. With respect to the Old Latin translations, Lachmann recognized that the best witnesses originated in Africa, that

---

ory, "Prolegomena," in Constantin von Tischendorf, *Novum Testamentum Graece ad antiquissimos testes denuo recensuit; Apparatum criticum apposuit Constantinus Tischendorf*, 8th ed. (Leipzig: Hinrichs, 1894), 3:258–66.

18. Caspar René Gregory, *Textkritik des Neuen Testamentes* (Leipzig; Hinrichs, 1900–1909), 2:966. So earlier Friedrich Lücke, review of *Novum Testamentum Graece et Latine*, by Karl Lachmann, *GGA* (1843): 1333.

19. Friedrich Lücke, review of *Novum Testamentum Graece*, by Karl Lachmann, *GGA* (1831): 657–76; H. C. M. Rettig, review of *Novum Testamentum Graece*, by Karl Lachmann, *ThStKr* 5 (1832): 861–901; August H. Hahn, review of *Novum Testamentum Graece*, by Karl Lachmann, *Jahrbücher für wissenschaftliche Kritik* (1838): 726–84.

20. Naturally comments from later editors of the New Testament are of great interest at this point, such as Constantin von Tischendorf, "Zur Kritik des Neuen Testaments," *ThStKr* 15 (1842): 496–511; Tischendorf, *Neue Jenaische Allgemeine Literaturzeitung* 2 (1843): 326–34; Samuel Prideaux Tregelles, *An Account of the Printed Text of the Greek New Testament: With Remarks on Its Revision upon Critical Principles: Together with a Collation of the Text of Griesbach, Scholz, Lachmann and Tischendorf with That in Common Use* (London: Bagster & Sons, 1854); Ziegler, "*Wahre strenghistorische Kritik*," notes numerous reviews; see pp. 314–43.

21. Ziegler, "*Wahre strenghistorische Kritik*," 163.

the Itala tradition represented a later stage, and that the Gallic tradition was to be distinguished from older traditions.[22]

Surprisingly a result of research on the work of Jerome was that better witnesses from the Itala tradition tended to reinforce the testimony of older representatives of the Greek transmission. Lachmann recognized that apart from the "translator of Irenaeus" he could rely on Cyprian, Hilary of Poitiers, and Lucifer of Cagliari, as well as on Primasius in the Apocalypse of John.[23] Of the Greek fathers he relied, on good grounds, exclusively on Origen.[24]

As indicated, Lachmann centered on his *recensio* of the ancient tradition of the fourth century. Moreover, in the preface to his major edition he commented on questions of necessary emendation. He cited passages in which arguably this tradition offered a corrupted text, but without emending.[25]

In the second volume he presented his own conjectures, again without taking them over into the printed text.[26] Words that he considered secondary additions he put in brackets (Matt 3:6, 16 and often).

The two prefaces for the major edition of the New Testament reveal that this scholar was heart-stricken over the malevolent and unjustified criticism of his contemporaries.[27] However, there was also remarkable recognition from many quarters. Friedrich Schleiermacher had warmly encouraged Lachmann so that at his command, as he said, he wrote the report for *Theologische Studien und Kritiken* (1830). The German theologians Friedrich Lücke (who represented Schleiermacher's hermeneutic independently and forcefully) and H. C. M. Rettig, C. K. J. Bunsen and Constantin von Tischendorf, the Dutchman J. I. Doedes, and the British scholars Samuel Prideaux Tregelles, Samuel Davidson, and Thomas Hartwell Horne, as well as the educator Matthew Arnold, spoke out in public.[28]

---

22. Ziegler, "*Wahre strenghistorische Kritik*," 172–75.

23. Lachmann, *Novum Testamentum*, ix.

24. Ziegler, "*Wahre strenghistorische Kritik*," 168, 171.

25. Lachmann, *Novum Testamentum*, xliv: Mark 8:26; 9:23; John 8:44; Jas 3:6, 12; 2 Cor 7:8; Heb 9:2.

26. Lachmann, *Novum Testamentum*, v–xiii: Matt 21:31; 27:28; Mark 1:1, 4; 9:23; Luke 14:5; John 8:44; Acts 4:25; 7:46; 8:7; 13:19, 27, 32; 20:4, 5; 21:5; 26:28; Jas 3:3; Rom 5:6; 6:16; 7:22–25; 10:16; 16:25; 1 Cor 8:1; 9:15; 14:33; 2 Cor 7:8; Gal 2:12; Eph 1:15.

27. Lücke, Review of *Novum Testamentum Graece et Latine*, 1331.

28. C. K. J. von Bunsen, *Die drei ächten und die vier unächten Briefe des*

Before the publication of the second volume Lücke had already declared, "There is now no Protestant university in Germany where Lachmann's work is not used and taken into consideration with all seriousness and respect by specialists and experts in exegetical studies, in lectures, seminars, and societies."[29]

All later editions accepted Lachmann's proposal in part, if not his method and specific mode of operation. Among later New Testament scholars especially Caspar René Gregory gave attention to Lachmann's achievements and results. Many of his prudent judgments remain until today.[30]

2. The Perception of Karl Lachmann in Classical Philology

As early as May 18, 1821, the leading classical scholar Gottfried Hermann wrote to Lachmann: "This matter must, indeed, be tackled in the way you did."[31] In the introduction to classical studies by Alfred Gercke and Eduard Norden, Ulrich von Wilamowitz-Moellendorff undertook to assess Lachmann's extraordinary achievements and found justifiable words of admiration.[32]

Until the beginning of the twentieth century, Lachmann's achievements were recognized without serious criticism.[33] His approach was

---

Ignatius von Antiochien: Hergestellter und vergleichender Text mit Anmerkungen (Hamburg: Agentur des Rauhen Hauses, 1847), v–viii; J. I. Doedes, *Verhandeling over de tekstkritiek des nieuwen verbonds* (Harlem: Bohn, 1844), 150–175; Thomas Hartwell Horne, *An Introduction to the Textual Criticism of the New Testament, with Analyses, of the Respective Books, and a Bibliographical List of Editions of the Scriptures in the Original Texts and the Ancient Versions*, rev. and ed. Samuel Prideaux Tregelles (London: Longman, 1856; repr., Cambridge: Cambridge University Press, 2013), 133–38; Ziegler, "*Wahre strenghistorische Kritik*," 198.

29. Friedrich Lücke, "Epimetron," *GGA* (1848): 504.

30. Gregory, "Prolegomena," 258–66; Gregory, *Textkritik des Neuen Testamentes*.

31. Albert Leitzmann, *Briefe an Karl Lachmann aus den Jahren 1814–50*, APAW.PH (Berlin: Reimer, 1915), 41–42.

32. Ulrich von Wilamowitz-Moellendorff, *Geschichte der Philologie: Mit einem Nachwort und Register von Albert Henrichs* (Stuttgart: Teubner, 1998), 58–59; cf. von Wilamowitz-Moellendorff, *History of Classical Scholarship*, ed. with introduction and notes by Hugh Lloyd-Jones (London: Duckworth, 1982).

33. "During the half-century or so that followed the publication of Lachmann's *Lucretius* in 1850 and the death of its editor in 1851 there was no serious challenge to the 'method' itself; there was, that is to say, no fundamental expres-

recommended under the designation "Lachmann's method" in classical philology, in Romance studies, [34] in Middle High German philology, wherever texts were transmitted by copying. Confidence grew in the ability to design genealogical stemmata of all known manuscripts by means of recognizing characteristic faults.

However, in 1928 the French literary critic Joseph Bédier published a most effective criticism on the editions of medieval French literature. After reviewing more than one hundred editions, he reproached editors for having arbitrarily manipulated genealogical stemmata.[35]

According to Bédier, in striking singularity stemmata that were presented demonstrated regularly two branches, regularly two ramifications, with the result that editors easily felt justified in giving preference to the witnesses that they favored. In avoiding any threefold or fourfold branch, critics alleviated their work. In connection with his critique, Bédier developed a statistical approach that disposed of philological critique and no longer designated readings as of higher quality or as textual errors, and finally focused on the numerical aspect of testimony. Bédier supported his position by the thorough analysis of the transmission of the *Lai de l'ombre*. He emphasized, of course, the exceptional position of medieval, especially French, traditions compared with texts dealt with in classical philology.

Dom Henri Quentin also developed his own different position from Lachmann's method that in important points was in contrast to procedures adhered to in classical philology.[36] Like Lachmann, he attached importance to separating *recensio* and *emendatio*, and further to refraining from any reference to good or bad readings, to errors or to connected faults.[37] Quentin was able to rely on his experience in the Vulgate Commission

---

sion of doubt as to its validity" (Edward John Kenney, *The Classical Text: Aspects of Editing in the Age of the Printed Book* [Berkeley: University of California Press, 1974], 130).

34. "Des 1866, Gaston Paris l'avait recommandée à l'attention des romanistes" (Joseph Bédier, "La tradition manuscrite du Lai de l'ombre: Réflexions sur l'art d'éditer les anciens textes," Romania 54 [1928]: 164 n. 1).

35. Joseph Bédier, *La tradition manuscrite du Lai de l' ombre* (Paris: Champion, 1929), 168–71.

36. Dom Henri Quentin, *Essais de critique textuelle (Ecdotique)* (Paris: Picard, 1926); Kenney, *Classical Text*, 135 n. 3, refers to the critical echo that this work received.

37. Quentin, *Essais de critique*, 11.

of Leo X that in exemplary fashion had collated an enormous number of Octateuch manuscripts and had examined the quality of this tradition.[38]

With a taxonomic approach that analyzes groups of three witnesses in selected passages, Quentin aimed at an archetype that in fact did not correspond to the text of New Testament authors, and yet came close to it.[39] Where philology has resources at its disposal to determine the texts of authors, these were not to be excluded, although in other cases an edition of the readings of the archetype was recommended, as these readings were entitled to a superior claim.[40] As his series of essays shows, Quentin considered his approach to be multifunctional.

As late as the 1970s, in view of an increasing attractiveness of computer assisted collations and text-processing programs, Lachmann's stemmatics method was adopted by the majority.[41] However, in the meantime it appears that this is changing. But this subject will not be discussed here.

A fundamental introduction to textual criticism for classical philologists, written by Paul Maas, was published in 1927 in Gercke's and Norden's *Einleitung in die Altertumswissenschaft*. Four editions came out before this work was replaced by Martin L. West, *Textual Criticism and Editorial Technique Applicable to Greek and Latin Texts*.[42] Both introductions could be described as topical presentations of Lachmann's method. Maas shows

---

38. *Biblia sacra iuxta latinam vulgata versionem ad codicum fidem cura et studio monachorum Pontificiae Abbatiae S. Hieronymi in Urbe edita* (Rome: Pontifical Biblical Institute, 1926–1994). Only the Old Testament has appeared.

39. "De ce classement résulte un canon critique qui impose pour l'établissement du texte une règle de fer et ainsi j'aboutis à la reconstitution de l'archétype qui, en somme, est la forme du texte la plus voisine de l'original à laquelle on puisse arriver par voie des manuscrits conservés" (Quentin, *Essais de critique*, 37).

40. "Mais dans les cas douteux le mieux sera évidemment de conserver la leçon de l'archétype, car nous ne possédons … pas de meilleur témoin de l'original que lui il en représente la copie la plus ancienne" (Quentin, *Essais de critique*, 52, cf. 43).

41. Kurt Gärtner, "Der Computer als Werkzeug und Medium in der Editionswissenschaft: Ein Rückblick," *Editio* 25 (2011): 39; Pieter M. W. Robinson, "Computer-Assisted Stemmatic Analysis and 'Best-Text' Historical Editing," in *Studies in Stemmatology*, ed. Pieter van Reenen and Margot Mulken (Amsterdam: Benjamins, 1996), 71–103.

42. Paul Maas, *Textkritik*, 4th ed. (Leipzig: Teubner, 1960); Martin L. West, *Textual Criticism and Editorial Technique Applicable to Greek and Latin Texts* (Stuttgart: Teubner, 1973).

which possibilities are opened up by various constellations of witnesses. He discusses the identification and use of connecting errors, a term not used by Lachmann.[43] A large collection of examples proves that young and isolated witnesses may be capable of preserving ancient and good readings. Newly discovered and edited papyri gave convincing proof. Some fragments from antiquity even justified felicitous emendations by outstanding scholars. Bernard P. Grenfell, in the course of a series of papyrus editions, and Eduard Schwartz, in the edition of Eusebius's *Ecclesiastical History*, demonstrated that an eclectic use of all available material is fully justified. New Testament textual criticism has long since adopted an eclectic position.

Neither Maas nor West mentions Lachmann. West, however, pointed out that Maas introduced the diagnostic value of emendations and of identified cruces into the relevant discussion.[44] West himself considered as his own contribution the admission that contamination within the transmission of texts is a normal and even frequent phenomenon. He made proposals for procedure in cases of partly contaminated and partly uncontaminated transmission.[45]

Giorgio Pasquali devoted the first chapter of his monumental *Geschichte der Textkritik* to Lachmann's method.[46] He emphasized his assured judgment, his ability to identify textual errors, his willingness to emend in a noteworthy manner. Lachmann's effort to locate ancient transmission precisely according to time and region as far as possible leads toward a convincing identification of the readings that are attested by Jerome and to the use of the tradition of the Latin fathers as well as that of the Itala.

The usefulness of this stance is demonstrated not least in the research developed by Hans von Soden and Heinrich Greeven on regional manuscript traditions.[47] Pasquali refers to the fact that as with Lachmann,

---

43. Maas, *Textkritik*, 26–30.

44. West, *Textual Criticism*, 58 n. 10.

45. West, *Textual Criticism*, 38–46. Academic discussion with regard to the editorial treatment of cruces and of conjectures is presently gaining attention; see Anne Bohnenkamp et al., eds., *Konjektur und Krux: Zur Methodenpolitik der Philologie* (Göttingen: Wallstein, 2010).

46. Pasquali, *Storia della tradizione*, 3–12.

47. Hans von Soden, reviews of *Novum Testamentum Graece*, by D. Eberhard Nestle and Erwin Nestle; *The Caesarean Text of the Gospel of Mark*, by Kirsopp Lake, Robert P. Blake, and Silva New, *Gnomon* 6 (1930): 199–212, see esp. 204–12;

so also in neolinguistics the preservation of ancient tradition in remote regions plays an important role.⁴⁸

Despite his wholehearted recognition of Lachmann, Pasquali did not shy away from criticizing his approach. Pasquali censured Lachmann for his readiness to exclude interpolated manuscripts from investigation.⁴⁹ He conceded, however, that for Propertius, Catullus, and Lucretius this had been only a minimal handicap.

Whereas Lachmann criticized the approach of Griesbach, Pasquali accentuated Griesbach's achievements. "Quentin recently positioned the importance of the *Prolegomena* ... of Professor J. J. Griesbach of Jena in the correct light (Halle, 1796). In addition, in my opinion the rules of the *Sectio tertia* formulated by him (pp. lixff.) deserve to be reprinted and disseminated among researchers and students of philology as a catechism."⁵⁰ Of course Pasquali also discussed the specific advances of text-critical work, which go back to Johann Jacob Wettstein (1730), Albrecht Bengel (1734), and Johann Salomo Semler (1765).

Sometime after Pasquali, indeed in 2000, the Latinist Peter Lebrecht Schmidt addressed anew Lachmann's achievements. First of all, he emphasized that he himself saw no reason to throw doubt upon the stemmatic method of philology, which Romanists challenged.⁵¹

Then he emphasized that Lachmann at the most should be named as one among many of a whole circle of scholars alongside J. C. Orelli, C. G. Zumpt, F. W. Ritschl, J. N. Madvig, and H. Sauppe.⁵² Schmidt criticized Lachmann explicitly. Lachmann judged the achievements of the editor Bernay on Lucretius and the significance of a further discovery of

---

Heinrich Greeven and Eberhard Güting, *Textkritik des Markusevangeliums*, Theologie, Forschung und Wissenschaft 11 (Münster: LIT, 2005).

48. Matteo Bartoli, *Introduzione alla neolinguistica: principi, scopi, metodi* (Geneva: Olschki, 1925), 3–9; Pasquali, *Storia della tradizione*, 8 n. 1.

49. Pasquali, *Storia della tradizione*, 4.

50. Pasquali, *Storia della tradizione*, 10.

51. Peter Lebrecht Schmidt, "Lachmann's Method: On the History of a Misunderstanding," in *Traditio Latinitatis: Studien zur Rezeption und Überlieferung der lateinischen Literatur*, ed. Joachim Fugmann, Martin Hose, and Bernhard Zimmermann (Stuttgart: Steiner, 2000), 11.

52. Timpanaro dealt with the antecedents of Lachmann's method extensively. See Sebastiano Timpanaro, *Die Entstehung der Lachmannschen Methode*, 2nd ed., trans. Dieter Irmer (Hamburg: Buske, 1971); ET: *The Genesis of Lachmann's Method*, ed. and trans. Glenn W. Most (Chicago: University of Chicago, 2005).

manuscripts of that time quite disparagingly.[53] Schmidt ascribed the genealogical method to a radical change of the early nineteenth century.

> The genealogical method, applied to Latin texts of antiquity, may be defined as the constitution of manuscript groups or families by means of shared errors of transmission. These families may lead back to an archetype, standing somewhere between the original and the medieval copies. Their historical relationship may then be illustrated by means of a stemmatic reconstruction of the historical process. The recognition of the primary importance of manuscript families constituted the real progress for the first generations of nineteenth-century philologists. F. A. W. Wolf's *Prolegomena*, which called for a complete reconstitution of the textual history of ancient authors, had already stressed the need for reducing complexity, an essential element of which was the grouping of manuscripts into *classes* or *familiae*.[54]

Whereas Lachmann himself and many other editors of his time and later were content with the discovery and editing of a "best" manuscript, genealogical research into the history of tradition and its stemmatic account was generally accepted from around 1880.[55]

In his critique of Lachmann's approach, which sometimes was, indeed, subject to criticism, Schmidt did not fail to accentuate positively Lachmann's achievement in one important respect: "All this may sound far too negative: there can be no doubt that Lachmann for the most part made excellent use of the manuscript material he chose or adopted. He read the manuscripts more carefully than most scholars at that time, presented the variants sensibly, even though a bit too sparingly for our liking, and established sound texts that, especially in Germanic studies, have become standard."[56]

Finally, Schmidt took exception to Bédier's criticism of Lachmann and of his influence on a particular school of Romance studies. "I call this misunderstanding paradoxical because Bédier's decision to exorcize the genealogical method as subjective, and his concentration on a 'manuscrit de base' resembles Lachmann's procedure much more closely than the method he was really attacking."[57]

---

53. Schmidt, "Lachmann's Method," 12 n. 11, 14 n. 17.
54. Schmidt, "Lachmann's Method," 13.
55. Schmidt, "Lachmann's Method," 16.
56. Schmidt, "Lachmann's Method," 14.
57. Schmidt, "Lachmann's Method," 18.

3. A Challenge to Karl Lachmann's Method by Means of Gerd Mink's Coherence-Based Genealogical Method

After a long period of preparatory work, the first two issues of the Editio Critica Maior of the New Testament appeared in 1997. A massive amount of material from Greek, Latin, Coptic, Syriac, Armenian, Old Church Slavonic, and Ethiopic manuscripts from editions of texts and writings of the fathers was arranged and presented. Each variant received an address that was accessible for computer programs. This edition of James had been long awaited and was welcomed in reviews. A complicated procedure was used for constituting the text that first of all dealt with all the material in the computer programs. These computer programs were presented in several publications. The underlying method was designated as the "coherence based genealogical method" and also described as a cladistic neo-Lachmannian approach. The interpretation of the approach just described is, however, not entirely simple. I will, therefore, confine myself to Gerd Mink's detailed descriptions, definitions, and explanations that appeared in an article that appeared in 2004.[58]

First of all, Mink's approach, developed in the Institut für Neutestamentliche Textforschung in Münster, arranges all witnesses according to their family relationships before individual readings are investigated in a local genealogical procedure. A difficulty is immediately encountered: fragmented manuscripts can be compared with completely preserved ones by computers only with difficulty. But some papyri, in particular some early ones, P^{20} (third century), P^{23} (third century), P^{54} (fifth/sixth century), P^{74} (seventh century), P^{100} (third/fourth century) are transmitted only as fragments.[59]

The kinship of two manuscripts is not, as is common in classical philology, determined on the basis of shared characteristic errors. Rather, it is calculated on the basis of the number of jointly transmitted correct or

---

58. Gerd Mink, "Problems of a Highly Contaminated Tradition: The New Testament Stemmata of Variants as a Source of a Genealogy for Witnesses," in *Studies in Stemmatology II*, ed. Pieter van Reenen, August den Hollander, and Margot van Mulken (Amsterdam: Benjamins, 2004), 13–85.

59. Mink also discusses difficulties with complete manuscripts that are available, for example the majuscule 04. In the process it is possible for circular relationships of dependence to appear at the point of family relationships. See Mink, "Problems of a Highly Contaminated Tradition," 71–72.

incorrect readings. Thus it is possible to determine nearer or more distant kinships for each manuscript in descending degrees of relationship. This approach favors manuscripts that are free from individual particularities, above all late witnesses of the largely consistently transmitted Byzantine form of the text.

A central problem of the transmission of the New Testament is the presence of contaminated witnesses, that is, of witnesses that alongside what is copied from the source manuscript contain readings from other witnesses. Mink aims to avoid unnecessary assumptions, to work with as few as possible, and these defensible.[60] However, one of his assumptions is highly debatable. He assumes that in addition to their own master copy, copyists would also normally check manuscripts from their immediate vicinity, with the effect that contaminations contain no severe changes in the text.[61] Of course this is not always the case.

In the first pages of his article the author explains his procedure in the construction of regional genealogical stemmata. A simple case occurs in Jas 4:12: witnesses that read εἷς ἐστιν ὁ νομοθέτης καὶ κριτής are exactly in accordance with the source text that the Editio Critica Maior reads: "The best hypothesis is that variant *a* [καὶ κριτής] represents the original text, since the word κριτής ('judge') is very important for the author's argument in the context."[62] The witnesses for this variant are: A Ψ 33 81 323 614 630 1241 1505 1739 lat sy co. Variant *b*, καὶ ὁ κριτής (supported by the witnesses 467 643 1848), supposedly depends on *a*. On the other hand *c*, κριτής (attested by 631), also supposedly depends on *a*. However, whether *c* concurrently depends on *a* through *d* (omit καὶ κριτής) or exclusively goes back directly to *a* is unclear (a dashed line calls attention to this possibility). Since the witnesses for *c* are closely related to the witnesses for *d*, this is not to be excluded. In addition, the ὁ before νομοθέτης exhibited

---

60. Mink, "Problems of a Highly Contaminated Tradition," 48.

61. "The contamination in the tradition is viewed as a process. The assumption is that, if contamination occurs, it emerges from those texts which were at the disposal of the scribe, i.e., texts in his direct environment, i.e., texts which are, for the most part, closely related with each other.… In a dense tradition, it is typical of contamination that a witness shares most of its variants with its closest relative and if it deviates from this relative the variants concerned can be found in other close relatives" (Mink, "Problems of a Highly Contaminated Tradition," 14 and 22).

62. Mink, "Problems of a Highly Contaminated Tradition," 14.

in A 044 and numerous primarily Byzantine minuscule manuscripts is accepted and accordingly incorporated as a part of the text.

However, it remains to verify whether the attestation supports this judgment. Vaticanus B reads εἷς ἐστιν νομοθέτης καὶ κριτής ὁ δυνάμενος σῶσαι καὶ ἀπολέσαι. This text with the absence of the article is impressive because of its style. The lack of the article before νομοθέτης is attested by ancient and extraordinarily good witnesses: P[74] P[100] B 025 as well as 88 621 720[vid] 915 1175 1241* 1243 1448 1852 2374 2492 2674 2805 *l*1281 Cyr. The reading not only has ancient attestation, but is also stylistically good.

En route to a complete stemmata collection of witnesses of the book of James, Mink presents an ideal substemma of the witness B/03. For this three potential "ancestors" are correlated. The predominant flow of the text runs from A (the *Ausgangstext*/initial text) toward B, as does the flow of the text of the fragments 0166 and 0173. A flow of the text from P[23] toward B cannot be substantiated. Mink comes to the conclusion that the fragmented manuscripts 0166 and 0173 (both fifth century) represented an older form of the text of B (fourth century).[63]

A new examination, however, produces another pattern. In Jas 1:11 (0166 is a witness here) B leaves out the second αὐτοῦ and stands almost alone with this error (03 1827 1893). In Jas 1:25–27 (0173 is a witness here) a secondary reading οὗτος (following παραμείνας) is not in either B or 0173. But it is found in the witnesses P Ψ sy[h] as well as in numerous further witnesses of the Byzantine form of the text. A secondary εἰ δέ τις instead of εἴ τις is attested by C P 0173[vid] 33 69 88 252 442 467 915 945 1175 1241 1243 1739 1848 2298 2444 2464 2492 *l*596. Here B does not participate in the insertion, unlike 0173. In verse 26, B and 0173 do not participate in the secondary insertion of ἐν ὑμῖν (so 049 and the majority text). However, again B has a singular error: χαλινῶν. On the basis of such errors a weak performance is ascribed to the manuscript B. However, this indicates that Mink's reconstruction of the relationships of dependence of the manuscript B cannot be satisfactory. The Byzantine manuscript A does not belong to the predecessors of the Alexandrian manuscript B either.

The author intimates that extensive inspection is demanded before a satisfactory interpretation of the computer data is possible.[64] Such a revisionary interpretation that can be based on the appraisal of all most likely

---

63. Mink, "Problems of a Highly Contaminated Tradition," 52.
64. Mink, "Problems of a Highly Contaminated Tradition," 46.

probabilities produces a complete genealogical stemma of the dominant flow of the text for James.[65] It may be that this stemma is supported by an enormous amount of data and evaluations. However, a reader may notice assumptions that must be viewed with skepticism. Twelve witnesses, majuscule and minuscule manuscripts, will be cited that supposedly stand as close as possible to the source text: P^{74} P^{100} 01 03 04 025 81 307 1175 1243 1739 1852.

The manuscript 02 supposedly goes back to the source text by way of transmission of a witness of the type 81: "But in James, 81 has a predominantly older textual state than 02. However, what is not visible in this case, is that 02 nonetheless has readings deriving from A [= source text] in 28 instances which do not occur in 81 and therefore cannot derive from 81."[66] Papyrus 20 from the third century supposedly goes back to 044 as a probable ancestor (ninth/tenth century). The majuscule manuscript 0246 (sixth century) is supposedly dependent on 1739. This is possible, since according to its well-known provenance, this minuscule reproduces a very ancient text. However, again manuscript 020 (ninth century) supposedly goes back through labyrinthine ways through 617, through 424, through 468, through 307 to the presumed starting point of the "textual flow."[67] Anyone who takes all of this as probable has much confidence in the procedures undertaken here.

4. Which Aspects of Karl Lachmann's Achievements Need to Be Emphasized?

Lachmann's method, a philological method, has been recognized and recommended for more than one hundred years. Its access to the material, a thought-out selection from sources, and its astute judgment are praised internationally. Perhaps one should also mention his untiring diligence.

Of course the availability of competently edited sources set limits for his research of that time. He recognized these limits. Today the sources available in the area of New Testament textual criticism have grown in a breath-taking manner. This is clearly due to the remarkable achievements of the Institut für neutestamentliche Textforschung in Münster. It seems to

---

65. Mink, "Problems of a Highly Contaminated Tradition," 48.
66. Mink, "Problems of a Highly Contaminated Tradition," 48–49.
67. Mink, "Problems of a Highly Contaminated Tradition," 47; fig. 16.

me that the philological skill of contemporary research has not kept pace with the current possibilities. What can one learn from Lachmann?

Lachmann read all texts as literary texts. He interpreted the procedure of the authors that he investigated as a literary skill, not in explaining but in editing them. This holds also for Mark as an author, to whom he turned in the framework of his editions of the New Testament.

He analyzed the structure of the Gospel of Mark, the structure of his narrative devices, the literary form of the whole, and he recognized that Mark is the oldest of the Synoptic Gospels, and therefore that it provided the exemplar for later gospels.[68]

If I am correct, no one has adequately appreciated one important element of his criticism until now, namely, a literary procedure that uses the author Mark's mode of representation to his readers as the basis for critical emendations. Lachmann recognizes that the author Mark does not confront his readers argumentatively; rather he strictly maintains the role of narrator. Mark 1:2 and 1:3, therefore, cannot possibly go back to the author in spite of their strong attestation.[69] As an editor one should take this into account.

It remains beyond dispute that new focal points for research, necessary shifts of paradigms, and transformations in all fields of study are to be welcomed. For their part editors must bring back to memory that which has been forgotten.

In 1981 in the first issue of the periodical *Text*, the distinguished historian of philosophy and editor Paul Oskar Kristeller presented his experience as editor in the form of a speech, quite impeccably, quite splendidly. He spoke about the merits and limits of Lachmann's method, and also about the significance of academic editing: "For the whole enterprise of history, and especially of intellectual history, rests on the belief, or rather the conviction, that the texts of the past contain a substance and a quality, philosophical, literary, and historical, that still speak to us if properly understood and that should not be reduced to the limits of our contemporary understanding, but should in turn help us to extend and overcome these limits."[70]

---

68. Ziegler, "*Wahre strenghistorische Kritik*," 243–75.

69. Lachmann, "Rechenschaft über seine Ausgabe," 844–45; Greeven and Güting, *Textkritik des Markusevangeliums*, 53–55.

70. Paul Otto Kristeller, "The Lachmann Method: Merits and Limitations," *Text* 1 (1981): 20.

Addendum

Studies concerning the history of medieval German have resulted in important insights into the method of Lachmann. Thomas Bein, a specialist in medieval studies, discussed Lachmann's approach and his achievements in the context of present methodology. Basic to more recent procedures is the realization that originals or even archetypes of medieval German texts are only rarely available for research. Transmitted texts that have been supplemented, altered, abridged, and improved are frequently hundreds of years distant from their origins.

Lachmann perceived that to investigate the grammar, meter, and topic of medieval texts at the same time is indispensable. Lachmann ventured to emend, but at the same time he appeared to hesitate in a characteristic manner. He reckoned with uncertainty in the transmission of texts. The tasks of editing, of sifting, of comparing, and of designing hierarchies of witnesses are discussed, following the lead of Lachmann, but cautious criticism is also presented. Work done by the author Magdalene Lutz-Hensel and by the editors Karl von Kraus and Christoph Cormeau is also cited.[71]

Bibliography

Aland, Barbara, and Kurt Aland, Johannes Karavidopoulos, Carlo M. Martini, and Bruce M. Metzger, eds. *Novum Testamentum Graece*, 27th ed. 8th printing corrected and extended to Papyri 99–116. Stuttgart: Deutsche Bibelgesellschaft, 2001.

———, eds. *Novum Testamentum Graece*. 28th ed. Stuttgart: Deutsche Bibelgesellschaft, 2012.

Bartoli, Matteo. *Introduzione alla neolinguistica: principi, scopi, metodi*. Geneva: Olschki, 1925.

Bédier, Joseph. *La tradition manuscrite du Lai de l' ombre*. Paris: Champion, 1929.

———. "La tradition manuscrite du Lai de l'ombre: Réflexions sur l'art d'éditer les anciens textes." *Romania* 54 (1928): 161–96, 321–56.

Bein, Thomas. *Textkritik: Eine Einführung in Grundlagen germanistisch-mediävistischer Editionswissenschaft*. Frankfurt am Main: Lang, 2008.

---

71. Thomas Bein, *Textkritik: Eine Einführung in Grundlagen germanistisch-mediävistischer Editionswissenschaft* (Frankfurt am Main: Lang, 2008), 73–84.

Biblia sacra iuxta latinam vulgata versionem ad codicum fidem cura et studio monachorum Pontificiae Abbatiae S. Hieronymi in Urbe edita. Rome: Pontifical Biblical Institute, 1926–1994.

Bohnenkamp, Anne, Kai Bremer, Uwe Wirth, and Irmgard R. Wirtz, eds. *Konjektur und Krux: Zur Methodenpolitik der Philologie.* Göttingen: Wallstein, 2010.

Bunsen, C. K. J. von. *Die drei ächten und die vier unächten Briefe des Ignatius von Antiochien: Hergestellter und vergleichender Text mit Anmerkungen.* Hamburg: Agentur des Rauhen Hauses, 1847.

Doedes, J. I. *Verhandeling over de tekstkritiek des nieuwen verbonds.* Harlem: Bohn, 1844.

Gärtner, Kurt. "Der Computer als Werkzeug und Medium in der Editionswissenschaft: Ein Rückblick." *Editio* 25 (2011): 32–41.

Greeven, Heinrich, and Eberhard Güting. *Textkritik des Markusevangeliums.* Theologie, Forschung und Wissenschaft 11. Münster: LIT, 2005.

Gregory, Caspar René. "Prolegomena." In *Novum Testamentum Graece ad antiquissimos testes denuo recensuit; Apparatum criticum apposuit Constantinus Tischendorf.* Edited by Constantin von Tischendorf. 8th ed. Leipzig: Hinrichs, 1894.

———. *Textkritik des Neuen Testamentes.* 3 vols. Leipzig: Hinrichs, 1900–1909.

Güting, Eberhard. "The Methodological Contribution of Günther Zuntz to the Text of Hebrews." *NovT* 48 (2006): 359–78. [Ch. 10 in this collection.]

Hahn, August H. Review of *Novum Testamentum Graece*, by Karl Lachmann. *Jahrbücher für wissenschaftliche Kritik* (1838): 726–84.

Hertz, Martin. *Karl Lachmann: Eine Biographie.* Berlin: Hertz, 1851.

Horne, Thomas Hartwell. *An Introduction to the Textual Criticism of the New Testament, with Analyses, of the Respective Books, and a Bibliographical List of Editions of the Scriptures in the Original Texts and the Ancient Versions.* Revised and edited by Samuel Prideaux Tregelles. London: Longman, 1856. Repr., Cambridge: Cambridge University Press, 2013.

Kenney, Edward John. *The Classical Text: Aspects of Editing in the Age of the Printed Book.* Berkeley: University of California Press, 1974.

Kristeller, Paul Otto. "The Lachmann Method: Merits and Limitations." *Text* 1 (1981): 11–20.

Lachmann, Karl, ed. *Novum Testamentum Graece et Latine.* 2nd ed. 2 vols. Berlin: Reimer, 1842–1850.

———. "Rechenschaft über seine Ausgabe des Neuen Testaments." *TSK* 3 (1830): 817–45.
Leitzmann, Albert. *Briefe an Karl Lachmann aus den Jahren 1814–50.* APAW.PH. Berlin: Reimer, 1915.
Lücke, Friedrich. "Epimetron." *GGA* (1848): 499–511.
———. Review *Novum Testamentum Graece* by Karl Lachmann. *GGA* (1831): 657–76.
———. Review of *Novum Testamentum Graece et Latine*, by Karl Lachmann. *GGA* (1843): 1330–52.
Maas, Paul. *Textkritik.* 4th ed. Leipzig: Teubner, 1960.
Mink, Gerd. "Problems of a Highly Contaminated Tradition: The New Testament Stemmata of Variants as a Source of a Genealogy for Witnesses." Pages 13–85 in *Studies in Stemmatology II.* Edited by Pieter van Reenen, August den Hollander, and Margot van Mulken. Amsterdam: Benjamins, 2004.
Pasquali, Giorgio. *Storia della tradizione e critica del testo.* 2nd ed. Firenze: Le lettere, 2003.
Quentin, Dom Henri. *Essais de critique textuelle (Ecdotique).* Paris: Picard, 1926.
Rettig, H. C. M. Review of *Novum Testamentum Graece*, by Karl Lachmann. *ThStKr* 5 (1832): 861–901.
Robinson, Pieter M. W. "Computer-Assisted Stemmatic Analysis and 'Best-Text' Historical Editing." Pages 71–103 in *Studies in Stemmatology.* Edited by Pieter van Reenen and Margot Mulken. Amsterdam: Benjamins, 1996.
Schmidt, Peter Lebrecht. "Lachmann's Method: On the History of a Misunderstanding." Pages 11–18 *Traditio Latinitatis: Studien zur Rezeption und Überlieferung der lateinischen Literatur.* Edited by Joachim Fugmann, Martin Hose, and Bernhard Zimmermann. Stuttgart: Steiner, 2000.
Soden, Hans von. Reviews of *Novum Testamentum Graece*, by D. Eberhard Nestle and Erwin Nestle; *The Caesarean Text of the Gospel of Mark*, by Kirsopp Lake, Robert P. Blake, and Silva New. *Gnomon* 6 (1930): 199–212.
Sparks, Irving Alan. "Lachmann, Karl (1793–1851)." *TRE* 20:368–70.
Timpanaro, Sebastiano. *Die Entstehung der Lachmannschen Methode.* 2nd ed. Translated by Dieter Irmer. Hamburg: Buske, 1971.
———. *The Genesis of Lachmann's Method.* Edited and translated by Glenn W. Most. Chicago: University of Chicago, 2005.

Tischendorf, Constantin von. *Neue Jenaische Allgemeine Literaturzeitung* 2 (1843): 326–34.

———. "Zur Kritik des Neuen Testaments." *ThStKr* 15 (1842): 496–511.

Tregelles, Samuel Prideaux. *An Account of the Printed Text of the Greek New Testament: With Remarks on Its Revision upon Critical Principles: Together with a Collation of the Text of Griesbach, Scholz, Lachmann and Tischendorf with That in Common Use.* London: Bagster and Sons, 1854.

West, Martin L. *Textual Criticism and Editorial Technique Applicable to Greek and Latin Texts.* Stuttgart: Teubner, 1973.

Wilamowitz-Moellendorff, Ulrich von. *Geschichte der Philologie: Mit einem Nachwort und Register von Albert Henrichs.* Stuttgart: Teubner, 1998.

———. *History of Classical Scholarship.* Edited with introduction and notes by Hugh Lloyd-Jones. London: Duckworth, 1982.

Ziegler, Winfried. *Die "wahre strenghistorische Kritik": Leben und Werk Carl Lachmanns und sein Beitrag zur neutestamentlichen Wissenschaft.* Hamburg: Kovac, 2000.

13
Print Editions and Online Editions of the *Novum Testamentum Graece*: Facing New Challenges

1. An Online Edition of the *Novum Testamentum Graece* Faces New Challenges

For years theological publishers have offered online access to journals and even to their whole publishing program. On receipt of the annual payment, subscribers to the *Theologische Literaturzeitung*, for example, receive a code through the mail by means of which they can obtain access to all articles and reviews for the years 1996 to 2013.[1] In addition, it is possible to search through the indexes for the volumes 1876 to 1995.[2] Similarly, an important reviewing tool does not appear in print but only as an online journal: *TC: A Journal of Biblical Textual Criticism*.[3]

The first online edition of the Greek New Testament edited with a critical text appeared in 2010. This edition was presented as *The Greek New Testament: SBL Edition* (SBLGNT).[4] At the same time, its text was offered as a printed edition. It was edited by Michael W. Holmes, with the assistance of Rick Brannan. This edition, according to the editors, was intended to serve practical requirements but would also suit the requirements of critical analysis. In more than 540 units of variation, the text differs from the widely used text of Nestle-Aland.[5] The text also differs frequently from

---

1. See http://www.thlz.com.
2. The full access to all volumes of this journal is being prepared; see *TLZ* 139 (2014): 146.
3. http://purl.org/TC.
4. http://www.sblgnt.com.
5. Michael W. Holmes, ed., *The Greek New Testament: SBL Edition* (Atlanta: Society of Biblical Literature; Bellingham, WA: Logos Bible Software, 2010), viii.

the textual decisions found in the Editio Critica Maior of the Institute for New Testament Textual Research, Münster.[6]

The textual apparatus names neither Greek nor Latin witnesses nor other ancient translations and does not quote fathers or early lectionaries. It does not mention known corruptions and abstains from emending or from recommending emendation, even where emendations have been accepted into modern Bible translations.[7] In a Panel Review Session that took place in San Francisco in 2011 and was later published, the editor explained in detail the considerations that determined the form of the apparatus.[8] Instead of witnesses, the text-critical decisions from four seminal editions are named throughout.[9] Here the marginal readings are considered, if regarded by editors as equally valid alternatives. Occasionally

---

6. Michael W. Holmes, "Appendix: The SBLGNT in comparison to ECM," in Holmes, *The Greek New Testament: SBL Edition*, 515–16.

7. Holmes, *Greek New Testament*, ix–xviii. Suggested emendations are not normally listed. An exception to the rule will be cited later. In 2 Pet 3:10 a reading accepted into the text of the ECM is quoted in the apparatus by the note *em*, but is not accepted into the critical text. The ECM relies here on several ancient translations that testify to a negation. Among the rare conjectures in NA[28], Holmes names in Acts 16:12 πρώτης μερίδος τῆς—an absolutely convincing emendation of Le Clerc, yet he does not accept it into his critical text. The twenty-eighth edition of the Nestle-Aland integrated it into the edited text; see Barbara Aland, Kurt Aland, Johannes Karavidopoulos, Carlo M. Martini, and Bruce M. Metzger, eds., *Novum Testamentum Graece*, 28th ed. (Stuttgart: Deutsche Bibelgesellschaft, 2012), 435. See also Jan Krans, "Conjectural Emendation and the Text of the New Testament," in *The Text of the New Testament in Contemporary Research: Essays on the Status Quaestionis*, ed. Bart D. Ehrman and Michael W. Holmes, 2nd ed., NTTS 42 (Leiden: Brill, 2013), 613–35. A careful discussion of the problems of emending together with a new conjecture is presented by Nathan Thiel, "The Old But New Command in 1 John 2:7–8? A Proposed Emendation," *TC* 19 (2014): 1–13.

8. Michael Holmes et al., "The SBL Greek New Testament: Papers from the 2011 SBL Panel Review Session," *TC* 17 (2012): 1–7, 21–24.

9. Samuel Prideaux Tregelles, ed., *The Greek New Testament Edited from Ancient Authorities, With Their Various Readings in Full and the Latin Version of Jerome* (London: Bagster, 1857–1879); Brook Foss Westcott and Fenton John Anthony Hort, eds., *The New Testament in the Original Greek, Volume 1: Text; Volume 2: Introduction [and] Appendix* (Cambridge: Macmillan, 1881; 2nd ed., 1896); Richard J. Goodrich and Albert L. Lukaszewski, eds., *A Reader's Greek New Testament* (Grand Rapids: Zondervan, 2003); Maurice A. Robinson and William

the edition is alone with its decisions, and this deserves full recognition. Examples of readings that Holmes adopts include: in Matt 6:25, omit ἢ τί πίητε; in Matt 27:15 and 16, Ἰησοῦν Βαραββᾶν and Ἰησοῦν τὸν Βαραββᾶν; in John 1:34, ὁ ἐκλεκτός; in Heb 2:9, χωρίς; in Heb 3:2, omit ὅλῳ; in Heb 3:6, ὅς οἶκος; in Heb 4:3, omit τήν; in Heb 11:39, omit οὗτοι; in Heb 12:27, om. τήν.[10]

I am prepared to approve of all of these decisions. In addition, text and notes were supplied with an "Extensible Markup Language," so that a reader is able to mark words or parts of the text, to cut out text or to make notes in the margins.[11] Readers are requested to add their name when they add marginal notes. The entire text can be obtained free of charge from the internet as a PDF file.

2. The Nestle-Aland Online Faces the Challenge of the Internet

The Nestle-Aland is also available from the twenty-eighth edition onward both in a print and an internet version.[12] The print edition is presented with an impressive richness. This applies to the critical apparatus as much as to the additional information in the margins, and for the four appendices (I Codices Graeci et Latini, II Variae lectiones minores, III Loci citati vel allegati, IV Signa et abbreviationes). The detailed introduction in English and German shows to what a great extent many specialists have collaborated: in the examination of the Coptic versions of the Gospel of John, in the examination of the Latin, Coptic, and Syriac notations in the area of

---

G. Pierpont, *The New Testament in the Original Greek: Byzantine Textform 2005* (Southborough, MA: Chilton, 2005).

10. There is good reason to regard the investigations of the classical scholar Günther Zuntz as indispensable; see Günther Zuntz, *The Text of the Epistles: A Disquisition upon the Corpus Paulinum*, Schweich Lectures of the British Academy 1946 (London: Oxford University Press, 1953); Eberhard Güting, "The Methodological Contribution of Günther Zuntz to the Text of Hebrews," *NovT* 48 (2006): 359–78 [ch. 10 in this collection].

11. Technical aspects of such work are presented by Fotis Jannidis, "Elektronische Edition," in *Editionen zu deutschsprachigen Autoren als Spiegel der Editionsgeschichte*, ed. Rüdiger Nutt-Kofoth and Bodo Plachta (Tübingen: Niemeyer, 2005), 2:457–70; and by David C. Parker, "Through a Screen Darkly: Digital Texts and the New Testament," *JSNT* 25 (2003): 395–411; repr., in *Manuscripts, Texts, Theology: Collected Papers 1977–2007*, ANTF 40 (Berlin: de Gruyter, 2009), 287–304.

12. http://www.uni-muenster.de/NTTextforschung.

the Catholic letters, and in the documentation of the patristic quotations in the area of the Catholic Letters (NA[28]). The most important innovation in this edition is that it includes the progress of the Editio Critica Maior in its research on the Catholic Epistles. In this part of the New Testament the text of the ECM[2] is offered together with a large number of variants, while the rest of the text presents the decisions made for the twenty-seventh edition. The Nestle-Aland together with a great number of its resources is also available via the internet.[13] The presentation on the website of the Institute is no less impressive than the print edition.[14] The twenty-eighth edition can be read online.[15] Access to a text without a textual apparatus is given. Even something one would not advise anyone to do is possible here. Also online access to the most important Coptic manuscripts and to extensive bibliographical data is granted: SMR Datenbank koptischer neutestamentlicher Handschriften (SMR database for Coptic New Testament manuscripts).[16]

Access to numerous transcripts of important witnesses has been available for some time now; the bibliography shows that this file was generated in 2003. If we open the file, we find on request positive witnesses together with a list of witnesses unable to give testimony. We can work our way through the text either verse by verse or word by word.[17] We can obtain either complete transcripts of the manuscripts we have accessed or careful descriptions regarding the verses covered by the specific fragment, and, additionally, numerous bibliographical data. For this file it was deemed necessary to inform the reader which requirements his home computer would have to meet, in order to use the file (the SBL Greek font; either Windows Internet Explorer 5.0 or a later version, Netscape 6.0, Opera 6.0 or the later versions; and for Macintosh at least the version Mac OS X 10.0).

---

13. Several internet sites offer revised versions of the twenty-eighth edition. These add lexical, grammatical, and text comparing notes. Upon opening such sites, one is confronted with distinctly economic interests. The materials are offered on DVDs and are meant to promote the sales of additional products. See http://www.accordancebible.com or http://www.olivetree.com or http://www.logos.com.

14. http://egora.uni-muenster.de/intf.

15. http://www.nestle-aland.com/en/read-na28-online.

16. http://intf.uni-muenster.de/smr/.

17. http://nttranscripts.uni-muenster.de

The Institute for New Testament Textual Research in Münster is interested in obtaining the help of external researchers for numerous tasks that are still unfinished. For instance, there are transcripts of Greek witnesses still to be made, and, if necessary, suggestions for improvements to be passed on to the Institute. In the journal *Early Christianity*, the director of the Institute has already noted the collaboration with the University of Birmingham in the operation of the Virtual Manuscript Room, and thus encouraged internet users to collaborate.[18] But in the meantime many of the internet addresses given there are out of date.

The local-genealogical method, developed by Gerd Mink, can be used to generate probabilities in the assessment of relationships between documents.[19] This, however, is a demanding task, which the file "Genealogical Queries 2.0" can introduce us to.[20]

3. A Challenge from the Local-Genealogical Method of Gerd Mink

Mink's Coherence-Based Genealogical Method (CBGM) contributed in a definitive way to the completion of the Editio Critica Maior of the Catholic Letters. Numerous transcriptions of witnesses and specific computer programs were necessary in order to overcome the editorial problems and to produce a justifiable, although hypothetical, basic text.[21] Mink emphasizes in his reports that philology and philological methods shape the "iterative"

---

18. Holger Strutwolf, "Der 'New Testament Virtual Manuscript Room'—eine Online Plattform zum Studium der neutestamentlichen Textüberlieferung," *Early Christianity* 2 (2011): 275–77.

19. Gerd Mink: "Contamination, Coherence, and Coincidence in Textual Transmission: The Coherence-Based Genealogical Method (CBGM) as a Complement and Corrective to Existing Approaches," in *The Textual History of the Greek New Testament: Changing Views in Contemporary Research*, ed. Klaus Wachtel and Michael Holmes, TCSt 8 (Atlanta: Society of Biblical Literature, 2011): 141–216.

20. http://intf.uni-muenster.de/cbgm/index.html. See also http://egora.uni-muenster.de/intf/projekte/ecm.shtml.

21. Barbara Aland, Kurt Aland, Gerd Mink, Holger Strutwolf, and Klaus Wachtel, eds., *Novum Testamentum Graecum: Editio Critica Maior; Edited by the Institute for New Testament Textual Research; IV. Catholic Letters; Part 1: Text; Part 2: Supplementary Material*, 2nd ed. (Stuttgart: Deutsche Bibelgesellschaft, 2013). On the internet, Gerd Mink introduces his "Coherence Based Genealogical Method" in detail: http://egora.uni-muenster.de/intf/service/downloads_en.shtml.

approach toward clarification of the genealogical relationships between textual witnesses.[22]

In this respect his method can only be an addition to traditional philology, because it must contend at the same time with the problem of contamination, as also with the problems of the development of numerous variant readings, and likewise with the enormous loss of ancient witnesses. However, a caveat by Mink should be treated with reservation. Mink argues that work done on the basis of three types of ancient text is in the meantime out of date.[23] This traditional division of the ancient texts into Alexandrian, Western, and Byzantine manuscripts, which has been used for so long, is the basis of the procedures used in the SBL edition. With the aid of these, remarkable text-critical decisions were made.

First, Mink's admittedly complicated techniques must be introduced in brief. These are intended to deal with the effects of early contamination. Mink proceeds on complete transcriptions of selected Greek manuscripts, which are not produced by hand but generated digitally by means of the COLLATE program.[24] To begin with, computer programs decide which manuscripts are possibly related to one another. The resulting data do not yet imply genealogical relationship, but serve to establish lists of witnesses dependent on one another. A number of variants show a textual flow, sometimes very clearly, sometimes without sufficient clarity. In order to handle such variants in computer programs, numerical addresses are assigned to each word of the basic text and to each blank space, a procedure that ensures the exact placing of all variant readings. Next, each witness receives numerical recognition on the basis of the quality of its

---

22. "In the course of a revision it will be checked carefully whether a relationship between variants that appears to be philologically and genealogically plausible was overlooked or whether a previously favored relationship conflicts with the overall picture. In such cases strong philological reasons will be required to sustain the original assumption" (Mink, "Contamination, Coherence, and Coincidence," 204).

23. "At any rate we should not try to impose the concept of text-types on evidence that is far too complex to be adequately sorted by it" (Mink, "Contamination, Coherence, and Coincidence," 148 n. 16).

24. As the volumes of the *Editio Critica Maior* appeared, procedures were developed and, in the course of time, refined. Compare Peter M. Head, "The Editio Critica Maior: An Introduction and Assessment," *TynBul* 61 (2010): 131–52. The software designed by Peter Robinson and named "Collate."

transmitted text. By drafting local stemmata and then by drafting stemmata of complete passages a basic text is aimed for.

A full criticism of this procedure can and will not be given.[25] But in the meantime the results and the collections of the Editio Critica Maior are available. It is possible to examine the text-critical decisions of these volumes cautiously and in a limited fashion.

It must be emphasized that, with the completion of this edition in its impressive richness, variants and their witnesses have been listed and arranged with great clarity. Beside the patristic quotations, ancient translations are among the witnesses. The editors maintain that in making text-critical decisions, it is not possible to claim the same degree of certainty throughout. In ECM² a "split guiding line" (in ECM¹ it was a pair of bold dots in the text line) alerts the reader to alternative readings that, from a critical viewpoint, are possibly preferable. The twenty-eighth edition of the Nestle-Aland uses for this purpose a ♦ (rhombus/diamond). Similarly the use of square brackets ([ ]) serves to emphasize this critical position.[26]

Besides the new developments in the field of New Testament textual criticism presented here, tried and tested philological approaches continue in use. The careful observation of the procedures of copyists belongs to these.[27]

4. The Impact of a "Digital Revolution" on the Interpretation of New Testament Texts

Digital editions of the New Testament open up new possibilities for scientific work on the texts. Further possibilities are becoming available now. In the course of the publication of the *Editio Critica Maior* much preparatory

---

25. For a discussion of Mink's procedure, see Scott Charlesworth's review of *The Textual History of the Greek New Testament: Changing Views in Contemporary Research*, ed. Klaus Wachtel and Michael W. Holmes, *TC:* (2013); https://tinyurl.com/sbl7012e; §§10–15 discuss Mink.

26. "Square brackets in the text (([]) except in the case of the Catholic Letters indicate that textual critics today are not completely convinced of the authenticity of the enclosed words.... Square brackets always reflect a great degree of difficulty in determining the text" (NA[28], 54*); "The sign ♦ (diamond) indicates passages where the guiding line is split in the second edition of the ECM, because there are two variants which in the editors' judgement could equally well be adopted in the reconstructed initial text" (NA[28], 55*).

27. Wachtel and Holmes, *Textual History of the Greek New Testament*.

work was included in the printed volumes, and in particular the result of collations covering test passages.[28] Also digital editions of manuscripts and of collections of variant readings[29] have been prepared or have already been published. The important Codex Sinaiticus has been available digitally for some time.[30] At present the main focus of work is on the analysis and presentation of the transmission of the Acts of the Apostles as well as on digital materials for the edition of the Gospel of John within the framework of the *Editio Critica Maior*.[31]

5. A Text-Critical Comparison of Two Online Editions

Two digital editions of the Greek New Testament are presently available. A comparison of their edited texts will be given in brief. Attention is centered upon the decisive arguments.[32]

---

28. Kurt Aland, ed., *Text und Textwert der griechischen Handschriften des Neuen Testaments*, ANTF 1-5, 9-11, 16-21, 27-31, 35-36 (Berlin: de Gruyter, 1987-2005).

29. Among the materials available is a collation of chapter 18 of the Gospel of John that covers two thousand manuscripts, as well as a collation of all majuscule manuscripts of the Gospel of John prepared by the International Greek New Testament Project: http://iohannes.com/transcriptions/index.html. Papyri and minuscule manuscripts have largely been transcribed and may be accessed online at the same location.

30. http://www.codexsinaiticus.org/en/.

31. Details concerning the above paragraph may be found in Hugh A. G. Houghton, "Recent Developments in New Testament Textual Criticism," *Early Christianity* 2 (2011): 245-58. For additional information see Krans, "Conjectural Emendation," 613-35; and Head, "Introduction and Assessment," 131-52.

32. Critical reviews of *Novum Testamentum Graecum: Editio Critica Maior, IV. Catholic Letters, Installment 1: James* (1997): J. Keith Elliott, *NovT* 40 (1998): 195-204; David C. Parker, *TLZ* 127 (2002): 297-300; Parker, "The Development of the Critical Text of the Epistle of James: From Lachmann to the *Editio Critica Maior*," in *New Testament Textual Criticism and Exegesis: Festschrift J. Delobel*, ed. Adelbert Denaux, BETL 161 (Leuven: Leuven University Press, 2002), 317-30. Reviews of *Installment 2: The Letters of Peter*: J. Keith Elliott, *NovT* 42 (2000): 328-39; David C. Parker, *TLZ* 127 (2002): 297-300; Elliott, "The *Editio Critica Maior*: One Reader's Reactions," in *Recent Developments in Textual Criticism: New Testament, Other Early Christian and Jewish Literature*, ed. Wim Weren and Dietrich-Alex Koch, STAR 8 (Assen: van Gorcum, 2003), 129-44. Review of *Installment 3: The First Letter of John*: J. Keith Elliott, *TLZ* 129 (2004): 1068-71.

James 2:4: Here the form of the argument and the specific variation of the testimony support the text of the SBLGNT (οὐ διεκρίθητε), at any rate if we give due weight to the Egyptian witnesses. In the ECM the Byzantine witnesses were given greater weight, so that now a different reading was chosen: καὶ οὐ διεκρίθητε.³³

James 2:14, 16: In the Editio Critica Maior, τί τὸ ὄφελος is preferred in 2:14 and in 2:16. Paul uses the expression similarly in the apodosis of a conditional phrase: τί μοι τὸ ὄφελος (1 Cor 15:32). The majuscules B and C* as also the minuscules 631 1175 L 593 Dam leave out the article (as does SBLGNT). In such a type of variation this testimony is not sufficient to decide against the large majority of witnesses supporting the ECM reading.

James 4:12: However, the testimony for a νομοθέτης lacking the article is strong: P⁷⁴ P¹⁰⁰ 01 02 03 025 044 and numerous minuscules. Here we prefer the anarthrous reading of the SBLGNT.

James 5:4: Bruce M. Metzger adopted the text of B* and ℵ, namely, ἀφυστερημένος, and argued in a minority vote for the rare wording, which was apparently later replaced by scribes.³⁴ Walter Bauer had also opted for this reading in his dictionary. So here we should fall in line with the SBLGNT.

1 Peter 1:16: Holmes apparently made a wrong decision here. διότι γέγραπται ἅγιοι ἔσεσθε, ὅτι ἐγὼ ἅγιος is correct (rather than γέγραπται ὅτι).

Reviews of *Installment 4: The Second and Third Letter of John; The Letter of Jude*: J. Keith Elliott, *TLZ* 131 (2006): 1156–59; Head, "Introduction and Assessment," 131–52.

Review of *Novum Testamentum Graecum: Editio Critica Maior*, IV. *Catholic Letters*, 2nd ed.: Karl-Wilhelm Niebuhr, *TLZ* 138 (2013): 1236–38.

Reviews of *Novum Testamentum Graece*, 28th ed.: Karl-Wilhelm Niebuhr, *TLZ* 138 (2013): 323–25; J. Keith Elliott, "A New Edition of Nestle-Aland, Greek New Testament," *JTS* 64 (2013): 48–65; Anthony J. Forte, "Observations on the 28th Revised Edition of Nestle-Aland's *Novum Testamentum Graece*," *Bib* 94 (2013): 268–92.

Review of *The Greek New Testament*, 5th ed.: Eberhard Güting, *TLZ* 140 (2015): 64–65.

33. Barbara Aland et al., *Testamentum Graecum: Editio Critica Maior; Edited by the Institute for New Testament Textual Research; IV. Catholic Letters/ Die Katholischen Briefe; Part 1, Text* (Stuttgart: Deutsche Bibelgesellschaft, 2000), 24* n. 4.

34. Bruce M. Metzger, *A Textual Commentary on the Greek New Testament: A Companion Volume to the United Bible Societies' Greek New Testament (Fourth Revised Edition)*, 2nd ed. (Stuttgart: Deutsche Bibelgesellschaft, 1994), 614.

1 Peter 1:22: The variants reveal that καθαρᾶς should be deleted. Holmes deleted it. Metzger's *Textual Commentary* remained undecided and printed the adjective in square brackets: [καθαρᾶς].[35] The NA[28] printed ⸱ καθαρᾶς καρδίας, using the rhombus (⸱) to signal uncertainty as to its status.

1 Peter 2:5: The testimony of this unit of variation and the language of the letter support θεῷ without the article. Accordingly the SBLGNT and the NA[28]—and now ECM[2]—omit it. ECM[1] offered τῷ θεῷ, and included the article between black dots to signal a possibly preferable alternative.

1 Peter 2:25: The text of this epistle originally had the elision ἀλλ', and not ἀλλά. Hence the text of the ECM and of the NA[28] is to be preferred.

1 Peter 3:1: γυναῖκες without the article is the better reading and claims the better testimony. We ought to agree with Holmes. Metzger's *Textual Commentary* stayed undecided and put the article in square brackets: [αἱ].[36] ECM[1] put the article between two black dots to signal a possibly preferable alternative; ECM[2], however, simply prints αἱ γυναῖκες.

1 Peter 3:22: The testimony of this unit of variation and the language of the epistle support θεοῦ without the article. Holmes decided accordingly. ECM[2] and NA[28] print τοῦ θεοῦ; ECM[1] had put the article between black dots.

1 Peter 4:16: ECM prints τῷ μέρει τούτῳ.[37] The alternative τῷ ὀνόματι τούτῳ (read by NA[27] and SBLGNT) commands strong external support (including P[72] ℵ A B 1739 latt sy co). The testimony for the former reading is rather strong, but is almost confined to Byzantine witnesses. It is an important issue, whether occasionally Byzantine readings may be accepted. Holmes often does accept such readings (though not in this instance).

1 Peter 5:9: ἐν τῷ κόσμῳ is to be preferred because of its testimony: P[72] ℵ B. Holmes prints it thus. ECM[1] printed ⸱ἐν κόσμῳ⸱ (the dots indicating a degree of uncertainty), while ECM[2] printed both readings on a split guiding line, leaving the textual decision undecided.

1 Peter 5:11 The brief εἰς τοὺς αἰῶνας is preferable. Thus the ECM[1]

---

35. Metzger, *Textual Commentary*, 618.
36. Metzger, *Textual Commentary*, 620.
37. For a discussion of the CBGM analysis underlying this decision, see Gerd Mink, "Problems of a Highly Contaminated Tradition: The New Testament Stemmata of Variants as a Source of a Genealogy for Witnesses," in *Studies in Stemmatology II*, ed. Pieter van Reenen, August den Hollander, and Margot van Mulken (Amsterdam: Benjamins, 2004), 43–45.

(with a dot, signaling uncertainty) and Metzger's *Textual Commentary*.[38] ECM², however, left the choice undecided.

2 Peter 1:9: Because of the frequency of abstract nouns ending in -μα, it appears that in v. 9 the original reading is ἁμαρτημάτων, and so SBLGNT prints. But the testimony in this unit of variation speaks against this assumption. The ECM¹ decided accordingly, but admitted uncertainty and for this reason printed between two black dots ἁμαρτιῶν. NA²⁸ likewise printed ἁμαρτιῶν. ECM² declined to make a decision.

2 Peter 2:6: Here Holmes accepted the convincing text and the stronger testimony: ἀσεβέσιν, with P⁷² 03 025 and among numerous minuscules 442 1175 1243 1852 sy. ECM¹ preferred ἀσεβεῖν, printed between dots; ECM² and NA²⁸ print ἀσεβεῖν. Metzger's *Textual Commentary* remained undecided: ἀσεβέ[σ]ιν.[39]

2 Peter 2:11 As παρὰ κυρίου has not been preserved firmly, the decision of the SBLGNT to print only αὐτῶν is justified. The ECM¹ preferred παρὰ κυρίῳ. ECM², however, prints παρὰ κυρίῳ on a split guiding line with its omission as the alternative, thereby declining to decide; thus NA²⁸ prints παρὰ κυρίῳ with a rhombus. Metzger supported the omission of the phrase in his minority vote, but did not argue assuredly.[40]

2 Peter 2:19: The Coptic text, among other good witnesses like P⁷² ℵ* B, justifies the omission of the additional καί. The ECM¹ decided accordingly, but signaled uncertainty with a dot. ECM² and NA²⁸ omit. SBLGNT followed ℵ² A C P Ψ 048 307 1735 1739, the Byzantine tradition, and vg sy in printing καί.

2 Peter 2:20: The phrase τοῦ κυρίου ἡμῶν καὶ σωτῆρος Ἰησοῦ Χριστοῦ is found repeatedly in the text of the author (1:11; 3:18). If we accept the pronoun ἡμῶν in the passage 2:20, we have here the comparable passage τοῦ κυρίου ἡμῶν καὶ σωτῆρος Ἰησοῦ Χριστοῦ. Occasionally words have been lost in the course of transmission, as, for instance, the omission of καθὼς καὶ ὁ κύριος ἡμῶν in 1:14 by ℵ. The phrase τοῦ κυρίου ἡμῶν, as found in 3:15, was transmitted in a defective form (τοῦ κυρίου) by P and, among other minuscules, 307 1175 1243 syᵖʰ boᵐˢ. Here in the passage 2:20, the pronoun ἡμῶν is missing in B 88 307 321 453 720 915 918 996 1661 1678 1751 2818 Byz PsOec. This seems to be in conflict with the regular language of the author,

---

38. Metzger, *Textual Commentary*, 628.
39. Metzger, *Textual Commentary*, 633.
40. Metzger, *Textual Commentary*, 633.

but we should not follow these witnesses here. The text of ECM¹ is to be preferred, τοῦ κυρίου ἡμῶν καὶ σωτῆρος Ἰησοῦ Χριστοῦ, even though ἡμῶν is placed between two black dots. Metzger's *Textual Commentary* decided differently. His verdict states ἡμῶν to be an addition,[41] and is followed by SBLGNT and ECM².

2 Peter 3:6: The context demands the reading of P 69 398 876 945 1067 1175 1729 2652 *l*590 vg^mss Aug, which must be followed: δι' ὅν; so ECM and NA²⁸. Holmes judged differently, printing δι' ὧν with P⁷² ℵ A B C Ψ 048 5 33 81 307 436 442 1735 1739 1852 2344 Byz lat sy co.

2 Peter 3:10: As can be gathered from diverse variants, the text has survived only in translations, in particular in the Sahidic: οὐχ εὑρεθήσεται sy^ph mss sa cv^vid. ECM and NA²⁸ printed their texts accordingly. Holmes decided differently. Metzger discussed the numerous variants and gave a list of modern emendations.[42]

2 Peter 3:16: The future tense is not really supported by the context. So we should follow with Holmes the simpler and well-supported στρεβλοῦσιν.

2 Peter 3:18: In the Festschrift for Heinz Schreckenberg I argued that the "Amen" should be retained at the end of 2 Peter.[43] The SBLGNT has also adhered to this text-critical judgment as against the ECM² and NA²⁸ (ECM¹ marked the omission with a dot). Metzger's *Textual Commentary* put the "Amen" in square brackets and expressed "a considerable measure of doubt as to its right to stand in the text."[44]

1 John 1:7: The testimony for a δέ is very impressive. To its omission testify Ψ, some minuscules, the original hand of the ancient Latin z*, and in addition manuscripts of the Bohairic translation, Cyrill, and MaxConf. That is not much. And yet the flow of parallel conditional phrases shows that no δέ is needed. A sequence seemingly continuing the text of verse 6 was the cause of the insertion. ECM¹ omitted it (but signaled uncertainty with a dot); SBLGNT included it; the editors of ECM² declined to make a decision.

1 John 2:6: The testimony for leaving out οὕτως is rather weak. B and

---

41. Metzger, *Textual Commentary*, 635–36.
42. Metzger, *Textual Commentary*, 636–37.
43. Eberhard Güting, "Amen, Eulogie, Doxologie: Eine textkritische Untersuchung," in *Begegnungen zwischen Christentum und Judentum in Antike und Mittelalter: Festschrift für Heinz Schreckenberg*, ed. Dietrich-Alex Koch and Hermannn Lichtenberger. SIJD 1 (Göttingen: Vandenhoeck & Ruprecht, 1993), 158–59 [ch. 4 in this collection].
44. Metzger, *Textual Commentary*, 638.

A are the two majuscules. But the testimony of the fathers is clear: Cl Cyr. And again the Itala witness z is among the witnesses. Therefore the οὕτως will have to be deleted, as in Holmes. Metzger's *Textual Commentary* remained irresolute: [οὕτως].[45] ECM¹ printed it; ECM² placing it on a split guiding line with its omission, declined to decide.

1 John 2:16: The SBLGNT prints ἀλλὰ ἐκ τοῦ κόσμου. Yet the author evidently seeks to avoid the hiatus, an endeavor in which he is not always successful. Several times we find ἀλλ' in his texts (2:7, 16, 19 [2x], 21, 27; 3:18; 4:18; 5:6, 19). We cannot rely on the testimony of B and C in such a matter. The ἀλλ' in the Editio Critica Maior is correct.

1 John 2:29: This καί is superfluous and disrupts the author's measured style. The testimonies of B and Ψ for its omission are strengthened by numerous Byzantine and non-Byzantine minuscules, by translations, and especially by the Itala witnesses. Holmes printed accordingly.

1 John 3:13: The evidence for the omission of καί, namely, B A and numerous minuscule manuscripts, is crucially strengthened by the Latin, the entire Coptic transmission, and sy^h. Holmes omits; Metzger's *Textual Commentary* remains undecided here ([καί])[46]; ECM¹ printed it between dots; ECM² includes it.

1 John 3:19: As in verse 13, the testimony of B A and more than twenty minuscules (including 436 623 1735 2344 2541) for the omission of καί is strengthened by the Latin and the Coptic transmission, by sy^h mss, by the redaction A1 of the Old Georgian, and here by Clement of Alexandria as well. καί should be deleted, as in the SBLGNT.

1 John 3:21: The unclear position of ἡμῶν before μὴ καταγινώσκῃ was the reason for not only the many alternative locations of the pronoun, but also for the discarding of the pronoun by B. The testimony of C is strengthened by 442 1852 *l*596, by Cl^lat and Or. The *Editio Critica Maior* (followed by NA²⁸) printed accordingly ἡμῶν μὴ καταγινώσκῃ. Metzger's *Textual Commentary* remained undecided: [ἡμῶν].[47]

1 John 5:10: It is not appropriate to print a reflexive αὐτῷ, as Holmes does. Nestle-Aland does not. The testimony of ℵ Ψ and some of the Byzantines (for ἐν ἑαυτῷ) is here not decisive. Accordingly, the Editio Critica

---

45. Metzger, *Textual Commentary*, 639–40.
46. Metzger, *Textual Commentary*, 642–43.
47. Metzger, *Textual Commentary*, 643–44.

Maior prints ἐν αὐτῷ. But the *Textual Commentary* of Metzger decided on ἐν ἑαυτῷ (the minority preferred αὐτῷ).[48]

Jude 15: πᾶσαν ψυχήν, by testimony of P[72] ℵ 1852 sa bo[mss] sy[ph mss], fits the context well. Byzantine and other witnesses (including A B C 044) accentuate the text and emphasize the element ἀσέβεια (reading πάντας τοὺς ἀσεβεῖς). The *Editio Critica Maior* offers a completely justifiable text here.

Jude 16: ἑαυτῶν cannot be justified in this sentence. We agree with Holmes.

6. Result of the Comparison

With the publication of two online editions, a new situation has arisen for the user of philologically edited New Testament texts, which affects the practical access to these texts in many ways. In view of this new development an important point may easily be overlooked. Each edition introduces its own approach. It should not be overlooked that the SBLGNT has appeared with a new approach, an approach that led to revised decisions in many places of textual variation. Holmes, the editor, has expressly focused on a comparison with the Editio Critica Maior. This challenge must be recognized. The Editio Critica Maior likewise presents a new text-critical approach, which undertakes a reevaluation of variants by means of sophisticated computer programs. Moreover this edition expressly emphasizes uncertainty in the evaluation of its results. These points should both be appreciated and ought to be considered. My comparison above of both texts seeks to point out decisive features for future discussion. This comparison also leads to its own provisional result: As the text-critical examination has shown, the use of both editions, insofar as they have edited the same texts, is to be recommended.

Bibliography

Aland, Barbara, Kurt Aland, Johannes Karavidopoulos, Carlo M. Martini, and Bruce M. Metzger, eds. *Novum Testamentum Graece*. 28th ed. Stuttgart: Deutsche Bibelgesellschaft, 2012.

Aland, Barbara, Kurt Aland, Gerd Mink, Holger Strutwolf, and Klaus Wachtel, eds. *Novum Testamentum Graecum: Editio Critica Maior;*

---

48. Metzger, *Textual Commentary*, 649.

Edited by the Institute for New Testament Textual Research; IV. Catholic Letters; Part 1: Text; Part 2: Supplementary Material. 2nd ed. Stuttgart: Deutsche Bibelgesellschaft, 2013.

———, eds., *Novum Testamentum Graecum: Editio Critica Maior; Edited by the Institute for New Testament Textual Research; Installment 2: Catholic Letters. VI.2. The Letters of Peter. Part 1: Text; Part 2: Supplementary Material.* Stuttgart: Deutsche Bibelgesellschaft, 2000.

———, eds., *Novum Testamentum Graecum: Editio Critica Maior; Edited by the Institute for New Testament Textual Research; Installment 3. Catholic Letters. IV.3. The First Letter of John. Part 1: Text; Part 2: Supplementary Material.* Stuttgart: Deutsche Bibelgesellschaft, 2003.

———, eds., *Novum Testamentum Graecum: Editio Critica Maior; Edited by the Institute for New Testament Textual Research; Installment 4. Catholic Letters. IV.4. The Second and Third Letter of John. The Letter of Jude. Part 1: Text, Part 2: Supplementary Material.* Stuttgart: Deutsche Bibelgesellschaft, 2005.

Aland, Kurt, ed. *Text und Textwert der griechischen Handschriften des Neuen Testaments.* ANTF 1–5, 9–11, 16–21, 27–31, 35–36. Berlin: de Gruyter, 1987–2005.

Charlesworth, Scott. Review of *The Textual History of the Greek New Testament: Changing Views in Contemporary Research*, edited by Klaus Wachtel and Michael W. Holmes. *TC* (2013). https://tinyurl.com/sbl7012e.

Elliott, J. Keith. "The *Editio Critica Maior*: One Reader's Reactions." Pages 129–49 in *Recent Developments in Textual Criticism: New Testament, Other Early Christian and Jewish Literature.* Edited by Wim Weren and Dietrich-Alex Koch. STAR 8. Assen: Van Gorcum, 2003.

———. "A New Edition of Nestle-Aland, *Greek New Testament*." *JTS* 64 (2013): 48–65.

———. Review of *Novum Testamentum Graecum: Editio Critica Maior, IV. Catholic Letters, Installment 1: James. NovT* 40 (1998): 195–204.

———. Review of *Novum Testamentum Graecum: Editio Critica Maior, IV. Catholic Letters, Installment 2: The Letters of Peter. NovT* 42 (2000): 328–39.

———. Review of *Novum Testamentum Graecum: Editio Critica Maior, IV. Catholic Letters, Installment 3: The First Letter of John. TLZ* 129 (2004): 1068–71.

———. Review of *Novum Testamentum Graecum: Editio Critica Maior, IV. Catholic Letters, Installment 4: The Second and Third Letter of John; The Letter of Jude*. *TLZ* 131 (2006): 1156–59.

Forte, Anthony J. "Observations on the 28th Revised Edition of Nestle-Aland's *Novum Testamentum Graece*." *Bib* 94 (2013): 268–92.

Goodrich, Richard J., and Albert L. Lukaszewski, eds. *A Reader's Greek New Testament*. Grand Rapids: Zondervan, 2003.

Güting, Eberhard. "Amen, Eulogie, Doxologie: Eine textkritische Untersuchung." Pages 133–62 in *Begegnungen zwischen Christentum und Judentum in Antike und Mittelalter: Festschrift Heinz Schreckenberg*. Edited by Dietrich-Alex Koch and Hermann Lichtenberger. SIJD 1. Göttingen: Vandenhoeck & Ruprecht, 1993. [chapter 4 in this collection]

———. "The Methodological Contribution of Günther Zuntz to the Text of Hebrews." *NovT* 48 (2006): 359–78. [chapter 10 in this collection]

———. Review of *The Greek New Testament*, 5th ed. *TLZ* 140 (2015): 64–65.

Head, Peter M. "The *Editio Critica Maior*: An Introduction and Assessment." *TynBul* 61 (2010): 131–52.

Holmes, Michael W. "Appendix: The SBLGNT in Comparison to ECM." In *The Greek New Testament: SBL Edition*. Edited by Michael W. Holmes. Atlanta: Society of Biblical Literature; Bellingham, WA: Logos Bible Software, 2010.

———, ed. *The Greek New Testament: SBL Edition*. Atlanta: Society of Biblical Literature; Bellingham, WA: Logos Bible Software, 2010.

Holmes, Michael W., David Parker, Harold Attridge, and Klaus Wachtel, "The SBL Greek New Testament: Papers from the 2011 SBL Panel Review Session." *TC* 17 (2012): 1–24.

Houghton, Hugh A. G. "Recent Developments in New Testament Textual Criticism." *Early Christianity* 2 (2011): 245–58.

Jannidis, Fotis. "Elektronische Edition." Pages 457–70 in vol. 2 of *Editionen zu deutschsprachigen Autoren als Spiegel der Editionsgeschichte*. Edited by Rüdiger Nutt-Kofoth and Bodo Plachta. 2 vols. Tübingen: Niemeyer, 2005.

Krans, Jan. "Conjectural Emendation and the Text of the New Testament." Pages 613–35 in *The Text of the New Testament in Contemporary Research: Essays on the Status Quaestionis*. Edited by Bart D. Ehrman and Michael W. Holmes. 2nd ed. NTTS 42. Leiden: Brill, 2013.

Metzger, Bruce M. *A Textual Commentary on the Greek New Testament: A Companion Volume to the United Bible Societies' Greek New Testament*

(Fourth Revised Edition). 2nd ed. Stuttgart: Deutsche Bibelgesellschaft, 1994.

Mink, Gerd. "Contamination, Coherence, and Coincidence in Textual Transmission: The Coherence-Based Genealogical Method (CBGM) as a Complement and Corrective to Existing Approaches." Pages 141–216 in *The Textual History of the Greek New Testament: Changing Views in Contemporary Research*. Edited by Klaus Wachtel and Michael W. Holmes. TCSt 8. Atlanta: Society of Biblical Literature, 2011.

———. "Problems of a Highly Contaminated Tradition: The New Testament Stemmata of Variants as a Source of a Genealogy for Witnesses." Pages 13–85 in *Studies in Stemmatology II*. Edited by Pieter van Reenen, August den Hollander, and Margot van Mulken. Amsterdam: Benjamins, 2004.

Niebuhr, Karl-Wilhelm. Review of *Novum Testamentum Graece*, 28th ed. *TLZ* 138 (2013): 323–25.

———. Review of *Novum Testamentum Graecum: Editio Critica Maior, IV. Catholic Letters*, 2nd ed. *TLZ* 138 (2013): 1236–38.

Parker, David C. "The Development of the Critical Text of the Epistle of James: From Lachmann to the *Editio Critica Maior*." Pages 317–30 in *New Testament Textual Criticism and Exegesis: Festschrift J. Delobel*. Edited by Adelbert Denaux. BETL 161. Leuven: Leuven University Press, 2002.

———. Review of *Novum Testamentum Graecum: Editio Critica Maior, IV. Catholic Letters, Installment 1: James*. *TLZ* 127 (2002): 297–300.

———. Review of *Novum Testamentum Graecum: Editio Critica Maior, IV. Catholic Letters, Installment 2: The Letters of Peter*. *TLZ* 127 (2002): 297–300.

———. "Through a Screen Darkly: Digital Texts and the New Testament." *JSNT* 25 (2003): 395–411. Repr., pages 287–304 in *Manuscripts, Texts, Theology: Collected Papers 1977–2007*. ANTF 40. Berlin: de Gruyter, 2009.

Robinson, Maurice A., and William G. Pierpont. *The New Testament in the Original Greek: Byzantine Textform 2005*. Southborough, MA: Chilton, 2005.

Strutwolf, Holger. "Der 'New Testament Virtual Manuscript Room'—eine Online Plattform zum Studium der neutestamentlichen Textüberlieferung." *Early Christianity* 2 (2011): 275–77.

Thiel, Nathan. "The Old But New Command in 1 John 2:7–8? A Proposed Emendation." *TC* 19 (2014): 1–13.

Tregelles, Samuel Prideaux, ed. *The Greek New Testament Edited from Ancient Authorities, with Their Various Readings in Full and the Latin Version of Jerome.* London: Bagster, 1857–1879.

Wachtel, Klaus, and Michael W. Holmes, eds. *The Textual History of the Greek New Testament: Changing Views in Contemporary Research.* TCSt 8. Atlanta: Society of Biblical Literature, 2011.

Westcott, Brooke Foss, and Fenton John Anthony Hort, eds. *The New Testament in the Original Greek: Volume 1, Text; Volume 2, Introduction [and] Appendix.* Cambridge: Macmillan, 1881. 2nd ed., 1896.

Zuntz, Günther. *The Text of the Epistles: A Disquisition upon the Corpus Paulinum.* Schweich Lectures of the British Academy 1946. London: Oxford University Press, 1953.

14
The Form of the New Testament Acclamation κύριος Ἰησοῦς: A Text-Critical Investigation

One of the most impressive, and perhaps the earliest of the ancient Christ *encomia* is found in the parting letter sent by St. Paul to the church in Philippi (Phil 2:6–11). This text compares with similar texts that deal with the topic of the divine mission of Jesus, all of them in an excellent stylistic form (Heb 1:1–2:1; 1 Tim 3:16; Col 1:15–20).[1]

The text quoted from the epistle to the Philippians exhibits a concise yet impressive style. Two sentences contrast the willing degradation of the Son and his subsequent restoration. This text heralds the acclamation of all beings under the sun, a process of eschatological dimension. "Regarding Philippians 2:6–11 we can demonstrate that this text in every respect is the earliest of all references compared ... and that here an exceptional tradition of the mission of the divine messenger was used."[2]

Other authors refer here to an ancient hymn that exalted Christ. The text of this hymn was identified as an early pre-Pauline hymn in a remarkable study by Ernst Lohmeyer.[3] In his New Testament commentary

---

1. Klaus Berger, *Formen und Gattungen im Neuen Testament* (Tübingen: Francke, 2005), 401–12; Larry W. Hurtado, *Lord Jesus Christ: Devotion to Jesus in Earliest Christianity* (Grand Rapids: Eerdmans, 2003); The specific approach to the history of religion used by this author has been discussed by Jörg Frey, "Eine neue religionsgeschichtliche Perspektive: Larry W. Hurtados Lord Jesus Christ und die Herausbildung der frühen Christologie," in *Reflections on the Early Christian History of Religion/Erwägungen zur frühchristlichen Religionsgeschichte*, ed. Cilliers Breytenbach and Jörg Frey, AGJU 81 (Leiden: Brill, 2013), 117–69.

2. Berger, *Formen und Gattungen*, 402, with reference to Berger, "Hellenistische Gattungen und Neues Testament," *ANRW* 25.2:1184–85 n. 159.

3. Ernst Lohmeyer, *Die Briefe an die Philipper, Kolosser und an Philemon*, 11th ed., KEK 9.1 (Göttingen: Vandenhoeck & Ruprecht, 1956); Lohmeyer and

Lohmeyer accounted for his views in detail. Lohmeyer considered Phil 2:6–11 to be a pre-Pauline text, carefully designed, but distinguished from Paul's speech. Lohmeyer referred to the use of κενοῦν *malo sensu* by Paul in distinction to its use in this hymn. He pointed to ταπεινοῦν used in a very specific way and to the non-Pauline terminology: ὑπερυψοῦν, μορφή, σχῆμα.[4] Some authors deny that Phil 2:6–11 is a pre-Pauline hymn, as for instance, Marius Reiser: "The assumption of a pre-Pauline hymn as an original independent text is quite improbable."[5]

My topic is a text-critical topic. There is no intention of studying the Christ *encomion* quoted in Philippians intensively. Here, therefore, the topic is not a detailed interpretation of its text but whether the last verse, Phil 2:11, has been transmitted correctly. On comparing all editions of the Greek New Testament since the days of Karl Lachmann, we find that all editors edited the same sequence: ὅτι κύριος Ἰησοῦς Χριστὸς εἰς δόξαν θεοῦ πατρός.

Textual variation is noted, but the texts of the editions are identical. No variant is accepted.[6] The impressive study of Jean-Baptiste Édart of the École Biblique et Archéologique de Jerusalem does not refer to the problem of the critical text; he quotes the words in the sequence given above.[7] The question of what meaning is to be given to the word "Christ" in this context is never asked.

Werner Schmauch, *Die Briefe an die Philipper, Kolosser und an Philemon*, 13th ed., KEK 9.1 (Göttingen: Vandenhoeck & Ruprecht, 1964). See the fundamental study by Ernst Lohmeyer: *Kyrios Jesus: Eine Untersuchung zu Phil. 2,5–11*, SHAW. PH 4 (Heidelberg: Winter, 1928; repr., Darmstadt: Wissenschaftliche Buchgesellschaft, 1962). Regarding the effects of this study see Jean-Baptiste Édart, *L' Épitre aux Philippiens, rhetorique et composition stylistique* (Paris: Gabalda, 2002): 128 n. 1; and Samuel Vollenweider, "Dienst und Verführung, Überlegungen zur Kommentierung des 'Briefs an die Philipper,'" in *Der Philipperbrief des Paulus in der hellenistischen Welt*, ed. Jörg Frey and Benjamin Schliesser, WUNT 353 (Tübingen: Mohr Siebeck, 2015), 376 n. 1. The argument of Ernst Lohmeyer was accepted by Hans-Dieter Betz, *Studies in Paul's Letter to the Philippians*, WUNT 343 (Tübingen: Mohr Siebeck, 2015), 10, 15.

4. Lohmeyer, *Briefe an die Philipper*, 90–99.

5. Marius Reiser, *Sprache und literarische Formen des Neuen Testaments: Eine Einführung* (Paderborn: Schöningh, 2001), 176.

6. This also holds true regarding the quotation of the passage by Betz, *Studies in Paul's Letter*, 43 n. 131, 44.

7. Édart, Épitre aux *Philippiens*, 168.

Clearly numerous authors have no qualms about quoting the standard text as edited by the Nestle-Aland edition. In contrast to the regular decision by all modern editions in favor of a secondary κύριος Ἰησοῦς Χριστός in the passage Phil 2:11 one needs to recall that Günther Zuntz in his pioneering investigation identified numerous weakly attested, yet original readings in the passages he examined.[8] It is necessary, therefore, to examine the ancient testimony.

Certainly, the title "ruler" is emphatically conferred on the subject.[9] But what follows disturbs the obvious sequence. The alternative testimony to merely two words, κύριος Ἰησοῦς, needs to be taken into account. The edition of Nestle-Aland quotes two majuscules, one minuscule, two Itala witnesses, some ancient witnesses to the early text of Origen, and, finally, one Sahidic manuscript.[10] The fifth edition of *The Greek New Testament* adds to the list; the combined testimony of the two editions includes: (A^c) F G 1505* *l*591 it$^{b, g, o}$ vg^{ms} sa^{ms} Origen^{lat½} Gregory-Nyssa$^{2/10}$ Didymus-$^{dub1/4}$ Hesychius$^{2/3}$ Novatian Rebaptism Cyprian Ambrosiaster Hilary$^{23/25}$ Priscillian$^{1/2}$ Ambrose Rufinus Jerome$^{3/5}$ Paulinus-Nola Augustine$^{2/7}$ Speculum Arnobius.[11]

Bruce M. Metzger printed his explanation for the omission of Χριστός: "Several witnesses, chiefly Western, omit Χριστός, perhaps in order to conform the expression to that in ver. 10."[12] Metzger considered this reading to be faulty. But on inspection of the witnesses quoted, it becomes evident that Χριστός is a secondary addition. Metzger's explanation is not acceptable. Similar interpolations are found in different sections of the early transmission. In Rom 10:9, for instance, we read ὅτι ἐὰν ὁμολογήσῃς ἐν τῷ

---

8. Günther Zuntz, *The Text of the Epistles: A Disquisition upon the Corpus Paulinum*, Schweich Lectures of the British Academy 1946 (London: Oxford University Press, 1953).

9. Reiser discusses in *Sprache und literarischen Formen*, 181–83 the correct form of the acclamation κύριος Ἰησοῦς, as found in Rom 10:3, in 1 Cor 12:3, and in an incorrect form of Phil 2:11.

10. NA^{28}, 606.

11. Barbara Aland et al, eds., *The Greek New Testament*, 5th ed. (Stuttgart: Deutsche Bibelgesellschaft; United Bible Societies, 2014), 654–55.

12. Bruce M. Metzger, *A Textual Commentary on the Greek New Testament: A Companion Volume to the United Bible Societies' Greek New Testament (Fourth Revised Edition)*, 2nd ed.(Stuttgart: Deutsche Bibelgesellschaft, 1994), 546.

στόματι σου κύριον Ἰησοῦν καί. Here P⁴⁶ A t add the word Χριστόν to the text. Further variant readings are found in this passage.

Faced with this testimony, it is necessary for us to check whether objections against the reading κύριος Ἰησοῦς should be raised on account of its weak transmission. On careful consideration, this is not the case. Indeed, the secondary word Χριστός added to the text of Phil 2:11 may be found elsewhere, so, for instance, in Matt 16:21 or in Rom 10:9, as quoted above.

Bibliography

Aland, Barbara, Kurt Aland, Johannes Karavidopoulos, Carlo M. Martini, and Bruce M. Metzger, eds. *The Greek New Testament*. 5th ed. Stuttgart: Deutsche Bibelgesellschaft; United Bible Societies, 2014.

Berger, Klaus. *Formen und Gattungen im Neuen Testament*. Tübingen: Francke, 2005.

———. "Hellenistische Gattungen und Neues Testament." *ANRW* 25.2:1178–89.

Betz, Hans-Dieter. *Studies in Paul's Letter to the Philippians*. WUNT 343. Tübingen: Mohr Siebeck, 2015.

Édart, Jean-Baptiste. *L' Épitre aux Philippiens, rhetorique et composition stylistique*. Paris: Gabalda, 2002.

Frey, Jörg. "Eine neue religionsgeschichtliche Perspektive: Larry W. Hurtados *Lord Jesus Christ* und die Herausbildung der frühen Christologie." Pages 117–69 in *Reflections on the Early Christian History of Religion/ Erwägungen zur frühchristlichen Religionsgeschichte*. Edited by Cilliers Breytenbach and Jörg Frey. AGJU 81. Leiden: Brill, 2013.

Hurtado, Larry W. *Lord Jesus Christ: Devotion to Jesus in Earliest Christianity*. Grand Rapids: Eerdmans 2003.

Lohmeyer, Ernst. *Die Briefe an die Philipper, Kolosser und an Philemon*. 11th ed. KEK 9.1. Göttingen: Vandenhoeck & Ruprecht, 1956.

———. *Kyrios Jesus: Eine Untersuchung zu Phil. 2,5-11*. SHAW.PH 4. Heidelberg: Winter, 1928. Repr., Darmstadt: Wissenschaftliche Buchgesellschaft, 1962.

Lohmeyer, Ernst, and Werner Schmauch. *Die Briefe an die Philipper, Kolosser und an Philemon*. 13th ed. KEK 9.1. Göttingen: Vandenhoeck & Ruprecht, 1964.

Metzger, Bruce M. *A Textual Commentary on the Greek New Testament: A Companion Volume to the United Bible Societies' Greek New Testament*

(Fourth Revised Edition). 2nd ed. Stuttgart: Deutsche Bibelgesellschaft, 1994.
Reiser, Marius. *Sprache und literarische Formen des Neuen Testaments: Eine Einführung*. Paderborn: Schöningh, 2001.
Vollenweider, Samuel. "Dienst und Verführung, Überlegungen zur Kommentierung des 'Briefs an die Philipper.'" Pages 373–93 in *Der Philipperbrief des Paulus in der hellenistischen Welt*. Edited by Jörg Frey and Benjamin Schliesser. WUNT 353. Tübingen: Mohr Siebeck, 2015.
Zuntz, Günther. *The Text of the Epistles: A Disquisition upon the Corpus Paulinum*. Schweich Lectures of the British Academy 1946. London: Oxford University Press, 1953.

Author Index

Abbot, Ezra 96, 113
Ackroyd, Peter R. 122, 140
Aejmelaeus, Anneli 233, 245
Aland, Barbara 1, 2, 4–5, 19–20, 23, 96, 109, 113, 121, 126–27, 131, 133–35, 139–40, 153, 158, 162–63, 167, 172, 192, 200, 202–3, 208, 210–11, 214–15, 224, 228, 239, 244, 248, 263–65, 268, 270, 282, 284–85, 295, 309, 314, 317, 321, 326–27, 333–34
Aland, Kurt 2, 5–6, 19–20, 23–24, 54, 56–57, 74–76, 81, 87, 101, 103, 113, 121–24, 126–28, 132–35, 139–40, 144, 150–53, 155, 162–63, 165, 175, 192, 195, 200–203, 208, 210, 224–25, 234, 239, 244, 268, 284–85, 309, 314, 317, 320, 326–27, 334
Alexanian, Joseph M. 172, 192
Amphoux, Christian-Bernard xiii, 2, 23, 133, 188, 193, 200, 203, 208, 228, 251, 269
Allen, Willoughby C. 150, 163
Althoff, Jochen 275, 286
Arkwright, W. 42, 48
Arndt, William F. xv
Arnold, Gerhard 181, 192
Arnold, Matthew 297
Attridge, Harold 328
Audet, Jean-Paul 83, 91, 113
Avi-Yonah, Michael 33, 50
Baarda, Tjitze 167, 192, 232, 244
Bachmann, Philipp 70, 76
Baer, Heinrich von 26, 43, 45
Balz, Horst 106, 113
Bammel, Caroline P. H. 67, 76

Bammel, Ernst 213, 225
Barnard, Mordaunt 130, 141
Barrett, Charles K. 26, 45
Barrett, David P. 23, 235, 244
Barth, Karl xvii, 94, 113
Bartoli, Matteo 302, 309
Bartsch, Hans-Werner 93, 94, 97, 113
Bauer, Walter xii, xv, 5, 20, 27, 48, 94, 107, 113, 251, 268, 321
Bauernfeind, Otto 27, 48
Becker, Jürgen 104, 113
Bédier, Joseph 299, 303, 309
Bein, Thomas xi, 309
Bell, H. Idris 53, 63–66, 73, 76–77
Belle, Gilbert van 196, 197
Bengel, Johann Albrecht 79, 81, 87, 100–106, 113, 123, 131, 135, 140, 154, 211, 257, 260, 267, 268, 302
Benson, George 219, 225
Bentley, Richard 93–94, 113, 123, 140, 202, 209, 218, 225, 266, 268, 269
Berger, Klaus 85, 99, 113, 331, 334
Best, Ernest 123, 139
Betz, Hans-Dieter xix, 100, 108–9, 114, 332, 334
Bickerman, Elias J. 83, 91, 98, 114
Biddle, Mark E. xx
Bihlmeyer, Karl 87, 114
Billerbeck, Paul xx
Birdsall, J. Neville 71, 122, 128–31, 133, 140, 154, 163, 213, 219–20, 225, 232–33, 244
Bishop, Eric Francis Fox 41, 48
Black, David Alan 122, 140, 200, 210, 225, 226

Black, Matthew   75–76, 123, 125, 139–40, 148, 163, 225, 268
Blake, Robert P.   301, 311
Blass, Friedrich   xv, 4, 6–7, 12, 15, 20, 26, 43, 48, 161, 163, 205, 251, 264, 268
Blau, Lajos   37, 49
Bleek, Friedrich   267–68
Böcher, Otto   25, 49
Boeder, Winfried   233
Bohnenkamp, Anne   301, 310
Boismard, Marie-Émile   137, 140, 188, 250, 268
Booras, Steven W.   283, 285
Borger, Rykle   131, 140
Boring, M. Eugene   180, 182, 192
Botterweck, G. Johannes   xx–xxi
Bousset, Wilhelm   89–90, 114
Bover, Joseph M.   103, 114, 122, 140
Brannan, Rick   313
Braun, Herbert   252, 256–57, 259, 261, 263–65, 268
Brawley, Robert L.   vii
Brecht, Martin   155, 165
Bremer, Kai   310
Breytenbach, Cilliers   vii, 331, 334
Brink, Charles O.   266, 269
Brixhe, Claude   39, 49
Brock, Sebastian P.   168, 192
Bromiley, Geoffrey W.   xx
Bruce, F. F.   xi, 27, 51, 101, 114
Bruder, Carl Hermann   6, 20
Buck, Erwin   xi
Buckler, William Hepburn   42, 45
Bultmann, Rudolf   170, 192, 220–21, 223, 225
Bunbury, Edward H.   40, 49
Bunsen, Christian Karl J. von   297, 310
Burkitt, Francis Crawford   39, 48, 129–30, 141, 157, 163, 213
Burton, Philip H.   23
Buttmann, Philip   294, 296
Cadbury, Henry J.   27, 51
Calder, William M.   42, 45
Camerarius, Joachim   276
Cancik, Hubert   198

Capelle, Bernard   93, 117
Caragounis, Chrys C.   241, 244
Carlson, Stephen C.   xiii, 108, 114
Catchpole, David C.   188
Cavallo, Guglielmo   57, 76, 275
Chen, Yen-Chun   xi
Charles, Robert H.   97, 114
Charlesworth, Scott   319, 327
Childers, Jeffrey Wayne   4, 21, 271, 287
Christophersen, Alf   25, 52
Clark, Albert C.   26, 49
Clemen, Carl   26, 49
Cobet, Carel   209, 248
Cockerell, Douglas   281
Colwell, Ernest C.   133, 141, 167, 184, 193
Comfort, Philip Wesley   xii, 23, 139, 141, 235–36, 244
Conzelmann, Hans   25–26, 29–31, 43, 46, 49, 66, 68, 76, 104, 113, 251, 269
Cormeau, Christoph   309
Cowley, Arthur Ernest   98, 114
Cranfield, Charles E. B.   94–95, 102, 114
Crellius, Samuel   94, 113
Crum, Walter E.   53, 73, 76–77
Dain, Alphonse   277, 285
Danker, Frederick W.   xv
Dautzenberg, Gerhard   69, 76
Davidson, Robert   125, 140
Davidson, Samuel   297
Davies, John Gordon   46, 49
Debrunner, Albert   7, 20, 251, 264, 268
Deichgräber, Reinhard   82–84, 88–91, 107, 114
Deissmann, Adolf   4, 275
Delobel, Joel   167, 192, 203, 214, 225, 228, 320, 329
Denaux, Adelbert   320, 329
Dibelius, Martin   27, 29, 41, 49, 103, 114, 205–6, 220–25
Dietrich, Albert   38, 50
Dietrich, Wolfgang   86, 116
Dobschütz, Ernst von   27, 37, 49, 104, 115, 155, 163
Dodd, Charles Harold   221

Doedes, Jakobus Isaak 297–98, 310
Donaldson, Amy M. 2, 20, 235, 244
Dorandi, Tiziano 275–76, 280, 286
Doutreleau, Louis 192
Dummer, Jürgen 193
Dunderberg, Ismo 188, 193
Dungan, David L. 148, 163
Durand, George Matthieu de 192
Dziatzko, Carl 275, 286
Eck, Werner vii
Édart, Jean-Baptiste 332, 334
Ehrman, Bart D. 2, 6–8, 12, 16, 20–22, 122–23, 125, 127, 141, 143–44, 168, 172–74, 188, 192–194, 196–97, 199–200, 225, 227, 232, 235, 244–46, 271, 286, 314, 329
Eissfeldt, Otto 30, 42, 49
Elbogen, Ismar 90, 115
Elliott, J. Keith 2, 11–12, 14, 20, 23–24, 54, 76, 81, 89–90, 115, 122, 124, 126–28, 132–35, 138, 141–42, 145, 148–49, 153, 156–57, 159, 161–68, 181–83, 193–94, 198, 210, 215, 225, 274, 280, 286, 289, 320–21, 327–28
Elliott, William J. 10, 14, 20, 22, 24, 168
Ellis, Arthur Ayres 94, 113, 218, 225, 266, 268
Ellis, E. Earle 171, 195
Epp, Eldon J. 2, 3, 16, 21, 101, 116, 122–24, 132, 138–39, 141–42, 153, 158–59, 163, 168, 194, 199–201, 207, 209–10, 216, 219, 222, 226, 228–29, 235, 244, 278, 286
Erasmus, Desiderius R. 79, 102–6, 115
Esh, Shaul 97, 115
Evans, Christopher F. 140
Fabry, Heinz-Josef xx–xxi
Farstad, Arthur L. 122, 143
Fee, Gordon D. 1, 6–8, 12, 20–21, 101, 116, 124, 126–27, 132, 139, 141–42, 153, 159, 163, 168, 194, 209–10, 219, 226, 228–29, 235, 244, 245, 278, 286
Fischer, Bonifatius 127, 143
Fitzmyer, Joseph A. 25, 49, 133, 143

Fleddermann, Harry T. 185, 187–88, 194, 196
Flower, Barbara 4, 21, 269, 287
Foakes-Jackson, Frederick J. 26, 27, 51, 52
Fornberg, Tord 174, 193
Forte, Anthony J. 321, 328
Fortna, Robert T. 223, 226
Frame, James E. 104, 115
Frankemölle, Hubert 106, 115
Frede, Hermann Josef 74, 76, 255, 260–61, 263–65, 269, 282, 286
Frey, Jean-Baptistes xvi
Frey, Jörg 331–32, 334–35
Friedrich, Gerhard xx–xxi, 103–4, 113, 180, 194
Friedrich, Johannes 94, 116
Fuchs, Eric 106, 115
Fugmann, Joachim 302, 311
Funk, Robert W. xv
Gärtner, Kurt 300, 310
Gager, John G. 25, 49
Gamble, Harry 74, 76, 98–101, 107, 115
Gasque, W. Ward 27, 45, 51
Gempf, Conrad 25, 52
Gercke, Alfred 298
Gershevitch, Ilya 37, 49
Gignac, Francis Thomas 133, 143
Gilbert, Gary 25, 49
Gill, David W. J. 25, 52
Gingrich, F. Wilbur xv
Gippert, Jost 233, 245
Glaue, Paul 83, 115
Globe, Alexander 176, 194
Goodrich, Richard J. 314, 328
Gore, Charles 154, 166
Goudge, Henry Leighton 154, 166
Graesser, Erich 29, 49, 171, 195, 256–57, 259
Grant, Frederick M. 184, 194
Greenslade, Stanley L. 140
Greetham, David C. 271, 272, 279, 286
Greeven, Heinrich v, xi, xvii, 3, 16, 21–22, 27, 49, 116, 124, 126, 128, 132, 137–38, 143, 148, 150–51, 154–56,

Greeven, Heinrich (cont.) 158–60, 162, 164, 168, 188, 193, 205, 213, 216, 225, 226, 231–35, 237–43, 245–46, 277, 286, 301–2, 308, 310
Grégory, Caspar René   128, 136, 143, 284, 286, 295–96, 298, 310
Grenfell, Bernard P.   301
Griesbach, Johann Jacob   16, 79, 102–3, 106, 115, 126, 131, 143, 158, 208, 211, 231, 239, 243, 245, 249, 250, 255, 257–58 260, 266, 269, 293, 296, 302, 312
Grundmann, Walter   106, 115
Grunewald, Winfried   105, 115, 133, 143
Guardina, Andrea   276, 288
Guelich, Robert A.   181, 194
Güting, Eberhard W.   xi–xiii, 3, 4, 5, 16–17 21–22, 27, 125, 134, 143, 148, 150–51, 154–56, 158–60, 162, 164, 194, 199, 201, 206, 209, 213, 216, 218, 222, 226, 233, 237–38, 240, 242, 245, 269, 271, 273, 277, 286, 295, 302, 308, 310, 315, 321, 324, 328
Guillaume, Alfred   154, 166
Gutbrod, Walter   43, 49
Gwynn, John   80, 88, 115
Haacker, Klaus   25, 49
Haas, Otto   38, 49
Haase, Wolfgang   xv
Haenchen, Ernst   26, 28–30, 43, 50, 206, 226
Hahn, August H.   296, 310
Hahn, Ferdinand   45, 50
Hall, Stuart George   83, 89, 114
Harder, Günther   94, 115
Harlfinger, Dieter   277, 283, 286, 287
Harnack, Adolf von   4, 26, 28, 40, 43, 50, 68–69, 76, 217, 220, 247, 253, 254, 267, 269
Hartman, Lars   174, 193
Hase, Karl Benedict   284
Hatch, William H. P.   74, 76, 122
Hauck, Friedrich   94, 119
Haussleiter, Johannes   176, 183, 198
Havet, Louis   133
Hawkins, John C.   148, 164

Head, Peter M.   174, 194, 318, 320–21, 328
Headlam, Arthur C.   95, 117
Heckel, Theo   273
Hedley, P. L.   150, 164
Heiberg, Johan Ludvig   285
Heichelheim, Fritz M.   38–39, 50
Heimerdinger, Jenny   2, 23, 200, 228
Hellholm, David   174, 193
Hengel, Martin   248, 273–75, 287
Henrichs, Albert   298, 312
Hermann, Gottfried   298
Hertz, Martin   294, 310
Heubeck, Alfred   38–39, 42
Hintmaier, Johann   24
Hodges, Zane C.   122, 143
Hoffmann, Lawrence A.   85, 115
Holl, Karl   38, 50, 176, 183, 193
Hollander, August den   304, 311, 322, 329
Holmes, Michael W.   vii, 1–2, 4, 6–8, 12, 20–21, 122, 127, 129, 138, 141, 143, 148, 151, 155, 157, 164, 168, 172, 192, 194, 196–97, 199, 225, 235, 244–45, 271, 276–77, 286–87, 313–15, 317, 319, 321–30
Holtz, Traugott   103–4, 115
Holtzmann, Heinrich J.   27, 43, 47, 50, 182, 194
Horgan, Maurya P.   133, 143
Horne, Thomas Hartwell   297–98, 310
Horner, George W.   80, 87, 115, 157
Horst, Pieter W. van der   25, 50
Hort, Fenton John Anthony   9, 23, 66–67 77, 79, 96, 101–3, 106, 119, 130, 138, 145, 153–54, 157, 158–59, 166, 178, 180, 198, 202, 212, 219, 221, 228, 232, 237, 238, 246, 251, 256, 259, 261–62, 264–65, 272, 278, 289, 314, 330
Hose, Martin   302, 311
Houghton, Hugh A. G.   23, 320, 328
Housman, Alfred E.   266, 269
Houwink ten Cate, Philo H. J.   39, 50
Howard, Wilbert Francis   196
Huck, Albert   xvii, 80, 116, 124, 128, 132, 137–38, 143, 231, 245

Author Index

Hurtado, Larry W.   101-2, 115, 127, 143, 200, 226, 271, 273, 275, 287, 331, 334
Irmer, Dieter   302, 311
Jacobson, Arland D.   185, 194
Janeras, Sebastià   150, 163
Jannidis, Fotis   315, 328
Jaros, Brigitte   24
Jaros, Karl   24, 272, 287
Jenkins, Claude   67, 76
Jenni, Ernst   xx
Jensen, Ragnar   283, 287
Jeremias, Joachim   20, 46, 50, 83, 86, 116
Jervell, Jacob   29, 50
Job, Michael   232, 245
Jones, Arnold H. M.   33, 42, 50
Jones, Henry Stuart   xviii
Jülicher, Adolf   24, 175, 195
Junack, Klaus   xiii, 13, 76, 105, 115, 133, 140, 143
Juster, Jean   37, 50
Justus, Bernhard   xi
Kabayashi, Nozomu   vii
Kadzaja, Lamara   232-33, 245
Käsemann, Ernst   82, 89, 94, 96, 98-99, 102, 116
Karavidopoulos, Johannes   19, 113, 139, 162, 192, 224, 239, 244, 268, 285, 309, 314, 326, 334
Kasting, Heinrich   37, 50
Kee, Howard C.   171, 185, 195
Kelber, Werner H.   171, 195
Kenney, Edward John   299, 310
Kenyon, Frederick G.   249, 274, 282, 287
Kertelge, Karl   74
Kharanauli, Anna   232, 245
Kilpatrick, George Dunbar   116, 121, 125-26, 138, 142, 144, 147, 148, 149, 156-57, 164, 168, 193-194, 209, 226, 256, 264, 269
Kittel, Gerhard   xx-xxi
Klauck, Hans-Josef   272, 276, 287
Klauser, Theodor   xix
Kleve, Knut   283, 287
Kobelski, Paul J.   133, 143

Koch, Dietrich-Alex   ix, xi, 3, 21, 125, 143, 187, 195, 211, 225, 320, 324, 327, 328
Köster, Beate   76, 140
Koester, Helmut   204, 227
Koetschau, Paul   196
Krans, Jan   314, 320, 328
Kraus, Karl von   309
Krause, Gerhard   xx, 83
Kremer, Jacob   25, 50
Kretschmer, Paul   39, 42, 50
Kristeller, Paul Oskar   308, 310
Kroll, Wilhelm   xix
Kümmel, Werner Georg   25, 155, 164, 171, 195, 223, 227
Kullmann, Wolfgang   275, 286
Kuss, Otto   94-96, 116
Lachmann, Karl   vi, xi, 1, 79, 81, 101-3, 106, 116, 125, 144, 177-80, 183, 189, 195, 200-202, 209, 221, 227, 249, 251, 257, 261, 264-66, 293-304, 307-12, 320, 329, 332
Lagrange, Marie-Josèphe   93, 96, 102, 116, 150, 153, 157, 161, 164, 180, 182, 195
Lake, Kirsopp   26, 27, 36, 50-52, 155, 164, 301, 311
Lambrecht, Jan   188
Lamouille, Arnaud   137, 140, 188
Lampe, Geoffrey W. H.   140
Lange, Joachim   21
Larson, Stan   128, 144
Leclerc, Jean   210, 314
Leitzmann, Albert   298, 311
Lichtenberger, Hermann   ix, xi, 3, 21, 125, 143, 324, 328
Liddell, Henry George   xviii
Lietzmann, Hans   67, 76, 96, 102, 116
Lightfoot, Robert B.   195, 218, 219, 227
Lindars, Barnabas   94, 117
Ling, Mary   27, 49
Livingstone, Elizabeth A.   74, 76
Lloyd-Jones, Hugh   298, 312
Lohmeyer, Ernst   170, 195, 331-32, 334
Lohse, Bernhard   88, 116

Lohse, Eduard 25, 27–28, 51
Loisy, Alfred F. 26, 51, 179, 195, 206
Longstaff, Thomas R. W. 126, 142, 239, 245
Lorimer, William Laughton 93, 116
Lucas, Francis 123
Lücke, Friedrich 294, 296–98, 311
Lühr, Franz-Frieder 33, 51
Lukaszewski, Albert L. 314, 328
Lumsden, Diana C. vii
Lutz-Hensel, Magdalene 309
Luz, Ulrich 187, 195
Maas, Paul 4, 21, 203, 227, 248–49, 269, 277, 287, 300–301, 311
Mace, Daniel 123, 125, 144, 201
Maclachlan, Rosalind F. 23
MacRae, George W. 123, 142
Madden, Frederic 274, 288
Madvig, Johan N. 302
Marmorstein, Arthur 90, 116
Martin, Ralph P. 27, 45, 51
Martin, Victor 13, 21
Martini, Carlo M. 19, 76, 113, 139, 162, 192, 214, 224, 238–39, 244, 246, 268, 285, 309, 314, 326, 334
Marxsen, Willi 103–4, 116, 179, 195
Matera, Frank J. 173, 189, 195
Mattill, Andrew J. 45, 51
Matzkow, Walter 24, 175, 195
Mayer, Günter 86, 116
Mealand, David L. xiii, 3, 5, 21, 134, 143, 218, 226
Merk, August 103, 116, 121, 144
Merk, Otto 220, 227
Merx, Adalbert 157, 164, 172, 195
Metzger, Bruce M. 2, 3, 7–8, 10, 16, 19, 22, 26–28, 51, 68, 70, 75–76, 94, 101–4, 108, 113, 116, 123–27, 129, 132, 134, 139, 141, 144, 150, 153, 157–59, 161–63, 165, 168, 173, 192, 194–97, 200, 202, 204, 206, 208, 209, 211, 214, 216–17, 219–20, 224–29, 232, 239, 244, 246, 250, 256, 258, 261–63, 265, 268–69, 285, 309, 314, 321–26, 329, 333–34

Metzger, Henri 42, 51
Meyer, Heinrich August W. 109, 117
Michel, Otto 95–96, 102, 117
Migne, Jacques-Paul xix
Milligan, George xviii
Milne, Herbert J. M. 53–54, 77, 280–81, 283, 288
Mink, Gerd 19, 224, 284, 289, 304, 311, 317–19, 322, 326–27, 329
Most, Glenn W. 302, 311
Moule, Charles Francis Digby 94, 116
Moulton, James H. xviii, 196
Müller, Gerhard xx
Mulken, Margot van 300, 310, 322, 329
Mullen, Roderic L. 1, 21, 127, 142, 235, 245
Mussner, Franz 108, 117
Nägeli, Theodor von 69, 77
Neirynck, Frans 170, 180, 187–88, 196–97
Nestle, Eberhard 3, 79, 96, 103, 117, 121, 131–32, 136, 144, 153, 155, 165, 205, 211, 227, 264, 301, 311
Nestle, Erwin 121, 131, 144, 211, 227, 301, 311
Netz, Reviel 283, 285, 288
Neumann, Günther 38–39, 42, 51
New, David S. 185, 196
New, Silva 301, 311
Nicklas, Tobias xii, 3, 22, 207, 214, 227
Niebuhr, Karl-Wilhelm 321, 329
Nimtz, Ulrich xiii, 143
Noel, William 283, 285, 288
Nolli, Giofranco 117, 122, 144
Norden, Eduard 298
North, J. Lionel 168–196
Nutt-Kofoth, Rüdiger 315, 328
Oakes, Peter 108, 117
O'Callaghan, José 122, 128, 140
Orchard, Bernard 126, 142, 239, 245
Orelli, Johann Caspar von 302
Omerzu, Heike 214, 227
Ore, Espen S. 283, 287
Outtier, Bernard 233, 246
Overbeck, Franz 47

Pallis, Alex 170, 196
Papathomas, Amphilochios 247, 270
Parker, David C. xii, xiii, 2–4, 10–11, 14, 16, 20–24, 122, 127, 145, 188, 192–93, 200, 207, 211, 227, 251, 269, 271, 279–80, 287–88, 315, 320, 328–29
Paris, Gaston 299
Pasquali, Giorgio 294, 301–2, 311
Pattie, Thomas Smith 67, 77
Pecere, Oronzo 276, 288
Perez, Gonzalo Aranda 149
Perrin, Norman 170, 196
Pervo, Richard I. 25–26, 50–51
Pesch, Rudolf 170–171, 173, 180, 196
Petersen, William L. 203–5, 227–28
Peterson, Erik 83, 117
Petzer, Jacobus H. 203, 215–16, 228
Pichlwagner, Karin 24
Pierpont, William G. 315, 329
Piper, Ronald A. 186–88, 196, 198
Plachta, Bodo 315, 328
Planck 243
Plümacher, Eckhard 31–32, 51
Plummer, Alfred 67, 77
Pöhlmann, Egert 202, 228, 272, 276, 284, 288
Porson, Richard 266, 269
Porter, Stanley E. 24
Porter, Wendy J. 24
Potin, Jean 37, 51
Preuschen, Erwin 196, 206
Pryke, E. J. 155, 161, 165
Quast, Ulrich 233, 245
Quentin, Henri 299–300, 302, 311
Ramsay, William Mitchell 42, 48
Rawlinson, Alfred Edward J. 182, 196
Reenen, Pieter van 300, 304, 311, 322, 329
Rehkopf, Friedrich 20, 268
Reiner, Erica 37, 51
Reiser, Marius 4, 6, 22, 332–33, 335
Rengstorf, Karl Heinrich xi, 86, 116
Rettig, Heinrich Christian M. 296–97, 311
Reymond, Pierre 106, 115
Reynolds, Leighton D. 272, 288
Rhodes, Errol F. 219, 228
Riesenfeld, Harald 155, 165
Rigaux, Béda 103, 117
Ringgren, Helmer xx–xxi
Rissi, Matthias 205, 228
Ritschl, Friedrich 302
Roberts, Colin H. 93, 117, 274, 288
Robertson, Archibald Thomas 67, 77
Robinson, James M. 180, 186–88, 196
Robinson, Maurice A. 314, 329
Robinson, Peter 318
Robinson, Pieter M. W. 300, 311
Roca-Puig, Ramon 150, 163
Roetzel, Calvin J. 100, 117
Roller, Otto 276–77, 288
Roos, Antoon G. 39
Ropes, James H. 27, 52
Ross, J. M. 155, 165
Royse, James R. 200, 228
Rück, Peter 281, 288
Sagnard, François Louis Marie Matthieu 194
Sand, Alexander 74, 77
Sanday, William 95, 117, 188, 197
Sanders, Henry A. 175, 197
Sarjveladze, Zurab 233, 245
Sauppe, Hermann 302
Schaefer, Karl Theodor 259, 270
Scharbert, Josef 81, 117
Schelkle, Karl Hermann 106, 117
Scherer, Jean 67, 77
Schlatter, Adolf xiii
Schleiermacher, Friedrich 297
Schlier, Heinrich 83, 103, 107–8, 117
Schliesser, Benjamin 332, 335
Schmauch, Werner 331, 334
Schmid, Josef 87, 117
Schmid, Ulrich B. xii, 14, 22, 24, 168, 194
Schmidt, Karl L. 27, 36, 43, 52, 89, 117, 161, 165
Schmidt, Peter Lebrecht 302–3, 311
Schmiedel, Wilhelm 136, 211

Schmitz, Franz-Jürgen xii, 284–85, 288–89
Schneckenburger, Matthias 45
Schneemelcher, Wilhelm 74, 77
Schnider, Franz 89, 98–99, 107–8, 117
Schniewind, Julius 94, 118
Scholz, Augustin 296, 312
Schrage, Wolfgang 3, 22, 66, 68–70, 77, 106, 113, 168, 193, 231, 246
Schreckenberg, Heinz ix, xi–xii, 3, 21, 125, 143, 324, 328
Schubert, Martin xiii, 10
Schwartz, Eduard 220, 301
Scott, James M. 25, 52
Scott, Robert xviii, 32
Scrivener, Frederick H. 79, 102, 104, 118
Seely, David R. 283, 285
Segbroeck, F. van 170, 180, 196–97
Semler, Johann Salomo 249, 302
Sesboüé, Bernard 192
Sherwin-White, Adrian N. 43, 52
Sickenberger, Joseph 174, 182, 197
Sider, David 275, 283, 289
Sieffert, Friedrich 109, 118
Siegert, Folker xii, 273, 286
Silva, Moisés 168, 197
Simon, Richard 123, 145
Skeat, Theodore C. 280–81, 283, 288–89
Slichtingius, Jonas 94, 118
Slomp, Jan 174, 197
Smith, Dennis E. 181, 197
Soden, Hermann von 101, 103, 118, 121, 124–25, 135, 137, 145, 174, 235, 264, 301, 311
Souter, Alexander 118
Sparks, Hedley F. D. 259, 270
Sparks, Irving Allen 295, 311
Stählin, Gustav 25, 49, 155, 165
Stanton, Graham 273
Stenger, Werner 25, 52, 89, 98, 99, 107–8, 117
Stingelin, Urs 24
Stolz, Michael xi
Strack, Hermann L. xx
Strecker, Georg 184, 198, 223, 228
Streeter, Burnett Hillman 122, 188, 197, 211, 227
Strugnell, John 208–9, 228
Strutwolf, Holger 19, 317, 326, 330
Stuiber, Alfred 81, 83, 87, 106–8, 118
Suhl, Alfred 185, 197
Swanson, Reuben J. 14, 22, 24
Tannehill, Robert C. 181, 197
Tasker, Randolph V. 121, 145, 155, 157, 165
Taylor, David G. K. xii, 16, 200, 209, 226, 272, 287
Taylor, Justin 25, 52
Taylor, Vincent 150, 160, 165, 180–82, 197
Telford, William R. 170, 195–97
Temporini, Hildegard xv
Theissen, Gerd 170, 192
Thiel, Nathan 314, 330
Thomas, Joel 31–33, 35, 52
Thompson, R. Campbell 53, 77
Tilly, Michael xii, 3, 22, 207, 214, 227
Timpanaro, Sebastiano 302, 311
Tischendorf, Constantin von 14–15, 22, 79, 81, 87, 101–3, 106, 118, 123, 125, 128, 130, 136, 140, 145, 149, 152, 157, 165, 174–76, 197, 202, 209, 235, 257, 264, 279, 281, 284, 296–97, 310, 312
Tolbert, Mary Ann 182, 197
Tregelles, Samuel Prideaux 79, 101–3, 106, 118, 202, 209, 257, 262, 264, 270, 296–98, 310, 312, 314, 330
Trocmé, Étienne 36–37, 52
Tschiedel, Hans Jürgen 47, 52
Tuckett, Christopher M. 167, 184, 196, 197
Tune, Ernest W. 167, 193
Turner, Cuthbert Hamilton 124, 145, 147–49, 153–61, 164–66, 182–83, 198, 215, 225
Turner, Eric G. 56–58, 77
Turner, Nigel 196
Uro, Risto 188, 198

Author Index

Vaganay, Léon   2, 23, 133, 145, 200, 203, 208, 228
Verheule, Anthonie F.   90, 114
Verheyden, Joseph   196–97, 214, 225
Victor, Ulrich   24
Vielhauer, Philipp   82, 89, 98–99, 118, 192
Vitelli, Girolamo   276, 289
Vööbus, Arthur   205
Vogels, Heinrich Joseph   103, 118, 121, 145, 257, 270
Vollenweider, Samuel   332, 335
Vorster, Willem S.   185, 198
Wach, Joachim   xiii
Wachtel, Klaus   4, 19, 23, 224, 248, 270, 277, 287, 317, 319, 326–30
Wedderburn, Alexander J. M.   25, 52
Weinstock, Stefan   28, 32, 52
Weische, Alfons   162
Weiss, Bernhard   2, 94, 103, 118, 121, 145, 150–53, 166, 209, 251, 256–57, 261, 263–64, 267, 270
Weiss, Hans Friedrich   254, 259, 263, 270
Weiss, Johannes   27, 31, 52, 93–94, 118, 170, 198
Weissbach, Franz Heinrich   38, 52
Weisse, Christian Hermann   179, 198
Wellhausen, Julius   26, 30, 52, 157, 159, 161, 166, 174, 179, 180, 198, 206, 220
Wells, Edward   123, 201, 202
Welte, Michael   76, 140
Wendland, Paul   89, 118
Weren, Wim   211, 225, 320, 327
Werner, Eric   82, 118
West, Martin L.   2, 23, 168, 198, 300–301, 312
Westcott, Brook Foss   9, 23, 66, 77, 79, 96, 101–3, 106, 119, 130, 138, 145, 153, 157–59, 166, 178, 198, 202, 205, 212, 219, 221, 228, 232, 237, 238, 246, 251, 256, 259, 261–65, 270, 272, 278, 289, 314, 330
Westermann, Claus   xx, 92, 119
Wettstein, Johann Jakob   93–94, 119, 302
White, Henry J.   259, 270
Widengren, Geo   38, 50
Wikgren, Allen P.   75–76, 140, 157, 210, 225, 229, 268
Wilamowitz-Moellendorff, Ulrich von   298, 312
Wilckens, Ulrich   31, 52, 95–96, 102, 119, 219, 229
Willis, John T.   xx
Wilson, Nigel G.   273, 288
Wilson, Robert M.   123, 139
Wilson, Stephen G.   27, 52
Windisch, Hans   106, 119
Winter, Bruce W.   25, 52
Wirth, G.   39
Wirth, Uwe   310
Wirtz, Irmgard R.   310
Wisselink, Willem Franciscus   126, 128, 145
Wissowa, Georg   xix
Witte, Klaus   xiii, 143
Woesler, Winfried   vii
Wohlenberg, Gustav   174, 198
Wolf, Friedrich August   303
Wolff, Christian   25, 52
Wordsworth, John   259, 270
Wrede, William   93–94, 119
Yarbro Collins, Adela   174, 176, 192
Young, Edward   201
Yutaka, Maekawa   ix, xii
Zahn, Theodor   94, 119
Zerwick, Max   182, 198
Ziegler, Winfried   293–98, 308, 312
Zimmermann, Bernhard   302, 311
Zumpt, Karl Gottlob   302
Zuntz, Günther   vi, xii, 4, 15–16, 21, 23, 67–68, 70, 77, 129, 145, 198, 203, 208–9, 211–13, 215, 217, 229, 238, 240, 243, 245, 246–68, 270, 273, 278, 280, 289, 295, 310, 315, 328, 330, 333, 335

www.ingramcontent.com/pod-product-compliance
Lightning Source LLC
Chambersburg PA
CBHW020607300426
44113CB00007B/541